WHAT CAN THIS BOOK DO FOR YOU?

Within a few years, your high school experience will lead you into the work world of adults. This book is designed to give you guidance, ideas, and answers about the many options life offers and the steps you will need to take for each.

WHAT FIRST?

Take a few minutes to claim ownership of this book. Write your name in it. In pencil, lay out your career and life goals as you see them today. Consider the obstacles you may have to overcome in order to achieve them. If you don't have a formal plan, that's ok. Answering these questions will spark your imagination and help you make one. The first steps might not be easy, but there are no right or wrong answers. As you continue working through this book, refer to these goals and feel free to fill in any blanks you left or to change your ideas.

WHAT NEXT?

Your needs, goals, ideas, and talents are unique to you. What is right for you may not be right for others. But the steps in the process of choosing a career direction (and understanding what education you might need to get there) are the same whether you aspire to repair car engines or design the next generation of space shuttles.

THINK OF THIS BOOK AS A ROAD MAP

Knowing where you want to go and what roads will lead you there is the first step in the process. You can always change your destination and chart a new course. We're providing the map. The rest is up to you.

GETTING A JUMP ON THE ROAD TO SUCCESS

Name_____

Age_____

Grade_____

Date Started_____

My current goal after I graduate from high school is to:_____

_____

Steps at school to reach my goal:

Curriculum planning:_____

_____

Clubs, teams, associations:_____

_____

Career research:_____

_____

Steps outside of school to reach my goal:

Volunteer work:_____

_____

Shadowing/mentor program:_____

_____

Job experience:_____

Extracurricular activities:_____

Challenges my goal presents:_____

_____

Ideas to overcome_____

_____

About The Thomson Corporation and Peterson's

With revenues of US$7.2 billion, The Thomson Corporation (www.thomson.com) is a leading global provider of integrated information solutions for business, education, and professional customers. Its Learning businesses and brands (www.thomsonlearning.com) serve the needs of individuals, learning institutions, and corporations with products and services for both traditional and distributed learning.

Peterson's, part of The Thomson Corporation, is one of the nation's most respected providers of lifelong learning online resources, software, reference guides, and books. The Education Supersite℠ at www.petersons.com—the Internet's most heavily traveled education resource—has searchable databases and interactive tools for contacting U.S.-accredited institutions and programs. In addition, Peterson's serves more than 105 million education consumers annually.

For more information, contact Peterson's, 2000 Lenox Drive, Lawrenceville, NJ 08648; 800-338-3282; or find us on the World Wide Web at www.petersons.com/about.

ACKNOWLEDGEMENTS: Peterson's would like to acknowledge the following authors for their contribution to this publication: Kenneth Edwards, Michele Kornegay, Emily Law, Brenna McBride, Charlotte Thomas, and Amy Tomcavage.

For permission to use material from this text or product, contact us by

Phone: 800-730-2214

Fax: 800-730-2215

Web: www.thomsonrights.com

ISBN: 0-7689-1038-2 (Middle Atlantic)   0-7689-1039-0 (Midwest)

0-7689-1040-4 (New England)   0-7689-1042-0 (South)

0-7689-1043-9 (Texas)   0-7689-1044-7 (West)

Printed in the United States of America

10 9 8 7 6 5 4 3 2 1   04 03 02

Dear Student:

Whether graduation seems light-years away or alarmingly close, it's never too early—or too late—to think about what comes after high school. Do you know what your next step will be?

Get a Jump can help you figure that out. This book is designed to help you launch your career, whether this means going on for more education or directly entering the workforce. You have a multitude of options and some crucial choices to make. In the pages that follow, we have tried to give you a jumpstart on planning the future that's right for you.

The book is arranged in four parts. Part One provides general introductory information about your options after high school and how to use your high school education to plan for the next phase of your life. Part Two offers more detailed information about postsecondary education, whether you choose a two-year, four-year, career, or technical college or the military. Part Three provides useful information about the world of work and how to handle stress, peer pressure, conflict, and other obstacles you may encounter in the real world. Finally, Part Four contains appendices for each state in your part of the United States, including valuable information on two- and four-year colleges and universities in your area and your state's high school graduation requirements, internships, scholarship and financial aid programs, summer opportunities, and vocational schools.

We hope you find this publication helpful as you begin thinking about the rest of your life. If you have questions or feedback on *Get a Jump*, please e-mail us at getajump@petersons.com.

Sincerely,

Peterson's Editorial Staff

Contents

PART THREE: YOU AND THE WORKPLACE

PART FOUR: APPENDICES.

Part **1**

JUMPSTART YOUR FUTURE

COME ON, ADMIT IT. You know that big question—what will I do when I graduate from high school?—is right around the corner. Some of your classmates know what they want to do, but you're freaking out about all of the decisions you have to make.

You've got a lot of possibilities from which to choose. Maybe you'll attend a two-year or four-year college or vocational or technical school. Or you'll join the armed forces. Or perhaps you'll go right into the workplace with a full-time job. But before you march across that stage to get your diploma, *Get a Jump* will help you to begin thinking about your options and to open up doors you never knew existed.

FIRST, A LOOK AT YOURSELF

Deciding what to do with your life is a lot like flying. Just look at the many ways you can fly and the many directions your life can take.

A TEACHER ONCE asked her students to bring something to class that flies. Students brought kites, balloons, and models of airplanes, blimps, hot-air balloons, helicopters, spaceships, gliders, and seaplanes. But when class began, the teacher explained that the lesson was about career planning, not flying.

She was making the point that your plans for life after high school can take many forms. Some people take direct flights via jets. Others are carried along by circumstances. How you will make the journey is an individual matter. That's why it's important to know who you are and what you want before taking off.

You may not choose your life's career by reading Get a Jump (GAJ), but you'll learn how to become part of the decision-making process and find resources that can help you plan your future.

Ready to Fly?

Just having a high school diploma is not enough for many occupations. But, surprise, surprise, neither is a college degree. Different kinds of work require different kinds of training. Knowing how to operate a particular type of equipment, for instance, takes special skills and work experience that you might not learn in college. Employers always want to hire the best-qualified people available, but this does not mean that they always choose those applicants who have the most education. The type of education and training you have is just as important as how much. Right now, you're at the point in your life where you can choose how much and what kind of education and training you want to get.

If you have a definite career goal in mind, like being a doctor, you probably already know what it will take in terms of education. You're looking at about four years of college, then four years of medical school, and, in most states, one year of residency. Cosmetologists, on the other hand, complete a state-approved training program that ranges from eight to eighteen months.

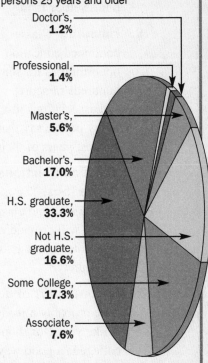

EDUCATIONAL ATTAINMENT
Highest level of education attained by persons 25 years and older

- Doctor's, **1.2%**
- Professional, **1.4%**
- Master's, **5.6%**
- Bachelor's, **17.0%**
- H.S. graduate, **33.3%**
- Not H.S. graduate, **16.6%**
- Some College, **17.3%**
- Associate, **7.6%**

Source: Digest of Educational Statistics, U.S. Department of Commerce, Bureau of the Census, Current Population Survey

But for most of you, deciding what to do after high school is not so easy. Perhaps you haven't chosen a field of work yet. You might just know for certain that you want a job that will give you status and a big paycheck. Or maybe you know what you want to do, but you're not sure what kind of education you'll need. For instance, you may love fixing cars, and the idea of being an auto mechanic sounds great. But you need to decide whether to learn on the job, attend a vocational school, seek an apprenticeship, or pursue a combination of these options.

THE TOP 10 REASONS TO CONTINUE YOUR EDUCATION

Continuing your education after high school is one choice that can give you a good start no matter what your final career decision is. There are many good reasons to do so. If you think college is not for you at all, take a look at this list. It might change your mind.

10. **Fulfill a dream—or begin one.** Some people hope to become teachers or scientists. For many, continuing their education provides the opportunity to make that wish a reality for one's self or family.

9. **Have fun.** Classes are an important part of continued education, but there are plenty of opportunities for some great times. There are hundreds of sports, clubs, groups, activities, and associations just waiting for you to join. Many people say that their college years were the best years of their lives.

8. **Make connections that can link you to future jobs.** The friends, professors, supervisors, and classmates you meet after high school will provide valuable ties for future jobs, committees, and associations within the community.

7. **Become part of a cultural stew.** As you have probably already figured out, not everyone is like you. Nor should they be. Being in college is a good way to expose yourself to many types of people from various backgrounds and geographic locations, with different viewpoints and opinions. You may discover that you like people and things you never knew existed.

6. **Meet new people.** By furthering your education, you will widen your circle of friends and, chances are, form meaningful lifelong relationships.

5. **Do what you love doing and get paid for it.** Have you ever taken a test during which everything clicked or played a video game and caught on immediately? This is what happens when you combine education and training with the right job. Work becomes more like play, which is far more satisfying and rewarding than just going through the motions.

4. **Exercise your mind.** Just as physical exercise keeps your body in shape, mental exercise keeps your mind free of cobwebs. No matter what your area of interest, education holds the key to the most interesting and challenging information you can imagine. Explore your outer limits and become a lifelong learner.

3. **Earn a higher income.** Although money isn't everything, it is necessary for survival. A good education prepares you to become a solid member of society. (See the chart "Increase Your Earning Power.")

2. **Learn critical-thinking and analytical skills.** More than any other skill, education teaches you to think. Furthering your learning will help you to think critically, organize and analyze information, and write clearly.

1. **You won't get left behind.** In the twenty-first century, you will need to be prepared to change jobs and continually learn new skills in order to keep up with changes in industry, communications, and technology. Education and training will give you a solid background.

INCREASE YOUR EARNING POWER

People with more education tend to earn more money. Look at the average yearly earnings of workers over the age of 25 by education level.

Professional Degree	$80,230
Doctoral Degree	$70,476
Master's Degree	$55,302
Bachelor's Degree	$46,276
Associate Degree	$35,389
Some College	$32,400
High School Diploma	$28,807
Less Than High School Diploma	$21,391

Source: Bureau of the Census; Bureau of Labor Statistics

Breaking Down the Barriers to Continuing Your Education

Some of you may say, "Forget the reasons why I should continue my education. I can't because (fill in the blank)." Let's see if your objections stand up to this list.

You say:

Nobody in my family has ever gone to college.

GAJ says:

You can be the first! It's a little scary and not always easy, but just think how great you'll feel being the first person in your family to receive a degree, diploma, or certificate.

You say:

My grades are not good enough.

GAJ says:

Don't let less-than-perfect grades stand in your way. Different institutions have different requirements, including what grades they accept. Schools also evaluate you for admission as a whole person, such as participation in extracurricular activities; your talents, such as academics and athletics; and your employment and volunteer history. There are also classes that you can take to improve your skills in various subject areas. Get a tutor now or form a study group in high school to improve your grades as much as possible. Talk to your guidance counselor about what the appropriate high school curriculum for you is so you'll have more options when making decisions about continuing your education.

You say:

I can't afford it.

GAJ says:

Many families cannot afford to pay education costs completely out of pocket. That's why there are so many opportunities for financial aid, scholarships, grants, and work-study programs. Federal, state, school-sponsored, private, and career-specific financial aid resources are available to students who take the time to look. Talk to a guidance counselor, go to the library, and look on the Internet. Read the "Financial Aid Dollars and Sense" section of GAJ for more information about how to finance your continued education. Be creative and persistent. It can happen for you.

You say:

I don't know how to apply or where I want to go.

GAJ says:

Fortunately, there are resources to help you decide which institution to select. Talk to friends, family members, neighbors, your guidance counselor, pastor, coach, or librarian. Take a look at the appendix at the back of GAJ for a guide to two-year and four-year colleges as well as vocational and technical schools in your state.

You say:

I think it may be too difficult for me.

GAJ says:

Think back to something you have done in your life that seemed too difficult in the beginning. Didn't you find that once you began, put your mind to it, and stuck with it that you succeeded? You can do almost anything if you set your mind to it and are willing to work for it.

You say:

I'm not sure I'll fit in.

GAJ says:

One of the best things about furthering your education is the chance to meet new people and be part of new experiences in new surroundings. Colleges and other continuing education options attract a wide variety of students from many different backgrounds. Chances are you won't have any problem finding someone else with interests that are similar to yours. Because schools differ in size, location, student body, and lifestyle, you'll surely find one that meets your needs. Advance visits and interviews can help you determine which school is right for you.

FASTEST-GROWING OCCUPATIONS

Want to have a career that's going places? Check out this chart to see which occupations are expected to grow the fastest by the year 2010 and what type of training you'll need to get the job.

Occupation	Expected Openings	Required Education
Computer Software Engineers, applications	760,000	Bachelor's degree
Computer Support Specialists	996,000	Associate degree
Computer Software Engineers, systems software	601,000	Bachelor's degree
Network and Computer Systems Administrators	416,000	Bachelor's degree
Network Systems and Data Communications Analysts	211,000	Bachelor's degree
Desktop Publishers	63,000	Postsecondary Vocational Training
Database Administrators	176,000	Bachelor's degree
Personal and Home Care Aides	672,000	On-the-job training
Computer Systems Analysts	689,000	Bachelor's degree
Medical Assistants	516,000	On-the-job-training
Social and Human Service Assistants	418,000	On-the-job training
Physician Assistants	89,000	Bachelor's degree
Medical Records and Health Information Technicians	202,000	Associate degree
Computer and Information Systems Managers	463,000	Master's degree
Home Health Aides	907,000	On-the-job training
Physical Therapist Aides	53,000	On-the-job training
Occupational Therapist Aides	12,000	On-the-job training
Physical Therapist Assistants	64,000	Associate degree
Audiologists	19,000	Master's degree
Fitness Trainers and Aerobics Instructors	222,000	Postsecondary Vocational Training
Computer and Information Scientists	39,000	Doctoral degree
Veterinary Assistants and Lab Animal Caretakers	77,000	On-the-job training
Occupational Therapist Assistants	23,000	Associate degree
Veterinary Technologists and Technicians	69,000	Associate degree
Speech-language Pathologists	122,000	Master's degree
Mental Health and Substance Abuse Social Workers	116,000	Master's degree
Dental Assistants	339,000	On-the-job training
Dental Hygienists	201,000	Associate degree
Special Education Teachers, grades Pre-K to 6	320,000	Bachelor's degree
Pharmacy Technicians	259,000	On-the-job training

Source: Bureau of Labor Statistics, Occupational Outlook Handbook

You say:

I don't even know what I want to do with my life.

GAJ says:

Many students don't know this about themselves until they get to experience some of the possibilities. Take the self-assessment on page 8 to help you determine what your interests and talents are. Read "How to Choose a Major" on page 101 for a listing of the most popular college majors and their related careers.

You say:

There is no way I can pursue my education full-time.

GAJ says:

Part-time students are becoming the norm. In fact, a recent study determined that 43 percent of undergraduate students attend school part-time. Most schools offer evening and weekend classes, and many offer work-study opportunities to help students pay for their education. Also, some employers will pay or reimburse you if you are working and want to further your education. If you are enrolled part-time, it takes longer to graduate. But if full-time enrollment is not an option for you, don't give up the opportunity to continue your education. There are many nontraditional ways to achieve your goals.

CHOOSING A CAREER YOU'LL BE HAPPY WITH

Did you know that of the estimated 15 million people searching for employment in the American job market, approximately 12 million are looking for a new occupation or a different employer? That's an awful lot of people who aren't happy with their jobs. Hopefully, you won't be one of them if you take some time to consider what it is you really want to do now, while you're still in school. Is there a particular type of job you've always dreamed of doing? Or perhaps you're one of the many high school students who say:

"I Kind of Know What I Want, But I'm Not Really Sure."

A good way to gather information about potential occupations is by talking with people who have achieved goals that are similar to yours. Talk to teachers, neighbors, and adult friends about their work experiences. The formal name for that activity is an "informational interview." You're interviewing them about the work they do—not to get a job from them but to gather information about their jobs.

If you don't have any contacts in a field that sparks your interest, do some poking around in the workplace. For instance, if you're interested in a career in nursing, you could visit a hospital, doctor's office, or nursing home. Most people love to talk about themselves, so don't be afraid to ask if they'll chat with you about their profession. Offering to volunteer your services can be the best way to know whether you'll be happy doing that type of work.

"I Haven't a Clue about What I Want to Do."

If you're completely unsure about what kind of work you'd like to do, contact a career counselor who can help you explore your options and possibly administer some interest and aptitude tests. You also might think about contacting a college career planning and placement office, a vocational school placement office, the counseling services of community agencies, or a private counseling service, which may charge you a fee. Many high schools offer job-shadowing programs, where students actually shadow someone in a particular occupation for an entire day or more. Don't forget that as a high school student, your best resource is your high school guidance counselor. Take a look at the list of the fastest-growing occupations on page 6 to get a sampling of the careers with the largest projected job growth in the coming years.

ON THE HUNT FOR INFORMATION

Regardless of how unsure you may be about what you want to do after high school, here's a list of things you can do to get the information you need to head in the right direction. Many people start off thinking they want one career and end up doing something completely different. But this is a good place to begin:

- Investigate careers both in and out of school. Participate in mentoring, job shadowing, and career day opportunities whenever possible.

- Get some on-the-job experience in a field that interests you.

- Research two-year and four-year colleges, vocational and technical schools, and apprenticeship programs.

- Participate in school and state career development activities.

- Prepare for and take aptitude and college entrance tests.

Here are a few Web sites where you can receive valuable direction by completing a career interest questionnaire or by reading about various occupations:

Peterson's

www.petersons.com

On Peterson's Web site, you can read helpful articles about the world of work and search for undergraduate academic and career-oriented degree and certificate programs.

Occupational Outlook Handbook

www.bls.gov/oco

The Bureau of Labor Statistics, an agency within the U.S. Department of Labor, produces this Web site, which offers more information than you'll ever need about a specific career.

SELF-ASSESSMENT INVENTORY

In addition to looking to outside sources for information, there's another rich source of data: yourself. Knowing what you want to do begins with knowing yourself—the real you. That's because the better you understand your own wants and needs, the better you will be able to make decisions about your career goals and dreams. This self-assessment inventory can help.

Who do you admire most, and why?

_____

What is your greatest strength?

_____

What is your greatest talent?

_____

What skills do you already have?

_____

DESCRIBE HOW YOU CURRENTLY USE THESE SKILLS IN YOUR LIFE:

Athletic ability_____

Mechanical ability_____

Ability to work with numbers_____

Leadership skills_____

Teaching skills_____

Artistic skills_____

Analytical skills_____

CHECK THE AREAS THAT MOST INTEREST YOU.

❑ Providing a practical service for people

❑ Self-expression in music, art, literature, or nature

❑ Organizing and record keeping

❑ Meeting people and supervising others

❑ Helping others in need, either mentally, spiritually, or physically

❑ Solving practical problems

❑ Working in forestry, farming, or fishing

❑ Working with machines and tools

❑ Taking care of animals

❑ Physical work out of doors

❑ Protecting the public via law enforcement or fire fighting

❑ Medical, scientific, or mathematical work

❑ Selling, advertising, or promoting

WHAT GIVES YOU SATISFACTION?

Answer the following questions True (T) or False (F).

T F I get satisfaction not from personal accomplishment, but from helping others.

T F I'd like to have a job in which I can use my imagination and be inventive.

T F In my life, money will be placed ahead of job security and personal interests.

T F It is my ambition to have a direct impact on other people's lives.

T F I am not a risk-taker and would prefer a career that offers little risk.

T F I enjoy working with people rather than by myself.

T F I would not be happy doing the same thing all the time.

WHAT MATTERS THE MOST TO YOU?

Rate the items on the list below from 1 to 10, with 10 being extremely important and 1 being not at all important.

___ Good health

___ Justice

___ Marriage/family

___ Faith

___ Fame

___ Beauty

___ Safety

___ Friendship

___ Respect

___ Accomplishment

___ Seeing the world

___ Love

___ Fun

___ Power

___ Individualism

___ Charity

___ Honor

___ Intelligence

___ Wealth

Mapping Your Future

www.mapping-your-future.org

On this site, you can find out how to choose a career and how to reach your career goals. You can also pick up useful tips on job hunting, resume writing, and job interviewing techniques. This site also provides a ten-step plan for determining and achieving your career goals.

University of Waterloo Career Development Manual

www.cdm.uwaterloo.ca/

This site provides a thorough online career interest survey, and you can use strategies to get the job that's right for you.

Motivational Appraisal of Personal Potential

www.assessment.com

Features a free 71-question career assessment that analyzes your motivation and points you to the ten best careers for you.

Monster.com

www.monster.com

Includes information about thousands of job and career fairs, advice on resumes, and much more.

WHAT WOULD YOU DO IF YOU WERE IN A BLIZZARD SURVIVAL SITUATION?

Check the one that would be your most likely role.

- ☐ The leader
- ☐ The one who explains the situation to the others
- ☐ The one who keeps morale up
- ☐ The one who invents a way to keep warm and melt snow for water
- ☐ The one who listens to instructions and keeps the supplies organized
- ☐ The one who positions sticks and rocks to signal SOS

LOOKING AHEAD AND LOOKING BACK

What are your goals for the next five years?

Where would you like to be in ten years?

What has been your favorite course, and why?

What was your least favorite course, and why?

Who was your favorite teacher, and why?

What are your hobbies?

What are your extracurricular activities?

What jobs have you held?

What volunteer work, if any, have you performed?

Have you ever shadowed a professional for a day? If so, what did you learn?

Do you have a mentor? If so, who? What have you learned from this person?

Do you want to stay close to home, or would you prefer to travel to another city after high school?

WHAT ARE YOUR CAREER GOALS?

My interests, skills, and knowledge supporting my career goals:

To fulfill my career goals, I will need additional skills and knowledge in:

I will obtain the additional skills and knowledge by taking part in the following educational activities:

I will need a degree, certification, and/or specialized training in:

When I look in the classified ads of the newspaper, the following job descriptions sound attractive to me:

WHAT WILL YOU NEED TO GET WHERE YOU'RE GOING?

The information I have given indicates that I will be selecting courses that are primarily:

- ☐ College path (Four-year or two-year education that offers liberal arts courses combined with courses in your area of interest.)
- ☐ Vocational path (One or more years of education that includes hands-on training for a specific job.)
- ☐ Combination of the two

WHAT ARE YOUR IMMEDIATE PLANS AFTER HIGH SCHOOL?

After high school, I plan to:

- ☐ work full-time
- ☐ work part-time and attend school
- ☐ attend college full-time
- ☐ attend technical college
- ☐ enter the military

MY PERFECT JOB WOULD BE ...

Let your imagination run wild. You can have any job you want. What's it like? Start by describing to yourself the following job conditions:

Work conditions: What hours are you willing to work? Do you feel most satisfied in an environment that is indoors/outdoors, varied/regular, noisy/quiet, or casual/traditional?

Duties: What duties do you feel comfortable carrying out? Do you want to be a leader, or do you perform best as a team player?

People: Do you want to work with other people or more independently? How much people contact do you want/need?

Education: How much special training or education is required? How much education are you willing to seek? Can you build upon the education or experience you have to date? Will you need to gain new education or experience?

Benefits: What salary and benefits do you expect? Are you willing to travel?

Disadvantages: There are disadvantages with almost any job. Can you imagine what the disadvantages may be? Can you confirm or disprove these beliefs by talking to someone or researching the industry or job further? If these disadvantages really exist, can you live with them?

Personal qualities: What qualities do you want in the employer you ultimately choose? What are the most important qualities that you want in a supervisor? In your coworkers?

Look over your responses to this assessment. Do you see recurring themes in your answers that start to show you what kind of career you might like? If not, there are many more places to get information to decide where your interests lie. You can go to your guidance counselor for advice. You can take the Campbell (TM) Interest and Skills Inventory, the Strong Interest Inventory, the Self-Directed Search, or other assessment tests that your guidance counselor recommends.

THE FIRST STEPS TO A CAREER

Don't be too surprised when your summer job turns into your career.

THE WORD "CAREER" has a scary sound to it when you're still in high school. Careers are for college graduates or those who have been in the workplace for years. But unless you grew up knowing for sure that you wanted to fly airplanes or be a marine biologist, what will you do? You'll be happy to know that interests you have now can very possibly lead to a college major or into a career. A job at a clothing store, for instance, could lead to a career designing clothes. Perhaps those hours you spend chasing Laura Croft, Tomb Raider, will lead to a career creating video games! Maybe you baby-sit and love being around kids, so teaching becomes an obvious choice. Perhaps cars fascinate you, and you find out you want to fix them for a living.

This section will show you how you can begin exploring your interests—sort of like getting into a swimming pool starting with your big toe, rather than plunging in. Vocational/career and tech-prep programs, summer jobs, and volunteering are all ways you can test various career paths to decide if you like them.

THE VOCATIONAL/CAREER EDUCATION PATH

If you're looking for a more real-world education, add yourself to the nearly 11 million youths and adults who are getting a taste of the workplace through vocational and career education programs offered in high schools across the nation. These programs are designed to help you develop competency in the skills you'll need in the workplace as well as in school.

What makes this kind of program different is that you learn in the classroom and in the "real world" of the workplace. Not only do you learn the academics in school, but you also get hands-on training by job shadowing, working under a mentor, and actually performing a job outside of school. Your interests and talents are usually taken into consideration, and you can choose from a variety of traditional, high-tech, and service industry training programs. Take a look at the following categories and see what piques your interest.

STUDENT COUNSEL

Q: What do you like about vocational training?

A: I jumped into the tech center my first year when I was a junior because I thought it was a good way to get out of school. But as the year went on, I said, "Hey, this is a good place to be because it's giving me job experience, and I'm learning how to dress and present myself like I was at a real job." I go during the first 3 or last 3 hours out of the school day. When we're in class, we get to do real jobs for people who ask our instructor for help. Then our teacher lets our creative minds go. We just designed a CD cover. One guy here designed a motorcycle and built it, and now he has three people asking him to come and work for them.

Trisha Younk
Tuscola County Tech Center
Reese High School
Reese, Michigan

Agricultural education. These programs prepare students for careers in agricultural production, animal production and care, agribusiness, agricultural and industrial mechanics, environmental management, farming, horticulture and landscaping, food processing, and natural resource management.

Business education. Students prepare for careers in accounting and finance and computer and data processing as well as administrative/secretarial and management/supervisory positions in professional environments (banking, insurance, law, public service).

Family and consumer sciences. These programs prepare students for careers in child care, food management and production, clothing and interiors, and hospitality and facility care. Core elements include personal development, family life and planning, resource management, and nutrition and wellness.

Trade and industrial and health occupations. Students prepare for careers in such fields as auto mechanics, the construction trades, cosmetology, electronics, graphics, public safety, and welding. Health occupation programs offer vocational training for careers in dental and medical assisting, practical nursing, home health care, and medical office assisting.

Marketing education. These programs prepare individuals for careers in sales, retail, advertising, food and restaurant marketing, and hotel management.

There are many vocational/career education programs available; the kinds listed above represent only a few of the possibilities. To find a program that suits your interests and that is located near you, refer to the listing of schools in the appendix of this book. Or, you can get more information about vocational education programs by calling 202-205-5451 or e-mailing the U.S. Department of Education, Office of Vocational and Adult Education via its Web site, www.ed.gov/offices/OVAE.

FROM THE GUIDANCE OFFICE

Q: What if going to college is not for me?

A: When adults ask kids what they want to do as a career, kids feel pressured. They think adults want them to identify with one single career. But there are more than 40,000 job titles a person can hold. We tell kids to pick a path first. When you exit high school, there are three paths you can take. One is to the workplace. One leads to the military as a career or as a stepping stone. The third leads to more education—a professional degree, a four-year degree, or a two-year degree. They have to determine which path they'll take.

One of the main selling points about getting career education in high school is that nearly every employer wants you to have some experience before you are hired. In career tech, students are in a workplace environment and can list their time as work experience, and they'll have previous employers who can vouch for them.

Lenore Lemanski
Counselor, Technology Center
Tuscola ISD
Caro, Michigan

THE TECH-PREP PATH

An even more advanced preparation for the workplace and/or an associate degree from a college is called tech prep. It's an educational path that combines college-prep and vocational/technical courses of study.

During the two-year course, the focus is on blending academic and vocational/technical competencies. When you graduate from high school, you'll be able to jump right into the workforce or get an associate degree. But if you want to follow this path, you've got to plan for it starting in the ninth grade. Ask your guidance counselor for more information.

USING THE SUMMER TO YOUR ADVANTAGE

When you're sitting in class, a summer with nothing to do might seem appealing. But after you've listened to all of your CDs, aced all of your video games, hung out at the same old mall, and talked to your friends on the phone about being bored, what's left? How about windsurfing on a cool, clear New England lake? Horseback riding along breathtaking mountain trails? Parlez en français in Paris? Trekking through spectacular canyon lands or living with a family in Costa Rica, Spain, Switzerland, or Japan? Exploring college majors or possible careers? Helping out on an archeological dig or community-service project? Along the way, you'll meet some wonderful people and maybe even make a couple of lifelong friends.

Interested? Get ready to pack your bags and join the 1 million kids and teens who will be having the summer of a lifetime at thousands of terrific camps, academic programs, sports clinics, arts workshops, internships, volunteer opportunities, and travel adventures throughout North America and abroad.

Oh, you don't have the money, you say? Not to worry. There are programs to meet every budget, from $50 workshops to $4,500 world treks and sessions that vary in length from just a couple of hours to a couple of months.

For a list of summer opportunities, take a look at the appendix in this book. You can also find out about summer opportunities by visiting www.petersons.com.

FROM THE GUIDANCE OFFICE

Q: What options are open to students who take high school career and technology classes and who feel they can't go to college?

A: Students have the opportunity to develop many skills through classes, student organizations, and career/technology classes during high school. These skills form an essential core that they can use to continue on to college, enter the job market, or participate in additional training after graduation. When students can identify those skills and make the connection by applying and expanding their skills as lifelong learners, then the possibilities are endless.

Linda S. Sanchez
Career and Technology Counselor
South San Antonio I.S.D.
Career Education Center
San Antonio, Texas

FLIP BURGERS AND LEARN ABOUT LIFE

A lot of teenagers who are anxious to earn extra cash spend their summers in retail or food service since those jobs are plentiful. If you're flipping burgers or helping customers find a special outfit, you might think the only thing you're getting out of the job is a paycheck. Think again. You will be amazed to discover that you have gained far more.

Being employed in these fields will teach you how to get along with demanding (and sometimes downright unpleasant) customers, how to work on a team, and how to handle money and order supplies. Not only do summer jobs teach you life skills, but they also offer ways to explore potential careers. What's more, when you apply to college or for a full-time job after high school graduation, the experience will look good on your application.

Sometimes, summer jobs become the very thing you want to do later in life. Before committing to a college major, summer jobs give you the opportunity to try out many directions. Students who think they want to be engineers, lawyers, or doctors might spend the summer shadowing an engineer, being a gofer in a legal firm, or volunteering in a hospital.

However, rather than grab the first job that comes along, find out where your interests are and build on what is natural for you. Activities you take for granted provide clues to what you are good at. What about that bookcase you built? Or those kids you love to baby-sit? Same thing with that big party you arranged. The environments you prefer provide other hints, too. Perhaps you feel best in the middle of a cluttered garage or surrounded by people. That suggests certain types of jobs.

Getting a summer job while in high school is the first step in a long line of work experiences to come. And the more experience you have, the better you'll be at getting jobs all your life. To search for summer jobs on the Internet, visit www.petersons.com, and click on the Summer Opportunities button.

TRY YOUR HAND AT AN INTERNSHIP

Each year, thousands of interns work in a wide variety of places, including corporations, law firms, government agencies, media organizations, interest groups, clinics, labs, museums, and historical sites. How popular are internships? Consider the recent trends. In the early 1980s, only 1 in 36 students completed an internship or other experiential learning program. Compare this to 2000, where one study found that 86 percent of college students had completed internships, with 69 percent reporting having had two or more. And an increasing number of high school students are signing up for internships now, too.

The Employer's Perspective

Employers consider internships a good option in both healthy and ailing economies. In healthy economies, managers often struggle to fill their positions with eager workers who can adapt to changing technologies. Internships offer a low-cost way to get good workers into "the pipeline" without offering them a full-time position up front. In struggling economies, on the other hand, downsizing often requires employers to lay off workers without thinking about who will cover their responsibilities. Internships offer an inexpensive way to offset position losses resulting from these disruptive layoffs.

The Intern's Perspective

If you are looking to begin a career or supplement your education with practical training, internships are a good bet for several reasons.

1. **Internships offer a relatively quick way to gain work experience and develop job skills.** Try this exercise. Scan the Sunday want ads of your newspaper. Choose a range of interesting advertisements for professional positions that you would consider taking. List the desired or required job skills and work experiences specified in the ads. How many of these skills and experiences do you have?

Chances are, if you are still in school or a recent graduate, you don't have most of the skills and experience that employers require of their new hires. What do you do?

The growing reality is that many entry-level positions require skills and experiences that schools and part-time jobs don't provide. Sure, you know your way around a computer. You have some customer service experience. You may even have edited your school's newspaper or organized your senior prom. But you still lack the relevant skills and on-the-job experiences that many hiring managers require. A well-chosen internship can offer a way out of this common dilemma by providing you job training in an actual career field. Internships help you take your existing knowledge and skills and apply them in ways that will help you compete for good jobs.

2. **Internships offer a relatively risk-free way to explore a possible career path.** Believe it or not, the best internship may tell you what you *don't* want to do for the next ten or twenty years. Think about it. If you put all your eggs in one basket, what happens if your dream job turns out to be the exact opposite of what you want or who you are? Internships offer a relatively low-cost opportunity to "try out" a career field to see if it's right for *you*.

3. **Internships offer real opportunities to do career networking and can significantly increase your chances of landing a good full-time position.** Have you heard the saying: "It's not what you know, but who you know"? For good or ill, the reality is that who you know (or who knows you) can make a big difference in your job search. Studies show fewer than 20 percent of job placements occur through traditional application methods, including newspaper and trade journal advertisements, employment agencies, and career fairs. Instead, 60 to 90 percent of jobs are found through personal contacts and direct application.

Career "networking" is the exchange of information with others for mutual benefit. Your career network can tell you where the jobs are and help you compete for them. Isn't it better to develop your networking skills now, when the stakes aren't as high, than later when you are competing with everyone else for full-time jobs? The internship hiring process and the weeks you actually spend on the job provide excellent opportunities to talk with various people about careers, your skills, and ways to succeed.

VOLUNTEERING IN YOUR COMMUNITY

You've probably heard the saying that money isn't everything. Well, it's true, especially when it comes to volunteering and community service. There are a number of benefits you'll get that don't add up in dollars and cents but do add up to open doors in your future.

Community service looks good on a college application. Admissions staff members look for applicants who have volunteered and done community service in addition to grades. You could have gotten top grades, but if that's all that's on your application, you won't come across as a well-rounded person.

Community service lets you try out careers. How will you know you'll like a certain type of work if you haven't seen it done? For instance, you might think you want to work in the health-care field. Volunteering in a hospital will let you know if this is really what you want to do.

Community service is an American tradition. You'll be able to meet some of your own community's needs and join with all of the people who have contributed their talents to our country. No matter what your talents, there are unlimited ways for you to serve your community. Take a look at your interests, and then see how they can be applied to help others.

Here are some ideas to get you started:

❑ **Do you like kids?** Volunteer at your local parks and recreation department, for a Little League team, or as a big brother or sister.

❑ **Planning a career in health care?** Volunteer at a blood bank, clinic, hospital, retirement home, or hospice. There are also several organizations that raise money for disease research.

❑ **Interested in the environment?** Volunteer to assist in a recycling program. Create a beautification program for your school or community. Plant trees and flowers or design a community garden.

❑ **Just say no.** Help others stay off drugs and alcohol by volunteering at a crisis center, hotline, or prevention program. Help educate younger kids about the dangers of drug abuse.

❑ **Lend a hand.** Collect money, food, or clothing for the homeless. Food banks, homeless shelters, and charitable organizations need your help.

❑ **Is art your talent?** Share your knowledge and skills with youngsters, the elderly, or local arts organizations that depend on volunteers to help present their plays, recitals, and exhibitions.

❑ **Help fight crime.** Form a neighborhood watch or organize a group to clean up graffiti.

❑ **Your church or synagogue may have projects that need youth volunteers.** The United Way, your local politician's office, civic groups, and special interest organizations also provide exceptional opportunities to serve your community. Ask your principal, teachers, or counselors for additional ideas.

For more information on joining in the spirit of youth volunteerism, write to the Consumer Information Center, CIC-00A, P.O. Box 100, Pueblo, Colorado 81002, and request the *Catch the Spirit* booklet, or call 719-948-3334. Also check out the CIC's Web site at www.pueblo.gsa.gov.

Part 2

THE ROAD TO MORE EDUCATION

SOME PEOPLE WAKE up at age three and announce that they want to be doctors, teachers, or marine biologists—and they do it.

They're the exceptions. Many high school students don't have a clue about what they want to be. They dread the question, "So, what are you doing after graduating from high school?" Unfortunately, some of those same people also end up in careers that don't satisfy them.

You don't have to plan the rest of your life down to the last detail, but you can start to take some general steps toward your future and lay the groundwork. Then, when you do decide what you want to do, you'll be able to seize hold of your dream and go with it.

Chapter 3

PLANNING YOUR EDUCATION IN HIGH SCHOOL

Some people are planners. They make a plan, and they follow it. Then there are the non-planners.

Non-planners see the words "plan" and "future" and say, "Yeah, yeah, I know." Meanwhile, they're running out the door for an appointment they were supposed to be at 5 minutes ago.

Unfortunately, when it comes time to really do something about those goals and future hopes, the non-planners often discover that much of what should have been done wasn't done—which is not good when they're planning their future after high school. What about those classes they should have taken? What about those jobs they should have volunteered for? What about that scholarship they could have had if only they'd found out about it sooner?

But there is hope for poor planners. Now that you've thought about yourself and the direction you might want to go after graduating, you can use this section to help you plan what you should be doing while still in high school and when you should be doing it.

Regardless of what type of education you're planning on after high school, here's a plan to help you get there.

YOUR EDUCATION TIMELINE

Use this timeline to help you make sure you're accomplishing everything you need to accomplish on time.

Ninth Grade

- As soon as you can, meet with your counselor to begin talking about colleges and careers.

- Make sure you are enrolled in the appropriate college-preparatory or tech-prep courses.

- Get off to a good start with your grades. The grades you earn in ninth grade will be included in your final high school GPA and class rank.

- College might seem a long way off now, but grades really do count toward college admission and scholarships.

- Explore your interests and possible careers. Take advantage of Career Day opportunities.

- Get involved in extracurricular activities (both school and non-school-sponsored).

- Talk to your parents about planning for college expenses. Continue or begin a savings plan for college.

- Look at the college information available in your counselor's office and library. Use the Internet to check out college Web sites. Visit Peterson's at www.petersons.com to start a list of colleges that might interest you.

- Tour a nearby college, if possible. Visit relatives or friends who live on or near a college campus. Check out the dorms, go to the library or student center, and get a feel for college life.

⏰ Investigate summer enrichment programs. Visit www.petersons.com for some neat ideas about summer opportunities.

Tenth Grade

Fall

⏰ In October, take the Preliminary SAT/National Merit Scholarship Qualifying Test (PSAT/NMSQT) for practice. When you fill out your test sheet, check the box that releases your name to colleges so you can start receiving brochures from them.

⏰ Ask your guidance counselor about the American College Testing program's PLAN (Pre-ACT) assessment program, which helps determine your study habits and academic progress and interests. This test will prepare you for the ACT Assessment next year.

⏰ Take geometry if you have not already done so. Take biology and a second year of a foreign language.

⏰ Become familiar with general college entrance requirements.

⏰ Participate in your school's or state's career development activities.

⏰ Visit Petersons.com for advice on test taking and general college entrance requirements.

Winter

⏰ Discuss your PSAT score with your counselor.

⏰ The people who read college applications aren't looking just for grades. Get involved in activities outside the classroom. Work toward leadership positions in the activities that you like best. Become involved in community service and other volunteer activities.

⏰ Read, read, read. Read as many books as possible from a comprehensive reading list, like the one on pages 24 and 25.

⏰ Read the newspaper every day to learn about current affairs.

⏰ Work on your writing skills—you'll need them no matter what you do.

⏰ Find a teacher or another adult who will advise and encourage you to write well.

Spring

⏰ Keep your grades up so you can have the highest GPA and class rank possible.

⏰ Ask your counselor about postsecondary enrollment options and Advanced Placement (AP) courses.

⏰ Continue to explore your interests and careers that you think you might like.

⏰ Begin zeroing in on the type of college you would prefer (two-year or four-year, small or large, rural or urban). To get an idea of what's available, take a look at college profiles on Petersons.com or read books about college.

⏰ If you are interested in attending a military academy such as West Point or Annapolis, now is the time to start planning and getting information.

⏰ Write to colleges and ask for their academic requirements for admission.

PARENT PERSPECTIVE

Q: When should parents and their children start thinking about preparing for college?

A: The discussion needs to start in middle school. If parents don't expose their children to these concepts at that time, then it can be too late in the game. Children need to take the right courses in high school. Many kids here end up going to junior colleges because they don't meet the minimum requirements when they graduate. Many universities and private colleges don't count some of the classes kids take in high school. You can't wait until the child is 18 and then say, "Maybe we should do something about getting into college."

Kevin Carr

Parent

Oak Park, California

- Visit a few more college campuses. Read all of the mail you receive from colleges. You may see something you like.

- Attend college fairs.

- Keep putting money away for college. Get a summer job.

- Consider taking SAT II Subject Tests in the courses you took this year while the material is still fresh in your mind. These tests are offered in May and June.

Eleventh Grade

Fall

- Meet with your counselor to review the courses you've taken, and see what you still need to take.

- Check your class rank. Even if your grades haven't been that good so far, it's never too late to improve. Colleges like to see an upward trend.

- If you didn't do so in tenth grade, sign up for and take the PSAT/NMSQT. In addition to National Merit Scholarships, this is the qualifying test for the National Scholarship Service and Fund for Negro Students and the National Hispanic Scholar Recognition Program.

- Make sure that you have a social security number.

- Take a long, hard look at why you want to continue your education after high school so you will be able to choose the best college or university for your needs.

- Make a list of colleges that meet your most important criteria (size, location, distance from home, majors, academic rigor, housing, and cost). Weigh each of the factors according to their importance to you.

- Continue visiting college fairs. You may be able to narrow your choices or add a college to your list.

PARENT PERSPECTIVE

Q: How involved should parents get in the selection of a college for their children?

A: Parents are getting more involved than ever before in supporting their children in the college process. This phenomenon is due to two factors:

This generation of parents has been much more involved with their children in dealing with the outside world than were their parents.

The investment made by today's parents is much more than that made by parents 20 or 30 years ago. As parents focus on the cost of this big-ticket item, there's interest to be more involved, to get the proper return.

Parents certainly should be involved in the college selection and application process. Studies clearly indicate that parental support in this process and throughout the college years can make a big difference in the success of a student. But this process also should be a learning opportunity in decision making for students. In that regard, parents shouldn't direct the student but provide input and the framework to assist their students.

Parents should not feel uncomfortable making suggestions to help their children through the thought and selection process—especially when it comes to identifying schools that their pocketbooks can accommodate. However, the child must be comfortable with the final decision and must have ultimate responsibility for the selection of the school. When students have made the final decision, it can help in their level of commitment because they've invested in it. They have a responsibility to do well and complete their academics at that location.

Richard Flaherty
President, College Parents of America

- Speak to college representatives who visit your high school.

- If you want to participate in Division I or Division II sports in college, start the certification process. Check with your counselor to make sure you are taking a core curriculum that meets NCAA requirements.

- If you are interested in one of the military academies, talk to your guidance counselor about starting the application process now.

SIX STUDY SKILLS THAT LEAD TO SUCCESS

1. **SET A REGULAR STUDY SCHEDULE.** No one at college is going to hound you to do your homework. Develop the study patterns in high school that will lead to success in college. Anyone who has ever pulled an all-nighter knows how much you remember when you are on the downside of your fifth cup of coffee and no sleep—not much! Nothing beats steady and consistent study habits.

2. **SAVE EVERYTHING.** To make sure your history notes don't end up in your math notebook and your English papers don't get thrown at the bottom of your friend's locker, develop an organized system for storing your papers. Stay on top of your materials, and be sure to save quizzes and tests. It is amazing how questions from a test you took in March can miraculously reappear on your final exam.

3. **LISTEN.** Teachers give away what will be on the test by repeating themselves. If you pay attention to what the teacher is saying, you will probably notice what is being emphasized. If what the teacher says in class repeats itself in your notes and in review sessions, chances are that material will be on the test. So really listen.

4. **TAKE NOTES.** If the teacher has taken the time to prepare a lecture, then what he or she says is important enough for you to write down. Develop a system for reviewing your notes. After each class, rewrite them, review them, or reread them. Try highlighting the important points or making notes in the margins to jar your memory.

5. **USE TEXTBOOKS WISELY.** What can you do with a textbook besides lose it? Use it to back up or clarify information that you don't understand from your class notes. Reading every word may be more effort than it is worth, so look at the book intelligently. What is in boxes or highlighted areas? What content is emphasized? What do the questions ask about in the review sections?

6. **FORM A STUDY GROUP.** Establish a group that will stay on task and ask one another the questions you think the teacher will ask. Compare notes to see if you have all the important facts. And discuss your thoughts. Talking ideas out can help when you have to respond to an essay question.

Winter

- Collect information about college application procedures, entrance requirements, tuition and fees, room and board costs, student activities, course offerings, faculty composition, accreditation, and financial aid. The Internet is a good way to visit colleges and obtain this information. Begin comparing the schools by the factors that you consider to be most important.

- Discuss your PSAT score with your counselor.

- Begin narrowing down your college choices. Find out if the colleges you are interested in require the SAT I, ACT Assessment, or SAT II Subject Tests for admission.

- Register for the SAT I and additional SAT II Subject Tests, which are offered several times during the winter and spring of your junior year (see the "Tackling the Tests" section for a schedule). You can take them again in the fall of your senior year if you are unhappy with your scores.

- Register for the ACT Assessment, which is usually taken in April or June. You can take it again late in your junior year or in the fall of your senior year, if necessary.

- Begin preparing for the tests you've decided to take.

- Have a discussion with your parents about the colleges in which you are interested. Examine financial resources, and gather information about financial aid. Check out the chapter on financial aid later in this book for a step-by-step explanation of the financial aid process.

- Set up a filing system with individual folders for each college's correspondence and printed materials.

Spring

- Meet with your counselor to review senior-year course selection and graduation requirements.

- Discuss ACT Assessment/SAT I scores with your counselor. Register to take the ACT Assessment and/or SAT I again if you'd like to try to increase your score.

- Discuss the college essay with your guidance counselor or English teacher.

- Stay involved with your extracurricular activities. Colleges look for consistency and depth in activities.

⊕ Consider whom you will ask to write your recommendations. Think about asking teachers who know you well and who will write positive letters about you. Letters from a coach, activity leader, or an adult who knows you well outside of school (e.g., volunteer work contact) are also valuable.

⊕ Inquire about personal interviews at your favorite colleges. Call or write for early summer appointments. Make necessary travel arrangements.

⊕ See your counselor to apply for on-campus summer programs for high school students. Apply for a summer job or internship. Be prepared to pay for college application, financial aid, and testing fees in the fall.

⊕ Request applications from schools you're interested in by mail or via the Internet.

Summer

⊕ Visit the campuses of your top-five college choices.

⊕ After each college interview, send a thank-you letter to the interviewer.

⊕ Talk to people you know who have attended the colleges in which you are interested.

⊕ Continue to read books, magazines, and newspapers.

⊕ Practice filling out college applications, and then type the final application forms or apply on line through the Web sites of the colleges in which you're interested.

⊕ Volunteer in your community.

⊕ Compose rough drafts of your college essays. Have a teacher read and discuss them with you. Polish them, and prepare final drafts. Proofread your final essays at least three times.

⊕ Develop a financial aid application plan, including a list of the aid sources, requirements for each application, and a timetable for meeting the filing deadlines.

ADMISSIONS ADVICE

Q: Other than grades and test scores, what are the most important qualities that you look for in students?

A: We consider the types of classes students have taken. A grade of a B in an honors class is competitive to an A in a regular course. We seek not only academically talented students but those who are well rounded. They need to submit their interests and activities, letters of recommendation, and writing samples in addition to their test scores. We look for someone that's involved in his or her community and high school, someone that holds leadership positions and has a balance of activities outside of academics. This gives us a look at that person as a whole.

Cheyenna Smith
Admission Counselor
University of Houston
Houston, Texas

Twelfth Grade

Fall

⊕ Continue to take a full course load of college-prep courses.

⊕ Keep working on your grades. Make sure you have taken the courses necessary to graduate in the spring.

⊕ Continue to participate in extracurricular and volunteer activities. Demonstrate initiative, creativity, commitment, and leadership in each.

⊕ To male students: you must register for selective service on your eighteenth birthday to be eligible for federal and state financial aid.

⊕ Talk to counselors, teachers, and parents about your final college choices.

⊕ Make a calendar showing application deadlines for admission, financial aid, and scholarships.

⊕ Check resource books, computer programs, and your guidance office for information on scholarships and grants. Ask colleges about scholarships for which you may qualify.

Check out Petersons.com for information on scholarships.

⊕ Give recommendation forms to the teachers you have chosen, along with stamped, self-addressed envelopes so your teachers can send them directly to the colleges. Be sure to fill out your name, address, and school name on the top of the form. Talk to your recommendation writers about your goals and ambitions.

⊕ Give School Report forms to your high school's guidance office. Fill in your name, address, and any other required information on top. Verify with your guidance counselor the schools to which transcripts, test scores, and letters are to be sent. Give your counselor any necessary forms at least two weeks before they are due or whenever your counselor's deadline is, whichever is earlier.

⊕ Register for and take the ACT Assessment, SAT I, or SAT II Subject Tests, as necessary.

⊕ Be sure you have requested (either by mail or on line) that your test scores be sent to the colleges of your choice.

⊕ Mail or send electronically any college applications for early decision admission by November 1.

⊕ If possible, visit colleges while classes are in session.

⊕ If you plan to apply for an ROTC scholarship, remember that your application is due by December 1.

⊕ Print extra copies or make photocopies of every application you send.

Winter

⊕ Attend whatever college-preparatory nights are held at your school or by local organizations.

⊕ Send midyear grade reports to colleges. Continue to focus on your schoolwork!

⊕ Fill out the Free Application for Federal Student Aid (FAFSA) and, if necessary, the Financial Aid Profile (FAP). These forms can be obtained from your guidance counselor or at www.ed.gov/offices/OPE/express.html to download the forms or to file electronically. These forms may not be processed before January 1, so don't send it before then.

⊕ Mail or send electronically any remaining applications and financial aid forms before winter break. Make sure you apply to at least one college that you know you can afford and where you know you will be accepted.

⊕ Follow up to make sure that the colleges have received all application information, including recommendations and test scores.

⊕ Meet with your counselor to verify that all applicable forms are in order and have been sent out to colleges.

Spring

⊕ Watch your mail between March 1 and April 1 for acceptance notifications from colleges.

⊕ Watch your mail for notification of financial aid awards between April 1 and May 1.

⊕ Compare the financial aid packages from the colleges and universities that have accepted you.

⊕ Make your final choice, and notify all schools of your intent by May 1. If possible, do not decide without making at least one campus visit. Send your nonrefundable deposit to your chosen school by May 1 as well. Request that your guidance counselor send a final transcript to the college in June.

⊕ Be sure that you have received a FAFSA acknowledgment.

⊕ If you applied for a Pell Grant (on the FAFSA), you will receive a Student Aid Report (SAR) statement. Review this Pell notice, and forward it to the college you plan to attend. Make a copy for your records.

🕐 Complete follow-up paperwork for the college of your choice (scheduling, orientation session, housing arrangements, and other necessary forms).

Summer

🕐 If applicable, apply for a Stafford Loan through a lender. Allow eight weeks for processing.

🕐 Receive the orientation schedule from your college.

🕐 Get residence hall assignment from your college.

🕐 Obtain course scheduling and cost information from your college.

🕐 Congratulations! You are about to begin the greatest adventure of your life. Good luck.

CLASSES TO TAKE IF YOU'RE GOING TO COLLEGE

Did you know that classes you take as early as the ninth grade will help you get into college? Make sure you take at least the minimum high school curriculum requirements necessary for college admission. Even if you don't plan to enter college immediately, take the most demanding courses you can handle.

Review the list of suggested courses on this page. Some courses, categories, and names might vary from state to state, but the following may be used as a guideline. Talk with your guidance counselor to select the curriculum that best meets your needs and skills.

Of course, learning also occurs outside of school. While outside activities will not make up for poor academic performance, skills learned from jobs, extracurricular activities, and volunteer opportunities will help you become a well-rounded student and will strengthen your college or job application.

Getting a Head Start on College Courses

You can take college courses while still in high school so that when you're in college, you'll be ahead of

SUGGESTED COURSES

College-Preparatory Curriculum

ENGLISH. Four units, with emphasis on composition (English 9, 10, 11, 12)

MATHEMATICS. Three units (algebra I, algebra II, geometry) are essential. Trigonometry, precalculus, calculus, and computer science are recommended for some fields of study.

SOCIAL SCIENCE. Three units (American history, world history, government/economics)

SCIENCE. Four units (earth science, biology, chemistry, physics)

FOREIGN LANGUAGE. Three units (at least 2 years in the same language)

FINE ARTS. One to 2 units

OTHER. Keyboarding, computer applications, computer science I, computer science II, physical education, health

College-Preparatory Curriculum Combined with a Career Education or Vocational Program

ENGLISH. Four units

MATHEMATICS. Three units (algebra I, algebra II, geometry)

SOCIAL SCIENCE. Three units (American history, world history, government/economics)

SCIENCE. Two units (earth science, biology)

FOREIGN LANGUAGE. Three units (at least 2 years in the same language)

FINE ARTS. One to 2 units

OTHER. Keyboarding, computer applications, physical education, and health and half-days at the Career Center during junior and senior year

everyone else. The formal name is postsecondary enrollment. What it means is that some students can take college courses and receive both high school and college credit for the courses taken. It's like a two-for-one deal!

Postsecondary enrollment is designed to provide an opportunity for qualified high school students to experience more advanced academic work. Participation in a postsecondary enrollment program is not intended to replace courses available in high school but rather to enhance the educational opportunities available to students while in high school. There are two options for postsecondary enrollment:

Option A: Qualified high school juniors and seniors take courses for college credit. Students enrolled under Option A must pay for all books, supplies, tuition, and associated fees.

Option B: Qualified high school juniors and seniors take courses for high school and college credit. For students enrolled under this option, the local school district covers the related costs, provided that the student completes the selected courses. Otherwise, the student and parent will be assessed the costs.

Certain preestablished conditions must be met for enrollment, so check with your high school counselor for more information.

SUGGESTED READING LIST FOR GRADES 9 THROUGH 12

Instead of flipping on the TV or putting on those headphones, how about picking up a book instead? Reading not only will take you to wonderful, unexplored worlds in your imagination, but there are practical reasons as well. Reading gives you a more well-rounded background. College admissions and future employers pick up on that. And you'll be able to answer the questions, "Did you read that book? What did you think of it?" How many of the books on this list have you read?

Adams, Richard
 Watership Down
Aesop
 Fables
Agee, James
 A Death in the Family
Anderson, Sherwood
 Winesburg, Ohio
Anonymous
 Go Ask Alice
Asimov, Isaac
 Short Stories
Austen, Jane
 Emma
 Northanger Abbey
 Pride and Prejudice
 Sense and Sensibility
Baldwin, James
 Go Tell It on the Mountain
Balzac, Honore de
 Pere Goriot
Beckett, Samuel
 Waiting for Godot
Bolt, Robert
 A Man for All Seasons
Brontë, Charlotte
 Jane Eyre
Brontë, Emily
 Wuthering Heights
Brooks, Gwendolyn
 In the Mecca
 Riot

Browning, Robert
 Poems
Buck, Pearl
 The Good Earth
Butler, Samuel
 The Way of All Flesh
Camus, Albert
 The Plague
 The Stranger
Cather, Willa
 Death Comes for the Archbishop
 My Antonia
Cervantes, Miguel
 Don Quixote
Chaucer, Geoffrey
 The Canterbury Tales
Chekhov, Anton
 The Cherry Orchard
Chopin, Kate
 The Awakening
Collins, Wilkie
 The Moonstone
Conrad, Joseph
 Heart of Darkness
 Lord Jim
 The Secret Sharer
 Victory
Crane, Stephen
 The Red Badge of Courage
Dante
 The Divine Comedy

Defoe, Daniel
 Moll Flanders
Dickens, Charles
 Bleak House
 David Copperfield
 Great Expectations
 Hard Times
 Oliver Twist
 A Tale of Two Cities
Dickinson, Emily
 Poems
Dinesen, Isak
 Out of Africa
Dostoevski, Fyodor
 The Brothers Karamazov
 Crime and Punishment
Douglas, Frederick
 The Life of Frederick Douglas
Dreiser, Theodore
 An American Tragedy
 Sister Carrie
Early, Gerald
 Tuxedo Junction
Eliot, George
 Adam Bede
 Middlemarch
 The Mill on the Floss
 Silas Marner

Eliot, T. S.
 Murder in the Cathedral
Ellison, Ralph
 Invisible Man
Emerson, Ralph Waldo
 Essays
Faulkner, William
 Absalom, Absalom!
 As I Lay Dying
 Intruder in the Dust
 Light in August
 The Sound and the Fury
Fielding, Henry
 Joseph Andrews
 Tom Jones
Fitzgerald, F. Scott
 The Great Gatsby
 Tender Is the Night
Flaubert, Gustave
 Madame Bovary
Forster, E. M.
 A Passage to India
 A Room with a View
Franklin, Benjamin
 The Autobiography of Benjamin Franklin
Galsworthy, John
 The Forsyte Saga

Golding, William
 Lord of the Flies
Goldsmith, Oliver
 She Stoops to Conquer
Graves, Robert
 I, Claudius
Greene, Graham
 The Heart of the Matter
 The Power and the Glory
Hamilton, Edith
 Mythology
Hardy, Thomas
 Far from the Madding Crowd
 Jude the Obscure
 The Mayor of Casterbridge
 The Return of the Native
 Tess of the D'Urbervilles
Hawthorne, Nathaniel
 The House of the Seven Gables
 The Scarlet Letter
Hemingway, Ernest
 A Farewell to Arms
 For Whom the Bell Tolls
 The Sun Also Rises
Henry, O.
 Stories

Hersey, John
 A Single Pebble
Hesse, Hermann
 Demian
 Siddhartha
 Steppenwolf
Homer
 The Iliad
 The Odyssey
Hughes, Langston
 Poems
 The Big Sea
Hugo, Victor
 Les Misérables
Huxley, Aldous
 Brave New World
Ibsen, Henrik
 A Doll's House
 An Enemy of the People
 Ghosts
 Hedda Gabler
 The Master Builder
 The Wild Duck
James, Henry
 The American
 Daisy Miller
 Portrait of a Lady
 The Turn of the Screw
Joyce, James
 Dubliners
 A Portrait of the Artist as a Young Man

Kafka, Franz
The Castle
The Metamorphosis
The Trial

Keats, John
Poems

Kerouac, Jack
On the Road

Koestler, Arthur
Darkness at Noon

Lawrence, Jerome, and Robert E. Lee
Inherit the Wind

Lewis, Sinclair
Arrowsmith
Babbitt
Main Street

Llewellyn, Richard
How Green Was My Valley

Machiavelli
The Prince

MacLeish, Archibald
J.B.

Mann, Thomas
Buddenbrooks
The Magic Mountain

Marlowe, Christopher
Dr. Faustus

Maugham, Somerset
Of Human Bondage

McCullers, Carson
The Heart Is a Lonely Hunter

Melville, Herman
Billy Budd
Moby-Dick
Typee

Miller, Arthur
The Crucible
Death of a Salesman

Monsarrat, Nicholas
The Cruel Sea

Naylor, Gloria
Bailey's Cafe
The Women of Brewster Place

O'Neill, Eugene
The Emperor Jones
Long Day's Journey Into Night
Mourning Becomes Electra

Orwell, George
Animal Farm
1984

Pasternak, Boris
Doctor Zhivago

Poe, Edgar Allan
Short Stories

Remarque, Erich
All Quiet on the Western Front

Rolvaag, O. E.
Giants in the Earth

Rostand, Edmond
Cyrano de Bergerac

Salinger, J. D.
The Catcher in the Rye

Sandburg, Carl
Abraham Lincoln: The Prairie Years
Abraham Lincoln: The War Years

Saroyan, William
The Human Comedy

Sayers, Dorothy
The Nine Tailors

Shakespeare, William
Plays and Sonnets

Shaw, George Bernard
Arms and the Man
Major Barbara
Pygmalion
Saint Joan

Sheridan, Richard B.
The School for Scandal

Shute, Nevil
On the Beach

Sinclair, Upton
The Jungle

Sophocles
Antigone
Oedipus Rex

Steinbeck, John
East of Eden
The Grapes of Wrath
Of Mice and Men

Stowe, Harriet Beecher
Uncle Tom's Cabin

Swift, Jonathan
Gulliver's Travels

Thackeray, William M.
Vanity Fair

Thoreau, Henry David
Walden

Tolstoy, Leo
Anna Karenina
War and Peace

Trollope, Anthony
Barchester Towers

Turgenev, Ivan
Fathers and Sons

Twain, Mark
Pudd'nhead Wilson

Updike, John
Rabbit, Run

Vergil
The Aeneid

Voltaire
Candide

Walker, Alice
The Color Purple
Meridian

Warren, Robert Penn
All the King's Men

Waugh, Evelyn
Brideshead Revisited
A Handful of Dust

Wharton, Edith
The Age of Innocence

White, T. H.
The Once and Future King
The Sword in the Stone

Wilde, Oscar
The Importance of Being Earnest
The Picture of Dorian Gray

Wilder, Thornton
Our Town

Williams, Tennessee
The Glass Menagerie
A Streetcar Named Desire

Wolfe, Thomas
Look Homeward, Angel

Woolf, Virginia
Mrs. Dalloway
To the Lighthouse

Wouk, Herman
The Caine Mutiny

Wright, Richard
Black Boy
Native Son

Source: The National Endowment for the Humanities.

For more book recommendations, see what college professors suggest in **Arco's Reading Lists for College-Bound Students**, *available at your local bookstore.*

4 Chapter

TACKLING THE TESTS

Unless you've been on another planet for the last two or three years, you've probably heard older high school students buzzing about the alphabet soup list of college entrance exams—SAT, ACT, and PSAT.

SOME OF THE STUDENTS who are getting ready to take one of these tests look like they're in various shades of hysteria. Others have been studying for months on end, so when they open their mouths, out pops the definition for "meretricious" or the answer to "What is the ratio of 3 pounds to 6 ounces?" Well, the talk that you've heard about the tests is partly true. They are a big deal and can be crucial to your academic plans. On the other hand, you don't have to walk in cold. Remember that word "planning"? It's a whole lot nicer than the word "panic." Preparing for the tests takes a lot of planning and time, but if you're reading this section, you're already ahead of the game.

A FEW FACTS ABOUT THE MAJOR TESTS

The major standardized tests students take in high school are the PSAT, SAT I, and ACT Assessment. Colleges across the country use them to get a sense of a student's readiness to enter their ivy-covered halls. These tests, or "boards" as they are sometimes called, have become notorious because of how important they can be. There is a mystique that surrounds them. People talk about the "magic number" that will get you into the school of your dreams.

Beware! There is a lot of misinformation out there. First and foremost, these are not intelligence tests; they are reasoning tests designed to evaluate the way you think. These tests assess the basic knowledge and skills you have gained through your classes in school, and they also gauge the knowledge you have gained through outside experience. The material on these tests is not curriculum-based, but the tests do emphasize those academic experiences that educational institutions feel are good indicators of your probable success in college.

THE ACT ASSESSMENT

The ACT Assessment is a standardized college entrance examination that measures knowledge and skills in English, mathematics, reading, and science reasoning and the application of these skills to future academic tasks. The ACT Assessment consists of four multiple-choice tests.

Test 1: English

- 75 questions, 45 minutes
- Punctuation
- Grammar and usage
- Sentence structure
- Strategy
- Organization
- Style

Test 2: Mathematics

- 60 questions, 60 minutes
- Pre-algebra
- Elementary algebra
- Intermediate algebra

- Coordinate geometry

- Plane geometry

- Trigonometry

Test 3: Reading

- 40 questions, 35 minutes

- Prose fiction

- Humanities

- Social studies

- Natural sciences

Test 4: Science Reasoning

- 40 questions, 35 minutes

- Biology

- Physical science

- Chemistry

- Physics

Each section is scored from 1 to 36 and is scaled for slight variations in difficulty. Students are not penalized for incorrect responses. The composite score is the average of the four scaled scores.

To prepare for the ACT Assessment, ask your guidance counselor for a free guidebook called *Preparing for the ACT Assessment*. Besides providing general test-preparation information and additional test-taking strategies, this guidebook describes the content and format of the four ACT Assessment subject area tests, summarizes test administration procedures followed at ACT Assessment test centers, and includes a practice test.

THE SAT

The SAT I measures developed verbal and mathematical reasoning abilities as they relate to successful performance in college. It is intended to supplement the secondary school record and other information about the student in assessing readiness for college. There is one unscored, experimental section on the exam, which is used for equating and/or

STUDENT COUNSEL

Q: What kept you from stressing out about the tests?

A: The best way I found to prepare was to take practice tests to get to know the questions. At first, I'd set the kitchen timer and practice while ignoring the time, just to see what I could do. Practice is the best because they don't really change the type of questions. You read that in every review book, and it's true.

My advice for dealing with the stress on test day? The night before, I watched movies and had popcorn. When you take the test, definitely bring candy. A candy bar in between each section helps.

Theresa-Marie Russo
Edgemont High School
Scarsdale, New York

pretesting purposes and can cover either the mathematics or verbal subject area.

Verbal Reasoning

- 78 questions, 75 minutes

- Analogies

- Sentence completions

- Critical reading passages

Mathematical Reasoning

- 60 questions, 75 minutes

- Student-produced responses

- Quantitative comparisons

- Regular math

Experimental Section

- 30 minutes

Students receive one point for each correct response and lose a fraction of a point for each incorrect response (except for student-produced responses). These points are totaled to produce the raw scores, which are then scaled to equalize the scores for slight variations in difficulty for various editions of the test. Both the verbal scaled score range and the math scaled

THE NEW SAT I

You've probably heard a rumor that the SAT I is changing. The rumor's true, but don't worry: Nothing will happen until 2005. In case you're not planning on taking the exam until then, here's what you have to look forward to:

- The dreaded Analogy questions in the Verbal section will disappear. Taking their place will be more Reading Comprehension passages.

- The Verbal section will get a new name: "Critical Reading."

- A third section, Writing, will be added. It will be similar to the SAT II Writing Test, with multiple-choice grammar usage questions and a 25-minute essay. Your essay will be read and scored, and then it will be posted on a Web site for college admissions officials to read when they review your college application package.

- Quantitative Comparisons will disappear from the Math section, replaced by multiple-choice math questions from Algebra II.

- The current test takes 3 hours to complete; the new SAT I will take 3½ hours.

- Instead of a top score of 1600 points, the new SAT I will have a top score of 2400 points.

score range are from 200 to 800. The total scaled score range is from 400 to 1600.

To prepare for the SAT I, you should carefully review the pamphlet, Taking the SAT I: Reasoning Test, which you should be able to get from your guidance counselor. Also, most libraries and bookstores stock a large selection of material about the SAT I and other standardized tests.

RECOMMENDED TEST-TAKING DATES

Sophomore Year

October	PSAT/NMSQT and PLAN For practice, planning, and preparation
May–June	SAT II Subject Tests (if necessary)

Junior Year

October	PSAT/NMSQT For the National Merit Scholarship Program and practice
January–June	ACT and/or SAT I, SAT II Subject Tests (if necessary) For college admission

Senior Year

October–December	ACT and/or SAT I, SAT II Subject Tests (if necessary) For college admission

Which Should I Take? The ACT vs. the SAT

It's not a bad idea to take both. This assures that you will have the test scores required for admission to all schools, because some colleges accept the results of one test and not the other. Some institutions use test results for proper placement of students in English and math courses.

You should take the ACT Assessment and SAT I during the spring of your junior year, if not earlier. This enables you to retake the test in the fall of your senior year if you're not satisfied with your scores. Also, this makes it possible for institutions to receive all test scores before the end of January. Institutions generally consider the better score when determining admission and placement. Because most scholarship applications are processed between December and April of the senior year, your best score results can then be included in the application.

THE PSAT/NMSQT

The Preliminary SAT/National Merit Scholarship Qualifying Test, better known as the PSAT/NMSQT, is a practice test for the SAT I. Many students take the PSAT more than once because scores tend to increase with repetition and because it allows students to become more comfortable with taking standardized tests. During the junior year, the PSAT is also used as a qualifying test for the National Merit Scholarship Program and the National Scholarship Service and Fund for Negro Students. It is also used in designating students for the National Hispanic Scholar Recognition Program. The PSAT includes a writing skills section, which consists entirely of multiple-choice questions. This section does not appear on the SAT.

Verbal Reasoning

- Approximately 50 questions, two 25-minute sections

- Analogies

- Sentence completion

- Critical reading passages

Mathematical Reasoning

- 40 questions, two 25-minute sections
- Student-produced responses
- Quantitative comparisons
- Regular math

Writing Skills

- 39 questions, one 30-minute section
- Identifying sentence errors
- Improving sentences
- Improving paragraphs

Students receive a score in each content area (verbal, math, and writing). Each score ranges from 20 to 80 and is totaled with the others for the combined score.

WHAT DOES IT TAKE TO GET IN?

College Admission Policy	Class Rank	Average ACT Range (1–36)	Average SAT Range (400–1600)
Highly Selective	Top 10% of class, very strong academic record	27–31	1220–1380
Selective	Top 25% of class, strong academic record	22–27	1150–1230
Traditional	Top 50% of class, good academic record	20–23	950–1070
Liberal	Many accepted from lower half of class	18–21	870–990
Open	All accepted to limit of capacity	17–20	830–950

The total score ranges from 60 to 240.

Selection Index (used for National Merit Scholarship purposes)

- Verbal + Math + Writing
- Score Range: 60 to 240
- Mean Junior Score: 147

National Merit Scholarship Program

- Semifinalist Status: Selection
- Index of 201 to 222
- Commended Student: Selection Index of 199

SAT II SUBJECT TESTS

Subject Tests are required by some institutions for admission and/or placement in freshman-level courses. Each Subject Test measures one's knowledge of a specific subject and the ability to apply that knowledge. Students should check with each institution for its specific requirements. In general, students are required to take three Subject Tests (one English, one mathematics, and one of their choice).

Subject Tests are given in the following areas:

ADMISSIONS ADVICE

Q: What can students who don't have the best grades do to improve their chances of getting into the college of their choice?

A: We encourage students to take the SAT or ACT more than once and see how they do. There are options for students who may not meet the academic requirements because they've had to work or are gifted in other areas, such as art or athletics, or who perhaps have been through something tragic. We ask them to submit letters or recommendations, a personal statement, and any other documentation that might help support their cases. What were the factors that affected their grades? What else can they offer the university?

We often encourage students who still may not meet the requirements to start at a community college and then transfer. We'll look at their college credit vs. their high school credit. They can prove to us that they can handle a college curriculum.

Cheyenna Smith
Admission Counselor
University of Houston
Houston, Texas

biology, chemistry, Chinese, English language proficiency, French, German, Italian, Japanese, Korean, Latin, literature, mathematics, modern Hebrew, physics, Spanish, U.S. history, world history, and writing. These tests are 1 hour long and are primarily multiple-choice tests. Three Subject Tests may be taken on one test date.

Scored like the SAT I, students gain a point for each correct answer and lose a fraction of a point for each incorrect answer. The raw scores are then converted to scaled scores that range from 200 to 800.

THE TOEFL TEST

The Test of English as a Foreign Language (TOEFL) is designed to help assess a student's grasp of English if it is not the student's first language. Performance on the TOEFL test may help interpret scores on the verbal section of the SAT I. The 3-hour test consists of four sections: listening comprehension, structure and written expression, reading comprehension, and a writing section. The test is given at more than 1,260 centers in 180 countries and is administered by Educational Testing Service (ETS). For further information, visit www.toefl.org.

WHAT OTHER TESTS SHOULD I KNOW ABOUT?

The AP Program

This program allows high school students to try college-level work and build valuable skills and study habits in the process. Subject matter is explored in more depth in AP courses than in other high school classes. A qualifying score on an AP test—which varies from school to school—can earn you college credit or advanced placement. Getting qualifying grades on enough exams can even earn you a full year's credit and sophomore standing at more than 1,400 higher-education institutions. There are currently thirty-two AP courses in eighteen different subject areas, including art, biology, and computer science. Speak to your guidance counselor for information about your school's offerings.

College-Level Examination Program (CLEP)

The CLEP enables students to earn college credit for what they already know, whether it was learned in school, through independent study, or through other experiences outside of the classroom. More than 2,800 colleges and universities now award credit for qualifying scores on one or more of the 34 CLEP exams. The exams, which are 90 minutes in length and are primarily multiple choice, are administered at participating colleges and universities. For more information, check out the Web site at www.collegeboard.com/clep.

Armed Services Vocational Aptitude Battery (ASVAB)

ASVAB is a career exploration program consisting of a multi-aptitude test battery that helps students explore their interests, abilities, and personal preferences. A career exploration workbook gives students information about the world of work, and a career information resource book helps students match their personal characteristics to the working world. Finally, an occupational outlook handbook describes in detail approximately 250 civilian and military occupations. Students can use ASVAB scores for military enlistment up to two years after they take the test. A student can take the ASVAB as a sophomore, junior, or senior, but students cannot use their sophomore scores to enter the armed forces. Ask your guidance counselor or your local recruiting office for more information. Also, see Chapter 10 of GAJ, "The Military Option."

General Educational Development (GED) Test

If you have not completed your high school education, you may earn an equivalence by taking the GED test, sponsored by your state Department of Education. However, taking the GED test is not a legitimate reason for dropping out of school. In fact, it is more difficult to get into the armed services with only a GED, and some employees have difficulty getting promoted without a high school diploma.

You're eligible to take the GED if you are not enrolled in high school, have not yet graduated from high school, are at least 16 years old, and meet your local requirements regarding age, residency, and length of time since leaving school.

There are five sections to the GED test, covering writing skills, social studies, science, interpreting literature and the arts, and mathematics. Part II of the Writing Skills Test requires writing an essay. The GED costs an average of $35 but can vary from state to state, and the application fee may be waived under certain circumstances. You should contact your local GED office to arrange to take the exam. Call 800-62-MYGED to find your local GED office and for more information.

WHAT CAN I DO TO PREPARE FOR THESE TESTS?

Know what to expect. Get familiar with how the tests are structured, how much time is allowed, and the directions for each type of question. Get plenty of rest the night before the test and eat breakfast that morning.

There are a variety of products, from books to software to videos, available to help you prepare for most standardized tests. Find the learning style that suits you best. As for which products to buy, there are two major categories—those created by the test makers and those created by private companies. The best approach is to talk to someone who has been through the process and find out which product or products he or she recommends.

Some students report significant increases in scores after participating in coaching programs.

Longer-term programs (40 hours) seem to raise scores more than short-term programs (20 hours), but beyond 40 hours, score gains are minor. Math scores appear to benefit more from coaching than verbal scores.

Preparation Resources

There are a variety of ways to prepare for standardized tests—find a method that fits your schedule and your budget. But you should definitely prepare. Far too many students walk into these tests cold, either because they find standardized tests frightening or annoying or they just haven't found the time to study. The key is that these exams are standardized. That means these tests are largely the same from administration to administration; they always test the same concepts. They have to, or else you couldn't compare the scores of people who took the tests on different dates. The numbers or words may change, but the underlying content doesn't.

So how do you prepare? At the very least, you should review relevant material, such as math formulas and commonly tested vocabulary words, and know the directions for each question type or test section. You should take at least one practice test and review your mistakes so you don't make them again on test day. Beyond that, you know best how much preparation you need. You'll also find lots of material in libraries or bookstores to help you: books and software from the test makers and from other publishers (including Peterson's) or live courses that range from national test-preparation companies to teachers at your high school who offer classes.

THE TOP 10 WAYS NOT TO TAKE THE TEST

10. Cramming the night before the test.
9. Not becoming familiar with the directions before you take the test.
8. Not becoming familiar with the format of the test before you take it.
7. Not knowing how the test is graded.
6. Spending too much time on any one question.
5. Not checking spelling, grammar, and sentence structure in essays.
4. Second-guessing yourself.
3. Forgetting to take a deep breath to keep from—
2. Losing It!
1. Writing a one-paragraph essay.

5 Chapter

THE COLLEGE SEARCH

Now that you have examined your interests, talents, wants, and needs in great detail, it's time to start investigating colleges.

THE BEST RESOURCES

There are hundreds of colleges and universities in the United States, so before you can start filling out applications, you need to narrow down your search. There are a number of sources that will help you do this.

BESTCOLLEGEPICKS: AN EASY WAY TO PICK A COLLEGE

College guides, brochures, Web sites, and the lists that rank colleges are necessary sources of information for applicants, but they only provide part of the picture. They give data about incoming students such as GPAs and required test scores. This information is useful, but those facts are similar to finding out what materials go into the production of a car, not the results from driving it. BestCollegePicks looks at the driving record of a college by surveying college graduates about how well their colleges prepared them for the real world.

After filling out a comprehensive survey that pinpoints your skills, abilities, goals, and personal preferences, you'll get a list of colleges whose graduates most closely fit your goals, aspirations, and values and whose size, location, and kind of institution best match what you're interested in.

Then, BestCollegePicks matches what you say you want with what graduates say they've gotten from a wide range of colleges and universities. You can take the survey more than once, each time setting different goals. Say you are not sure if you want to go into law or business. You can take the survey twice—once for law and once for business—by signing in under a different name each time. When you get the list of schools, you can compare them to see which schools overlap. If you choose to attend one of those schools, you'll know that either way, a high percentage of graduates from that school have been successful in business or law.

The benefits of BestCollegePicks are enormous. You will be led to lesser-known schools you might never have thought of whose graduates match your future plans. And the vague ideas that you have about what you want out of college will take shape. You can get to BestCollegePicks by going to www.bestcollegepicks.com.

Your Guidance Counselor

Your guidance counselor is your greatest asset in the college search process. She has access to a vast repository of information, from college bulletins and catalogs to financial aid applications. She knows how well graduates from your high school have performed at colleges across the country, and she has probably even visited many of the colleges to get some first-hand knowledge about the places she has sent her students to. The more your guidance counselor sees you and learns about you, the easier it is for her to help you. So make sure you stop by her office often, whether it's to talk about your progress or just to say "hi."

Your Teachers

Use your teachers as resources, too. Many of them have had twenty to thirty years of experience in their field. They have taught thousands of students and watched them go off to college and careers. Teachers often stay in contact with graduates and know about their experiences in college and may be familiar with the schools you are interested in attending. Ask your teachers how they feel about the match between you and your choice schools and if they think you will be able to succeed in that environment.

Mom and Dad

Your parents or guardians need to be an integral part of the college selection process, whether they are financing your education or not. They have opinions and valuable advice. Listen to them carefully. Try to take in all their information and see if it applies to you. Does it fit with who you are and what you want?

What works and what doesn't work for you? Is some of what they say dated? How long ago were their experiences, and how relevant are they today? Take in the information, thank them for their concern, compare what they have said with the information you are gathering, and discard what doesn't fit.

Colleges and Universities

Don't forget to go to college fairs. Usually held in large cities in the evening, they are free and sponsored by your local guidance counselors' association and the National Association of College Admissions Counselors (NACAC). The admissions counselors of hundreds of colleges, vocational/technical schools, and universities attend college fairs each year. Whether your questions are as general as what the overall cost of education is at a particular institution or as specific as how many biology majors had works published last year, the admissions office works to assist you in locating the people who can answer your questions. Bring a shopping bag for all the information you will get.

Admissions officers also visit high schools. Don't forget to attend these meetings during your junior and senior years. Generally, college admissions counselors come to a school to get a general sense of the high school and the caliber and personality of the student body. Although it is difficult to make an individual impression at these group sessions, the college counselors do take names on cards for later contact, and you will occasionally see them making notes on the cards when they are struck by an astute questioner. It is helpful to attend these sessions because consistent contact between a student and a college is tracked by colleges and universities. An admissions decision may come down to examining the size of your admissions folder and the number of interactions you have had with the school over time.

College and university brochures and catalogs are a good place to look, too. After reading a few, you will discover that some offer more objective information than others. You will also start to learn what information colleges think is essential to present. That's important. If a college's brochure does not present the same information as most of the other college brochures, you have to ask yourself why.

PARENT PERSPECTIVE

Q: Now that you've been through the process of getting three of your children into college, what's your best advice for parents and teens?

A: Apply early and meet deadlines. Both of our older sons were sitting there after high school graduation wondering why they were on college waiting lists: "I have good grades. I can't figure it out." At eighteen, they don't see tomorrow, much less way down the line, but do you want to deal with their heartbreak at not getting into the college where they want to be? It's their future. It's hard because they're in their senior year and you want it to be fun for them. However, you see the reality out there that they will be facing for the rest of their lives. They don't want to look at it, but you have to keep bringing them back to it—not in a preachy way. If they start earlier than their senior year, it won't be as much of a shock when they become seniors.

Jeanette and Amedee Richard
San Antonio, Texas

What might this say about the college's academic offerings, athletic or extracurricular programs, or campus life? What does the campus look like? How is the campus environment presented in the brochure? The brochures should present clues to what schools feel are their important majors, what their mission is, and which departments they are spending their budgets on. Take the time to do these informational resources justice. They have a great deal to say to the careful reader.

A college's Web site can give you a glimpse of campus life that does not appear in the college's brochure and catalog. It is true that the virtual tour will show you the shots that the college marketing department wants you to see and that shows the campus in the best light, but you can use the home page to see other things, too. Read the student newspaper. Visit college-sponsored chat rooms. Go to the department in the major you are investigating. Look at the Course Bulletin to see what courses are required.

ONLINE HELP

To help you find two-year and four-year colleges or universities in your specific region, take a look at the

CRITERIA TO CONSIDER

Depending on your personal interests, the following characteristics should play a role in helping you narrow down the field of colleges.

AFFILIATION
Public
Private, independent
Private, church affiliated
Proprietary

SIZE
Very small (fewer than 1,000 students)
Small (1,000–3,999 students)
Medium (4,000–8,999 students)
Large (9,000–19,999 students)
Very large (more than 20,000 students)

COMMUNITY
Rural
Small town
Suburban
Urban

LOCATION
In your hometown
Less than 3 hours from home
More than 3 hours from home

HOUSING
Dorm
Off-campus apartment
Home
Facilities and services for students with disabilities

STUDENT BODY
All male
All female
Coed
Minority representation
Primarily one religious denomination
Primarily full-time students
Primarily part-time students
Primarily commuter students
Primarily residential students

ACADEMIC ENVIRONMENT
Majors offered
Student-faculty ratio
Faculty teaching reputation
Instruction by professors versus teaching assistants
Facilities (such as classrooms and labs)
Libraries
Independent study available
International study available
Internships available

FINANCIAL AID
Scholarships
Grants
Loans
Work-study program
Part-time or full-time jobs

SUPPORT SERVICES
Academic counseling
Career/placement counseling
Personal counseling
Student health facilities

ACTIVITIES/SOCIAL CLUBS
Clubs, organizations
Greek life
Athletics, intramurals
Other

ATHLETICS
Division I, II, or III
Sports offered
Scholarships available

SPECIALIZED PROGRAMS
Gifted student services
Services for students with disabilities or special needs

appendix in the back of this book for a table of schools in each state of your region. Then check out the following online resources for additional information on college selection, scholarships, student information, and much more.

Peterson's Undergraduate Channel. Petersons.com provides information and tools that will help you prepare, search, and pay for college. You can find the schools that BestCollegePicks matched you to in order to view in-depth profiles or do a side-by-side comparison of selected colleges. Or you can search for a school by name or location. In addition to college search and selection tools, the undergraduate channel on Petersons.com also offers tips on financial aid, test preparation, and online applications.

The National Association for College Admission Counseling. This home page offers information for professionals, students, and parents. The Internet address is www.nacac.com.

U.S. Department of Education. This federal agency's National Center for Education Statistics produces reports on every level of education, from elementary to postgraduate. Dozens are available for downloading. You can hook up with these and other links at www.ed.gov.

CAMPUS VISITS

You've heard the old saying, "A picture is worth a thousand words." Well, a campus visit is worth a thousand brochures. Nothing beats walking around a campus to get a feel for it. Some students report that all they needed to know that they loved or hated a campus was to drive through it. Then there is the true story of the guy who applied to a school because it had a prestigious name. Got accepted. Didn't visit, and when he arrived to move into the dorms, discovered to his horror it was an all-male school. A visit would have taken care of that problem.

The best time to experience the college environment is during the spring of your junior year or the fall of your senior year. Although you may have more time to make college visits during your summer off, your observations will be more accurate when you can see the campus in full swing. Open houses are a good idea and provide you with opportunities to talk to students, faculty members, and administrators. Write or call in advance to take student-conducted campus tours. If possible, stay overnight in a dorm to see what living at the college is really like.

Bring your transcript so that you are prepared to interview with admission officers. Take this opportunity to ask questions about financial aid and other services that are available to students. You can get a good snapshot of campus life by reading a copy of the student newspaper. The final goal of the campus visit is to study the school's personality and decide if it matches yours. Your parents should be involved with the campus visits so that you can share your impressions. Here are some additional campus visit tips:

- Read campus literature prior to the visit.
- Ask for directions, and allow ample travel time.
- Make a list of questions before the visit.
- Dress in neat, clean, casual clothes and shoes.
- Ask to meet one-on-one with a current student.
- Ask to meet personally with a professor in your area of interest.
- Ask to meet a coach or athlete in your area of interest.
- Offer a firm handshake.
- Use good posture.
- Listen, and take notes.
- Speak clearly, and maintain eye contact with people you meet.
- Don't interrupt.
- Be honest, direct, and polite.
- Be aware of factual information so that you can ask questions of comparison and evaluation.
- Be prepared to answer questions about yourself. Practice a mock interview with someone.
- Don't be shy about explaining your background and why you are interested in the school.
- Ask questions about the background and experiences of the people you meet.
- Convey your interest in getting involved in campus life.
- Be positive and energetic.
- Don't feel as though you have to talk the whole time or carry the conversation yourself.
- Relax, and enjoy yourself.
- Thank those you meet, and send thank-you notes when appropriate.

After you have made your college visits, use the "College Comparison Worksheet" on page 38 to rank the schools in which you're interested. This will help

WRITING TO A COLLEGE FOR INFORMATION

If neither you nor your guidance counselor has an application for a college that you are interested in, write a brief letter to the college admissions office to request an application.

Date

Your Name
Street Address
City, State, Zip

Office of Admission
Name of College
Street Address
City, State, Zip

To Whom It May Concern:

I am a (freshman, sophomore, junior, senior) at (name of your school) and plan to graduate in (month) (year).

Please send me the following information about your college: a general information brochure, program descriptions, an admission application, financial aid information, and any other information that might be helpful. I am considering _____ as my major field of study (optional, if you know your major).

I am interested in visiting your campus, taking a campus tour, and meeting with an admission counselor and a financial aid officer. I would also like to meet with an adviser or professor in the (your preferred field of study) department, if possible (optional, if you know your major). I will contact you in a week to set up a time that is convenient.

If you would like to contact me directly, I can be reached at (your phone number with area code). Thank you.

Sincerely,

(Signature)

Name

you decide not only which ones to apply to, but also which one to attend once you receive your acceptance letters.

THE COLLEGE INTERVIEW

Not all schools require or offer an interview. However, if you are offered an interview, use this one-on-one time to evaluate the college in detail and to sell

(Continued on page 38)

IT'S ALL ABOUT *YOU!* Read each question and respond by circling Y (Yes), N (No), or C (Combination). Complete all the questions and return to the top. Highlight each action that coordinates with your answer, and then read it. Where you chose C, read both actions. Is there a pattern? Do the questions seem to lead to a certain type of college or university? Certain size? Certain location? Read the suggestions at the end of "The Matching Game" for more ideas.

Question	Yes/No/ Combination	Action
1. Do I have a goal in life?	Y/N/C	Y: State it._____. N: Don't worry, many students start college without knowing what they want to do. Look into colleges that specialize in the arts and sciences.
2. Do I know what I want to achieve with a college diploma?	Y/N/C	Y: List specifically what those goals are. _____ N: Think about what college can offer you.
3. Do I want to broaden my knowledge?	Y/N/C	Y: Consider a liberal arts college. N: You might need to consider other options or educational opportunities.
4. Do I want specific training?	Y/N/C	Y: Investigate technical colleges or professional training programs in universities. N: You don't know what you want to study. Only 20 percent of seniors who apply to college are sure.
5. Am I willing to work hard?	Y/N/C	Y: When you are visiting colleges, ask students about handling the work load. N: Check the work load carefully. If no one is on campus on a sunny day, it may not be the school for you
6. Am I self-directed enough to finish a four-year college program?	Y/N/C	Y: Consider only four-year colleges and universities. N: Maybe a two-year junior or community college is a better way to begin your college experience. Also consider a tech/vocational school.
7. Do I know what I do well?	Y/N/C	Y: Consider how your abilites relate to majors. Identify some. _____ N: Spend a little more time asking yourself questions about your interests. Speak to your counselor and do an interest inventory.
8. Do I like to spend time learning any one subject more than others?	Y/N/C	Y: Check to see what some majors are in that area. _____ _____ N: Look at your high school courses. Do you like any of them better than others? Which ones? _____
9. Do I know what matters to me and what my values are?	Y/N/C	Y: Look for the schools that talk about the values on their campus. Do they have an honor code for students? Do the values confirm or conflict with your values? N: Values are less important to you, so places that really expound their values may seem confining to you.
10. Do I need to be in affluent surroundings?	Y/N/C	Y: Look at the schools that deliver that package. Check the small, private liberal arts colleges. N: How strong is your reaction against this setting? If it is strong, check larger, more diverse settings, like an urban school.
11. Am I going to college for the financial gains?	Y/N/C	Y: What majors are going to give you the payback you want? Look at business colleges and professional programs, like premed. N: If a big financial payback does not interest you, look at social service majors, like counseling, teaching, and social work.
12. Am I focused?	Y/N/C	Y: Search out the programs that will offer you the best options. N: Avoid those schools whose programs are not strong in your focused area.
13. Am I conservative in my views and behavior?	Y/N/C	Y: The political policies of schools are important. Look into them carefully. You might look at the schools in the Midwest or the South. N: If you're a liberal, look closely at the political climate. Check the schools in the Northeast and the West Coast.

14. Do I need to be around people who are similar to me?	Y/N/C	Y: If you are African American, check the historically black colleges. If socioeconomic level or a certain look is important to you, study the student populations carefully during campus visits. If it is religious orientation you are interested in, look into religiously sponsored colleges and universities. N: Look at large, midsize, and small universities in urban settings.
15. Are the name and prestige of the school important to me?	Y/N/C	Y: Look into the Ivies and the competitive schools to see if you are eligible and what they offer you. Broaden your search to include other colleges and compare their offerings for your specific needs and interests. N: Don't exclude the well-known institutions if they fit in every other way.
16. Do I like sports?	Y/N/C	Y: Large universities with Division I teams will give you all the sports you need—as a competitor or a fan. If you do not want to compete at that level, check schools in other divisions. Look at the liberal arts colleges for athletes. N: Look into smaller universities and liberal arts colleges with good teams.
17. Am I a techie?	Y/N/C	Y: Check for computer engineering courses at technical universities and large universities near research centers and major computer business areas. Ask about hardwiring, e-mail, and computer packages before you enroll. N: It still helps to know what computer services are available where you enroll.
18. Do I need to live in or be near a city?	Y/N/C	Y: How close to a city do you need to be? In the city or an hour away? Do you still want a campus feel? Consider these questions as you visit campuses. N: Do you need space, natural beauty, and peaceful surroundings to think? Look into small liberal arts schools in rural and suburban settings. Explore universities in the Midwest and South.
19. Will I need counseling for support?	Y/N/C	Y: Investigate the quality of student services and the mechanism for accessing them. Smaller schools often pride themselves on their services. Look at liberal arts colleges. Universities connected to medical centers often provide extensive services. N: It is still good to know what is offered.
20. Do I need an environment in which questioning is important?	Y/N/C	Y: Liberal arts colleges, honors colleges, and smaller universities place an emphasis on academic inquiry. N: You like to hear others discuss issues, gather as much information and opinions as you can, and think it over by yourself. Try the university setting.

Suggestions

Here are some ideas for you to consider based on the way you answered the questions.

1. If you answered *no* to numbers 2 and 3, why not investigate apprenticeships, vocational/technical schools, military enlistment options, and certification or two-year college programs?

2. If you answered *yes* to numbers 4, 11, and 17, technical or professional colleges and universities with hands-on training may give you the direction you are looking for.

3. If you answered *yes* to numbers 9, 10, and 20, you are leaning toward a liberal arts setting.

4. If you answered *yes* to numbers 5 and 6, examine the competitive and Ivy League colleges.

5. If you answered *no* to numbers 9, 10, 14, and 20 and yes to 16, 17, and 18, larger universities may offer you the best options.

Once you have completed your self-evaluation, made a decision whether college is for you, have some ideas about your personality and likes and dislikes, and can relate them to the different personalities of colleges, it is time to gather information. It needs to be quality information from the right sources. The quality of information you put into the search now will determine whether your list of colleges will represent a good or a bad match.

yourself to the admission officer. The following list of questions can help you collect the information you may need to know.

☑ How many students apply each year? How many are accepted?

☑ What are the average GPA and average ACT or SAT I score(s) for those accepted?

☑ How many students in last year's freshman class returned for their sophomore year?

☑ What is the school's procedure for credit for Advanced Placement high school courses?

☑ As a freshman, will I be taught by professors or teaching assistants?

☑ How many students are there per teacher?

☑ When is it necessary to declare a major?

☑ Is it possible to have a double major or to declare a major and a minor?

☑ What are the requirements?

☑ How does the advising system work?

☑ Does this college offer overseas study, cooperative programs, or academic honors programs?

☑ What is the likelihood, due to overcrowding, of getting closed out of the courses I need?

☑ What technology is available?

☑ How well equipped are the libraries and laboratories?

☑ Are internships available?

☑ How effective is the job placement service of the school?

☑ What is the average class size in my area of interest?

☑ Have any professors in my area of interest recently won any honors or awards?

☑ What teaching methods are used in my area of interest (lecture, group discussion, fieldwork)?

COLLEGE COMPARISON WORKSHEET

Fill in your top five selection criteria and any others that may be of importance to you. Once you narrow your search of colleges to five, fill in the colleges across the top row. Using a scale of 1 to 5, where 1 is poor and 5 is excellent, rate each college by your criteria. Total each column to see which college rates the highest based upon your criteria.

SELECTION CRITERIA	COLLEGE 1	COLLEGE 2	COLLEGE 3	COLLEGE 4	COLLEGE 5
1.					
2.					
3.					
4.					
5.					
OTHER CRITERIA					
6.					
7.					
8.					
9.					
10.					
TOTAL					

Sample criteria: (Use this list as a starting point—there may be other criteria important to you not listed here.) Arts facilities, athletic facilities, audiovisual center, campus setting, class size, classrooms/lecture halls, computer labs, dining hall, dorms, financial aid, fraternity/sorority houses, majors offered, religious facilities, professor profiles, student-professor ratio, student profile, student union, surrounding community.

- How many students graduate in four years in my area of interest?

- What are the special requirements for graduation in my area of interest?

- What is the student body like? Age? Sex? Race? Geographic origin?

- What percentage of students live in dormitories? Off-campus housing?

- What percentage of students go home for the weekend?

- What are some of the regulations that apply to living in a dormitory?

- What are the security precautions taken on campus and in the dorms?

- Is the surrounding community safe?

- Are there problems with drug and alcohol abuse on campus?

- Are there dorms available that are free of any use of drugs and alcohol?

- Do faculty members and students mix on an informal basis?

- How important are the arts to student life?

- What facilities are available for cultural events?

- How important are sports to student life?

- What facilities are available for sporting events?

- What percentage of the student body belongs to a sorority/fraternity?

- What is the relationship between those who belong to the Greek system and those who don't?

- Are students involved in the decision-making process at the college? Do they sit on major committees?

- What other activities can students get involved in?

- What percentage of students receive financial aid based on need?

- What percentage of students receive scholarships based on academic ability?

- What percentage of a typical financial aid offer is in the form of a loan?

- If my family demonstrates financial need on the FAFSA (and FAF, if applicable), what percentage of the established need is generally awarded?

- How much did the college increase the cost of room, board, tuition, and fees from last year?

- Do opportunities for financial aid, scholarships, or work-study increase each year?

- When is the application deadline?

- When does the school notify you of the admission decision?

- If there is a deposit required, is it refundable?

Keep in mind that you don't need to ask all these questions—in fact, some of them may have already been answered for you in the catalog, on the Web site, or in the interview. Ask only the questions for which you still need answers.

SHOULD YOU HEAD FOR THE IVY LEAGUES?

Determining whether to apply to one of the eight Ivy League schools is something you should think long and hard about. Sure, it can't hurt to toss your application into the ring if you can afford the application fee and the time you'll spend writing the essays. But if you want to figure out if you'd be a legitimate candidate for acceptance at one of these top-tier schools, you should understand the type of student that they look for and how you compare, says John Machulsky, a guidance counselor at Lawrence High School in New Jersey. Take a look at these statistics:

- Only 30 percent or fewer applicants are accepted at these highly competitive colleges each year.

- Most Ivy League students have placed in the top 10 percent of their class and have SAT I scores in the 700 levels for math and verbal each or ACT scores of 29 or higher.

- Because Ivy League schools are so selective, they want a diverse student population. That means they want students that represent not only the fifty states but also a wide selection of other countries.

Lirio Jimenez, a guidance counselor at New Brunswick High School in New Jersey, says that being accepted by an Ivy League school is a process that starts early in the ninth grade. You should select demanding courses and maintain good grades in those courses throughout all four years of high school. Get involved in extracurricular activities as well, and, of course, do well on your standardized tests. When it comes time to apply for college, select at least three schools: one ideal, one possible, and one shoe-in. Your ideal can be an Ivy League if you wish.

GAJ certainly doesn't want to discourage you from applying to one of these prestigious schools. We're in your corner and want to see you get the best education possible. However, students are sometimes more concerned about getting accepted than with taking a hard look at what a school has to offer them. Often, a university or college that is less competitive than an Ivy League may have exactly what you need to succeed in the future. Keep that in mind as you select the colleges that would offer you what you need.

MINORITY STUDENTS GO TO COLLEGE

African-American, Hispanic/Latino, and Native-American high school students have a lot of doors into higher education opening for them. In fact, most colleges want to respond to the social and economic disadvantages of certain groups of Americans. They want to reflect the globalization of our economy. They want their student populations to look like the rest of America, which means people from many different backgrounds and ethnic groups. This isn't just talk either. You'll find that most colleges have at least one member of the admissions staff who specializes in recruiting minorities.

One of the reasons college admissions staff are recruiting minorities and want to accommodate their needs is because there are more minorities thinking of attending college—and graduating. Let's put some numbers to these statements. According to the Department of Education, in 1976, 16 percent of college students were minorities, compared to 27 percent in 1997. Much of the change can be attributed to rising numbers of Hispanic and Asian students. The proportion of Asian and Pacific Islander students rose from 2 percent to 6 percent, and the Hispanic proportion rose from 4 percent to 9 percent during that same time period. The proportion of black students fluctuated during most of the early part of the period before rising slightly to 11 percent in 1997, the last year for which data was collected on this subject.

STUDENT COUNSEL

Q: What made you choose to apply to an Ivy League school?

A: My mother recommended that I apply to Princeton. She said, "Why not just try? What do you have to lose? All they can tell you is no." I was afraid of being rejected. I wasn't a straight-A student, and I thought they weren't going to want me—they get thousands of applications. Through the whole college process I had a whole lot of self-doubt. Looking back, I realize that you won't know if you don't try. Take the chance and fill out the application. If you don't get in, it doesn't mean you're less intelligent. It just wasn't the correct fit.

Zoelene Hill, College Freshman
Princeton University

SHOULD YOU ATTEND A HISTORICALLY BLACK COLLEGE OR UNIVERSITY?

Choosing which college to attend is usually a difficult decision for anyone to make, but when an African-American student is considering attending a historically black college or university (HBCU), a whole other set of family and cultural issues are raised.

There are many valid reasons that favor one or the other. Some are obvious differences. Parents and their children have to be honest with themselves and take a long, hard look at the needs of the student and how the campus environment can fulfill them. To help you decide, here are some questions to ask:

DO I KNOW WHAT'S REALLY IMPORTANT TO ME?

Look at the reasons why you want a degree and what you want to achieve with it. Is the choice to attend an HBCU yours or your family's? Do you have a particular field of study you want to pursue? Sometimes students can get so caught up in applying to a particular institution, they don't realize it doesn't even offer their major.

HOW WILL THIS CAMPUS FIT MY PLANS FOR THE FUTURE?

There's no substitute for doing your homework about the campuses you're seriously considering. Know the reputation of those campuses in the community and among employers and the general population. Find out about graduation, retention, and placement rates.

DOES THIS CAMPUS HAVE THE FACILITIES AND LIVING CONDITIONS THAT SUIT MY COMFORT LEVEL?

Finding a campus where you're comfortable is a big factor in choosing a college. What do you want in campus facilities and living conditions? For instance, if you currently attend a small private high school in a suburban setting, perhaps you wouldn't like living on a large urban campus with peers who don't mirror your kind of background.

WHAT LEVEL OF SUPPORT WILL I GET ON CAMPUS?

Students considering institutions where few people are like them should look at the available support systems and organizations that will be available to them. Parents need to feel comfortable with the contact person on campus.

When all the factors that determine the choice of a college are laid out, the bottom line is which institution best meets your needs. For some African-American students, an HBCU is the best choice. For others, it's not. African-American students reflect many backgrounds, and there is no single decision that will be right for everyone.

GAJ has a lot of information in this section to help you make decisions about college and paying for college. Perhaps the most important information we can give you is that if you want to go to college, you can. There are a lot of organizations ready to assist you. So go for it. See the list of organizations in this section and check with the colleges in which you're interested to connect with the minority affairs office.

Academic Resources for Minority Students

In addition to churches, sororities and fraternities, and college minority affairs offices, minority students can receive information and assistance from the following organizations:

ASPIRA

An association of community-based organizations that provide leadership, development, and educational services to Latino youths.

1444 Eye Street, NW, Suite 800
Washington, D.C. 20005
202-835-3600
www.aspira.org

INROADS

A national career-development organization that places and develops talented minority students (African American, Hispanic American, and Native American) in business and industry.

10 South Broadway, Suite 700
St. Louis, Missouri 63102
314-241-7488
www.inroadsinc.org

National Action Council for Minorities in Engineering (NACME)

An organization that aims to increase the number of minorities who earn bachelor's degrees in engineering by offering an Incentive Grants Program, Summer Engineering Employment Project, field services, and publications for parents and students.

The Empire State Building
350 Fifth Avenue, Suite 2212
New York, New York 10118-2299
212-279-2626
www.nacme.org

STUDENT COUNSEL

Q: How did you make the decision to attend a historically black college or university?

A: Selecting a college was one of the hardest decisions I've ever had to make. As a recipient of the National Achievement Scholarship and a National History Day winner, I was offered scholarships to a number of colleges across the country, including many HCBUs. I tried to figure out which institution would be able to give me the most help in achieving my goals. I finally decided on Florida A&M University (FAMU) in my hometown of Tallahassee.

There are many pluses to attending college in my hometown. By living on campus, I have the freedom to make my own decisions and live as a young adult while being close to the loving support of my parents. Also, FAMU will help me succeed in my objective of obtaining a bachelor's degree in broadcast journalism. As I look back, I am glad that I, unlike some of my other high school peers, did not rush to judgment during the process of choosing a college. I am very happy with my decision.

Larry Rivers
Florida A&M University

National Association for the Advancement of Colored People (NAACP)

The purpose of the NAACP is to improve the political, educational, social, and economic status of minority groups; to eliminate racial prejudice; to keep the public aware of the adverse effects of racial discrimination; and to take lawful action to secure its elimination, consistent with the efforts of the national organization.

> 4805 Mt. Hope Drive
> Baltimore, Maryland 21205
> 410-358-8900
> www.naacp.org

The National Urban League

The Education and Youth Services Department of the Urban League provides services for African Americans and economically disadvantaged people. These services include basic academic development, GED test preparation for youths and adults, after-school tutoring for children, parent training classes, scholarships, an annual tour of historically black colleges and universities, and summer employment

for youths. Call individual Urban League offices in your state.

> 120 Wall Street
> 8th Floor
> New York, New York 10005
> 212-558-5300 (national office)
> www.nul.org

United Negro College Fund (UNCF)

The UNCF provides scholarships for undergraduates who attend one of forty private, historically black colleges. Students must be accepted first and then nominated by the college's financial aid director. Programs and services include summer learning programs, internships, precollege and mentoring programs, and international programs.

> 8260 Willow Oaks Corporate Drive
> Fairfax, Virginia 22031
> 800-331-2244 (toll-free)
> www.uncf.org

Online Resources

Hispanic Association of Colleges and Universities
www.hacu.com

The American Indian Higher Education Consortium
www.aihec.org

Minority On-Line Information Service (MOLIS)
www.sciencewise.com/molis

STUDENTS WITH DISABILITIES GO TO COLLEGE

The Americans with Disabilities Act (ADA) requires educational institutions at all levels, public and private, to provide equal access to programs, services, and facilities. Schools must be accessible to students, as well as to employees and the public, regardless of any disability. To ensure such accessibility, they must follow specific requirements for new construction, alterations or renovations, academic programs, and institutional policies, practices, and procedures. Students with specific disabilities have the right to request and expect accommodations, including auxiliary aids and services that enable them to participate in and benefit from all programs and activities offered by or related to a school.

To comply with ADA requirements, many high schools and universities offer programs and information to answer questions for students with disabilities and to assist them both in selecting appropriate colleges and in attaining full inclusion once they enter college. And most colleges and universities have disabilities services offices to help students negotiate the system. When it comes time to apply to colleges, write to the ones that you're interested in to find out what kinds of programs they have in place. When it comes time to narrow down your choices, make a request for a visit.

What is Considered a Disability?

A person is considered to have a disability if he or she meets at least one of three conditions. The individual must:

1. have a documented physical or mental impairment that substantially limits one or more major life activities, such as personal self-care, walking, seeing, hearing, speaking, breathing, learning, working, or performing manual tasks;

2. have a record of such an impairment; or

3. be perceived as having such an impairment.

Physical disabilities include impairments of speech, vision, hearing, and mobility. Other disabilities, while less obvious, are similarly limiting; they include diabetes, asthma, multiple sclerosis, heart disease, cancer, mental illness, mental retardation, cerebral palsy, and learning disabilities.

Learning disabilities refer to an array of biological conditions that impede a person's ability to process and disseminate information. A learning disability is commonly recognized as a significant deficiency in

DIRECTORY FOR STUDENTS WITH DISABILITIES

The following resources can help students, families, and schools with the legal requirements for accommodating disabilities. They can also link you with other groups and individuals that are knowledgeable in students' rights and the process of transition into postsecondary education.

Also, there are special interest, education, support, and advocacy organizations for persons with particular disabilities. Check with your counselor or contact one of the following organizations for information:

ACT Assessment Administration

Special Testing
P.O. Box 4028
Iowa City, Iowa 52243
319-337-1332
www.act.org

Association on Higher Education and Disability (AHEAD)

University of Massachusetts Boston
100 Morrissey Boulevard
Boston, Massachusetts 02125-3393
617-287-3880
www.ahead.org

Attention Deficit Disorder Association (ADDA)

1788 Second Street, Suite 200
Highland Park, Illinois 60035
847-432-ADDA
www.add.org

Children and Adults with Attention Deficit Disorders (CHADD)

8181 Professional Place, Suite 201
Landover, Maryland 20785
800-233-4050 (toll-free)
www.chadd.org

ERIC Clearing House on Disabilities and Gifted Children

1110 North Glebe Road
Arlington, Virginia 22201-5704
800-328-0272 (toll-free)

Council for Learning Disabilities (CLD)

P.O. Box 40303
Overland Park, Kansas 66204
913-492-8755

HEATH Resource Center National Clearinghouse on Postsecondary Education for Individuals with Disabilities

American Council on Education
One Dupont Circle, NW, Suite 800
Washington, D.C. 20036
800-544-3284 (toll-free)
www.heath-resource-center.org

International Dyslexia Association The Chester Building

8600 LaSalle Road, Suite 382
Baltimore, Maryland 21286-2044
800-222-3123 (toll-free)
www.interdys.org

Learning Disabilities Association of America, Inc. (LDA)
4156 Library Road
Pittsburgh, Pennsylvania 15234-1349
412-341-1515
www.ldanatl.org

Learning Disabilities Association of Canada (LDAC)

323 Chapel Street, Suite 200
Ottawa, Ontario K1N 7Z2
613-238-5721
www.ldac-taac.ca

National Center for Law and Learning Disabilities (NCLLD)

P.O. Box 368
Cabin John, Maryland 20818
301-469-8308

National Center for Learning Disabilities (NCLD)

381 Park Avenue South, Suite 1401
New York, New York 10016
888-575-7373 (toll-free)
www.ncld.org

National Information Center for Children and Youth with Disabilities

P.O. Box 1492
Washington, D.C. 20013
800-695-0285 (toll-free)
www.nichcy.org

Recording for the Blind & Dyslexic
20 Roszel Road
Princeton, New Jersey 08540
609-452-0606
www.rfbd.org

SAT Services for Students with Disabilities

The College Board
P.O. Box 6226
Princeton, New Jersey 08541-6226
609-771-7137
www.collegeboard.com

TIPS FOR STUDENTS WITH DISABILITIES

- Document your disability with letters from your physician(s), therapist, case manager, school psychologist, and other service providers.

- Get letters of support from teachers, family, friends, and service providers that detail how you have learned to work despite your disability.

- Learn the federal laws that apply to students with disabilities.

- Research support groups for peer information and advocacy.

- Visit several campuses.

- Determine the best point in the admissions process at which to identify yourself as having a disability.

- Look into the services available, the pace of campus life, and the college's expectations for students with disabilities.

- Ask about orientation programs, including specialized introductions for or about students with disabilities.

- Ask about flexible, individualized study plans.

- Ask if the school offers technology such as voice synthesizers, voice recognition, and/or visual learning equipment to its students.

- Ask about adapted intramural/social activities.

- Ask to talk with students who have similar disabilities to hear about their experiences on campus.

- Once you select a college, get a map of the campus and learn the entire layout.

- If you have a physical disability, make sure the buildings you need to be in are accessible to you. Some, even though they comply with the ADA, aren't as accessible as others.

- Be realistic. If you use a wheelchair, for example, a school with an exceptionally hilly campus may not be your best choice, no matter what other accommodations it has.

one or more of the following areas: oral expression, listening comprehension, written expression, basic reading skills, reading comprehension, mathematical calculation, or problem solving. Individuals with learning disabilities also may have difficulty with sustained attention, time management, or social skills.

If you have a disability, you will take the same steps to choose and apply to a college as other students, but you should also evaluate each college based on your special need(s). Get organized, and meet with campus specialists to discuss your specific requirements. Then, explore whether the programs, policies, procedures, and facilities meet your specific situation.

It is usually best to describe your disability in a letter attached to the application so the proper fit can be made between you and the school. You may even want to have your psychoeducational evaluation and testing record sent to the school. Some colleges help with schedules and offer transition courses, reduced course loads, extra access to professors, and special study areas to help address your needs.

Remember, admission to college is a realistic goal for any motivated student. If you invest the time and effort, you can make it happen.

STUDENT COUNSEL

The following quotes are from students who attend a college that offers services for learning disabled students.

"I have delayed development. I need help getting things done, and I need extra time for tests. As long as I'm able to go up to teachers and ask questions, I do well on tests."

—Anita

"I have dyslexia. I thought the term 'disabilities services' was for people with visual and hearing impairments. But when I got here, I found it covered a variety of disabilities. It was like Christmas. You got everything you wanted and more."

—Debra

"I am hard of hearing. I was always afraid I wouldn't be able to hear what [teachers] said. It's hard to read lips and listen at the same time. With note takers, I still get what I need even if the teacher moves around. They want you to make it through."

—Jeannette

Chapter 6

APPLYING TO COLLEGE

The big moment has arrived. It's time to make some decisions about where you want to apply.

ONCE THAT LIST IS FINALIZED, the worst part is filling out all the forms accurately and getting them in by the deadlines. Because requirements differ, you should check with all the colleges that you are interested in attending to find out what the specific requirements are at those schools.

WHAT SCHOOLS LOOK FOR IN PROSPECTIVE STUDENTS

As if you were sizing up the other team to plan your game strategy, understand what admissions committees want from you as you assemble all the pieces of your application.

Academic record: Admission representatives look at the breadth (how many), diversity (which ones), and difficulty (how challenging) of the courses on your transcript.

Grades: You should show consistency in your ability to work to your potential. If your grades are not initially good, colleges look to see that significant improvement has been made. Some colleges have minimum grade point averages that they are willing to accept.

Class rank: Colleges consider the academic standing of a student in relation to the other members of his or her class. Are you in the top 25 percent of your class? Top half? Ask your counselor for your class rank.

Standardized test scores: Colleges look at test scores in terms of ranges. If your scores aren't high but you

did well academically in high school, you shouldn't be discouraged. There is no set formula for admission. Even at the most competitive schools, some students' test scores are lower than you would think.

Out-of-class activities: Colleges look for depth of involvement (variety and how long you participated), initiative (leadership), and creativity demonstrated in activities, service, or work.

Recommendations: Most colleges require a recommendation from your high school guidance counselor. Some ask for references from teachers or other adults. If your counselor or teachers don't know you well, you should put together a student resume, or

---

PARENT PERSPECTIVE

Q: How did you help your daughter get into college?

A: The key is to start early, like in the junior year. We didn't do that. At this point in the fall of our daughter's senior year, deadlines are coming up, and we haven't really looked at any colleges yet or gone on visits. It's kind of like choosing a house to buy without going to the house. The parent's role is to ask a lot of questions to get your child to figure out exactly what it is he or she wants to do. It's a big decision.

We hired a financial aid consultant who is helping us look at different colleges. The biggest worry is the FAFSA form. If you get it wrong, and they send it back to you—you have to start all over again. In the meantime, you're behind and others are getting grants. The whole process is very confusing, and there's no one to walk you through it. We've looked at different colleges on the Internet, and college fairs are a good resource. Plus, our daughter has done a lot on her own.

Doug and Judy Ames
Colorado Springs, Colorado

PARENT PERSPECTIVE

Q: What can parents do to help their children make decisions about colleges?

A: Parents and teens should visit college campuses early and trust their gut feelings about whether the campus feels right. Above all, don't be blinded by name-brand colleges and the strong peer pressure that seems to steer your teen in the direction of prestigious colleges. Just as in shopping for clothing: Would you rather have a name brand or something that fits you well and makes you feel comfortable?

Ask your teen some questions. Do you really want to live in a pressure-cooker for the next four years? Some students thrive in a highly competitive environment, but many do not—even if they are excellent students. Before making a final decision, a teen should spend three or four days at the two colleges that interest him or her the most.

Senior year in high school is a time when teens go through many changes and experiment with many different roles. This can be bewildering to parents. Be patient. Realize that the time is equally bewildering to your son or daughter. Parents can be supportive and understanding, even though their teen may seem to be pushing them away. Offer guidance about choosing the right college, even though your teen might seem to be rejecting it. Teens hear everything, though they might not show it.

Marilyn Wedge, Ph.D.

Parent, family therapist, and educational consultant

Agoura Hills, California

brag sheet, that outlines what you have done during your four years of high school. In this section, you'll find a worksheet that will help you put together your resume.

College interview: Required by most colleges with highly selective procedures. For further information, see "The College Interview" in the previous section.

ADMISSION PROCEDURES

Your first task in applying is to get application forms. That's easy. You can get them from your high school's guidance department, at college fairs, or by calling or writing to colleges and requesting applications. (See "Writing to a College for Information" in the previous section.) The trend, however, is leaning toward online applications, which you can do at the school's Web site. Admission information can also be gathered from college representatives, catalogs, Web sites, and directories; alumni or students attending the college; and campus visits. Take a look at "Do's and Don'ts for Filling out an Application" on page 51 for some guidelines.

Which Admissions Option Is Best for You?

One of the first questions you will be asked on applications for four-year colleges and universities is which admission option you want. What they're talking about is whether you want to apply early action, early decision, etc.

If you're going to a two-year college, this doesn't apply to you. Two-year colleges usually have an "open-door" admission policy, which means that high school graduates may enroll as long as space is available. Sometimes vo-tech schools are somewhat selective, and competition for admission may be fairly intense for programs that are highly specialized.

Four-year institutions generally offer the following admissions options:

Early admission: A student of superior ability is admitted into college courses and programs before completing high school.

Early decision: A student declares a first-choice college, requests that the college decide on acceptance early (between November and January), and agrees to enroll if accepted. Students with a strong high school record who are sure they want to attend a certain school should consider early decision admission. (See "More on Early Decision," on the next page.)

Early action: Similar to early decision, but if a student is accepted, he or she has until the regular admission deadline to decide whether or not to attend.

Early evaluation: A student can apply under early evaluation to find out if the chance of acceptance is good, fair, or poor. Applications are due before the regular admission deadline, and the student is given an opinion between January and March.

Regular admission: This is the most common option offered to students. A deadline is set when all applications must be received, and all notifications are sent out at the same time.

Rolling admission: The college accepts students who meet the academic requirements on a first-come, first-served basis until it fills its freshman class. No strict application deadline is specified. Applications are reviewed and decisions are made immediately (usually within two to three weeks). This method is commonly used at large state universities, so students should apply early for the best chance of acceptance.

Open admission: Virtually all high school graduates are admitted, regardless of academic qualifications.

Deferred admission: An accepted student is allowed to postpone enrollment for a year.

More on Early Decision

Early decision is a legally binding agreement between you and the college. If the college accepts you, you pay a deposit within a short period of time and sign an agreement stating that you will not apply to other colleges. To keep students from backing out, some colleges mandate that applicants' high school counselors cannot send transcripts to other institutions.

In many ways, early decision is a win-win for both students and colleges. Students can relax and enjoy their senior year of high school without waiting to see if other colleges have accepted them. And colleges know early in the year who is enrolled and can start planning the coming year.

When Is Early Decision the Right Decision?

For good and bad reasons, early decision is a growing trend, so why not just do it? Early decision is an excellent idea that comes with a warning. It's not a good idea unless you have done a thorough college search and know without a shred of doubt that this is the college for you. Don't go for early decision unless you've spent time on the campus, in classes and

dorms, and you have a true sense of the academic and social climate of that college.

Early decision can get sticky if you change your mind. Parents of students who have signed agreements and then want to apply elsewhere get angry at high school counselors, saying they've taken away their rights to choose among colleges. They try to force them to send out transcripts even though their children have committed to one college. To guard against this scenario, some colleges ask parents and students to sign a statement signifying their understanding that early decision is a binding plan. Even some high schools now have their own form for students and parents to sign acknowledging that they completely realize the nature of an early decision agreement.

The Financial Reason Against Early Decision

Another common argument against early decision is that if an institution has you locked in, there's no incentive to offer applicants the best financial packages. The consensus seems to be that if you're looking to play the financial game, don't apply for early decision.

STUDENT COUNSEL

Q: What made you want to apply to college early decision?

A: I visited lots of schools in Pennsylvania, but the minute I walked on the campus at Gettysburg, I knew I wanted to come here. I liked the way the campus was set up. It was small, and everything was together. The student-teacher ratio was low, and it had a good political science program. It had everything that I wanted.

But if you want to go early decision, you have to visit the schools to be able to compare and contrast the different campuses. Many of the schools will have the same things, like small class size, but the way you feel about the campus is the largest factor because that's where you will be living. I visited Gettysburg four times, so when I went early decision, I was confident about it. I realized it was a huge step and knew I had to be sure. But after visiting here so many times, I knew I'd be unhappy anywhere else.

Kelly Keegan
Gettysburg College

However, some folks argue that the best financial aid offers are usually made to attractive applicants. Generally, if a student receives an early decision offer, they fall into that category and so would get "the sweetest" financial aid anyway. That doesn't mean that there aren't colleges out there using financial incentives to get students to enroll. A strong candidate who applies to six or eight schools and gets admitted to them all will look at how much money the colleges throw his or her way before making a decision.

Before You Decide...

If you're thinking about applying for early decision at a college, ask yourself these questions first. You'll be glad you did.

☑ Why am I applying early decision?

☑ Have I thoroughly researched several colleges and know what my options are?

☑ Do I know why I'm going to college and what I want to accomplish there?

☑ Have I visited several schools, spent time in classes, stayed overnight, and talked to professors?

☑ Do the courses that the college offers match my goals?

☑ Am I absolutely convinced that one college clearly stands out above all others?

MORE MUMBO JUMBO

Besides confusing terms like deferred admission, early decision, and early evaluation discussed previously in this section, you'll most likely stumble upon some additional terms that might bamboozle you. Here, we explain a few more:

Academic Calendar

Traditional semesters: Two equal periods of time during a school year.

Early semester: Two equal periods of time during a school year. The first semester is completed before Christmas.

Trimester: Calendar year divided into three equal periods of time. The third trimester replaces summer school.

Quarter: Four equal periods of time during a school year.

4-1-4: Two equal terms of about four months separated by a one-month term.

Accreditation

Accreditation is recognition of a college or university by a regional or national organization, which indicates that the institution has met its objectives and is maintaining prescribed educational standards. Colleges may be accredited by one of six regional associations of schools and colleges and by any one of many national specialized accrediting bodies.

Specialized accreditation of individual programs is granted by national professional organizations. This is intended to ensure that specific programs meet or exceed minimum requirements established by the professional organization. States may require that students in some professions that grant licenses graduate from an accredited program as one qualification for licensure.

Accreditation is somewhat like receiving a pass/fail grade. It doesn't differentiate colleges and universities that excel from those that meet minimum requirements. Accreditation applies to all programs within an institution, but it does not mean that all programs are of equal quality within an institution. Accreditation does not guarantee transfer recognition by other colleges. Transfer decisions are made by individual institutions.

Affiliation

Not-for-profit colleges are classified into one of the following categories: state-assisted, private/independent, or private/church-supported. The institution's affiliation does not guarantee the quality or nature of the institution, and it may or may not have an effect on the religious life of students.

State-assisted colleges and universities and private/independent colleges do not have requirements related to the religious activity of their students.

The influence of religion varies among private/church-supported colleges. At some, religious services or study are encouraged or required; at others, religious affiliation is less apparent.

Articulation Agreement

Articulation agreements facilitate the transfer of students and credits among state-assisted institutions of higher education by establishing transfer procedures and equitable treatment of all students in the system.

One type of articulation agreement links two or more colleges so that students can continue to make progress toward their degree, even if they must attend different schools at different times. For example, some states' community colleges have agreements with their universities that permit graduates of college parallel programs to transfer with junior standing.

A second type of articulation agreement links secondary (high school) and postsecondary institutions to allow students to gain college credit for relevant vocational courses. This type of agreement saves students time and tuition in the pursuit of higher learning.

Because articulation agreements vary from school to school and from program to program, it is recommended that students check with their home institution and the institution they are interested in attending in order to fully understand the options available to them and each institution's specific requirements.

Cross-Registration

Cross-registration is a cooperative arrangement offered by many colleges and universities for the purpose of increasing the number and types of courses offered at any one institution. This arrangement allows students to cross-register for one or more courses at any participating host institution. While specific cross-registration program requirements may vary, typically a student can cross-register without having to pay the host institution additional tuition.

If your college participates in cross-registration, check with your home institution concerning any additional tuition costs and request a cross-registration form. Check with your adviser and registrar at your home institution to make sure that the course you plan to take is approved, and then contact the host institution for cross-registration instructions. Make sure that there is space available in the course you want to take at the host institution, as some host institutions give their own students registration priority.

To participate in cross-registration, you may need to be a full-time student (some programs allow part-time student participation) in good academic and financial standing at your home institution. Check with both colleges well in advance for all of the specific requirements.

THE COMPLETE APPLICATION PACKAGE

Freshman applications can be filed any time after you have completed your junior year of high school. Colleges strongly recommend that students apply by April (at the latest) of their senior year in order to be considered for acceptance, scholarships, financial aid, and housing. College requirements may vary, so always read and comply with specific requirements. In general, admission officers are interested in the following basic materials:

- A completed and signed application and any required application fee.

- An official copy of your high school transcript, including your class ranking and grade point average. The transcript must include all work completed as of the date the application is submitted. Check with your guidance counselor for questions about these items. If you apply on line, you must inform your guidance counselor and request that he or she send your transcript to the schools you're applying to. Your application will not be processed without a transcript.

- An official record of your ACT or SAT I scores.

COLLEGE APPLICATION CHECKLIST Keep track of your applications by inserting a check mark or the completion date in the appropriate column and row.

	College 1	College 2	College 3	College 4
Campus visit				
Campus interview				
Letters of recommendation				
NAME:				
Date requested				
Follow-up				
NAME:				
Date requested				
Follow-up				
NAME:				
Date requested				
Follow-up				
Counselor recommendation form to counselor				
Secondary school report form to counselor				
Test scores requested				
Transcripts sent				
Application completed				
Essay completed				
All signatures collected				
Financial aid forms enclosed				
Application fee enclosed				
Postage affixed/copies made/return address on envelope				
Letters of acceptance/denial/wait list received				
Colleges notified of intent				
Tuition deposit sent				
Housing and other forms submitted to chosen college				
Orientation scheduled				

- Other items that may be required include letters of recommendation, an essay, the secondary school report form and midyear school report (sent in by your guidance counselor after you fill out a portion of the form), and any financial aid forms required by the college.

Use the "College Application Checklist" on the previous page to make sure you have everything you need before you send off that application.

Filling out the Forms

Filling out college applications can seem like a daunting task, but there are six easy steps to follow for the successful completion of this part of your college selection process.

Step 1: Practice Copies

Make a photocopy of each college's application that you plan to apply to. Since the presentation of your application may be considered an important aspect in the weighting for admission, you don't want to erase, cross out, or use white-out on your final application. Make all your mistakes on your copies. When you think you have it right, then transfer the information to your final original copy or go on line to enter it on the college's electronic application. If you are mailing in your applications, try to use a word processor. But if you have to type your applications, make the effort to line up your responses in those tiny spaces. Remember, at the larger universities, the application packet may be the only part of you they see.

Step 2: Decide on Your Approach

What is it about your application that will grab the admission counselor's attention so that it will be pulled out of the sea of applications on his or her desk for consideration? Be animated and interesting in what you say. Be memorable in your approach to your application, but don't overdo it. You want the admissions counselor to remember you, not your Spanish castle made of popsicle sticks. Most

DO'S AND DON'TS FOR FILLING OUT YOUR APPLICATIONS

One of the most intimidating steps of applying for admission to college is filling out all the forms. This list of do's and don'ts will help you put your best foot forward on your college applications.

DO

- Read applications and directions carefully.
- Make sure that everything that is supposed to be included is enclosed.
- Fill out your own applications. Type the information yourself to avoid crucial mistakes.
- Start with the simple applications and then progress to the more complex ones.
- Make copies of applications, and practice filling one out before you complete the original.
- Type or neatly print your answers, and then proofread the applications and essays several times for accuracy. Also ask someone else to proofread it for you.
- If asked, describe how you can make a contribution to the schools to which you apply.
- Be truthful, and do not exaggerate your accomplishments.
- Keep a copy of all forms you submit to colleges.
- Be thorough and on time.

DON'T

- Use correction fluid. If you type your application, use a correctable typewriter or the liftoff strips to correct mistakes. Better yet, fill out your application on line.
- Write in script. If you don't have access to a computer or typewriter, print neatly.
- Leave blank spaces. Missing information may cause your application to be sent back or delayed while admission officers wait for complete information.
- Be unclear. If the question calls for a specific answer, don't try to dodge it by being vague.
- Put it off! Do it early.

importantly, be honest and don't exaggerate your academics and extracurricular activities. Approach this process with integrity every step of the way. First of all, it is the best way to end up in a college that is the right match for you. Second, if you are less than truthful, the college will eventually learn about it. How will they know? You have to request that support materials accompany your application, things like transcripts and recommendations. If you tell one story and they tell another, the admissions office will notice the disparity—another red flag!

Step 3: Check the Deadlines

In September of your senior year, organize your applications in chronological order. Place the due dates for your final list of schools next to their names on your stretch, target, and safety list and on your "College Application Checklist." Work on the earliest due date first.

Step 4: Check the Data on You

You need to make sure that the information you will be sending to support your applications is correct. The first thing to double-check is your transcript. This is an important piece because you must send a transcript with each application you send to colleges. Take a trip to the guidance office and ask for a "Transcript Request Form." Fill out the request for a formal transcript indicating that you are requesting a copy for yourself and that you will pick it up. Pay the fee if there is one.

When you get your transcript, look it over carefully. It will be several pages long and will include everything from the titles of all the courses that you have taken since the ninth grade along with the final grade for each course to the community service hours you have logged each year. Check the information carefully. It is understandable that with this much data, it is easy to make an input error. Because this information is vital to you and you are the best judge of accuracy, it is up to you to check it. Take any corrections or questions you have back to your guidance counselor to make the corrections. If it is a

questionable grade, your counselor will help you find out what grade should have been posted on your transcript. Do whatever needs to be done to make sure your transcript has been corrected no later than October 1 of your senior year.

Step 5: List Your Activities

When you flip through your applications, you will find a section on extracurricular activities. It is time to hit your word processor again to prioritize your list of extracurricular activities and determine the best approach for presenting it to your colleges. Some students will prepare a resume and include this in every application they send. Other students will choose to develop an "Extracurricular, Academic, and Work Experience Addendum" and mark those specific sections of their application, "See attached Addendum."

If you are a powerhouse student with a great deal to say in this area, it will take time to prioritize your involvement in activities and word it succinctly yet interestingly. Your "Brag Sheet" will help (see "The Brag Sheet" on page 53). Put those activities that will have the strongest impact, show the most consistent involvement, and demonstrate your leadership abilities at the top of the list. This will take time, so plan accordingly. If you feel you have left out important information because the form limits you, include either an addendum or your resume as a back-up.

Step 6: Organize Your Other Data

What other information can you organize in advance of sitting down to fill out your applications?

The Personal Data Section

Most of this section is standard personal information that you will not have any difficulty responding to, but some items you will need to think about. For example, you may find a question that asks, "What special college or division are you applying to?" Do you have a specific school in mind, like the College of Engineering? If you are not sure about your major, ask yourself what interests you the most and then enter

THE BRAG SHEET

At the beginning of this section, we described how a student resume can help your guidance counselors and teachers write their letters of recommendation for you. Putting together a list of your accomplishments will also help you organize all of the information you will need to include when you fill out your college applications.

ACADEMICS

GPA (Grade Point Average) _____

THE HONORS COURSES I HAVE TAKEN ARE:

English _____

History _____

Math _____

Science _____

Language _____

Electives _____

STANDARDIZED TEST SCORES

PSAT _____

1st SAT I _____

2nd SAT I _____

ACT _____

THE AP COURSES I HAVE TAKEN ARE:

English _____

History _____

Math _____

Science _____

Language _____

Electives _____

SAT II SUBJECT TESTS

Test 1 _____ Score _____

Test 2 _____ Score _____

Test 3 _____ Score _____

SPECIAL TALENTS

I have received the following academic awards:

_____

_____

_____

I have performed in various theatrical productions: _____

I am lettered in the following sports: _____

_____

I have played on the following traveling teams: _____

_____

I am a member of the following musical groups: _____

_____

EXTRACURRICULAR ACTIVITIES

I participate on a regular basis in the following extracurricular activities: _____

_____

I have held the following offices: _____

_____

_____

I have established the following extracurricular organizations:

_____

I have held the following after-school and summer jobs: _____

_____

GOALS

I plan to major in the following area in college: _____

_____

that college. Once you are in college and have a better a sense of what you want to do, you can always change your major later.

The application will provide an optional space to declare ethnicity. If you feel you would like to declare an area and that it would work to your advantage for admission, consider completing this section of the application.

You are also going to need your high school's College Entrance Examination Board (CEEB) number. That is the number you needed when you filled out your test packets. It is stamped on the front of your SAT and ACT packets, or, if you go to the guidance department, they'll tell you what it is.

The Standardized Testing Section

Applications ask you for your test dates and scores. Get them together accurately. All your College Board scores should be recorded on the latest test results you received. Your latest ACT record will only have the current scores unless you asked for all your past test results. If you have lost this information, call these organizations or go to your guidance department. Your counselor should have copies. Be sure the testing organizations are sending your official score reports to the schools to which you're applying. If you are planning to take one of these tests in the future, the colleges will want those dates, too; they will wait for those scores before making a decision. If you change your plans, write the admissions office a note with the new dates or the reason for canceling.

The Senior Course Load Section

Colleges will request that you list your present senior schedule by semester. Set this information up in this order: List any AP or honors-level full-year courses first; these will have the most impact. Then list other required full-year courses and then required semester courses, followed by electives. Make sure you list first-semester and second-semester courses appropriately. Do not forget to include physical education if you are taking it this year.

Your Recommendation Writers

Most schools will require you to submit two or three letters of recommendation from adults who know you well.

Guidance Counselor Recommendations

Nearly all colleges require a letter of recommendation from the applicant's high school guidance counselor. Some counselors will give students an essay question that they feel will give them the background they need in order to structure a recommendation. Other counselors will canvass a wide array of individuals who know a student in order to gather a broader picture of the student in various settings. No one approach is better than the other. Find out which approach is used at your school. You will probably get this information as a handout at one of those evening guidance programs or in a classroom presentation by your school's guidance department. If you are still not sure you know what is expected of you or if the dog has eaten those papers, ask your guidance counselor what is due and by what date. Make sure that you complete the materials on time and that you set aside enough of your time to do them justice.

Teacher Recommendations

In addition to the recommendation from your counselor, colleges may request additional recommendations from your teachers. Known as formal recommendations, these are sent directly to the colleges by your subject teachers. Most colleges require at least one formal recommendation in addition to the counselor's recommendation. However, many competitive institutions require at least two, if not three, academic recommendations. Follow a school's directions regarding the exact number.

Approach your recommendation writers personally to request that they write for you. If they agree, provide them with a copy of your Brag Sheet. On the other hand, you may be met with a polite refusal on the order of "I'm sorry, but I'm unable to write for you. I've been approached by so many seniors already that it would be difficult for me to accomplish your recommendation by your due dates." This teacher may really be overburdened with requests for recommendations, especially if this is a senior English teacher, or the teacher may be giving you a signal that someone else may be able to write a stronger piece for you. Either way, accept the refusal politely, and seek another recommendation writer.

How do you decide whom to ask? Here are some questions to help you select your writers:

- How well does the teacher know you?

- Has the teacher taught you for more than one course? (A teacher who taught you over a two- to three-year period has seen your talents and skills develop.)

- Has the teacher sponsored an extracurricular activity in which you made a contribution?

- Do you get along with the teacher?

- Does the college/university indicate that a recommendation is required or recommended from a particular subject-area instructor?

- If you declare an intended major, can you obtain a recommendation from a teacher in that subject area?

TIP: Provide recommendations from two subject areas (e.g., English and math).

Other Recommendation Writers

Consider getting recommendations from your employer, your rabbi or pastor, the director of the summer camp where you worked for the last two summers, and so on—but only if these additional letters are going to reveal information about you that will have a profound impact on the way a college will view your candidacy. Otherwise, you run the risk of overloading your application with too much paper.

Writing the Application Essay

Application essays show how you think and how you write. They also reveal additional information about you that is not in your other application material. Not all colleges require essays, and those that do often have a preferred topic. Make sure you write about the topic that is specified and keep to the length of pages or words. If the essay asks for 300 words, don't submit 50 or 500. Some examples of essay topics include:

Tell us about yourself. Describe your personality and a special accomplishment. Illustrate the unique aspects of who you are, what you do, and what you want out of life. Share an experience that made an impact on you, or write about something you have learned from your parents.

Tell us about an academic or extracurricular interest or idea. Show how a book, experience, quotation, or idea reflects or shapes your outlook and aspirations.

Tell us why you want to come to our college. Explain why your goals and interests match the programs and offerings of that particular school. This question requires some research about the school. Be specific.

Show us an imaginative side of your personality. This question demands originality but is a great opportunity to show off your skills as a writer. Start writing down your thoughts and impressions well before the essay is due. Think about how you have

FROM THE GUIDANCE OFFICE

Q: Why are essays so important to the college application?

A: Students focus more on grades than anything else. They think grades are the be-all and end-all and that an SAT score will get them in. For most selective schools, that's just one piece of the pie. Many of the schools in the upper 20 percent of competitive schools consider the essay more heavily. Essays show whether the student is a thinker, creative, and analytical. They're looking for the type of personality that can shine rather than one that simply can spit out names and dates. When everyone has high SATs in a pool of applicants, the essay is what makes one student stand out over another.

Patsy Lovelady
Counselor
MacArthur High School
San Antonio, Texas

changed over the years so that if and when it comes time to write about yourself, you will have plenty of information. Write about something that means a lot to you, and support your thoughts with reasons and examples. Then explain why you care about your topic.

The essay should not be a summary of your high school career. Describe yourself as others see you, and use a natural, conversational style. Use an experience to set the scene in which you will illustrate something about yourself. For example, you might discuss how having a disabled relative helped you to appreciate life's simple pleasures. Or you may use your athletic experiences to tell how you learned the value of teamwork. The essay is your chance to tell something positive or enriching about yourself, so highlight an experience that will make the reader interested in you.

Outline in the essay what you have to offer the college. Explain why you want to attend the institution and how your abilities and goals match the strengths and offerings at the university. Write, rewrite, and edit. Do not try to dash off an essay in one sitting. The essay will improve with time and thought. Proofread and concentrate on spelling, punctuation, and content. Have someone else take a look at your essay. Make copies and save them after mailing the original.

Admission officers look for the person inside the essay. They seek students with a breadth of knowledge and experiences, someone with depth and perspective. Inner strength and commitment are admired, too. Not everyone is a winner all the time. The essay is a tool you can use to develop your competitive edge. Your essay should explain why you should be admitted over other applicants.

As a final word, write the essay from the heart. It should have life and not be contrived or one-dimensional. Avoid telling them what they want to hear; instead, be yourself.

SAMPLE APPLICATION ESSAY

Here is one student's college application essay. She answered the question, "Indicate a person who has had a significant influence on you, and describe that influence."

Mrs. Morrone did not become my guidance counselor until my sophomore year of high school. During my first meeting with her, I sat across from her in an uncomfortable vinyl chair and refused to meet her eyes as I told her about my long and painful shyness, how I detested oral reports, and how I feared raising my hand in class or being called on to answer a question—all because I didn't want to be the center of attention.

She did not offer me advice right away. Instead, she asked me more about myself—my family, my friends, what kinds of music, books, and movies I liked. We talked easily, like old friends, and it was not long before I began to look forward to our weekly meetings. Her office was one of the few places where I felt like I could be myself and let my personality shine through, where I knew that I was accepted and liked unconditionally.

In November of that year, the drama club announced auditions for the spring play, The Glass Menagerie. I had studied it in English class and it was one of my favorites; not surprisingly, I identified strongly with the timid Laura. I talked with Mrs. Morrone about the play and how much I liked theater. At one point I sighed, "I'd love to play Laura."

"Why don't you try out for the show?" Mrs. Morrone suggested.

The very idea of performing, onstage, in a spotlight, in front of dozens of people frightened me. She did not press the matter, but at the end of the session she encouraged me to bring a copy of the play to our next few meetings and read some of the character's lines, "just for fun." I did, and found myself gradually transforming into Laura as I recited her lines with increasing intensity.

After a couple of these amateur performances, she told me that I was genuinely good as Laura, and she would love to see me at least audition for the part. "I would never force you to do it," she said, "but I would hate to see you waste your potential." I insisted that I was too frightened, but she promised that she would come and watch my audition. She told me to pretend she was the only person in the audience.

A week later, I did read for the part of Laura. Mrs. Morrone beamed with pride in the back of the auditorium. I discovered that I truly enjoyed acting; slipping into another character cracked the shell that I had built around myself. I did not get the part, but I had found a passion that enriched my life in immeasurable ways. I owe Mrs. Morrone so much for putting me on the path to becoming a professional actress and for helping me to finally conquer my shyness. Without her quiet support and strength, none of this would have come to pass.

SPECIAL INFORMATION FOR ATHLETES

If you weren't a planner before, but you want to play sports while in college or go to college on an athletic scholarship, you'd better become a planner now. There are many regulations and conditions you need to know ahead of time so that you don't miss out on possible opportunities.

First, think about whether or not you have what it takes to play college sports. It's a tough question to ask, but it's a necessary one. In general, playing college sports requires the basic skills and natural ability, a solid knowledge of the sport, overall body strength, speed, and sound academics. Today's athletes are stronger and faster because of improved methods of training and conditioning. They are coached in skills and techniques, and they begin training in their sport at an early age. Remember, your talents will be compared with those from across the U.S. and around the world.

Second, know the background. Most college athletic programs are regulated by the National Collegiate Athletic Association (NCAA), an organization that has established rules on eligibility, recruiting, and financial aid. The NCAA has three membership divisions: Division I, Division II, and Division III. Institutions are members of one or another division according to the size and scope of their athletic programs and whether they provide athletic scholarships.

If you are planning to enroll in college as a freshman and you wish to participate in Division I or Division II athletics, you must be certified by the NCAA Initial-Eligibility Clearinghouse. The Clearinghouse was established as a separate organization by the NCAA member institutions to ensure consistent interpretation of NCAA initial-eligibility requirements for all prospective student athletes at all member institutions.

You should start the certification process when you are a junior in high school. Check with your counselor to make sure you are taking a core curriculum that meets NCAA requirements. Also, register to take the ACT or SAT I as a junior. Submit your Student Release Form (available in your

---

FROM THE GUIDANCE OFFICE

Q: What's a big mistake high school athletes make when thinking about college?

A: Some athletes think that their athletic ability alone will get them a scholarship and do not believe that their academics must be acceptable. The Division I or II schools cannot offer scholarships if the student has not met the academic standards required by the school for admission. Our counselors start reminding students in the freshman year and every year after that the courses they take do make a difference in how colleges view their transcripts. Students can't start preparing in their senior year of high school.

Sue Bradshaw
Guidance Counselor
Sterling High School
Baytown, Texas

---

guidance counseling office) to the Clearinghouse by the beginning of your senior year.

Initial Eligibility of Freshman Athletes for Division I and II

Students who plan to participate in NCAA Division I or II college sports must obtain the Student Release Form from their high school, complete it, and send it to the NCAA Clearinghouse. This form authorizes high schools to release student transcripts, including test scores, proof of grades, and other academic information, to the Clearinghouse. It also authorizes the Clearinghouse to release this information to the colleges that request it. The form and corresponding fee must be received before any documents will be processed. (Fee waivers are available for economically disadvantaged students. Check with your counselor for fee waiver information.)

Students must also make sure that the Clearinghouse receives ACT and/or SAT I score reports. Students can have score reports sent directly to the Clearinghouse by entering a specific code (9999) printed in the ACT and SAT I registration packets.

Once a year, high schools will send an updated Form 48-H, which lists each course offering that meets NCAA core course requirements. The Clearinghouse personnel will validate the form.

ATHLETIC RESUME

Name _____

Address _____

_____

High school address and phone number

_____

_____

_____

Coach's name _____

Height/weight _____

Foot speed (by specific event) _____

Position played _____

Weight classification _____

GPA _____

Class rank _____

ACT or SAT I scores (or when you plan to take them)

_____

Athletic records _____

_____

All-state teams _____

Special awards _____

Off-season accomplishments _____

Weightlifting exercises _____

Vertical jumps _____

Push-ups _____

Bench jumps _____

Shuttle run _____

Leadership characteristics _____

Former successful athletes from your high school

_____

Outstanding capabilities_____

Citizenship _____

Alumni parents/relatives _____

Include the following with your resume:

- **Team schedule with dates and times**

- **Videotape with jersey number identified**

- **Newspaper clippings about you or your team**

Thereafter, the Clearinghouse will determine each student's initial eligibility. Collegiate institutions will request information from the Clearinghouse on the initial eligibility of prospective student-athletes. The Clearinghouse will make a certification decision and report it directly to the institution.

Three types of eligibility are possible

1. Certification of eligibility for expense-paid campus visits.

2. Preliminary certification of eligibility to participate in college sports (appears likely to meet all NCAA requirements but not yet graduated).

3. Final certification granted when proof of graduation is received.

Additional information about the Clearinghouse can be found in the *Guide for the College-Bound Student-Athlete*, published by the NCAA. To get a copy of this guide, call 800-638-3731 (toll-free).

You can also visit the NCAA Web site at www.ncaa.org.

National Association of Intercollegiate Athletics (NAIA) Regulations

The National Association of Intercollegiate Athletics (NAIA) has different eligibility requirements for student-athletes. To be eligible to participate in intercollegiate athletics as an incoming freshman, two of the following three requirements must be met:

1. Have a 2.0 (C) or higher cumulative final grade point average in high school.

2. Have a composite score of 18 or higher on the ACT or an 860 total score or higher on the SAT I on a single test administered on a national test date.

3. Have a top-half final class rank in his or her high school graduating class.

Student-athletes must also have on file at the college an official ACT or SAT I score report from the appropriate national testing center. Results reported on the student's high school transcript are not acceptable. Students must request that their test scores be forwarded to the college's admission office.

If you have additional questions about NAIA eligibility, write to:
NAIA
6120 South Yale Avenue
Suite 1450
Tulsa, Oklahoma 74136
Telephone: 918-494-8828
Or visit their Web site at *www.naia.org*

AUDITIONS AND PORTFOLIOS

If you decide to study the arts, such as theater, music, or fine arts, you may be required to audition or show your portfolio to admissions personnel. The following tips will help you showcase your talents and skills when preparing for an audition or portfolio review.

Music Auditions

High school students who wish to pursue a degree in music, whether it is vocal or instrumental, typically must audition. If you're a singer, prepare at least two pieces in contrasting styles. One should be in a foreign language, if possible. Choose from operatic, show music, or art song repertories, and make sure you memorize each piece. If you're an instrumentalist or pianist, be prepared to play scales and arpeggios, at least one etude or technical study, and a solo work. Instrumental audition pieces need not be memorized. In either field, you may be required to do sight-reading.

When performing music that is sight-read, you should take time to look over the piece and make certain of the key and time signatures before proceeding with the audition. If you're a singer, you should bring a familiar accompanist to the audition.

"My advice is to ask for help from teachers, try to acquire audition information up front, and know more than is required for the audition," says one student. "It is also a good idea to select your audition time and date early."

"Try to perform your solo in front of as many people as you can as many times as possible," says another student. "You may also want to try to get involved in a high school performance."

Programs differ, so students are encouraged to call the college and ask for audition information. In general, music departments seek students who

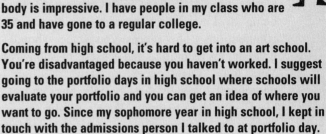

STUDENT COUNSEL

Q: What's it like going to an art school?

A: This is not your normal college experience. You totally immerse yourself in art and commit all your time to it. It's intense and can be stressful. The teachers are great. Most are working professionals. The student body is impressive. I have people in my class who are 35 and have gone to a regular college.

Coming from high school, it's hard to get into an art school. You're disadvantaged because you haven't worked. I suggest going to the portfolio days in high school where schools will evaluate your portfolio and you can get an idea of where you want to go. Since my sophomore year in high school, I kept in touch with the admissions person I talked to at portfolio day. She followed me along and saw my interest.

Eric Davidson
Art Center
Pasadena, California

demonstrate technical competence and performance achievement.

Admission to music programs varies in degree of competitiveness, so you should audition at a minimum of three colleges and a maximum of five to amplify your opportunity. The degree of competitiveness varies also by instrument, especially if a renowned musician teaches a certain instrument. Some colleges offer a second audition if you feel you did not audition to your potential. Ideally, you will be accepted into the music program of your choice, but keep in mind that it's possible to not be accepted. You must then make the decision to either pursue a music program at another college or consider another major at that college.

Dance Auditions

At many four-year colleges, an open class is held the day before auditions. A performance piece that combines improvisation, ballet, modern, and rhythm is taught and then students are expected to perform the piece at auditions. Professors look for coordination, technique, rhythm, degree of movement, and body structure. The dance faculty members also assess your ability to learn and your potential to complete the curriculum. Dance programs vary, so check with the college of your choice for specific information.

Art Portfolios

A portfolio is simply a collection of your best pieces of artwork. The pieces you select to put in your portfolio should demonstrate your interest and aptitude for a serious education in the arts. A well-developed portfolio can help you gain acceptance into a prestigious art college and increase your chances of being awarded a scholarship in national portfolio competitions. The pieces you select should show diversity in technique and variety in subject matter. You may show work in any medium (oils, photography, watercolors, pastels, etc.) and in either black-and-white or color. Your portfolio can include classroom assignments as well as independent projects. You can also include your sketchbook.

Specialized art colleges request that you submit an average of ten pieces of art, but remember that quality is more important than quantity. The admission office staff will review your artwork and transcripts to assess your skill and potential for success. Usually, you will present your portfolio in person; however, some schools allow students to mail slides if distance is an issue. There is no simple formula for success other than hard work. In addition, there is no such thing as a "perfect portfolio," nor any specific style or direction to achieve one.

Tips to Pull Your Portfolio Together:

☞ Try to make your portfolio as clean and organized as possible.

☞ It is important to protect your work, but make sure the package you select is easy to handle and does not interfere with the viewing of the artwork.

☞ Drawings that have been rolled up are difficult for the jurors to handle and view. You may shrink-wrap the pieces, but it is not required.

☞ Avoid loose sheets of paper between pieces.

☞ If you choose to mount or mat your work (not required), use only neutral gray tones, black, or white.

☞ Never include framed pieces or three smudge.

☞ A slide portfolio should be presented in a standard 8 × 11 plastic slide sleeve, which can be purchased at any photo or camera supply store.

☞ Be sure paintings are completely dry before you place them in your portfolio.

☞ Label each piece with your name, address, and high school.

Theater Auditions

Most liberal arts colleges do not require that students who audition be accepted into the theater department unless the college offers a Bachelor of Fine Arts (B.F.A.) degree in theater. You should apply to the college of your choice prior to scheduling an audition. You should also consider spending a full day on campus so that you may talk with theater faculty members and students, attend classes, meet with your admission counselor, and tour the facilities.

Although each college and university has different requirements, you should prepare two contrasting monologues taken from plays of your choice if you're auditioning for a B.F.A. acting program. The total length of both pieces should not exceed 5 minutes, and you should take a theater resume and photo to the audition with you.

Musical theater requirements generally consist of one up-tempo musical selection and one ballad as well as one monologue from a play or musical of your choice. The total of all your pieces should not exceed 5 minutes. Music for the accompanist, a resume of your theater experience, and a photo are also required.

Tips to Get You Successfully through an Audition:

☞ Choose material suitable for your age.

☞ If you choose your monologue from a book of monologues, you should read the entire play and be familiar with the context of your selection.

☞ Select a monologue that allows you to speak directly to another person; you should play only one character.

☞ Memorize your selection.

☞ Avoid using characterization or style, as they tend to trap you rather than tapping deeper into inner resources.

Chapter 7

FINANCIAL AID DOLLARS AND SENSE

Getting financial aid can be intimidating—but don't let that stop you.

It's COMPLICATED, and there are a lot of pieces to this puzzle. Leave a few out or put too many in, and the puzzle doesn't come out right. However, if you look at each piece separately rather than trying to understand the whole process all at once, it will be much easier to absorb. The trick is to start early, be organized, and plan ahead.

Finding the money you need to attend a two- or four-year institution or vocational or trade school is a challenge, but you can do it if you devise a strategy well before you actually start applying to college. Financial aid comes from a lot of different sources. But this is where GAJ comes in. You'll find lots of help here to locate those sources and find out where to get advice. Financial aid is available to help meet both direct educational costs (tuition, fees, books) and personal living expenses (food, housing, transportation).

PROJECTED COLLEGE EXPENSES

The following chart estimates the cost of one year of college education, including tuition, room, and board. Estimates are based on a 6 percent annual increase.

School Year	Public 4-Year	Private 4-Year
2002–2003	$12,712	$27,289
2006–2007	15,452	33,291
2010–2011	18,782	40,466
2014–2015	22,829	49,186

Source: The College Entrance Examination Board

Times have changed to favor the student in the financial aid process. Because the pool of potential traditional college students has diminished, colleges and universities are competing among themselves to attract good students. In fact, some colleges and universities no longer use financial aid primarily as a method to help students fund their college education but rather as a marketing and recruitment tool. This puts students and families at an advantage, one that should be recognized and used for bargaining power.

It used to be that colleges and universities offered need-based and merit-based financial aid to only needy and/or academically exceptional students. Now some schools offer what might be called incentive or discount aid to encourage students to choose them over another college. This aid, which is not necessarily based on need or merit, is aimed at students who meet the standards of the college but who wouldn't necessarily qualify for traditional kinds of aid.

A BIRD'S-EYE VIEW OF FINANCIAL AID

You and your family should be assertive in negotiating financial aid packages. It used to be that there was no room for such negotiation, but in today's environment, it is wise to be a comparison shopper. Families should wait until they've received all of their financial offers and then talk to their first-choice college to see if the college can match the better offers from other colleges.

To be eligible to receive federal/state financial aid, you must maintain satisfactory academic progress

FINANCIAL AID GLOSSARY

ASSETS. The amount a family has in savings and investments. This includes savings and checking accounts, a business, a farm or other real estate, and stocks, bonds, and trust funds. Cars are not considered assets, nor are such possessions as stamp collections or jewelry. The net value of the principal home is counted as an asset by some colleges in determining their own awards but is not included in the calculation for eligibility for federal funds.

CITIZENSHIP/ELIGIBILITY FOR AID. To be eligible to receive federally funded college aid, a student must be one of the following:

1. A United States citizen

2. A non-citizen national

3. A permanent resident with an I-151 or I-551 without conditions

4. A participant in a suspension of deportation case pending before Congress

5. A holder of an I-94 showing one of the following designations: "Refugee," "Asylum Granted," "Indefinite Parole" and/or "Humanitarian Parole," "Cuban/Haitian Entrant, Status Pending," or "Conditional Entrant" (valid if issued before April 1, 1980).

Individuals in the U.S. on an F1 or F2 visa only or on a J1 or J2 exchange visa only cannot get federal aid.

COOPERATIVE EDUCATION. A program offered by many colleges in which students alternate periods of enrollment with periods of employment, usually paid, and that can lengthen the usual baccalaureate program to five years.

EXPECTED FAMILY CONTRIBUTION (EFC) OR PARENTAL CONTRIBUTION. A figure determined by a congressionally mandated formula that indicates how much of a family's resources should be considered "available" for college expenses. Factors such as taxable and nontaxable income and the value of family assets are taken into account to determine a family's financial strength. Allowances for maintaining a family and future financial needs are then taken into consideration before determining how much a family should be able to put toward the cost of college.

INDEPENDENT STUDENT. A student who reports only his or her own income (and that of a spouse, if relevant) when applying for federal financial aid. Students who will be 24 or older by December 31, 2002, will automatically be considered "independent" for 2002–2003. Students who are under 24 will be considered independent if they are:

- married and not claimed as a dependent on their parents' 2002 federal income tax return

- the supporter of a legal dependent other than a spouse

- a veteran of the U.S. Armed Forces

- an orphan or ward of the court

- classified as independent by a college's financial aid administrator because of other unusual circumstances

- a graduate or professional student

MERIT-BASED AID. Any form of financial aid awarded on the basis of personal achievement or individual characteristics without reference to financial need.

SUBSIDIZED LOAN. A loan for which the borrower is not responsible for all of the interest payments. For Subsidized Federal Stafford and/or Direct Loans, the government pays interest to the lender on behalf of the borrower while the student is in college and during approved grace periods.

toward a degree or certificate. This criterion is established by each college or university. You'll also need a valid social security number, and all male students must register for selective service on their eighteenth birthday.

Once you apply for federal aid, your application will be processed in approximately four weeks (one week if applying electronically). You'll then receive a Student Aid Report (SAR) in the mail, which will report the information from your application and your expected family contribution (EFC—the number used in determining your eligibility for federal student aid). Each school you listed on the application will also receive your application information.

You must reapply for federal aid every year. Also, if you change schools, your aid doesn't necessarily go with you. Check with your new school to find out what steps you must take to continue receiving aid.

Once you've decided to which schools you want to apply, talk to the financial aid officers of those schools. There is no substitute for getting information from the source when it comes to understanding your financial aid options. That personal contact can lead you to substantial amounts of financial aid.

If you qualify, don't let the sticker price of the college or program scare you away, because you may get enough outside money to pay for the education you want. Don't rule out a private institution until you have received the financial aid package from the school. Private colleges, in order to attract students from all income levels, offer significant amounts of financial aid. Public-supported institutions tend to offer less financial aid because the lower tuition acts as a form of assistance (see "Projected College Expenses"). In addition, students attending school in their home state often have more aid possibilities than if they attend an out-of-state college. Use the "College Funds Available" chart to determine how much you and your family can contribute to your education and the "College Cost Comparison" table to figure out which schools best suit you financially.

TYPES OF FINANCIAL AID

Be sure that you understand the differences between the types of financial aid so you are fully prepared to apply for each. One or more of these financial resources may make it possible to pursue the education you want.

Grants: Grants are given for athletics (Division I only), academics, demographics, special talent potential, and/or need. Repayment is not required.

Scholarships: Scholarships, also called "merit aid," are awarded for academic excellence. Repayment is not required.

COLLEGE FUNDS AVAILABLE

Use this chart to estimate your family's resources that will be available for college expenses. Check your progress at the end of your sophomore and junior years to see if your plans for seeking financial aid need to be revised.

YOUR RESOURCES	Estimated amount available	Actual amount: 11 grade	Actual amount: 12th grade
Savings and other assets			
Summer earnings			
Part-time work during school year			
Miscellaneous			
PARENTS' RESOURCES			
From their current income			
From college savings			
Miscellaneous (insurance, annuities, stocks, trusts, home equity, property assets)			
TOTAL			

Source: American College Testing Program

Loans: Student loans, which have lower interest rates, may be college sponsored or federally sponsored or may be available through commercial financial institutions. Loans must be repaid, generally after you have graduated or left school.

College work-study: College work-study is a federally sponsored program that enables colleges to hire students for employment. If eligible, students work a limited number of hours throughout the school year. Many private colleges offer forms of self-help employment aid as their own supplement to the diminishing supply of federally funded work-study.

FEDERAL FINANCIAL AID PROGRAMS

A number of sources of financial aid are available to students from the federal government, state governments, private lenders, foundations and private agencies, and the colleges and universities themselves. In addition, as discussed earlier, there are four different forms of aid: grants, scholarships, loans, and work-study.

COLLEGE COST COMPARISON WORKSHEET

Chart your course to see which college or university best fits your financial resources. Your totals in expenses and funds available should be the same amount. If not, you have a funding gap, meaning that you have more expenses than funds available and will need to take out a loan (most likely), or vice versa (less likely).

	College 1	College 2	College 3	College 4
EXPENSES				
Tuition and fees	$	$	$	$
Books and supplies	$	$	$	$
Room and board	$	$	$	$
Transportation	$	$	$	$
Miscellaneous	$	$	$	$
TOTAL	$	$	$	$
FUNDS AVAILABLE				
Student and parent contributions	$	$	$	$
Grants	$	$	$	$
Scholarships	$	$	$	$
Work-study	$	$	$	$
TOTAL	$	$	$	$
Funding gap	$	$	$	$

The federal government is the single largest source of financial aid for students, making more than an estimated $60 billion available in loans, grants, and other aid to millions of students. Following are listings of federal financial aid programs available to you.

FEDERAL GRANTS

The federal government offers a number of educational grants, which are outlined below:

Federal Pell Grant

The Federal Pell Grant is the largest grant program in the nation; about 4 million students receive awards annually. This grant is intended to be the base or starting point of assistance for lower-income families. Eligibility for a Federal Pell Grant depends on the EFC, or Expected Family Contribution. (See the "Financial Aid Glossary" for a description of commonly used terms.) The amount you receive will depend on your EFC, the cost of education at the college or university you attend, and whether you attend full-time or part-time. The highest award depends on how much the program is funded. The maximum for the 2002–2003 school year was $4,000. How much you get will depend not only on your financial need but also on your cost of attending school, whether you're a full-time or part-time student, and whether you attend school for a full academic year or less.

Note that the actual maximum for each of these academic years will be determined by the amount Congress appropriates for the program. Historically, the amount appropriated has resulted in maximum awards that are greater than the awards in previous years but less than the authorized award.

Federal Supplemental Educational Opportunity Grant

As its name implies, the Federal Supplemental Educational Opportunity Grant (FSEOG) provides additional need-based federal grant money to supplement the Federal Pell Grant. Each participating college is given funds to award to especially needy students. The maximum award is $4,000 per year, but the amount a student receives depends on the college's policy, the availability of FSEOG funds, the total cost of education, and the amount of other aid awarded.

Federal Scholarships

The following comprise the scholarships available through the federal government:

ROTC Scholarships

The Armed Forces (Army, Air Force, Navy, Marines) may offer up to a four-year scholarship that pays full college tuition plus a monthly allowance; however, these scholarships are very competitive and based upon GPA, class rank, ACT or SAT scores, and physical qualifications. Apply as soon as possible before December 1 of your senior year. Contact the headquarters of each of the armed forces for more information: Army, 800-USA-ROTC; Air Force, 800-423-USAF; Navy, 800-USA-NAVY; Marines, 800-MARINES (all numbers are toll-free).

Scholarships from Federal Agencies

Federal agencies, such as the CIA, NASA, Department of Agriculture, and Office of Naval Research, offer an annual stipend as well as a scholarship. In return, the student must work for the agency for a certain number of years or else repay all the financial support. See your counselor for more information.

Robert C. Byrd Honors Scholarship

To qualify for this scholarship, you must demonstrate outstanding academic achievement and excellence in high school as indicated by class rank, high school grades, test scores, and leadership activities. Award amounts of $1,500 are renewable for four years. Contact your high school counselor for application information. Deadlines may vary per state, so contact your state's Department of Education.

National Science Scholars Program (NSSP)

To qualify, you must be a graduating high school senior with a minimum 3.5 GPA and an ACT score of at least 25 or SAT I score of at least 1100 and demonstrate excellence and achievement in the physical, life, or computer sciences; mathematics; or engineering. Scholarships are as much as $5,000 per year or the student's cost of attendance, whichever is less, for up to five years of study. Awards are made to two students from each congressional district. Contact your high school counselor or NSSP coordinators at your state's Department of Education for application and deadline information.

Federal Loans

Following are methods through which you may borrow money from the federal government:

Federal Perkins Loan

This loan provides low-interest (5 percent) aid for students with exceptional financial need (students with the lowest expected family contribution). The Federal Perkins Loans are made through the college's financial aid office—that is, the college is the lender. For undergraduate study, you may borrow a maximum of $4,000 per year for up to five years of undergraduate study and may take up to ten years to repay the loan, beginning nine months after you graduate, leave school, or drop below half-time status. No interest accrues while you are in school and, under certain conditions (e.g., if you teach in a low-income area, work in law enforcement, are a full-time nurse or medical technician, or serve as a Peace Corps or VISTA volunteer), some or all of your loan can be canceled within fourteen days after the date that your school sends notice of crediting the transaction, or by the first day of the payment period, whichever is later. Payments also can be deferred under certain conditions, such as unemployment.

FINANCIAL AID ADVICE

Q: What do you wish students and their parents knew about financial aid?

A: They don't know they should get their financial application filed early enough, so if we run into snags, it can be corrected. They make mistakes, such as not answering the question about the amount of taxes paid the previous year. A lot of parents think that if they didn't send in a check to the IRS, they didn't pay taxes. Something as simple as that causes a lot of problems. If their financial information is recorded incorrectly, it can really mess them up. They should read all the information on the financial aid form, and if they have questions, they should ask someone. Speaking from my experience, if you can't get in touch with the college you're child is thinking of attending, then call a local college. Any time an application doesn't go through the system smoothly, it can cause major problems.

Now that you can apply over the Internet, the applications are much simpler and worded in layman's terms. If applicants miss filling in some information, that will trigger a warning that they omitted something. I realize that not all students have access to the Internet, but they can go to the public library and look into getting onto the Internet there.

Trudy Masters, Financial Aid Officer
Lee College
Baytown, Texas

FFEL Stafford Student Loan

An FFEL Stafford Student Loan may be borrowed from a participating commercial lender, such as a bank, credit union, or savings and loan association. The interest rate varies annually (it has gone up to a maximum of 8.25 percent). If you qualify for a need-based subsidized FFEL Stafford Student Loan, the interest is paid by the federal government while you are enrolled in school. There is also an unsubsidized FFEL Stafford Student Loan that is not based on need and for which you are eligible, regardless of your family income.

The maximum amount you may borrow as a dependent in any one year is $2,625 when you're a freshman, $3,500 when you're a sophomore, and $5,500 when you're a junior or senior, with a maximum of $23,000 for the total undergraduate program. The maximum amount you may borrow as an independent is $6,625 when you're a freshman (no more than $2,625 in subsidized Stafford Loans), $7,500 when you're a sophomore (no more than $3,500 in subsidized Stafford Loans), and $10,500 when you're a junior or senior (no more than $5,500 in subsidized Stafford Loans). You will be required to pay a 4 percent fee, which is deducted from the loan proceeds.

To apply for an FFEL Stafford Student Loan, you must first complete a FAFSA to determine eligibility for a subsidized loan and then complete a separate loan application that is submitted to a lender. The financial aid office can help you select a lender, or you can contact your state's Department of Higher Education to find a participating lender. The lender will send you or your parents a promissory note that you must sign indicating that you agree to repay the loan. The proceeds of the loan, less the origination fee, will be sent to your college to be either credited to your student account or paid to you directly.

If you qualify for a subsidized Stafford Loan, you don't have to pay interest while in school. For an unsubsidized FFEL Loan, you will be responsible for paying the interest from the time the loan is established. However, some FFEL lenders will permit you to delay making payments and will add the interest to your loan. Once the repayment period

THINKING AHEAD TO PAYING BACK YOUR STUDENT LOAN

More than ever before, loans have become an important part of financial assistance. The majority of students find that they must borrow money to finance their education. If you accept a loan, you are incurring a financial obligation. You will have to repay the loan in full, along with all of the interest and any additional fees (collection, legal, etc.). Since you will be making loan payments to satisfy the loan obligation, carefully consider the burden your loan amount will impose on you after you leave college. Defaulting on a student loan can jeopardize your financial future. Borrow intelligently.

SOME REPAYMENT OPTIONS

A number of repayment options are available to borrowers of federally guaranteed student loans.

The Standard Repayment Plan: requires fixed monthly payments (at least $50) over a fixed period of time (up to ten years). The length of the repayment period depends on the loan amount. This plan usually results in the lowest total interest paid because the repayment period is shorter than under the other plans.

The Extended Repayment Plan: allows loan repayment to be extended over a period from generally twelve to thirty years, depending on the total amount borrowed. Borrowers still pay a fixed amount each month (at least $50), but usually monthly payments will be less than under the Standard Repayment Plan. This plan may make repayment more manageable; however, borrowers usually will pay more interest because the repayment period is longer.

The Graduated Repayment Plan: allows payments to start out low and increase every two years. This plan may be helpful to borrowers whose incomes are low initially but will increase steadily. A borrower's monthly payments must be at least half but may not be more than one-and-a-half times what he or she would pay under Standard Repayment. As in the Extended Repayment Plan, the repayment period will usually vary from twelve to thirty years, depending on the total amount borrowed. Again, monthly payments may be more manageable at first because they are lower, but borrowers will pay more interest because the repayment period is longer.

The Income Contingent Repayment Plan: bases monthly payments on adjusted gross income (AGI) and the total amount borrowed. This is currently only available to students who participate in Direct Loans; however, some FFEL lenders and guaranty agencies provide income-sensitive repayment plans. As income rises or falls each year, monthly payments will be adjusted accordingly. The required monthly payment will not exceed 20 percent of the borrower's discretionary income as calculated under a published formula. Borrowers have up to twenty-five years to repay; after that time, any unpaid amount will be discharged, and borrowers must pay taxes on the amount discharged. In other words, if the federal government forgives the balance of a loan, the amount is considered to be part of the borrower's income for that year.

starts, whether you're a borrower of either subsidized or unsubsidized FFEL Loans, you will have to pay a combination of interest and principal monthly for up to a ten-year period.

William D. Ford Direct Stafford Loans

The Federal Direct Stafford Student Loan is basically the same as the Federal Stafford Student Loan Program. The difference is that the U.S. Department of Education, rather than a bank, is the lender. If your college does not participate in this program, you can still apply for an FFEL Stafford Student Loan.

Many of the terms of the Direct Stafford Loan are similar to those of the FFEL Stafford Loan. In particular, the interest rate, loan maximums, deferments, and cancellation benefits are the same. However, under the terms of the Direct Stafford Student Loan, you have a choice of repayment plans. You may choose:

- A standard fixed monthly repayment for up to ten years

- An extended repayment plan with lower fixed monthly payments for twelve to thirty years at a rate with a higher total amount of interest payment

- A graduated monthly repayment plan for twelve to thirty years in which payments grow from 50 percent to 150 percent of the standard plan

- Or an income contingent repayment plan with monthly payments based on your yearly income and family size

- You cannot receive both a Direct Stafford Loan and an FFEL Stafford Loan for the same period of time but may receive both in different enrollment periods.

PLUS Loans

The PLUS loans are for parents of dependent students and are designed to help families with cash-flow problems. There is no needs test to qualify, and the loans are made by FFEL lenders or directly by the Department of Education. The loan has a variable interest rate that cannot exceed 9 percent, and there is no specific yearly limit; your parents can borrow up to the cost of your education, less other financial aid received. Repayment begins sixty days after the money is advanced. A 4 percent fee is subtracted from the proceeds. Parent borrowers must generally have a good credit record to qualify for PLUS loans.

The PLUS loan will be processed under either the Direct or the FFEL system, depending on the type of loan program for which the college has contracted.

Federal Direct Lending

Provisions are identical to the Federal Stafford Student Loan programs. However, the primary lending institution is the college or university participating in the Federal Direct Lending Program, as opposed to a bank or other financial institution.

Lender of Last Resort

This program assists students who have tried to obtain a Federal Stafford Student Loan and have been denied by two lending institutions. Eligible students must be enrolled at an eligible postsecondary educational institution.

Nursing Student Loan Program

Awarded to nursing students with demonstrated financial need. This loan has a 5 percent interest rate, repayable after completion of studies. Repayment is to be completed within ten years. Contact your college's financial aid office for deadline and other information, including maximum borrowing amounts.

Other Federal Programs

The following programs offer alternative ways to earn money for college:

Federal Work-Study (FWS)

This program provides jobs for students who need

financial aid for their educational expenses. The salary is paid by funds from the federal government and the college (or the employer). You work on an hourly basis in jobs on or off campus and must be paid at least the federal minimum wage. You may earn only up to the amount awarded, which depends on the calculated financial need and the total amount of money available to the college.

AmeriCorps

AmeriCorps is a national service program for a limited number of students. Participants work in a public or private nonprofit agency that provides service to the community in one of four priority areas: education, human services, the environment, and public safety. In exchange, they earn a stipend for living expenses and up to $4,725 for up to two years to apply toward college expenses. Students can work either before, during, or after they go to college and can use the funds to either pay current educational expenses or repay federal student loans. If you successfully complete one full-time term of service (at least 1,700 hours over one year or less), you will be eligible for an award of $4,725. If you successfully complete one part-time term of service (at least 900 hours over two years or less), you will be eligible for an award of $2,362.50. You should speak to your

college's financial aid office for more details about this program and any other new initiatives available to students.

FAMILIES' GUIDE TO TAX CUTS FOR EDUCATION

Many new tax benefits for adults who want to return to school and for parents who are sending or planning to send their children to college will be available due to the balanced budget that was signed into law in 1997. These tax cuts effectively make the first two years of college universally available, and they give many more working Americans the financial means to go back to school if they want to choose a new career or upgrade their skills. About 12.9 million students benefit—5.8 million under the "HOPE Scholarship" tax credit and 7.1 million under the Lifetime Learning tax credit.

HOPE Scholarship Tax Credit

The HOPE Scholarship tax credit helps make the first two years of college or career school universally available. Students receive a 100 percent tax credit for the first $1,000 of tuition and required fees and a 50 percent credit on the second $1,000. This credit is available for tuition and required fees minus grants, scholarships, and other tax-free educational assistance and became available for payments made after December 31, 1997, for college enrollment after that date.

This credit is phased out for joint filers who have between $80,000 and $100,000 of adjusted gross income and for single filers who have between $40,000 and $50,000 of adjusted gross income. The credit can be claimed in two years for students who are in their first two years of college or career school and who are enrolled on at least a half-time basis in a degree or certificate program for any portion of the year. The taxpayer can claim a credit for his own tuition expense or for the expenses of his or her spouse or dependent children.

The Lifetime Learning Tax Credit

This tax credit is targeted at adults who want to go back to school, change careers, or take a course or two to upgrade their skills and to college juniors, seniors, graduate and professional degree students. A family will receive a 20 percent tax credit for the first $5,000 of tuition and required fees paid each year through 2002 and for the first $10,000 thereafter. Just like the HOPE Scholarship tax credit, the Lifetime Learning Tax Credit is available for tuition and required fees minus grants, scholarships, and other tax-free educational assistance; families may claim the credit for amounts paid on or after July 1, 1998, for college or career school enrollment beginning on or after July 1, 1998. The maximum credit is determined on a per-taxpayer (family) basis, regardless of the number of postsecondary students in the family, and is phased out at the same income levels as the HOPE Scholarship tax credit. Families will be able to claim the Lifetime Learning tax credit for some members of their family and the HOPE Scholarship tax credit for others who qualify in the same year.

NATIONAL, STATEWIDE, AND LOCAL SCHOLARSHIPS

Requirements for the financial resources listed below are approximate and may vary. Check with your guidance counselor for the most up-to-date information regarding the availability of these resources and the requirements to qualify.

National Scholarships

Following is an abridged list of national scholarship programs:

Coca-Cola Scholars Program

Awards to seniors planning to attend an accredited college or university. Based on academics, school and community activities, and motivation to serve and succeed in all endeavors. Call for deadline and application information at 800-306-2653 (toll-free) or check www.cocacola.com.

Duracell/National Science Teachers Association Scholarship Competition

Open to all students in grades 9 through 12. Student must design and build a device powered by Duracell batteries. Call 703-243-7100 for application and deadline information.

Elks National Scholarship

Awards more than $1 million to "most valuable students" nationwide. To qualify, you must be in the upper 5 percent of your class and have an A average. Awards are based upon scholarship, leadership, and financial need. Call 773-755-4732 for application and deadline information or visit their Web site at www.elks.org.

National Foundation for Advancement in the Arts/Arts Recognition and Talent Search (NFAA/ARTS)

Awards are based on talent in dance, music, theater, visual arts, writing, voice, jazz, or photography. Call 800-970-2787 (toll-free). Early application is June 1 of junior year, and the final application deadline is October 1 of senior year.

National Merit Scholarship Program

Based on the PSAT exam taken in the junior year. Also investigate the National Honor Society Scholarship.

National Society of Professional Engineers

Awarded to high school seniors who plan to study engineering in college. Applications are accepted from August 1 through December 1, and the scholarships are awarded in January. Must be a U.S. citizen planning to attend an engineering program in the United States approved by the Accreditation Board for Engineering and Technology. Visit the NSPE's Web site at www.nspe.org for more information.

National Association of Secondary School Principals

The NASSP sponsors scholarships that recognize

students who are involved in activities such as student council, the National Honor Society, community service, and athletics. Contact the National Association of Secondary School Principals at 703-860-0200 for application and deadline information, or visit their Web site at www.nassp.org.

Tylenol

This award is based 40 percent on leadership in school and community, 50 percent on grade point average, and 10 percent on clear statement of goals. Call 800-676-8437 (toll-free) for an application. Deadline: January.

State and Local Scholarships

It is not possible within the scope of this book to list all of the sources of state and local scholarship dollars. The following are excellent resources for seeking financial assistance:

- ☑ Your guidance counselor
- ☑ A high school teacher or coach
- ☑ Your high school and elementary school PTA (yes, many elementary school PTAs award scholarships to alumni)
- ☑ The local librarian
- ☑ College admissions office
- ☑ Your parents' alma mater
- ☑ Your employer
- ☑ Your parents' employer
- ☑ Professional and social organizations in your community

SCHOLARSHIPS FOR MINORITY STUDENTS

The following is just a sample of the many scholarships available to minority students.

Blackfeet Tribal Education Grants

Available to members of the Blackfeet Tribe. Up to $3,500 in awards.
P.O. Box 850
Browning, Montana 59417
406-338-7521

Bureau of Indian Affairs Office of Indian Education Programs

Available to undergraduates in a federally recognized tribe. Award amounts vary.
1849 C Street, NW, MS 3512-MIB
Washington, D.C. 20240
202-208-6123

Hispanic Scholarship Fund General Program

Limited to Hispanic students enrolled at a two- or four-year institution. Up to $2,000 in awards.
Scholarship Committee
Hispanic Scholarship Fund
One Sansome Street, Suite 1000
San Francisco, California 94104
415-445-9930

National Achievement Scholarship Corporation

Limited to African-American high school students who have taken the PSAT/NMSQT. Up to $2,000 in awards.
Achievement Program
1560 Sherman Avenue, Suite 200
Evanston, Illinois 60201
847-866-5100

National Association of Minority Engineering Program Administrators National Scholarship Fund

Limited to African-American, Hispanic, and Native-American/Eskimo students with interest and potential for an undergraduate degree in engineering. Up to $30,000.
National Scholarship Selection
Committee Chair
NAMEPA National Scholarship Foundation
1133 West Mores Boulevard
Suite 201
Winter Park, Florida 32789-3788
407-647-8839

Jackie Robinson Foundation Scholarship

For minority students accepted to a four-year college and with demonstrated academic achievement and financial need. Award up to $6,000. Visit the Web site at www.jackierobinson.org for more information.

APPLYING FOR SCHOLARSHIPS

Here are some tips to help make a success of your scholarship hunt.

1. **Start early**. Your freshman year is not too early to plan for scholarships academically, choose extracurricular activities that will highlight your strengths, and get involved in your church and community—all things that are important to those who make scholarship decisions.

2. **Search for scholarships**. A couple of hours a week in the public library will help you learn about hundreds of scholarships and assess those for which you might qualify.

3. **Apply, apply, apply**. One student applied for nearly sixty scholarships and was fortunate enough to win seven. "Imagine if I'd applied for five and only gotten one," she says.

4. **Plan ahead**. It takes time to get transcripts and letters of recommendation. Letters from people who know you well are more effective than letters from prestigious names who know you only vaguely.

5. **Be organized**. In the homes of scholarship winners, you can often find a file box where all relevant information is stored. This method allows you to review deadlines and requirements every so often. Computerizing the information, if possible, allows you to change and update information quickly.

6. **Follow directions**. Make sure that you don't disqualify yourself by filling the forms out incorrectly, missing the deadline, or failing to supply important information. Type your applications, if possible, and have someone proofread them.

WHAT YOU NEED TO KNOW ABOUT ATHLETIC SCHOLARSHIPS

Whether you're male or female or interested in baseball, basketball, crew, cross-country, fencing, field hockey, football, golf, gymnastics, lacrosse, sailing, skiing, soccer, softball, swimming and diving, tennis, track and field, volleyball, or wrestling, there may be scholarship dollars available for you. But, there's that word again—planning. You must plan ahead if you want to get your tuition paid for in return for your competitive abilities.

At the beginning of your junior year, ask your guidance counselor to help you make sure that you take the required number and mix of academic courses and to inform you of the SAT I and ACT score minimums that must be met to play college sports. Also ask your counselor about academic requirements, because you must be certified by the NCAA Initial-Eligibility Clearinghouse, and this process must be started by the end of your junior year.

But before you do all that, think. Do you want and need an athletic scholarship? Certainly, it is prestigious to receive an athletic scholarship, but some athletes compare having an athletic scholarship to having a job at which you are expected to perform. Meetings, training sessions, practices, games, and (don't forget) studying take away from social and leisure time. Also, with very few full-ride scholarships available, you will most likely receive a partial scholarship or a one-year renewable contract. If your scholarship is not renewed, you may be left scrambling for financial aid. So ask yourself if you are ready for the demands and roles associated with accepting an athletic scholarship.

If you decide that you want an athletic scholarship, you need to market yourself to beat the stiff competition. Think of yourself as a newly designed sports car, and you're selling the speed, look, and all those other goodies to a waiting public. The point is that you're going to have to sell, or market, your abilities to college recruiters. You're the product, and the college recruiter is the buyer. What makes you stand out from the rest?

College recruiters look for a combination of the following attributes when awarding athletic scholarships: academic excellence, a desire to win, self-motivation, ability to perform as a team player, willingness to help others, cooperation with coaching staff, attitude in practice, attitude in games/matches, toughness, strength, optimal height and weight, and excellence.

In order to successfully sell your skills to a college or university, you'll need to take three main steps: 1) locate the colleges and universities that offer scholarships in your sport, 2) contact the institution in a formal manner, and 3) follow up each lead.

TYPES OF ATHLETIC SCHOLARSHIPS

Colleges and universities offer two basic types of athletic scholarships: the institutional grant, which is an agreement between the athlete and the college, and the conference grant, which also binds the college to the athlete. The difference is that the athlete who signs an institutional grant can change his or her mind and sign with another team. The athlete who signs a conference contract cannot renegotiate another contract with a school that honors conference grants. Here are the various ways that a scholarship may be offered.

Full four-year. Also known as full ride, these scholarships pay for room, board, tuition, and books. Due to the high cost of awarding scholarships, this type of grant is being discouraged by conferences around the country in favor of the one-year renewable contract or the partial scholarship.

Full one-year renewable contract. This type of scholarship, which has basically replaced the four-year grant, is automatically renewed at the end of each school year for four years if the conditions of the contract are met. The recruiter will probably tell you in good faith that the intent is to offer a four-year scholarship, but he is legally only allowed to offer you a one-year grant. You must ask the recruiter as well as other players what the record has been of renewing scholarships for athletes who comply athletically, academically, and socially. Remember—no athlete can receive more than a full scholarship.

One-year trial grant (full or partial). A verbal agreement between you and the institution that at the end of the year, your renewal will be dependent upon your academic and athletic performance.

Partial scholarship. The partial grant is any part of the total cost of college. You may be offered room and board but not tuition and books, or you may be offered just tuition. The possibility exists for you to negotiate to a full scholarship after you complete your freshman year.

Waiver of out-of-state fees. This award is for out-of-state students to attend the college or university at the same fee as an in-state student.

Finding and Getting Athletic Scholarships

Ask your coach or assistant coaches for recommendations; learn about the conference or institution from newspaper or television coverage; ask your guidance counselor; review guidebooks, reference books (check out Peterson's *Sports Scholarships and College Athletics Programs*), and the Internet; ask alumni; or attend a tryout or campus visit. You can also call the NCAA to request a recruiting guide for your sport. The following steps can help you snag that scholarship.

1. **Contact the school formally.** Once you make a list of schools in which you are interested, get the name of the head coach and write a letter to the top twenty schools on your list. Then compile a factual resume of your athletic and academic accomplishments. Put together 10 to 15 minutes of video highlights of your athletic performance (with your jersey number noted), get letters of recommendation from your high school coach and your off-season coach, and include a season schedule.

2. **Ace the interview.** When you meet a recruiter or coach, exhibit self-confidence with a firm handshake, by maintaining eye contact, and by making sure that you are well groomed. According to recruiters, the most effective attitude is quiet confidence, respect, sincerity, and enthusiasm.

3. **Ask good questions.** Don't be afraid to probe the recruiter by getting answers to the following questions: Do I qualify athletically and academically? If I am recruited, what would the parameters of the scholarship be? For what position am I being considered? It's okay to ask the recruiter to declare what level of interest he or she has in you.

4. **Follow up.** Persistence pays off when it comes to seeking an athletic scholarship, and timing can be everything. There are four good times when a follow-up letter from your coach or a personal letter from you is extremely effective: prior to your senior season, during or just after the senior season, just prior to or after announced conference-affiliated signing dates or national association signing dates, and late summer, in case scholarship offers have been withdrawn or declined.

To sum up, you know yourself better than anyone, so you must look at your skills—both athletic and academic—objectively. Evaluate the skills you need to improve, and keep the desire to improve alive in your heart. Develop your leadership skills, and keep striving for excellence with your individual achievements. Keep your mind open as to what school you want to attend, and keep plugging away, even when you are tired, sore, and unsure. After all, athletes are trained to be winners!

MYTHS AND MISCONCEPTIONS ABOUT SCHOLARSHIPS AND FINANCIAL AID

The scholarship and financial aid game is highly misunderstood by many high school students. And high school guidance counselors, overburdened with paperwork and complaints, often lack the time to fully investigate scholarship opportunities and to inform students about them. The myths and misconceptions persist while the truth about scholarships remains hidden, the glittering prizes and benefits unknown to many teenagers.

Myth 1: Scholarships are rare, elusive awards won only by valedictorians, geniuses, and whiz kids.

The truth is that with proper advice and strategies, private scholarships are very much within the grasp of high school students who possess talent and ability in almost any given field. Thousands of high school students like you compete and win.

Myth 2: My chances of being admitted to a college are reduced if I apply for financial aid.

The truth is that most colleges have a policy of "need-blind" admissions, which means that a student's financial need is not taken into account in the admission decision. However, there are a few colleges that do consider ability to pay before deciding whether or not to admit a student. There are a few more that look at ability to pay of those whom they placed on a waiting list to get in or those students who applied late. Some colleges will mention this in their literature, others may not. In making decisions about the college application and financing process, however, families should apply for financial aid if the student needs the aid to attend college.

Myth 3: All merit scholarships are based on a student's academic record.

The truth is that many of the best opportunities are in such areas as writing, public speaking, leadership, science, community service, music and the arts, foreign languages, and vocational-technical skills. So that means you don't always have to have a 3.99 GPA to win if you excel in a certain area.

Myth 4: You have to be a member of a minority group to get a scholarship.

The truth is that there are indeed some scholarships that are targeted toward women and minority students. There are also scholarships for which you must be a member of a specific national club or student organization (such as 4-H and the National Honor Society), which makes these scholarships just as exclusive. But most scholarship opportunities are not exclusive to any one segment of the population.

Myth 5: If you have need for and receive financial aid, it's useless to win a scholarship from some outside organization because the college will just take away the aid that the organization offered.

It's true that if you receive need-based aid, you can't receive more than the total cost of attendance (including room and board, books, and other expenses, not just tuition). If the financial aid that you've been awarded meets the total cost and you win an outside scholarship, colleges have to reduce something. But usually, they reduce the loan or work-study portion of your financial aid award before touching the grant portion that they've awarded you. This means that you won't have to borrow or earn as much. Also, most colleges don't meet your full financial need when you qualify for need-based financial aid. So, if you do win an outside scholarship, chances are that your other aid will not be taken away or reduced.

SCHOLARSHIP SCAMS

Unfortunately for prospective scholarship seekers, the private aid sector exists virtually without patterns or rules. Regrettably, the combination of the urgency to locate money, limited time, and a complex and bewildering system has created opportunities for fraud. Although most scholarship sponsors and most scholarship search services are legitimate, schemes that pose as either legitimate scholarship search services or scholarship sponsors have cheated thousands of families.

These fraudulent businesses advertise in campus newspapers, distribute flyers, mail letters and postcards, provide toll-free phone numbers, and even have sites on the Web. The most obvious frauds operate as scholarship search services or scholarship clearinghouses. Another quieter segment sets up as a scholarship sponsor, pockets the money from the fees and charges that are paid by thousands of hopeful scholarship seekers, and returns little, if anything, in proportion to the amount it collects. A few of these frauds inflict great harm by gaining access to individuals' credit or checking accounts with the intent to extort funds.

The Federal Trade Commission (FTC), in Washington, D.C., has a campaign called Project $cholar$cam to confront this type of fraudulent activity. There are legitimate services. However, a scholarship search service cannot truthfully guarantee that a student will receive a scholarship, and students almost always will fare as well or better by doing their own homework using a reliable scholarship information source, such as Peterson's *Scholarships, Grants & Prizes*, than by wasting money and time with a search service that promises a scholarship.

The FTC warns you to be alert for these six warning signs of a scam:

1. **"This scholarship is guaranteed or your money back."** No service can guarantee that it will get you a grant or scholarship. Refund guarantees often have impossible conditions attached. Review a service's refund policies in writing before you pay a fee.

2. **"The scholarship service will do all the work."** Unfortunately, nobody else can fill out the personal information forms, write the essays, and supply the references that many scholarships may require.

3. **"The scholarship will cost some money."** Be wary of any charges related to scholarship information services or individual scholarship applications, especially in significant amounts. Before you send money to apply for a scholarship, investigate the sponsor.

4. **"You can't get this information anywhere else."** In addition to Peterson's, scholarship directories from other publishers are available in any large bookstore, public library, or high school guidance office.

5. **"You are a finalist"** or **"You have been selected by a national foundation to receive a scholarship."** Most legitimate scholarship programs almost never seek out particular applicants. Most scholarship sponsors

will contact you only in response to an inquiry because they generally lack the budget to do anything more than this. Should you think that there is any real possibility that you may have been selected to receive a scholarship, before you send any money, investigate first to be sure that the sponsor or program is legitimate.

6. **"The scholarship service needs your credit card or checking account number in advance."** Never provide your credit card or bank account number on the telephone to the representative of an organization that you do not know. Get information in writing first. An unscrupulous operation does not need your signature on a check. It will scheme to set up situations that will allow it to drain a victim's account with unauthorized withdrawals.

In addition to the FTC's six signs, here are some other points to keep in mind when considering a scholarship program:

- Fraudulent scholarship operations often use official-sounding names, containing words such as *federal, national, administration, division, federation,* and *foundation.* Their names are often a slight variant of the name of a legitimate government or private organization. Do not be fooled by a name that seems reputable or official, an official-looking seal, or a Washington, D.C., address.

- If you win a scholarship, you will receive written official notification by mail, not by telephone. If the sponsor calls to inform you, it will follow up with a letter in the mail. If a request for money is made by phone, the operation is probably fraudulent.

- Be wary if an organization's address is a box number or a residential address. If a bona fide scholarship program uses a post office box number, it usually will include a street address and telephone number on its stationery.

- Beware of telephone numbers with a 900-area code. These may charge you a fee of several dollars a minute for a call that could be a long

recording that provides only a list of addresses or names.

- Watch for scholarships that ask you to "act now." A dishonest operation may put pressure on an applicant by saying that awards are on a "first-come, first-serve" basis. Some scholarship programs will give preference to the earlier qualified applications. However, if you are told, especially on the telephone, that you must respond quickly but that you will not hear about the results for several months, there may be a problem.

- Be wary of endorsements. Fraudulent operations will claim endorsements by groups with names similar to well-known private or government organizations. The Better Business Bureau (BBB) and government agencies do not endorse businesses.

- Don't pay money for a scholarship to an organization that you've never heard of before or whose legitimacy you can't verify. If you have already paid money to such an organization and find reason to doubt its authenticity, call your bank to stop payment on your check, if possible, or call your credit card company and tell it that you think you were the victim of consumer fraud.

To find out how to recognize, report, and stop a scholarship scam, you may write to the Federal Trade Commission's Consumer Response Center at 600 Pennsylvania Avenue NW, Washington, D.C. 20580. On the Web, go to www.ftc.gov, or call 877-FTC-HELP (toll-free). You can also check with the Better Business Bureau (BBB), which is an organization that maintains files of businesses about which it has received complaints. You should call both your local BBB office and the BBB office in the area of the organization in question; each local BBB has different records. Call 703-276-0100 to get the telephone number of your local BBB, or look at www.bbb.org for a directory of local BBBs and downloadable BBB complaint forms.

APPLYING FOR FINANCIAL AID

Applying for financial aid is a process that can be made easier when you take it step by step.

1. You must complete the Free Application for Federal Student Aid (FAFSA) to be considered for federal financial aid. Pick up the FAFSA from your high school guidance counselor or college financial aid office or download it from the Department of Education's Web site at www.fafsa.ed.gov. The FAFSA is due any time after January 1 of the year you will be attending school. Submit the form as soon as possible but never before the first of the year. If you need to estimate income tax information, it is easily amended later in the year.

2. Apply for any state grants.

3. Complete the PROFILE in addition to the FAFSA, because many four-year private colleges and some public universities require it. The PROFILE is a need analysis report, not an aid application. Some institutions have developed their own need analysis report. Check with your college or university to see what is required. The PROFILE registration is a one-page form available from your guidance counselor or through the College Board at www.collegeboard.com.

4. Complete individual colleges' required financial aid application forms on time. These deadlines are usually before March 15, but check with your institution to be sure.

5. Make sure your family completes the required forms during your senior year of high school.

6. Always apply for grants and scholarships before applying for student loans. Grants and scholarships are essentially free money. Loans must be repaid with interest.

Use the "Checklist for Seniors" to keep track of the financial aid application process.

FINANCIAL AID ON THE WEB

A number of good financial aid resources exist on the Web. It is quick and simple to access general financial aid information, links to relevant Web sites, loan information, employment and career information, advice, scholarship search services, interactive worksheets, forms, and free expected family contribution (EFC) calculators.

Also visit the Web sites of individual colleges to find more school-specific financial aid information.

FAFSA Online

The Free Application for Federal Student Aid can be downloaded from the U.S. Department of Education's World Wide Web page and filed electronically. The address is www.ed.gov/offices/OSFAP/Students/apply/express.html.

The Education Resource Institute (TERI)

TERI is a private, not-for-profit organization that was founded to help middle-income Americans afford a college education. This site contains a database describing more than 150 programs that aim to increase college attendance from underrepresented groups. (The target population includes students from low-income families and those who are the first in their family to pursue postsecondary education.) Visit TERI's Web site at www.teri.org.

FinAid

Sponsored by the National Association of Student Financial Aid Administrators, it includes a comprehensive alphabetical index of all financial aid resources on the Web. You can find the site at www.finaid.org.

Student Financial Assistance Information, Department of Education

This page takes you to some of the major publications

A CHECKLIST FOR SENIORS

Applying for financial aid can become confusing if you don't record what you've done and when. Use this chart to keep track of important information. Remember to keep copies of all applications and related information.

COLLEGE APPLICATIONS	COLLEGE 1	COLLEGE 2	COLLEGE 3	COLLEGE 4
Application deadline				
Date sent				
Official transcript sent				
Letters of recommendation sent				
SAT/ACT scores sent				
Acceptance received				
INDIVIDUAL COLLEGE FINANCIAL AID AND SCHOLARSHIP APPLICATIONS				
Application deadline				
Date sent				
Acceptance received				
FREE APPLICATION FOR FEDERAL STUDENT AID (FAFSA), FINANCIAL AID FORM (FAF), AND/OR PROFILE				
Form required				
Date sent				
School's priority deadline				
FAFSA ACKNOWLEDGMENT				
Date received				
Correct (Y/N)				
Date changes made, if needed				
Date changes were submitted				
STUDENT AID REPORT				
Date received				
Correct (Y/N)				
Date changes made, if needed				
Date changes were submitted				
Date sent to colleges				
FINANCIAL AWARD LETTERS				
Date received				
Accepted (Y/N)				

Source: The Dayton-Montgomery County Scholarship Program

on student aid, including the latest edition of the Student Guide. Visit www.ed.gov/finaid.html.

Petersons.com

Get advice on finding sources to pay for college and search for scholarships at www.petersons.com/resources/finance.html.

AESmentor.com

American Education Services works with nearly 4 million students through its guaranty, servicing, and financial aid processing system. Its Web site provides information on paying and saving for college as well as an application process for securing student loans.

FINANCIAL AID DIRECTORY

You can use these numbers for direct access to federal and state agencies and processing services. However, your guidance counselor may have the answers or information you need.

FEDERAL STUDENT AID INFORMATION CENTER

Provides duplicate student aid reports and aid applications to students. Also answers questions on student aid, mails Department of Education publications, makes corrections to applications, and verifies college federal aid participation. Write to the Federal Student Aid Information Center, P.O. Box 84, Washington, D.C. 20044-0084 or call 800-4-Fed-Aid (toll-free).

UNITED STUDENT AID FUNDS (USAF)

Provides aid application forms and information on loan amounts. Also provides information on guarantee dates and assists students in filling out application forms. Write to P.O. Box 6180, Indianapolis, Indiana 46206-6180, or call 877-USA-Group (toll-free).

VETERANS BENEFITS ADMINISTRATION

Provides dependent education assistance for children of disabled veterans. College-bound students should call the VBRO to determine whether or not they qualify for assistance, what the benefits are, and if a parent's disability qualifies them for benefits. Call 800-827-1000 (toll-free) or visit their Web site at www.gibill.va.gov.

ACT FINANCIAL AID NEED ESTIMATOR (FANE)

Mails financial tabloids to students, provides information on filling out financial aid forms, and estimates financial aid amounts. Also mails financial need estimator forms. Forms are also accessible on line. Go to www.ACT.org or write to P.O. Box 4029, Iowa City, Iowa 52243-4029, or call 319-337-1615.

COLLEGE SCHOLARSHIP SERVICE (PROFILE)

Provides free applications and registration forms for federal student aid. Helps students fill out applications. Write to P.O. Box 6350, Princeton, NJ 08541-6350 or call 800-239-5888 (toll-free).

Chapter 8

WHAT TO EXPECT IN COLLEGE

If you were going on a long trip, wouldn't you want to know what to expect once you reached your destination? The same should hold true for college.

GET A JUMP CAN'T FILL IN all the details of what you'll find once you begin college. However, we can give you information about some of the bigger questions you might have, such as how to choose your classes or major and how you can make the most of your life outside the classroom.

CHOOSING YOUR CLASSES

College is designed to give you freedom, but at the same time, it teaches you responsibility. You will probably have more free time than in high school, but you will also have more class material to master. Your parents may entrust you with more money, but it is up to you to make sure there's enough money in your bank account when school fees are due. The same principle applies to your class schedule: You will have more decision-making power than ever, but you also need to know and meet the requirements for graduation.

To guide you through the maze of requirements, all students are given an adviser. This person, typically a faculty member, will help you select classes that meet your interests and graduation requirements. During your first year or two at college, you and your adviser will focus on meeting general education requirements and selecting electives, or non-required classes, that meet your interests. Early on, it is a good idea to take a lot of general education classes. They are meant to expose you to new ideas and help you explore possible majors. Once you have selected a major, you will be given an adviser for that particular area of study. This person will help you understand and meet the requirements for that major.

In addition to talking to your adviser, talk to other students who have already taken a class you're interested in and who really enjoyed the professor. Then try to get into that professor's class when registering. Remember, a dynamic teacher can make a dry subject engaging. A boring teacher can make an engaging subject dry.

As you move through college, you will notice that focusing on the professor is more important than focusing on the course title. Class titles can be cleverly crafted. They can sound captivating. However, the advice above still holds true: "Pop Culture and Icons" could turn out to be awful when "Beowulf and Old English" could be a blast.

When you plan your schedule, watch out how many heavy reading classes you take in one semester. You don't want to live in the library or the dorm study lounge. In general, the humanities, such as history, English, philosophy, and theology, involve a lot of reading. Math and science classes involve less reading; they focus more on solving problems.

Finally, don't be afraid to schedule a fun class. Even the most intense program of study will let you take a few electives. So take a deep breath, dig in, and explore!

CHOOSING YOUR MAJOR

You can choose from hundreds of majors—from accounting to zoology—but which is right for you?

Should you choose something traditional or select a major from an emerging area? Perhaps you already know what career you want, so you can work backward to decide which major will best help you achieve your goals.

If you know what you want to do early in life, you will have more time to plan your high school curriculum, extracurricular activities, jobs, and community service to coincide with your college major. Your college selection process may also focus upon the schools that provide strong academic programs in a certain major.

Where Do I Begin?

Choosing a major usually starts with an assessment of your career interests. Once you have taken the self-assessment test in Section 1, you should have a clearer understanding of your interests, talents, values, and goals. Then review possible majors, and try several on for size. Picture yourself taking classes, writing papers, making presentations, conducting research, or working in a related field. Talk to people you know who work in your fields of interest and see if you like what you hear. Also, try reading the classified ads in your local newspaper. What jobs sound interesting to you? Which ones pay the salary that you'd like to make? What level of education is required in the ads you find interesting? Select a few jobs that you think you'd like and then consult the following list of majors to see which major(s) coincide. If your area of interest does not appear here, talk to your counselor or teacher about where to find information on that particular subject.

Majors and Related Careers

Agriculture

Many agriculture majors apply their knowledge directly on farms and ranches. Others work in industry (food, farm equipment, and agricultural supply companies), federal agencies (primarily in the Departments of Agriculture and the Interior), and state and local farm and agricultural agencies. Jobs might be in research and lab work, marketing and sales, advertising and public relations, or journalism and radio/TV (for farm communications media). Agriculture majors also pursue further training in biological sciences, animal health, veterinary medicine, agribusiness, management, vocational agriculture education, nutrition and dietetics, and rural sociology.

Architecture

Architecture and related design fields focus on the built environment as distinct from the natural environment of the agriculturist or the conservationist. Career possibilities include drafting, design, and project administration in architectural, engineering, landscape design, interior design, industrial design, planning, real estate, and construction firms; government agencies involved in construction, housing, highways, and parks and recreation; and government and nonprofit organizations interested in historic or architectural preservation.

Area/Ethnic Studies

The research, writing, analysis, critical thinking, and cultural awareness skills acquired by Area/Ethnic Studies majors, combined with the expertise gained in a particular area, make this group of majors valuable in a number of professions. Majors find positions in administration, education, public relations, and communications in such organizations as cultural, government, international, and (ethnic) community agencies; international trade (import-export); social service agencies; and the communications industry (journalism, radio, and TV). These studies also provide a good background for further training in law, business management, public administration, education, social work, museum and library work, and international relations.

Arts

Art majors most often use their training to become practicing artists, though the settings in which they work vary. Aside from the most obvious art-related career—that of the self-employed artist or craftsperson—many fields require the skills of a visual artist. These include advertising; public relations; publishing; journalism; museum work; television, movies, and theater; community and social service agencies concerned with education, recreation, and entertainment; and teaching. A background in art is also useful if a student wishes to pursue art therapy, arts or museum administration, or library work.

Biological Sciences

The biological sciences include the study of living organisms from the level of molecules to that of populations. Majors find jobs in industry; government agencies; technical writing, editing, or illustrating; science reporting; secondary school teaching (which usually requires education courses); and research and laboratory analysis and testing. Biological sciences are also a sound foundation for further study in medicine, psychology, health and hospital administration, and biologically oriented engineering.

Business

Business majors comprise all the basic business disciplines. At the undergraduate level, students can major in a general business administration program or specialize in a particular area, such as marketing or accounting. These studies lead not only to positions in business and industry but also to management positions in other sectors. Management-related studies include the general management areas (accounting, finance, marketing, and management) as well as special studies related to a particular type of organization or industry. Management-related majors may be offered in a business school or in a department dealing with the area in which the management skills are to be applied. Careers can be found throughout the business world.

Communication

Jobs in communication range from reporting (news and special features), copywriting, technical writing, copyediting, and programming to advertising, public relations, media sales, and market research. Such positions can be found at newspapers, radio and TV stations, publishing houses (book and magazine), advertising agencies, corporate communications departments, government agencies, universities, and firms that specialize in educational and training materials.

Computer, Information, and Library Sciences

Computer and information science and systems majors stress the theoretical aspects of the computer and emphasize mathematical and scientific disciplines. Data processing, programming, and computer technology programs tend to be more practical; they are more oriented toward business than to scientific applications and to working directly with the computer or with peripheral equipment. Career possibilities for computer and information sciences include data processing, programming, and systems development or maintenance in almost any setting: business and industry, banking and finance, government, colleges and universities, libraries, software firms, service bureaus, computer manufacturers, publishing, and communications.

STUDENT COUNSEL

Q: Why did you choose a seven-year premed program instead of a traditional four-year college program?

A: I'm one of those people who knew what I wanted to do since I was very little, so that made choosing easier. If I was not 100 percent sure that I wanted to go into medicine, I would not be in this seven-year program. For students who are interested but not really sure that they want to go into medicine, they should pick a school they will enjoy, get a good education, and then worry about medical school. That way, if they decide in their junior year that medicine is not for them, they have options.

Elliot Servais
Premed
Boston University

Library science gives preprofessional background in library work and provides valuable knowledge of research sources, indexing, abstracting, computer technology, and media technology, which is useful for further study in any professional field. In most cases, a master's degree in library science is necessary to obtain a job as a librarian. Library science majors find positions in public, school, college, corporate, and government libraries and research centers; book publishing (especially reference books); database and information retrieval services; and communications (especially audiovisual media).

Education

Positions as teachers in public elementary and secondary schools, private day and boarding schools, religious and parochial schools, vocational schools, and proprietary schools are the jobs most often filled by education majors. However, teaching positions also exist in noneducational institutions, such as museums, historical societies, prisons, hospitals, and nursing homes as well as jobs as educators and

(Continued on page 86)

trainers in government and industry. Administrative (nonteaching) positions in employee relations and personnel, public relations, marketing and sales, educational publishing, TV and film media, test development firms, and government and community social service agencies also tap the skills and interests of education majors.

Engineering and Engineering Technologies

Engineering and science technology majors prepare students for practical design and production work rather than for jobs that require more theoretical, scientific, and mathematical knowledge. Engineers work in a variety of fields, including aeronautics, bioengineering, geology, nuclear engineering, and quality control and safety. Industry, research labs, and government agencies where technology plays a key role, such as in manufacturing, electronics, construction communications, transportation, and utilities, hire engineering as well as engineering technology and science technology graduates regularly. Work may be in technical activities (research, development, design, production, testing, scientific programming, or systems analysis) or in nontechnical areas where a technical degree is needed, such as marketing, sales, or administration.

Foreign Language and Literature

Knowledge of foreign languages and cultures is becoming increasingly recognized as important in today's international world. Language majors possess a skill that is used in organizations with international dealings as well as in career fields and geographical areas where languages other than English are prominent. Career possibilities include positions with business firms with international subsidiaries; import-export firms; international banking; travel agencies; airlines; tourist services; government and international agencies dealing with international affairs, foreign trade, diplomacy, customs, or immigration; secondary school foreign language teaching and bilingual education (which usually require education courses); freelance translating and

MAKING THAT MAJOR DECISION: REAL-LIFE ADVICE FROM COLLEGE SENIORS

Somewhere between her junior and senior year in high school, Karen Gliebe got the psychology bug. When choosing a major in college, she knew just what she wanted. Justin Bintrim, on the other hand, did a complete 180. He thought he'd study physics, then veered toward philosophy. It wasn't until he took survey courses in literature that he found where his heart really lay, and now he's graduating with a degree in English.

You might find yourself at either end of this spectrum when choosing a major. Either you'll know just what you want or you'll try on a number of different hats before finally settling on one. To give you a taste of what it could be like for you, meet four college seniors who have been through the trials and errors of choosing their majors. Hopefully you'll pick up some pointers from them or at least find out that you don't have to worry so much about what your major will be.

From Grove City College, a liberal arts school in Pennsylvania, meet Karen Gliebe, who will graduate with a degree in psychology, and English major Justin Bintrim. From Michigan State University, meet computer engineering major Seth Mosier and Kim Trouten, who is finishing up a zoology degree. Here's what they had to say:

HOW THEY CHOSE THEIR MAJORS

Karen: During high school, I volunteered at a retirement center, and my supervisor gave me a lot of exposure to applied psychology. After my freshman year in college, I talked to people who were using a psychology degree. You put in a lot of work for a degree and can wonder if it's worth all the work. It helps to talk to someone who has gone through it so you can see if that's what you want to be doing when you graduate.

Justin: I wasn't sure about what my major would be. One professor told me to take survey courses to see if I was interested in the subject. I took English literature, math, psychology, and philosophy. I liked English the best and did well in it. The next semester, I took two English courses and decided to switch my major. My professors told me not to worry about choosing a major. They said to get my feet wet and we'll talk about your major in two years. I decided that if they're not worried about a major, I wouldn't be either, but I still had it on my mind. I was around older students who were thinking about their careers, so I talked to them about the jobs they had lined up.

Seth: I liked computers in high school. In college, I started out in computer science but got sick of coding. My interest in computers made me pick computer science right off the bat. I didn't know about computer engineering until I got to college.

Kim: I wanted to be a veterinarian but after two years decided that I didn't want to go to school for that long. I was still interested in animals and had two options. One was in animal science, which is working more with farm animals, or going into zoology. I decided to concentrate on zoo and aquarium science. Besides being a vet, the closest interaction with animals would be being a zookeeper.

THE ELECTIVES THEY TOOK AND WHY

Karen: My adviser told me to take different classes, so I took philosophy, art, religion, and extra psychology classes that weren't required.

Justin: I was planning to do a double major, but my professors said to take what interested me. English majors have lots of freedom to take different courses, unlike science majors.

Seth: Because I'm in computer engineering, I don't get to take a lot of electives. I am taking a swimming class right now and took a critical incident analysis class where we look at major accidents. I wanted something that wasn't computer engineering-related but extremely technical.

Kim: I took some kinesiology classes, which was pretty much an aerobics class. I needed to work out and figured I could get credit for it. I also took sign language because I'm interested in it.

WHAT THEY'RE GOING TO DO WITH THEIR DEGREES

Karen: I want to go to graduate school and hopefully get some experience working with kids.

Justin: I'm applying to graduate

school in English literature and cultural studies. I want to do research and become a college professor.

Seth: I'm going to work for the defense department. It's not the highest offer I've gotten, but it will be the most fun, which is more important to me than the money.

Kim: My goals have changed again. I don't plan on using my degree. I just got married a year ago, and my husband and I want to go into full-time ministry. I'll use my degree to get a job and then we'll go overseas.

THE CHANGES THEY WOULD MAKE IN THE CLASSES THEY TOOK IF THEY COULD

Karen: There are classes I wouldn't necessarily take again. But even though I didn't learn as much as I wanted to, it was worth it. I learned how to work and how to organize my efforts.

Justin: I should have worried less about choosing a major when I first started college. I didn't have the perspective as to how much time I had to choose.

Seth: I have friends who would change the order in which they took their humanities classes. I was lucky enough to think ahead and spread those classes out over the entire time. Most [engineering] students take them their freshman year to get them all out of the way. Later on, they're locked in the

engineering building all day. Because I didn't, it was nice for me to get my mind off engineering.

Kim: Something I can't change are the labs. They require a lot of work, and you only get one credit for 3 hours. Some labs take a lot of work outside of class hours. I had a comparative anatomy lab, which kept me busy over entire weekends. I suggest you don't take a lot of classes that require labs all at once.

THEIR ADVICE FOR YOU

Karen: You don't have to know what you want to do with the rest of your life when you get to college. Most people don't even stay with the major they first choose. Colleges recognize that you will see things you may have not considered at first. Some high school students say they won't go to college unless they know what they want to do.

Justin: If it's possible, take a little of this and a little of that. If you're an engineering student, you'll have it all planned out [for you], but if you're a liberal arts major and are not sure, you probably can take something from each department.

Seth: If possible, take AP exams in high school. You'll be able to make a decision about a major. Freshmen who think they want to do engineering suffer through math and physics classes. Then by their sophomore or junior year, they realize they don't want to be

engineers. If they'd taken AP classes, they'd know by their freshman year.

Kim: When I changed my major, I was worried that I might have spent a year in classes that wouldn't count toward my new major. But you shouldn't be scared to change majors because if you stick with something you don't like, you'll have to go back and take other classes anyway.

Though these four seniors arrived at a decision about which major they wanted in different ways, they had similar things to say:

- **It's okay to change your mind about what you want out of college.**

- **To find out which major you might want, start with what you like to do.**

- **Talk to professionals who have jobs in the fields that interest you.**

- **Ask your professors about what kinds of jobs you could get with the degree you're considering.**

- **Talk to seniors who will be graduating with a degree in the major you're considering.**

- **Take electives in areas that interest you, even though they may have nothing to do with your major.**

- **College is a time to explore many different options, so take advantage of the opportunity.**

interpreting (high level of skill necessary); foreign language publishing; and computer programming (especially for linguistics majors).

Health Sciences

Health professions majors, while having a scientific core, are more focused on applying the results of scientific investigation than on the scientific disciplines themselves. Allied health majors prepare graduates to assist health professionals in providing diagnostics, therapeutics, and rehabilitation. Medical science majors, such as optometry, pharmacy, and the premedical profession sequences, are, for the most part, preprofessional studies that compose the scientific disciplines necessary for admission to graduate or professional school in the health or medical fields. Health service and technology majors prepare students for positions in the health fields that primarily involve services to patients or working with complex machinery and materials. Medical technologies cover a wide range of fields, such as cytotechnology, biomedical technologies, and operating room technology.

Administrative, professional, or research assistant positions in health agencies, hospitals, occupational health units in industry, community and school health departments, government agencies (public health, environmental protection), and international health organizations are available to majors in health fields, as are jobs in marketing and sales of health-related products and services, health education (with education courses), advertising and public relations, journalism and publishing, and technical writing.

Home Economics and Social Services

Home economics encompasses many different fields—basic studies in foods and textiles as well as consumer economics and leisure studies—that overlap with aspects of agriculture, social science, and education. Jobs can be found in government and community agencies (especially those concerned with education, health, housing, or human services), nursing homes, child-care centers, journalism, radio/TV, educational media, and publishing. Types of work also include marketing, sales, and customer service in consumer-related industries, such as food processing and packaging, appliance manufacturing, utilities, textiles, and secondary school home economics teaching (which usually requires education courses).

Majors in social services find administrative aide or assistant positions in government and community health, welfare, and social service agencies, such as hospitals, clinics, YMCAs and YWCAs, recreation commissions, welfare agencies, and employment services. See the "Law and Legal Studies" section for information on more law-related social services.

Humanities (Miscellaneous)

The majors that constitute the humanities (sometimes called "letters") are the most general and widely applicable and the least vocationally oriented of the liberal arts. They are essentially studies of the ideas and concerns of human kind. These include classics, history of philosophy, history of science, linguistics, and medieval studies. Career possibilities for humanities majors can be found in business firms, government and community agencies, advertising and public relations, marketing and sales, publishing, journalism and radio/TV, secondary school teaching in English and literature (which usually requires education courses), freelance writing and editing, and computer programming (especially for those with a background in logic or linguistics).

Law and Legal Studies

Students of legal studies can use their knowledge of law and government in fields involving the making, breaking, and enforcement of laws; the crimes, trials, and punishment of law breakers; and the running of all branches of government at local, state, and federal levels. Graduates find positions in all types in law firms, legal departments of other organizations, the court or prison system, government agencies (such as law enforcement agencies or offices of state and federal attorneys general), and police departments.

Mathematics and Physical Sciences

Mathematics is the science of numbers and the abstract formulation of their operations. Physical sciences involve the study of the laws and structures of physical matter. The quantitative skills acquired through the study of science and mathematics are especially useful for computer-related careers. Career possibilities include positions in industry (manufacturing and processing companies, electronics firms, defense contractors, consulting firms); government agencies (defense, environmental protection, law enforcement); scientific/technical writing, editing, or illustrating; journalism (science reporting); secondary school teaching (usually requiring education courses); research and laboratory analysis and testing; statistical analysis; computer programming; systems analysis; surveying and mapping; weather forecasting; and technical sales.

Natural Resources

A major in the natural resources field prepares students for work in areas as generalized as environmental conservation and as specialized as groundwater contamination. Jobs are available in industry (food, energy, natural resources, and pulp and paper companies), consulting firms, state and federal government agencies (primarily the Departments of Agriculture and the Interior), and public and private conservation agencies. See also the "Agriculture" and "Biological Sciences" sections for more information on natural resources-related fields.

Psychology

Psychology majors involve the study of behavior and can range from the biological to the sociological. Students can study individual behavior, usually that of humans, or the behavior of crowds. Students of psychology do not always go into the more obvious clinical fields, the fields in which psychologists work with patients. Certain areas of psychology, such as industrial/organizational, experimental, and social, are not clinically oriented. Psychology and counseling careers can be in government (such as mental health

agencies), schools, hospitals, clinics, private practice, industry, test development firms, social work, and personnel. The careers listed in the general "Social Sciences" section are also pursued by psychology and counseling majors.

Religion

Religion majors are usually seen as preprofessional studies for those who are interested in entering the ministry. Career possibilities for religion also include casework, youth counseling, administration in community and social service organizations, teaching in religious educational institutions, and writing for religious and lay publications. Religious studies also prepare students for the kinds of jobs other humanities majors often pursue.

Social Sciences

Social sciences majors study people in relation to their society. Thus, social science majors can apply their education to a wide range of occupations that deal with social issues and activities. Career opportunities are varied. People with degrees in the social sciences find careers in government, business, community agencies (serving children, youth, senior citizens), advertising and public relations, marketing and sales, secondary school social studies teaching (with education courses), casework, law enforcement, parks and recreation, museum work (especially for anthropology, archaeology, geography, and history majors), preservation (especially for anthropology, archaeology, geography, and history majors), banking and finance (especially for economics majors), market and survey research, statistical analysis, publishing, fundraising and development, and political campaigning.

Technologies

Technology majors, along with trade fields, are most often offered as two-year programs. Majors in technology fields prepare students directly for jobs; however, positions are in practical design and production work rather than in areas that require more theoretical, scientific, and mathematical knowledge. Engineering technologies prepare students with the basic training in specific fields (e.g., electronics, mechanics, or chemistry) that are necessary to become technicians on the support staffs of engineers. Other technology majors center more on maintenance and repair. Work may be in technical activities, such as production or testing, or in nontechnical areas where a technical degree is needed, such as marketing, sales, or administration. Industries, research labs, and government agencies in which technology plays a key role—such as in manufacturing, electronics, construction, communications, transportation, and utilities—hire technology graduates regularly.

Still Unsure?

Relax! You don't have to know your major before you enroll in college. More than half of all freshmen are undecided when they start school and prefer to get a feel for what's available at college before making a decision. Most four-year colleges don't require students to formally declare a major until the end of their sophomore year or beginning of their junior year. Part of the experience of college is being exposed to new subjects and new ideas. Chances are your high school never offered anthropology. Or marine biology. Or applied mathematics. So take these classes and follow your interests. While you're fulfilling your general course requirements, you might stumble upon a major that appeals to you, or maybe you'll discover a new interest while you're volunteering or involved with other extracurricular activities. Talking to other students might even lead you to a decision.

Can I Change My Major if I Change My Mind?

Choosing a major does not set your future in stone, nor does it necessarily disrupt your life if you need to change your major. However, there are advantages to choosing a major sooner rather than later. If you wait too long to choose, you may have to take additional classes to satisfy the requirements, which may cost you additional time and money.

THE OTHER SIDE OF COLLEGE: HAVING FUN!

There is more to college than writing papers, reading books, and sitting through lectures. Social life plays an integral part in forming your college experience.

Meeting New People

The easiest time to meet new people is at the beginning of something new. New situations shake people up and make them feel just uncomfortable enough to take the risk of extending their hand in friendship. Fortunately for you, college is filled with new experiences. There are the first weeks of being the newest students. This can be quickly followed by being a new member of a club or activity. And with each passing semester, you will be in new classes with new teachers and new faces. College should be a time of constantly challenging and expanding yourself, so never feel that it is too late to meet new people.

But just how do you take that first step in forming a relationship? It's surprisingly easy. The first few weeks of school will require you to stand in many lines. Some will be to buy books; others will be to get meals. One will be to get a student I.D. card. Another will be to register for classes. While standing in line, turn around and introduce yourself to the person behind you. Focus on what you have in common and try to downplay the differences. Soon you will find the two of you have plenty to talk about. When it is time to leave the line, arrange to have coffee later or to see a movie. This will help you form relationships with the people you meet.

Be open to the opportunities of meeting new people and having new experiences. Join clubs and activities that pique your interest. Investigate rock-climbing. Try ballet. Write for the school paper. But most of all, get involved.

Campus Activities

College life will place a lot of demands on you. Your classes will be challenging. Your professors will expect more responsibility from you. You will have to budget and manage your own money. But there is a plus side you probably haven't thought of yet: college students have a lot of free time.

The average student spends about three hours a day in class. Add to this the time you will need to spend studying, eating, and socializing, and you will still have time to spare. One of the best ways to use this time is to participate in campus activities.

Intramural Sports

Intramurals are sports played for competition between members of the same campus community. They provide competition and a sense of belonging without the same level of intensity in practice schedules. Anyone can join an intramural sport. Often there are teams formed by dormitories, sororities, or fraternities that play games such as soccer, volleyball, basketball, flag-football, baseball, and softball. There are also individual intramural sports such as swimming, golf, wrestling, and diving. If you want to get involved, just stop by the intramural office. Usually it is located near the student government office. If not, they should be able to tell you where to go.

Student Government

Student government will be set up in a way that is probably similar to your high school. Students form committees and run for office. However, student government in college has more power than in high school. The officers address all of their class's concerns directly to the President of the college or university and the Board of Trustees. Most student governments have a branch responsible for student activities that brings in big name entertainers and controversial speakers. You may want to get involved to see how such contacts are made and such appearances negotiated.

Community Service

Another aspect of student life is volunteering, commonly called community service. Many colleges offer a range of opportunities. Some allow you to simply commit an afternoon to a cause, such as passing out food at a food bank. Others require an ongoing commitment. For example, you might decide to help an adult learn to read every Thursday at 4 p.m. for three months. Some colleges will link a service commitment with class credit. This will enhance your learning, giving you some real-world experience. Be sure to stop by your community service office and see what is available.

Clubs

There are a variety of clubs on most college campuses spanning just about every topic you can imagine. Amnesty International regularly meets on most campuses to write letters to help free prisoners in foreign lands. Most college majors band together in a club to discuss their common interests and career potential. There are also clubs based on the use of certain computer software or that engage in outdoor activities like sailing or downhill skiing. The list is endless. If you cannot find a club for your interest, consider starting one of your own. Stop by the student government office to see what rules you will need to follow. You will also need to find a location to hold meetings and post signs to advertise your club. When you hold your first meeting, you will probably be surprised at how many people are willing to take a chance and try a new club.

Greek Life

A major misconception of Greek life is that it revolves around wild frat parties and alcohol. In fact, the vast majority of fraternities and sororities focus on instilling values of scholarship, friendship, leadership, and service in their members. From this point forward, we will refer to both fraternities and sororities as fraternities.

Scholarship

A fraternity experience helps you make the academic transition from high school to college. Although the classes taken in high school are challenging, they'll be even harder in college. Fraternities usually require members to meet certain academic standards. Many hold mandatory study times, old class notes and exams are usually kept on file for study purposes, and personal tutors are often available. Members of a fraternity have a natural vested interest in seeing that other members succeed academically, so older members often assist younger members with their studies.

Friendship

Social life is an important component of Greek life. Social functions offer an excellent opportunity for freshmen to become better acquainted with others in the chapter. Whether it is a Halloween party or a formal dance, there are numerous chances for members to develop poise and confidence. By participating in these functions, students enrich friendships and build memories that will last a lifetime. Remember, social functions aren't only parties; they can include such activities as intramural sports and Homecoming.

Leadership

Because fraternities are self-governing organizations, leadership opportunities abound. Students are given hands-on experience in leading committees, managing budgets, and interacting with faculty members and administrators. Most houses have as many as ten officers, along with an array of committee members. By becoming actively involved in leadership roles, students gain valuable experience that is essential for a successful career. Interestingly, although Greeks represent less than 10 percent of the undergraduate student population, they hold the majority of leadership positions on campus.

Service

According to the North-American Interfraternity Council, fraternities are increasingly becoming involved in philanthropies and hands-on service projects. Helping less fortunate people has become a major focus of Greek life. This can vary from work with Easter Seals, blood drives, and food pantry collections to community upkeep, such as picking up trash, painting houses, or cleaning up area parks.

Greeks also get involved in projects with organizations such as Habitat for Humanity, the American Heart Association, and Children's Miracle Network. By being involved in philanthropic projects, students not only raise money for worthwhile causes, but they also gain a deeper insight into themselves and their responsibility to the community.

Roommates

When you arrive on campus, you will face a daunting task: to live peacefully with a stranger for the rest of the academic year.

To make this task easier, most schools use some type of room assignment survey. This can make roommate matches more successful. For example, two people who prefer to stay up late and play guitar can be matched, while two people who prefer to rise at dawn and hit the track can be a pair. Such differences are easy to ask about on a survey and easy for students to report. However, surveys cannot ask everything, and chances are pretty good that

HOMESICKNESS

Homesickness in its most basic form is a longing for the stuff of home: your parents, friends, bedroom, school, and all of the other familiar people and objects that make you comfortable. But on another level, homesickness is a longing to go back in time. Moving away to college forces you to take on new responsibilities and begin to act like an adult. This can be scary.

While this condition is often described as a "sickness," no pill will provide a quick fix. Instead, you need to acknowledge that your feelings are a normal reaction to a significant change in your life. Allow yourself to feel the sadness of moving on in life and be open to conversations about it that may crop up in your dorm or among your new friends. After all, everyone is dealing with this issue. Then, make an effort to create a new home and a new life on campus. Create new habits and routines so that this once-strange place becomes familiar. Join activities and engage in campus life. This will help you to create a feeling of belonging that will ultimately be the key to overcoming homesickness.

something about your roommate is going to get on your nerves.

In order to avoid conflict, plan ahead. When you first meet, work out some ground rules. Most schools have roommates write a contract together and sign it during the first week of school. Ground rules help eliminate conflict from the start by allowing each person to know what is expected. You should consider the following areas: privacy, quiet time, chores, and borrowing.

When considering privacy, think about how much time alone you need each day and how you will arrange for each person to have private time. Class schedules usually give you some alone time. Be aware of this; if your class is cancelled, consider going for a cup of coffee or a browse in the bookstore instead of immediately rushing back to the room. Privacy also relates to giving your roommate space when he or she has had a bad day or just needs time to think. Set up clear hours for quiet time. Your dorm will already have some quiet hours established. You may choose to simply reiterate those or add additional time. Just be clear.

Two other potentially stormy issues are chores and borrowing. If there are cleaning chores that need to be shared, make a schedule and stick to it. No one appreciates a sink full of dirty dishes or a dingy shower. Remember the golden rule: do your chores as you wish your roommate would. When it comes to borrowing, set up clear rules. The safest bet is to not allow it; but if you do, limit when, for how long, and what will be done in case of damage.

Another issue many students confront is whether or not to live with a best friend from high school who is attending the same college. Generally, this is a bad idea for several reasons. First, you may think you know your best friend inside and out, but you may be surprised by her personal living habits. There is nothing like the closeness of a dorm room to reveal the annoying routines of your friend. Plus, personalities can change rapidly in college. Once you are away from home, you may be surprised at how you or your friend transforms from shy and introverted to late night partygoer. This can cause

conflict. A final downfall is that the two of you will stick together like glue in the first few weeks and miss out on opportunities to meet other people who are also new, vulnerable, and open to new friendships.

Armed with this information, you should have a smooth year with your new roommate. But just in case you are the exception, most colleges will allow students who absolutely cannot get along to move. Prior to moving, each student must usually go through a dispute resolution process. This typically involves your Resident Adviser, you, and your roommate trying to work through your problems in a structured way.

Living with a roommate can be challenging at times, but the ultimate rewards—meeting someone new, encountering new ideas, and learning how to compromise—will serve you well later in life. Enjoy your roommate and all the experiences you will have, both good and bad, for they are all part of the college experience.

Commuting from Home

For some students, home during the college years is the same house they grew up in. Whether you are in this situation because you can't afford to live on campus or because you'd just rather live at home with your family, some basic guidelines will keep you connected with campus life.

By all means, do not just go straight home after class. Spend some of your free time at school. Usually there is a student union or a coffee shop where students gather and socialize. Make it a point to go there and talk to people between classes. Also, get involved in extracurricular activities, and visit classmates in the dorms.

If you drive to school, find other students who want to carpool. Most schools have a Commuter's Office or Club that will give you a list of people who live near you. Sharing a car ride will give you time to talk and form a relationship with someone else who knows about the challenges of commuting.

Commuter's clubs also sponsor a variety of activities throughout the year. Try out these activities.

Be sure also to consider the variety of activities open to all members of the student body, ranging from student government to community service to intramural sports. You may find this takes a bit more effort on your part, but the payoff in the close friendships you'll form will more than make up for it.

WHAT IF YOU DON'T LIKE THE COLLEGE YOU PICK

In the best of all worlds, you compile a list of colleges, find the most compatible one, and are accepted. You have a great time, learn a lot, graduate, and head off to a budding career. However, you may find the college you chose isn't the best of all worlds. Imagine these scenarios:

1. Halfway through your first semester of college, you come to the distressing conclusion that you can't stand being there for whatever reason. The courses don't match your interests. The campus is out in the boonies, and you don't ever want to see another cow. The selection of extracurricular activities doesn't cut it.

2. You have methodically planned to go to a community college for two years and move to a four-year college to complete your degree. Transferring takes you nearer to your goal.

3. You thought you wanted to major in art, but by the end of the first semester, you find yourself more interested in English lit. Things get confusing, so you drop out of college to sort out your thoughts and now you want to drop back in, hoping to rescue some of those credits.

4. You didn't do that well in high school— socializing got in the way of studying. But you've wised up, have gotten serious about your future, and two years of community college have brightened your prospects of transferring to a four-year institution.

Circumstances shift, people change, and, realistically speaking, it's not all that uncommon to transfer. Many people do. The reasons why students transfer run the gamut, as do the institutional policies that govern them. The most common transfers are students who move from a two-year to a four-year university or the person who opts for a career change midstream.

Whatever reasons you might have for wanting to transfer, you will be doing more than just switching academic gears. Aside from losing credits, time, and money, transferring brings up the problem of adjusting to a new situation. This affects just about all transfer students, from those who made a mistake in choosing a college to those who planned to go to a two-year college and then transferred to a four-year campus. People can choose colleges for arbitrary reasons. That's why admissions departments try to ensure a good match between the student and campus before classes begin. Unfortunately, sometimes students don't realize they've made a mistake until it's too late.

The best way to avoid having to transfer is to extensively research a college or university before choosing it. Visit the campus and stay overnight, talk to admissions and faculty members, and try to learn as much as you can.

OTHER OPTIONS AFTER HIGH SCHOOL

Thirty years ago, most young people went directly to work after high school. Today, most young people first go to school for more training, but the majority don't go to traditional four-year colleges.

Ａ CCORDING TO SHANNON MCBRIDE, Director of the Golden Crescent Tech Prep Partnership in Victoria, Texas, "Only 40 percent of high school graduates attempt to go to a four-year college, and of those, only 25 percent get their degree. And of that 25 percent, only 37 percent use the degree they got in that area."

So why aren't the remaining 60 percent of students choosing a traditional four-year college? The reasons are as varied as the students. Life events can often interfere with plans to attend college. Responsibilities to a family may materialize that make it impossible to delay earning an income for four years. One may have to work and go to school. And traditional colleges demand certain conventions, behaviors, and attitudes that don't fit every kind of person. Some people need a lot of physical activity to feel satisfied, while others just aren't interested in spending day after day sitting, reading, memorizing, and analyzing. Years of strict time management and postponed rewards are more than they can stand.

If any of these reasons ring true with you, there are still postsecondary options for you, all of which will not only allow you to pursue further education but also will train you for a career. Let's take a look at some of these educational directions you can follow.

DISTANCE LEARNING

As a future college student, can you picture yourself in any of these scenarios?

1. You need some information, but the only place to find it is at a big state university. Trouble is, it's hundreds of miles away. No problem. You simply go to your local community college and hook up electronically with the university. Voila! The resources are brought to you.

2. That ten-page paper is due in a few days, but you still have some last-minute questions to ask the professor before you turn it in. Only one problem: you won't be able to see the professor until after the paper is due. Being a night owl, you also want to work on it when your roommate is asleep. Not to worry. Since you have the professor's e-mail address, just like all the other students in the class, you simply e-mail your question to her. She replies. You get your answer, finish the paper, and even turn it in electronically.

3. After graduating from high school, you can't go to college right away, but your employer has a neat hook up with a college that offers courses via the Internet. During your lunch hours, you and several of your work buddies log in to a class and get college credit.

Not too long ago, if you'd offered these scenarios to high school graduates as real possibilities, they would have thought you were a sci-fi freak. Distance education was not common at all—or if it was, it usually meant getting courses via snail mail or on videotape. Well, today you are in the right place at the right time. Distance education is a reality for countless high school graduates.

What distance education now means is that you can access educational programs and not have to physically be in a classroom on a campus. Through such technologies as cable or satellite television, videotapes and audiotapes, fax, computer modem, computer conferencing and videoconferencing, and other means of electronic delivery, the classroom comes to you—sometimes even if you're sitting in your room in your bunny slippers and it's 2 in the morning.

Distance learning expands the reach of the classroom by using various technologies to deliver university resources to off-campus sites, transmit college courses into the workplace, and enable you to view class lectures in the comfort of your home.

Where and How Can I Take Distance Learning Courses?

The technology for new, cheaper telecommunications technology is getting better all the time, and there is a growing demand for education by people who can't afford either the time or money to be a full-time, on-campus student. To fill that demand, educational networks also are growing and changing how and when you can access college courses.

Most states have established new distance learning systems to advance the delivery of instruction to schools, postsecondary institutions, and state government agencies. Colleges and universities are collaborating with commercial telecommunications entities, including online information services such as America Online and cable and telephone companies, to provide education to far-flung student constituencies. Professions such as law, medicine, and accounting, as well as knowledge-based industries, are utilizing telecommunications networks for the transmission of customized higher education programs to working professionals, technicians, and managers.

Ways in Which Distance Learning May Be Offered:

- **Credit courses.** In general, if these credit courses are completed successfully, they may be applied toward a degree.

- **Noncredit courses and courses offered for professional certification.** These programs can help you acquire specialized knowledge in a concentrated, time-efficient manner and stay on top of the latest developments in your field. They provide a flexible way for you to prepare for a new career or study for professional licensure and certification. Many of these university programs are created in cooperation with professional and trade associations so that courses are based on real-life workforce needs, and the practical skills learned are immediately applicable in the field.

What Else Does Distance Learning Offer?

Distance learning comes in a variety of colors and flavors. Along with traditional college degrees, you can earn professional certification or continuing education credits (CEUs) in a particular field.

Professional Certification

Certificate programs often focus on employment specializations, such as hazardous waste management or electronic publishing, and can be helpful to those seeking to advance or change careers. Also, many states mandate continuing education for professionals such as teachers, nursing home administrators, or accountants. Distance learning offers a convenient way for many individuals to meet professional certification requirements. Health care, engineering, and education are just a few of the many professions that take advantage of distance learning to help their professionals maintain certification.

Many colleges offer a sequence of distance learning courses in a specific field of a profession. For instance, within the engineering profession, certificate programs in computer integrated manufacturing, systems engineering, test and evaluation, and waste management education and research consortium are offered via distance learning.

Business offerings include distance learning certification in information technology, total quality management, and health services management.

Within the field of education, you'll find distance learning certificate programs in areas such as early reading instruction and special education for the learning handicapped. There are opportunities for you to earn degrees at a distance at the associate, baccalaureate, and graduate levels. Two-year community college students are now able to earn baccalaureate degrees—without relocating—by transferring to distance learning programs offered by four-year universities. Corporations are forming partnerships with universities to bring college courses to worksites and encourage employees to continue their education. Distance learning is especially popular among people who want to earn their degree part-time while continuing to work full-time. Although on-campus residencies are sometimes required for certain distance learning degree programs, they generally can be completed while employees are on short-term leave or vacation.

Continuing Education Units (CEUs)

If you choose to take a course on a noncredit basis, you may be able to earn continuing education units (CEUs). The CEU system is a nationally recognized system to provide a standardized measure for accumulating, transferring, and recognizing participation in continuing education programs. One CEU is defined as 10 contact hours of participation in an organized continuing education experience under responsible sponsorship, capable direction, and qualified instruction.

The Way Distance Learning Works

Enrolling in a distance learning course may simply involve filling out a registration form, making sure that you have access to the equipment needed, and paying the tuition and fees by check, money order, or credit card. In these cases, your applications may be accepted without entrance examinations or proof of prior educational experience.

Other courses may involve educational prerequisites and access to equipment not found in all geographic locations. Some institutions offer detailed information about individual courses, such as a course outline, upon request. If you have access to the Internet and simply wish to review course descriptions, you may be able to peruse an institution's course catalogs electronically by accessing the institution's home page on the Web.

Time Requirements

Some courses allow you to enroll at your convenience and work at your own pace. Others closely adhere to a traditional classroom schedule. Specific policies and time limitations pertaining to withdrawals, refunds, transfers, and renewal periods can be found in the institutional catalog.

Admission to a Degree Program

If you plan to enter a degree program, you should consult the academic advising department of the institution of your choice to learn about entrance requirements and application procedures. You may find it necessary to develop a portfolio of your past experiences and of your accomplishments that may have resulted in college-level learning.

How Do I Communicate with My Instructor?

Student-faculty exchanges occur using electronic communication (through fax and e-mail). Many institutions offer their distance learning students access to toll-free numbers so students can talk to their professors or teaching assistants without incurring any long-distance charges.

Responses to your instructor's comments on your lessons, requests for clarification of comments, and all other exchanges between you and your instructor will take time. Interaction with your instructor—whether by computer, phone, or letter—is important, and you must be willing to take the initiative.

COMMUNITY COLLEGES

Two-year colleges—better known as community colleges—are often called "the people's colleges." With their open-door policies (admission is open to individuals with a high school diploma or its equivalent), community colleges provide access to higher education for millions of Americans who might otherwise be excluded from higher education. Community college students are diverse, of all ages, races, and economic backgrounds. While many community college students enroll full-time, an equally large number attend on a part-time basis so they can fulfill employment and family commitments as they advance their education.

Today, there are more than 1,100 community colleges in the United States. They enroll more than 5.6 million students, who represent 45 percent of all undergraduates in the United States. Nearly 55 percent of all first-time freshmen begin their higher education in a community college.

Community colleges can also be referred to as either technical or junior colleges, and they may either be under public or independent control. What unites these two-year colleges is that they are regionally accredited, postsecondary institutions, whose highest credential awarded is the associate degree. With few exceptions, community colleges offer a comprehensive curriculum, which includes transfer, technical, and continuing education programs.

Important Factors in a Community College Education

The student who attends a community college can count on receiving quality instruction in a supportive learning community. This setting frees the student to pursue his or her own goals, nurture special talents, explore new fields of learning, and develop the capacity for lifelong learning.

From the student's perspective, four characteristics capture the essence of community colleges:

- They are community-based institutions that work in close partnership with high schools, community groups, and employers in extending high-quality programs at convenient times and places.

- Community colleges are cost effective. Annual tuition and fees at public community colleges average approximately half those at public four-year colleges and less than 15 percent of private four-year institutions. In addition, since most community colleges are generally close to their students' homes, these students can also save a significant amount of money on the room, board, and transportation expenses traditionally associated with a college education.

- They provide a caring environment, with faculty members who are expert instructors, known for excellent teaching and for meeting students at the point of their individual needs, regardless of age, sex, race, current job status, or previous academic preparation. Community

A SCHOLARSHIP FOR CAREER COLLEGE STUDENTS

The Imagine America Scholarship can help those who dream of a career but might not be able to achieve it through traditional college education.

What Is the Imagine America Scholarship?

Introduced in 1998 by the Career Training Foundation, the Imagine America Scholarship aims to reduce the growing "skills gap" in America. Any graduating high school senior can be considered for selection for one of the two scholarships awarded to his or her high school. The Imagine America Scholarship gives 10,000 graduating high school seniors scholarships of $1,000 to be used at more than 300 participating career colleges and schools across the country.

You Can Participate in the Imagine America Scholarship If:

- You attend any private postsecondary institution that is accredited by an agency recognized by the U.S. Department of Education.

- You are graduating from high school this year.

To find out more about the Imagine America Scholarship Program, talk to your high school counselor or visit www.petersons.com/cca for more information.

colleges join a strong curriculum with a broad range of counseling and career services that are intended to assist students in making the most of their educational opportunities.

- Many offer comprehensive programs, including transfer curricula in such liberal arts programs as chemistry, psychology, and business management, that lead directly to a baccalaureate degree and career programs that prepare students for employment or assist those already employed to upgrade their skills. For those students who need to strengthen their academic skills, community colleges also offer a wide range of developmental programs in mathematics, languages, and learning skills, designed to prepare the student for success in college studies.

Getting to Know Your Two-Year College

The best way to learn about your college is to visit in person. During a campus visit, be prepared to ask a lot of questions. Talk to students, faculty members, administrators, and counselors about the college and its programs, particularly those in which you have a special interest. Ask about available certificates and associate degrees. Don't be shy. Do what you can to dig below the surface. Ask college officials about the transfer rate to four-year colleges. If a college emphasizes student services, find out what particular assistance is offered, such as educational or career guidance. Colleges are eager to provide you with the information you need to make informed decisions.

The Money Factor

For many students, the decision to attend a community college is often based on financial factors. If you aren't sure what you want to do or what talents you have, community colleges allow you the freedom to explore different career interests at a low cost. For those students who can't afford the cost of university tuition, community colleges let them take care of their basic classes before transferring to a four-year institution. Many two-year colleges can now offer you instruction in your own home through cable television or public broadcast stations or through home study courses that can save both time and money. Look into all your options, and be sure to add up all the costs of attending various colleges before deciding which is best for you.

Working and Going to School

Many two-year college students maintain full-time or part-time employment while they earn their degrees. Over the past decades, a steadily growing number of students have chosen to attend community colleges while they fulfill family and employment responsibilities. To enable these students to balance the demands of home, work, and school, most community colleges offer classes at night and on weekends.

For the full-time student, the usual length of time it takes to obtain an associate degree is two years. However, your length of study will depend on the course load you take: the fewer credits you earn each

MOST POPULAR MAJORS FOR COMMUNITY COLLEGE GRADS

The American Association of Community Colleges conducted a survey in the year 2000 to see what the most popular majors for community college students were. The top 15 majors and their average starting salaries follow:

MAJOR	AVERAGE STARTING SALARY
1. Registered Nursing	$32,757
2. General Computer Technologies	$34,242
3. Computer Networking	$38,767
4. Engineering–Electric/Electronics	$29, 464
5. Computer Technician/Networking	$36,092
6. Manufacturing Technology	$30,291
7. Radiology Technology	$32,478
8. Digital Media	$35,409
9. Computer Programming	$30,838
10. General Skilled Trades	$25,598
11. Law Enforcement	$27,975
12. Dental Hygiene	$41,907
13. Computer-Aided Design	$27,968
14. Automotive	$29,305
15. General Allied Health	$24,781

term, the longer it will take you to earn a degree. To assist you in moving more quickly to your degree, many community colleges now award credit through examination or for equivalent knowledge gained through relevant life experiences. Be certain to find out the credit options that are available to you at the college in which you are interested. You may discover that it will take less time to earn a degree than you first thought.

Preparation for Transfer

Studies have repeatedly shown that students who first attend a community college and then transfer to a four-year college or university do at least as well academically as the students who entered the four-year institutions as freshmen. Most community colleges have agreements with nearby four-year institutions to make transfer of credits easier. If you are thinking of transferring, be sure to meet with a counselor or faculty adviser before choosing your courses. You will want to map out a course of study with transfer in mind. Make sure you also find out the credit-transfer requirements of the four-year institution you might want to attend.

New Career Opportunities

Community colleges realize that many entering students are not sure about the field in which they want to focus their studies or the career they would like to pursue. Often, students discover fields and careers they never knew existed. Community colleges have the resources to help students identify areas of career interest and to set challenging occupational goals.

Once a career goal is set, you can be confident that a community college will provide job-relevant, quality occupation and technical education. About half of the students who take courses for credit at community colleges do so to prepare for employment or to acquire or upgrade skills for their current job. Especially helpful in charting a career path is the assistance of a counselor or a faculty adviser, who can discuss job opportunities in your chosen field and help you map out your course of study.

In addition, since community colleges have close ties to their communities, they are in constant contact with leaders in business, industry, organized labor, and public life. Community colleges work with these individuals and their organizations to prepare students for direct entry into the world of work. For example, some community colleges have established partnerships with local businesses and industries to provide specialized training programs. Some also provide the academic portion of apprenticeship training, while others offer extensive job-shadowing and cooperative education opportunities. Be sure to examine all of the career-preparation opportunities offered by the community colleges in which you are interested.

VOCATIONAL/CAREER COLLEGES

Career education is important for every employee as technology continues to change, and the traditional large employers are facing serious downsizing. No one is immune from this downsizing. From the largest employers, such as the U.S. military, defense contractors, IBM, aviation, and health care, down to the company with one and two employees, issues of keeping up with technology and producing goods and services cheaper, faster and at less cost requires—indeed demands—a skilled, world-class workforce. In good or bad economic times, you will always have a distinct advantage if you have a demonstrable skill and can be immediately productive while continuing to learn and improve. If you know how to use technology, work collaboratively, and find creative solutions, you will always be in demand.

Career colleges offer scores of opportunities to learn the technical skills required by many of today's and tomorrow's top jobs. This is especially true in the areas of computer and information technology, health care, and hospitality (culinary arts, travel and tourism, and hotel and motel management). Career colleges range in size from those with a handful of students to universities with thousands enrolled. They are located in every state in the nation and share one common objective—to prepare students for a successful career in the world of work through a focused, intensive

SNAPSHOT OF A CAREER COLLEGE STUDENT
Katrina Dew
Network Systems Administration
Silicon Valley College
Fremont, California

WHAT I LIKE ABOUT BEING A CAREER STUDENT:

"Career colleges are for fast-track-oriented students who want to get out in the work field and still feel that they have an appropriate education."

ABOUT KATRINA

Right after high school, Katrina headed for junior college, but she felt like she was spinning her wheels. She wanted something that was goal-oriented. Community college offered too many options. She needed to be focused in one direction.

At first, Katrina thought she would become a physical therapist. Then she realized how much schooling she would need to begin working. Turning to the computer field, she saw some definite benefits. For one, she had messed around with them in high school. She could get a degree and get out in two years. She saw that computer careers are big and getting bigger. Plus, there weren't a lot of women in that field, which signaled more potential for her. But before she switched schools, she visited the career college, talked to students, and sat in on lectures. She really liked the way the teachers related to their students. Along with her technical classes, she's taken algebra, psychology, English composition, and management communication.

Nicholas Cecere
Automotive Techniques Management
Education America/Vale Technical Institute
Blairsville, Pennsylvania

WHAT I LIKE ABOUT BEING A CAREER STUDENT:

"I compare career college to a magnifying glass that takes the sun and focuses it. You learn just what you need to learn."

ABOUT NICHOLAS

Nicholas has completely repainted his 1988 Mercury Topaz, redone all the brakes, put in a brand-new exhaust system, and lots of smaller stuff here and there. But he says that's nothing compared to the completely totaled cars some of his classmates haul into the school. Talk about hands-on: they're able to completely restore them while going through the program.

Nicholas didn't always have gasoline running through his veins. In fact, he just recently discovered how much he likes automotives. After graduating from high school, he went to a community college, and after one semester, he left to work at a personal care home. Standing over a sink of dirty dishes made him realize he wanted more than just a job. He started thinking about what he wanted to do and visited a few schools, including the body shop where his brother worked. Where others might see twisted car frames, Nicholas saw opportunity and enrolled in the program.

curriculum. America's career colleges are privately owned and operated for-profit companies. Instead of using tax support to operate, career colleges pay taxes. Because career colleges are businesses, they must be responsive to the workforce needs of their communities or they will cease to exist.

Generally, these schools prepare you for a specific career. Some will require you to take academic courses such as English or history. Others will relate every class you take to a specific job, such as computer-aided drafting or interior design. Some focus specifically on business or technical fields. Bob Sullivan, a career counselor at East Brunswick High School in East Brunswick, New Jersey, points out that the negative side to this kind of education is that if you haven't carefully researched what you want to do, you could waste a lot of time and money. "There's no room for exploration or finding yourself as opposed to a community college where you can go to find yourself and feel your way around," he explains.

So how do you find the right career college for you? A good place to start is knowing generally what you want to do. You don't have to know the fine details of your goals, but you should have a broad idea, such as a career in allied health or business or computing. Once you make that decision, most career colleges will help you define your initial decisions.

After you've crossed that hurdle, the rest is easy. Since professional training is the main purpose of career colleges, its graduates are the best measure of a school's success. Who hires the graduates? How do their jobs relate to the education they received? Career colleges should be able to provide that data to prospective students. "Career colleges have a different customer than other institutions," notes Stephen Friedheim, President of ESS College of Business in Dallas, Texas. In addition to focusing on the needs of their students, career colleges also want to ensure they meet the needs of the employers who are hiring their graduates. "The assumption is that if you can please the employer, you will please the student," Friedheim explains.

Checking the credentials of a career college is one of the most important steps you should take in your career college search. Though not every career college has to be accredited, it is a sign that the college has gone through a process that ensures quality. It also means that students can qualify for federal grant and loan programs. Furthermore, you should see if the college has met the standards from professional training organizations. In fields such as court reporting and health-related professions, those criteria mean a lot.

FINANCIAL AID OPTIONS FOR CAREER AND COMMUNITY COLLEGES

The financial aid process is basically the same for students attending a community college, a career college, or a technical institute as it is for students attending a four-year college. However, there are some details that can make the difference between getting the maximum amount of financial aid and only scraping by.

As with four-year students, the federal government is still your best source of financial aid. Most community colleges and career and technical schools participate in federal financial aid programs. To get detailed information about federal financial aid programs and how to apply for them, read through Chapter 7: "Financial Aid Dollars and Sense." Here are some quick tips on where to look for education money.

Investigate federal financial aid programs. You should definitely check out a Federal Pell Grant, which is a need-based grant available to those who can't pay the entire tuition themselves. The Federal Supplemental Educational Opportunity Grant (FSEOG) is for those students with exceptional financial need. You also can take advantage of the Federal Work-Study programs that provide jobs for students with financial aid eligibility to work in return for part of their tuition. Many two-year institutions offer work-study, but the number of jobs tends to be limited. Also, federal loans make up a substantial part of financial aid for two-year students. Student loans, which have lower interest rates, may be sponsored by the institution or federally sponsored, or they may be available through commercial financial institutions.

WHAT TO LOOK FOR IN A CAREER COLLEGE

A tour of the college is a must! While visiting the campus, do the following:

- **Get a full explanation of the curriculum, including finding out how you will be trained.**

- **Take a physical tour of the classrooms and laboratories and look for cleanliness, modern equipment/computers, and size of classes. Observe the activity in classes: are students engaged in class, and are lectures dynamic?**

- **Ask about employment opportunities after graduation. What are the placement rates (most current) and list of employers? Inquire about specific placement assistance: resume preparation, job leads, etc. Look for "success stories" on bulletin boards, placement boards, and newsletters.**

- **Find out about tuition and other costs associated with the program. Ask about the financial aid assistance provided to students.**

- **Find out if an externship is part of the training program. How are externships assigned? Does the student have any input as to externship assignment?**

- **Ask if national certification and registration in your chosen field is available upon graduation.**

- **Inquire about the college's accreditation and certification.**

- **Also find out the associations and organizations the college belongs to. Ask what awards or honors the college has achieved.**

- **Ask if the college utilizes an advisory board to develop employer relationships.**

- **Ask about the rules and regulations. What GPA must be maintained? What is the attendance policy? What are grounds for termination? What is the refund policy if the student drops or is terminated? Is there a dress code? What are the holidays of the college?**

Source: Arizona College of Allied Health, Phoenix, Arizona

They are basically the same as those for the traditional four-year college student, such as the Federal Perkins Loan and the Subsidized and Unsubsidized Federal Stafford Student Loans. In fact, some private career colleges and technical institutes only offer federal loans. You also can find more specific information about federal loans in Chapter 7.

Don't overlook scholarships. What many two-year students don't realize is that they could be eligible for scholarships. Regrettably, many make the assumption that scholarships are only for very smart students attending prestigious universities. You'd be surprised to learn how many community and career colleges have scholarships. It's critical to talk to the financial aid office of each school you plan to attend to find out what scholarships might be available. The Imagine America scholarship program is offered to students who attend select career colleges around the country. See "A Scholarship for Career College Students" on page 95 for more information.

Check in with your state. Two-year students should find out how their states can help them pay for tuition. Every state in the union has some level of state financial aid that goes to community college students. The amounts are dependent on which state you live in, and most are in the form of grants.

APPRENTICESHIPS

Some students like working with their hands and have the skill, patience, and temperament to become expert mechanics, carpenters, or electronic repair technicians. If you think you'd enjoy a profession like this and feel that college training isn't for you, then you might want to think about a job that requires apprenticeship training.

To stay competitive, America needs highly skilled workers. But if you're looking for a soft job, forget it. An apprenticeship is no snap. It demands hard work and has tough competition, so you've got to have the will to see it through. An apprenticeship is a program formally agreed upon between a worker and an employer where the employee learns a skilled trade through classroom work and on-the-job training. Apprenticeship programs vary in length, pay, and intensity among the various trades. A person completing an apprenticeship program generally becomes a journeyperson (skilled craftsperson) in that trade.

The advantages of apprenticeships are numerous. First and foremost, an apprenticeship leads to a lasting lifetime skill. As a highly trained worker, you can take

BUREAU OF APPRENTICESHIP AND TRAINING OFFICES

National Office:

**U.S. Department of Labor
Frances Perkins Building
200 Constitution Avenue, NW
Washington, D.C. 20210**

**Northeast Regional Office
Suite 1815 East
170 South Independence Mall West
Philadelphia, Pennsylvania 19106**

**Southern Regional Office
Room 6T71
61 Forsyth Street, SW
Atlanta, Georgia 30303**

**Midwestern Regional Office
Room 656
230 South Dearborn Street
Chicago, Illinois**

**Southwestern Regional Office
Room 317
Federal Building
525 Griffin Street
Dallas, Texas 75202**

**Western Regional Office
Room 465721
U.S. Custom House
19th Street
Denver, Colorado 80202**

your skill anywhere you decide to go. The more creative, exciting, and challenging jobs are put in the hands of the fully skilled worker, the all-around person who knows his or her trade inside out.

Skilled workers advance much faster than those who are semiskilled or whose skills are not broad enough to equip them to assume additional responsibilities in a career. Those who complete an apprenticeship have also acquired the skills and judgment that are necessary to go into business for themselves if they choose.

What to Do if You're Interested in an Apprenticeship

If you want to begin an apprenticeship, you have to be at least 16 years old, and you must fill out an application for employment. These applications may be available year-round or at certain times during the year, depending on the trade you're interested in. Because an apprentice must be trained in an area where work actually exists and where a certain pay scale is guaranteed upon completion of the program, the wait for application acceptance may be pretty long in areas of low employment. This standard works to your advantage, however. Just think: you wouldn't want to spend one to six years of your life learning a job where no work exists or where the wage is the same as, or just a little above, that of common laborer.

Federal regulations prohibit anyone under the age of 16 from being considered for an apprenticeship. Some programs require a high school degree or certain course work. Other requirements may include passing certain aptitude tests, proof of physical ability to perform the duties of the trade, and possession of a valid driver's license.

Once you have met the basic program entrance requirements, you'll be interviewed and awarded points on your interest in the trade, your attitude toward work in general, and personal traits, such as appearance, sincerity, character, and habits. Openings are awarded to those who have achieved the most points.

If you're considering an apprenticeship, the best sources of assistance and information are vocational or career counselors, local state employment security agencies, field offices of state apprenticeship agencies, and regional offices of the Bureau of Apprenticeship and Training (BAT). Apprenticeships are usually registered with the BAT or a state apprenticeship council. Some apprenticeships are not registered at all, although that doesn't necessarily mean that the program isn't valid. To find out if a certain apprenticeship is legitimate, contact your state's apprenticeship agency or a regional office of the BAT. Addresses and phone numbers for these regional offices are listed above. You can also visit the Bureau's Web site at www.doleta.gov/atels_bat.

10 Chapter

THE MILITARY OPTION

Bet you didn't know that the United States military is the largest employer in the country. There's got to be a good reason that so many people get their paychecks from Uncle Sam.

SHOULD I OR SHOULDN'T I WORK FOR THE LARGEST EMPLOYER IN THE U.S.?

Every year, thousands of young people pursue a military career and enjoy the benefits it offers. Yet thousands more consider joining the military and decide against it. Their reasons vary, but many choose not to enlist because they lack knowledge of what a career in the military can offer. Others simply mistrust recruiters based on horror stories they've heard. Sadly, many make the decision against joining the military without ever setting foot in the recruiting office.

But if you are an informed "shopper," you will be able to make an informed choice about whether the military is right for you.

People rarely buy anything based on their needs: Instead, they buy based on their emotions. We see it on a daily basis in advertising, from automobiles to soft drinks. We rarely see an automobile commercial that gives statistics about how the car is engineered, how long it will last, the gas mileage, and other technical specifications. Instead, we see people driving around and having a good time.

The reason for this is that advertising agencies know that you will probably buy something based on how you feel rather than what you think. Because of this tendency to buy with emotion rather than reason, it is important to separate the feelings from the facts. That way, you can base your decision about whether to join the military primarily on the facts.

There are two big questions that you must answer before you can come to any conclusions. First, is the military right for me, and second, if the first answer is yes, which branch is right for me?

Suppose that you have to decide whether to buy a new car or repair your current car. The first choice you make will determine your next course of action. You will have to weigh the facts to determine if you will purchase a new car or not. Once you've decided to buy a car rather than repair your old one, you must then decide exactly what make and model will best suit your needs.

NO HYPE, JUST THE FACTS

So you didn't wake up one morning and know for sure that you're going to join the Navy. One minute you think you'd like the Army, but then you talk to your cousin who convinces you to follow him into the Air Force. But then the neighbor down the street is a Marine, and he's gung ho for you to join up with them. What to do?

Well, a helpful Web site is the answer. Go to www.spear.navy.mil/profile for some really straightforward and non-partisan information about each branch of the military. You'll be able to compare the benefits that each service offers plus pick up other helpful tips and information. The Web site is designed specifically for high school students considering the military.

"Normally the first question we get from people interested in the Air Force is 'What does the Air Force have to offer me?' But I back off and ask them about their qualifications. Sometimes it's easier to go to an Ivy League school than to join the Air Force because of our stringent requirements."

**Master Sergeant Timothy Little
United States Air Force**

You should make a list of the reasons why you want to join the military before you ever set foot in the recruiter's office. Whether your list is long—containing such items as money for college, job security, opportunity to travel, technical training, and good pay—or contains only one item, such as having full-time employment, the number of items on your list is not what's important. What is important is that you are able to satisfy those reasons, or primary motivators.

Whatever your list contains, the first course of action is to collect your list of reasons to join the military and put them in order of importance to you. This process, known as rank-ordering, will help you determine if you should proceed with the enlistment process.

"Take two people with the same qualifications who are looking for jobs. The person with the Army background will be that much more competitive. That's due to the fact that he or she is disciplined and knows how to act without being told what to do."
Staff Sergeant Max Burda
United States Army

Rank-ordering your list is a simple process of deciding which motivators are most important to you and then listing them in order of importance. List your most important motivator as number one, your next most important as number two, and so on.

If we apply the car-buying scenario here, your primary motivators may be finding a car that costs under $20,000, has a four-cylinder engine, gets at least 30 miles to the gallon, has leather interior, is available in blue, and has a sunroof. If you put those motivators in rank order, your list might look something like this:

1. Costs under $20,000

2. Gets at least 30 mpg

3. Has a sunroof

4. Has leather interior

5. Available in blue

You'll notice that the number one, or most important, motivator in this case is cost, while the last, or least important, motivator is color. The more important the motivator, the less likely you'll be willing to settle for something different or to live without it altogether.

After you've rank-ordered your motivators, go down your list and determine whether those motivators can be met by enlisting in the military. If you find that all your motivators can be met by enlisting, that's great; but even if only some of your motivators can be met, you may still want to consider it. Seldom does a product meet all our needs and wants.

CHOOSING WHICH BRANCH TO JOIN

"If you like to travel, we offer more than anyone else. The longest you're underway is generally two to three weeks, with three to four days off in every port and one day on the ship. Prior to pulling in, you can even set up tours."
Chief Petty Officer Keith Horst
United States Navy

If you are seriously considering joining the military, you probably have checked out at least two of the branches. Check them all out, even if it means just requesting literature and reviewing it. A word of caution though: Brochures do not tell the complete story, and it is very difficult to base your decision either for or against a military branch on the contents of a brochure alone. Would you buy a car based solely on the information contained in a brochure? Probably not!

"I tell people that you get paid the same in all the services, and the benefits are the same. What's different about each branch is the environment."
Sergeant Ian Bonnell, Infantry Sergeant
United States Marines

I'M JOINING THE AIR FORCE

It didn't take Brian Filipek long to decide he wanted to join the Air Force. But that's if you don't count the times he talked to people who had served in the Air Force or the research he did on the Internet to gather information—and that was before he even set foot inside the recruiter's office. By the time an Air Force recruiter responded to a card Brian had sent in, he was pretty sure he liked what he'd seen so far. "The recruiter didn't have to do any work to convince me," says Brian. After that, it was a matter of going through the pre-qualifying process, like whether he met the height and weight qualifications, and the security forms he had to fill out.

After he enlisted, Brian didn't stop gathering information. Long before he was sent to Basic Training, he found out about Warrior Week, which is held on one of the last weeks in Basic Training. He was already looking forward to it. "I'm an outdoors kind of person," he says. "I want to do the obstacle course and ropes course."

Though the idea of testing his endurance and strength appeals to him, being away from family will be hard. "Granted, your food is cooked for you, but you're still on your own," he says. However, he knows that it's worth it to achieve his goal of education and free job training. Brian acknowledges that the military is not for everyone, but as far as he's concerned, he's sure he's made the right choice.

Brian Filipek, Enlistee
U.S. Air Force

"In the Army, you can get training in everything from culinary arts to truck driving and all the way to aviation mechanics, military intelligence, and computer networking."
Staff Sergeant Max Burda
United States Army

Length and type of training—How long will your training take? Usually the longer the training, the more in-depth and useful it is. You'll also want to consider how useful the training will be once you've left the military.

Enlistment bonuses—Be careful when using an enlistment bonus as the only factor in deciding which branch to choose. If it comes down to a tie between two branches and only one offers a bonus, it's not a bad reason to choose that branch.

Additional pay and allowances—There may be additional pay you'd be entitled to that can only be offered by a particular branch. For instance, if you join the Navy, you may be entitled to Sea Pay and Submarine Pay, something obviously not available if you join the Air Force.

Ability to pursue higher education—While all the military branches offer educational benefits, you must consider when you will be able to take advantage of these benefits. If your job requires 12-hour shifts and has you out in the field a lot, when will you be able to attend classes?

"Everyone in the Navy learns how to fight a fire. You get qualified in First Aid and CPR. That's mandatory for every sailor. The only jobs we don't have in the Navy are veterinarians, forest rangers, and rodeo stars."
Chief Petty Officer Keith Horst
United States Navy

The process of choosing the right branch of the military for you is basically the same process that you used to determine if joining the military was right for you. You should start with your list of primary motivators and use the "yes/no" method to determine whether each branch can meet all or some of those motivators. Once you've determined which branch or branches can best meet your motivators, it's time to compare those branches. Remember to look for the negative aspects as well as the motivators of each of the branches as you compare.

After making your comparisons, you may still find yourself with more than one choice. What do you do then? You could flip a coin, but that's not the wisest idea! Instead, look at some of these factors:

Length of enlistment—Some branches may require a longer term for offering the same benefits that you could receive from another branch.

Advanced pay grade—You may be entitled to an advanced rank in some branches based on certain enlistment options.

Once you have considered these factors, and perhaps some of your own, you should be able to decide which branch is right for you. If you still haven't been able to select one branch over another, though, consider the following:

- Ask your recruiter if you can speak to someone who has recently joined.

- If there is a base nearby, you may be able to get a tour to look at its facilities.

- If you are well versed in Internet chat rooms, you may want to look for ones that cater to military members—then ask a lot of questions.

- Talk to friends and family members who are currently serving in the military. Be careful, however, not to talk to people who have been out of the military for a while, as they probably aren't familiar with today's military. Also, avoid people who left the military under less-than-desirable conditions (for example, someone who was discharged from Basic Training for no compatibility).

If you choose to continue with processing for enlistment, your next step will probably be to take the Armed Services Vocational Aptitude Battery (ASVAB).

THE ASVAB

The ASVAB, a multiple-aptitude battery designed for use with students in their junior or senior year in high school or in a postsecondary school, was developed to yield results useful to both students and the military. The military uses the results to determine the qualifications of young people for enlistment and to help place them in military occupational programs. Schools use ASVAB test results to assist their students in developing future educational and career plans.

Frequently Asked Questions about the ASVAB

What is the Armed Services Vocational Aptitude Battery (ASVAB)?

The ASVAB, sponsored by the Department of Defense, is a multi-aptitude test battery consisting of ten short individual tests covering Word Knowledge, Paragraph Comprehension, Arithmetic Reasoning, Mathematic Knowledge, General Science, Auto and Shop Information, Mechanical Comprehension, Electronics Information, Numerical Operations, and Coding Speed. Your ASVAB results provide scores for each individual test, as well as three academic composite scores—Verbal, Math, and Academic Ability—and two career exploration composite scores.

Why should I take the ASVAB?

As a high school student nearing graduation, you are faced with important career choices. Should you go on to college, technical, or vocational school? Would it be better to enter the job market? Should you consider a military career? Your ASVAB scores are measures of aptitude. Your composite scores measure your aptitude for higher academic learning and give you ideas for career exploration.

When and where is the ASVAB given?

ASVAB is administered annually or semiannually at more than 14,000 high schools and postsecondary schools in the United States.

Is there a charge or fee to take the ASVAB?

ASVAB is administered at no cost to the school or to the student.

How long does it take to complete the ASVAB?

ASVAB testing takes approximately 3 hours. If you miss class, it will be with your school's approval.

If I wish to take the ASVAB but my school doesn't offer it (or I missed it), what should I do?

See your school counselor. In some cases, arrangements may be made for you to take it at another high school. Your counselor should call 800-323-0513 (toll-free) for additional information.

How do I find out what my scores mean and how to use them?

Your scores will be provided to you on a report called the ASVAB Student Results Sheet. Along with your scores, you should receive a copy of *Exploring*

Careers: The ASVAB Workbook, which contains information that will help you understand your ASVAB results and show you how to use them for career exploration. Test results are returned to participating schools within thirty days.

What is a passing score on the ASVAB?

No one "passes" or "fails" the ASVAB. The ASVAB enables you to compare your scores to those of other students at your grade level.

If I take the ASVAB, am I obligated to join the military?

No. Taking the ASVAB does not obligate you to the military in any way. You are free to use your test results in whatever manner you wish. You may use the ASVAB results for up to two years for military enlistment if you are a junior, a senior, or a

postsecondary school student. The military services encourage all young people to finish high school before joining the armed forces.

If I am planning to go to college, should I take the ASVAB?

Yes. ASVAB results provide you with information that can help you determine your capacity for advanced academic education. You can also use your ASVAB results, along with other personal information, to identify areas for career exploration.

Should I take the ASVAB if I plan to become a commissioned officer?

Yes. Taking the ASVAB is a valuable experience for any student who aspires to become a military officer. The aptitude information you receive could assist you in career planning.

Should I take the ASVAB if I am considering entering the Reserve or National Guard?

Yes. These military organizations also use the ASVAB for enlistment purposes.

What should I do if a service recruiter contacts me?

You may be contacted by a service recruiter before you graduate. If you want to learn about the many opportunities available through the military service, arrange for a follow-up meeting. However, you are under no obligation to the military as a result of taking the ASVAB.

Is the ASVAB administered other than in the school testing program?

Yes. ASVAB is also used in the regular military enlistment program. It is administered at approximately sixty-five Military Entrance Processing Stations located throughout the United States. Each year, hundreds of thousands of young men and women who are interested in enlisting in the uniformed services (Army, Navy, Air Force, Marines, and Coast Guard) but who did not take the ASVAB while in school are examined and processed at these military stations.

Is any special preparation necessary before taking the ASVAB?

Yes. A certain amount of preparation is required for taking any examination. Whether it is an athletic competition or a written test, preparation is a *must* in order to achieve the best results. Your test scores reflect not only your ability but also the time and effort in preparing for the test. The uniformed services use ASVAB to help determine a person's qualification for enlistment and to help indicate the vocational areas for which the person is best suited. Achieving your maximum score will increase your vocational opportunities. So take practice tests to prepare.

BASIC TRAINING: WHAT HAVE I GOTTEN MYSELF INTO?

The main objective of Basic Training is to transform civilians into well-disciplined military personnel in a matter of weeks. Performing such a monumental task takes a lot of hard work, both mentally and physically. For most people, Basic Training ends with a parade on graduation day. For others, though, it ends somewhere short of graduation. It is those "horror stories" that make Basic Training probably the one biggest fear, or anxiety, for those considering military enlistment.

Unlike the boot camp you may have heard about from your Uncle Louie or seen on television, today's Basic Training doesn't include the verbal and physical abuse of yesterday. All of the military branches are ensuring that new enlistees are treated fairly and with dignity. Not that enlistees aren't yelled at (because they are); however, the vulgarity and demeaning verbal attacks are a thing of the past. There are, from time to time, incidents involving instructors who contradict the military's policies. These violations, however, receive a lot of attention, are thoroughly investigated, and usually end up with disciplinary action taken against those involved in the abuse.

I SURVIVED BASIC TRAINING

Although Michael Hipszky was eager to join the Navy, it didn't take long for doubts about his decision to hit him. While he was riding the bus to the Navy's Basic Training facility, he asked himself THE QUESTION—"Why am I putting myself through this mess?" Recalls Michael, "It crosses everyone's mind. As far as I know, in my division, everyone had the same thought. 'I want to go home.' Those first few days are intense."

He figures it's because you lose control the minute you walk through the door on the first day of Basic Training. Someone's telling you (in a very loud voice) how to stand at attention, how to stand in line, how to do just about everything. "So many things go through your head," says Michael. He soon found that if he followed three rules, life got a whole lot easier:

1. KEEP YOUR MOUTH SHUT. "Your mouth is your biggest problem," he warns, "talking when you aren't supposed to and saying dumb things."

2. PAY ATTENTION TO DETAIL. "They'll say things like, 'Grab the door knob, turn it half to the right, and go through.' A lot of people will just pull it open and get yelled at. They teach you how to fold your clothes and clean the head (toilet). Everything is paying attention to detail," Michael advises.

3. DON'T THINK FOR YOURSELF. "Wait to be told what to do," Michael says, recalling the time his group was handed a form and told to wait until ordered to fill it out. Many saw that the form was asking for information like name, date, and division and began filling it out, only to get in trouble because they didn't wait.

Having been through Basic Training, he now knows that every little thing—from folding T-shirts the exact way he'd been told to do (arms folded in), to sweeping the floor, to marching—is all part of the training process. "You don't realize it until you're done," he says.

Despite all the yelling and push-ups, Michael values the training he got in the classes. He learned how to put out different kinds of fires, how to manage his money, how to identify aircraft—even etiquette. And that's just for starters.

His lowest point was about halfway through Basic, which, he found out, usually happens for everyone at the same time. "The first half of Basic, everything is so surreal. Then you get halfway through, and finishing up Basic seems so far away. You're always busy, whether you're stenciling your clothes or marching. You march a lot," he says. But then he reached his highest point, which was pass-in review at the end of the training and winning awards. He knew he'd done well. Looking into his future with the Navy, Michael says, "I want to see the world and have the experiences that the Navy can give you." Having finished Basic Training, he's well on his way.

Airman Michael Hipszky
United States Navy

"A lot of kids are worried about Marine boot camp. They've seen movies or heard stories. Boot camp is not set up to make you fail. It's challenging, but that's the purpose of it. You're learning that no matter what life throws at you, you will be able to improvise, adapt, and overcome."

**Sergeant Ian Bonnell, Infantry Sergeant
United States Marines**

If you are still uncertain of which branch you'd like to join, do not allow the type of Basic Training you'll receive to be your only deciding factor. If, for example, the Marine Corps meets all your needs and is clearly your first choice, do not select the Air Force because its Basic Training seems easier. Conversely, if the Air Force is clearly your first choice, do not select the Marine Corps because it has the "toughest" Basic Training, and you want to prove you are up to the challenge. Basic Training is a means to transform you from civilian life to military life. It happens in a relatively short period of time compared to the entire length of your enlistment.

Some Words on Getting through Basic Training

No matter what you may have heard or read elsewhere, there are no secrets to getting through Basic Training; only common sense and preparation will get you through. Here are some do's and don'ts that should help you survive Basic Training for any of the services. Although following these guidelines will not ensure your success at Basic Training, your chances for success will be greatly improved by following them.

Before Arriving at Basic Training

DO:

- Start an exercise program
- Maintain a sensible diet
- Stay out of trouble (pay any traffic fines promptly before leaving for Basic Training)
- Ensure that all of your financial obligations are in order

- Bring the required items that you'll be told to bring
- Give up smoking

DON'T:

- Skip preparing yourself physically because you think that Basic Training will whip you into shape
- Abuse drugs and/or alcohol
- Have a big send-off party and get drunk the night before you leave for Basic Training
- Leave home with open tickets, summonses, or warrants
- Get yourself into heavy debt (such as buying a new car)
- Bring any prohibited items
- Have your hair cut in a radical manner (This includes having your head shaved. Men will receive a "very close" haircut shortly after arriving at Basic Training.)
- Have any part of your body pierced, tattooed, or otherwise altered

PAYING FOR COLLEGE THROUGH THE ARMED SERVICES

You can take any of the following three paths into the armed services—all of which provide opportunities for financial assistance for college.

Enlisted personnel

All five branches of the armed services offer college-credit courses on base. Enlisted personnel can also take college courses at civilian colleges while on active duty.

"In the Air Force, you're not only getting an education, but also experience. You could go to school for a degree in avionics technology, but in the Air Force, you get the teaching and the experience— real-world, hands-on experience—that makes your education marketable."

**Master Sergeant Timothy Little
United States Air Force**

ROTC

More than 40,000 college students participate in Reserve Officers' Training Corps (ROTC). Two-, three-, and four-year ROTC scholarships are available to outstanding students. You can try ROTC at no obligation for two years or, if you have a four-year scholarship, for one year. Normally, all ROTC classes, uniforms, and books are free. ROTC graduates are required to serve in the military for a set period of time, either full-time on active duty or part-time in the Reserve or National Guard. Qualifying graduates can delay their service to go to graduate or professional school first.

Officer Candidate School

Openings at the U.S. service academies are few, so it pays to get information early. Every student is on a full scholarship, but free does not mean easy—these intense programs train graduates to meet the demands of leadership and success.

West Point. The U.S. Army Academy offers a broad-based academic program with nineteen majors in twenty-five fields of study. Extensive training and leadership experience go hand in hand with academics.

Annapolis. The U.S. Naval Academy is a unique blend of tradition and state-of-the-art technology. Its core curriculum includes eighteen major fields of study, and classroom work is supported by practical experience in leadership and professional operations.

Air Force Academy. The U.S. Air Force Academy prepares and motivates cadets for careers as Air Force officers. The academy offers a B.S. degree in twenty-six majors. Graduates receive a reserve commission as a second lieutenant in the Air Force.

Coast Guard Academy. This broad-based education, which leads to a B.S. degree in eight technical or professional majors, includes a thorough grounding in the professional skills necessary for the Coast Guard's work.

WHAT'S MY JOB?—OH, I JUST DRIVE AN ARMORED CARRIER AROUND

Justin Platt thought maybe he would join the Army, but first he had a few doubts to overcome. A big one was his reluctance to be away from friends and family. Another one was the overseas duty—something he definitely didn't want. But his desire to get his foot in the door of medical training won out. When he found out that he could get an education in the Army to become a nurse, his fears flew out the window, and Justin joined the Army. He's glad he did.

Stationed at Fort Carson in Colorado, Justin's been through Basic Training and is on his first stint of active duty working in—you guessed it—the medical field. "I work in an aid station, which is like a mini hospital," he says. He's the one who does the screening for anyone in his battalion who comes into sick call. Okay, it's from 5 a.m. to 7 a.m., but Justin doesn't mind.

Justin's job on active duty doesn't just consist of handing out Band-Aids and cough drops. He's also learning how to drive an armored carrier—not your usual medical training. But in the field, Army medics have to be able to pick up the wounded, which means knowing how to drive what he describes as a souped-up SUV—only instead of tires, it has tracks.

Justin plans to get enough rank to go from green to gold—enlisted to officer. "I'll have to take additional college courses to get a four-year degree," he says. It'll take him about seven years, including his Army duty. Not bad for someone who once had doubts about joining the military.

Private First Class Justin Platt
Fort Carson, Colorado

Financing Higher Education through the U.S. Armed Forces

The U.S. military provides a number of options to help students and their parents get financial aid for postsecondary education.

The Montgomery G.I. Bill

Available to enlistees in all branches of the service, the G.I. Bill pays up to $23,400 toward education costs at any accredited two- or four-year college or vocational school, for up to ten years after discharge.

There are two options under the bill:

1. **Active Duty.** If you serve on active duty, you will allocate $1,200 of your pay ($100 a month for twelve months) to your education fund.

Then, under the G.I. Bill, the federal government pays out up to $23,400.

2. **Reserve Duty.** If you join a Reserve unit, you can receive up to $9,180 to offset your education costs.

You can visit the Veteran's Affairs Web page at www.va.gov.

The Department of Defense

The U.S. Department of Defense offers a large number of education benefits to those enrolled in the U.S. military or employed by the Department of Defense, including scholarships, grants, tuition assistance, and internships. Visit their Web site at http://web.lmi.org/edugate for complete information.

Tuition Assistance

All branches of the military pay up to 75 percent of tuition for full-time, active-duty enlistees who take courses at community colleges or by correspondence during their tours of duty. Details vary by service.

The Community College of the Air Force

Members of the armed forces can convert their technical training and military experience into academic credit, earning an associate degree, an occupational instructor's certificate, or a trade school certificate. Participants receive an official transcript from this fully accredited program. You can visit the Community College of the Air Force on line at www.au.af.mil/au/ccaf.

Educational Loan-Repayment Program

The Armed Services can help repay government-insured and other approved loans. One third of the loan will be repaid for each year served on active duty.

Other Forms of Tuition Assistance

Each branch of the military offers its own education incentives. To find out more, check with a local recruiting office.

Part 3

YOU AND THE WORKPLACE

SOME OF YOU WILL GO TO COLLEGE first and then look for jobs. Some of you might work for a few years and then go to college. And many of you will go immediately into the workplace and bypass college altogether. Whenever you become an employee, you'll want to know what you can do to succeed on the job and move to both higher levels of responsibility and more pay.

Chapter 11

JUMP INTO WORK

Almost everyone ends up in the workplace at some point. No matter when you plan to receive that first full-time paycheck, there are some things you'll need to do to prepare yourself for the world of work.

AT EACH GRADE LEVEL, there are specific steps you should take regardless of whether or not you plan to attend college immediately following high school. In fact, college and career timelines should coincide, according to guidance counselors and career specialists, and students should take college-preparatory courses, even if they aren't planning on attending college.

THE CAREER TIMELINE

The following timeline will help you meet college requirements and still prepare for work. In an effort to make sure that you are adequately preparing for both school and work, incorporate these five steps into your career/college timeline:

1. **Take an aptitude test.** You can do this as early as the sixth grade, but even if you're in high school now, it's not too late. By doing so, you will begin to get a feel for what areas you might be good at and enjoy. Your guidance counselor should have a test in his or her office for you to take, or you can try the ASVAB (see page 105). Thousands of high school students take this test every year to discover possible career paths—and taking the ASVAB doesn't require you to join the military!

2. **Beginning in middle school, you should start considering what your options are after high school.** However, if you're only starting to think about this in high school, that's

okay, too. Keep a notebook of information gathered from field trips, job-shadowing experiences, mentoring programs, and career fairs to help you make sense of the possibilities open to you. This process should continue through high school. Many schools offer job shadowing and internship programs for students to explore different vocational avenues. Take advantage of these opportunities if you can. Too often, students don't explore the workplace until after they've taken the courses necessary to enter a particular profession, only to discover it wasn't the career they dreamed of after all.

3. **No later than the tenth grade, visit a vocational center to look at the training programs offered.** Some public school systems send students to vocational and career program centers for career exploration.

4. **During your junior and senior years, be**

TAKING A BREAK BETWEEN HIGH SCHOOL AND COLLEGE

Because of the soaring costs of college tuition today, college is no longer a place to "find yourself." It is a costly investment in your future. The career you choose to pursue may or may not require additional education; your research will determine whether or not it's required or preferred. If you decide not to attend college immediately after high school, however, don't consider it to be a closed door. Taking some time off between high school and college is considered perfectly acceptable by employers. Many students simply need a break after thirteen years of schooling. Most experts agree that it's better to be ready and prepared for college; many adults get more out of their classes after they've had a few years to mature.

Source: Street Smart Career Guide: A Step-by-Step Program for Your Career Development.

sure to create a portfolio of practice resumes, writing samples, and a list of work skills. This portfolio should also include your high school transcript and letters of recommendation. It will serve as a valuable reference tool when it comes time to apply for jobs.

5. **By tenth or eleventh grade, you should begin focusing on a specific career path.** More employers today are looking for employees who have both the education and work experience that relates to the career field for which they're interviewing. If you are looking for part-time employment, you should consider jobs that pertain to your field of study. Until you start interacting with people in the field, you won't have a realistic feel of what's involved in that profession. It adds to the importance of the learning. If you're planning on heading into the workplace right after high school, take a look at the previous two pages for a list of careers that don't require a four-year degree.

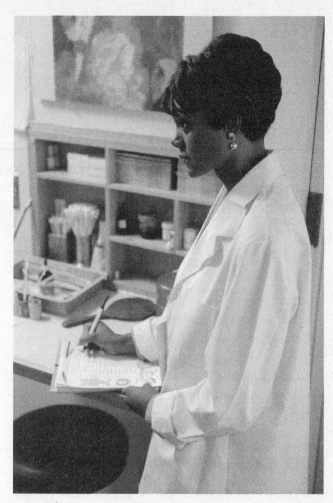

WRITING YOUR RESUME

Resumes are a critical part of getting a job. Chances are you'll have to submit one before you get interviewed. A resume is an introduction of your skills to a potential employer. For that reason, your resume must stand out in a crowd because some employers receive dozens of resumes in the mail each week. A resume that is too long, cluttered, or disorganized may find its way to the "circular file," also known as the trash can. You can avoid this hazard by creating a resume that is short, presentable, and easy to read.

Remember that a resume is a summary of who you are and an outline of your experiences, skills, and goals. While writing it, you may discover some talents that you weren't aware you had and that will help boost your confidence for the job search.

Begin by collecting facts about yourself, including where you went to high school, your past and present jobs, activities, interests, and leadership

(Continued on page 117)

roles. Next to the individual activities, write down what responsibilities you had. For example, something as simple as babysitting requires the ability to settle disagreements and supervise others.

Next, decide on how you would like to format your resume. Most hiring managers expect to see one of two types of resumes: chronological or functional. The chronological resume is the most traditional, supplying the reader with a sequential listing (from present to past) of your accomplishments. Because the emphasis here is on past employment experience, high school and college students with little or no employment history might want to avoid this type. A functional resume, on the other hand, highlights a person's abilities rather than his or her work history. Entry-level candidates who want to focus on skills rather than credentials should consider using a functional resume.

CAREERS WITHOUT A FOUR-YEAR DEGREE

Some students spend a few years in the workplace before going to college. Others begin their career with a high school diploma, a vocational certificate, or up to two years of education or training after high school.

With that in mind, sometimes it's easier to know what you don't want than what you do want. Take a look at the list below, and check off the careers that interest you. Perhaps you've thought of something you'd like to do that isn't on this list. Well, don't dump your hopes. There are many different levels of training and education that can lead you to the career of your dreams. Since this list is not all-inclusive, you should check with your high school counselor or go on line to research the training you'll need to achieve the job or career you want—without a four-year degree.

Then talk to your guidance counselor, teacher, librarian, or career counselor for more information about the careers on the list below or those you've researched on your own.

AGRICULTURE AND NATURAL RESOURCES

High school/vocational diploma
- Fisher
- Groundskeeper
- Logger
- Pest Controller

Up to two years beyond high school
- Fish and Game Warden
- Tree Surgeon

APPLIED ARTS (VISUAL)

High school/vocational diploma
- Floral Arranger
- Merchandise Displayer
- Painter (artist)

Up to two years beyond high school
- Cartoonist
- Commercial Artist
- Fashion Designer
- Interior Decorator
- Photographer

APPLIED ARTS (WRITTEN AND SPOKEN)

High school/vocational diploma
- Proofreader

Up to two years beyond high school
- Advertising copywriter
- Legal assistant

BUSINESS MACHINE/COMPUTER OPERATION

High school/vocational diploma
- Data Entry
- Statistical Clerk
- Telephone Operator
- Typist

Up to two years beyond high school
- Computer Operator
- Motion Picture Projectionist
- Word Processing Machine Operator

CONSTRUCTION AND MAINTENANCE

High school/vocational diploma
- Bricklayer
- Construction Laborer
- Elevator Mechanic
- Floor Covering Installer
- Heavy Equipment Operator
- Janitor
- Maintenance Mechanic

Up to two years beyond high school
- Building Inspector
- Carpenter

- Electrician
- Insulation Worker
- Lather
- Painter (construction)
- Pipefitter
- Plumber
- Roofer
- Sheet Metal Worker
- Structural Steel Worker
- Tile Setter

CRAFTS AND RELATED SERVICES

High school/vocational diploma
- Baker/Cook/Chef
- Butcher
- Furniture Upholsterer
- Housekeeper (hotel)
- Tailor/Dressmaker

Up to two years beyond high school
- Dry Cleaner
- Jeweler
- Locksmith
- Musical Instrument Repairer

CREATIVE/PERFORMING ARTS

High school/vocational diploma
- Singer
- Stunt Performer

Up to two years beyond high school
- Actor/Actress
- Dancer/Choreographer
- Musician
- Writer/Author

EDUCATION AND RELATED SERVICES

High school/vocational diploma
- Nursery School Attendant
- Teacher's Aide

ENGINEERING AND RELATED TECHNOLOGIES

High school/vocational diploma
- Biomedical Equipment Technician
- Laser Technician

Up to two years beyond high school
- Aerospace Engineer Technician
- Broadcast Technician
- Chemical Laboratory Technician
- Civil Engineering Technician
- Computer Programmer
- Computer Service Technician
- Electronic Technician
- Energy Conservation Technician

- Industrial Engineering Technician
- Laboratory Tester
- Mechanical Engineering Technician
- Metallurgical Technician
- Pollution Control Technician
- Quality Control Technician
- Robot Technician
- Surveyor (land)
- Technical Illustrator
- Tool Designer
- Weather Observer

FINANCIAL TRANSACTIONS

High school/vocational diploma
- Accounting Clerk
- Bank Teller
- Cashier
- Payroll Clerk
- Travel Agent

Up to two years beyond high school
- Bookkeeper
- Loan Officer

HEALTH CARE (GENERAL)

High school/vocational diploma
- Dental Assistant
- Medical Assistant
- Nursing/Psychiatric Aide

Up to two years beyond high school
- Dietetic Technician
- Nurse (practical)
- Nurse (registered)
- Optometric Assistant
- Physical Therapist's Assistant
- Physician's Assistant
- Recreation Therapist

HEALTH-CARE SPECIALTIES AND TECHNOLOGIES

High school/vocational diploma
- Dialysis Technician

Up to two years beyond high school
- Dental Hygienist
- Dental Laboratory Technician
- EEG Technologist
- EKG Technician
- Emergency Medical Technician
- Medical Laboratory Technician
- Medical Technologist
- Nuclear Medicine Technologist
- Operating Room Technician
- Optician

❑ Radiation Therapy Technologist
❑ Radiologic Technologist
❑ Respiratory Therapist
❑ Sonographer

HOME/BUSINESS EQUIPMENT REPAIR
High school/vocational diploma
❑ Air-Conditioning/Refrigeration/
   Heating Mechanic
❑ Appliance Servicer
❑ Coin Machine Mechanic
Up to two years beyond high school
❑ Communications Equipment Mechanic
❑ Line Installer/Splicer
❑ Office Machine Servicer
❑ Radio/TV Repairer
❑ Telephone Installer

INDUSTRIAL EQUIPMENT OPERATIONS AND REPAIR
High school/vocational diploma
❑ Assembler
❑ Blaster
❑ Boilermaker
❑ Coal Equipment Operator
❑ Compressor House Operator
❑ Crater
❑ Dock Worker
❑ Forging Press Operator
❑ Furnace Operator
❑ Heat Treater
❑ Machine Tool Operator
❑ Material Handler
❑ Miner
❑ Sailor
❑ Sewing Machine Operator
Up to two years beyond high school
❑ Bookbinder
❑ Compositor/Typesetter
❑ Electronic Equipment Repairer
❑ Electroplater
❑ Firefighter
❑ Instrument Mechanic
❑ Lithographer
❑ Machine Repairer
❑ Machinist
❑ Millwright
❑ Molder
❑ Nuclear Reactor Operator
❑ Patternmaker
❑ Photoengraver
❑ Power House Mechanic
❑ Power Plant Operator
❑ Printing Press Operator
❑ Stationery Engineer
❑ Tool and Die Maker
❑ Water Plant Operator
❑ Welder
❑ Wire Drawer

MANAGEMENT AND PLANNING
High school/vocational diploma
❑ Administrative Assistant

❑ Food Service Supervisor
❑ Postmaster
❑ Service Station Manager
Up to two years beyond high school
❑ Benefits Manager
❑ Building Manager
❑ Caterer
❑ Contractor
❑ Credit Manager
❑ Customer Service Coordinator
❑ Employment Interviewer
❑ Executive Housekeeper
❑ Funeral Director
❑ Hotel/Motel Manager
❑ Importer/Exporter
❑ Insurance Manager
❑ Manager (small business)
❑ Office Manager
❑ Personnel Manager
❑ Restaurant/Bar Manager
❑ Store Manager
❑ Supermarket Manager

MARKETING AND SALES
High school/vocational diploma
❑ Auctioneer
❑ Bill Collector
❑ Driver (route)
❑ Fashion Model
❑ Product Demonstrator
❑ Salesperson (general)
❑ Sample Distributor
Up to two years beyond high school
❑ Claims Adjuster
❑ Insurance Worker
❑ Manufacturer's Representative
❑ Real Estate Agent
❑ Sales Manager
❑ Travel Agent
❑ Travel Guide

PERSONAL AND CUSTOMER SERVICE
High school/vocational diploma
❑ Barber
❑ Bartender
❑ Beautician
❑ Child-care Worker
❑ Counter Attendant
❑ Dining Room Attendant
❑ Electrologist
❑ Flight Attendant
❑ Host/Hostess
❑ Houseparent
❑ Manicurist
❑ Parking Lot Attendant
❑ Porter
❑ Private Household Worker
❑ Waiter/Waitress

RECORDS AND COMMUNICATIONS
High school/vocational diploma
❑ Billing Clerk
❑ Clerk (general)

❑ File Clerk
❑ Foreign Trade Clerk
❑ Hotel Clerk
❑ Meter Reader
❑ Postal Clerk
❑ Receptionist
❑ Stenographer
Up to two years beyond high school
❑ Court Reporter
❑ Legal Secretary
❑ Library Assistant
❑ Library Technician
❑ Medical Records Technician
❑ Medical Secretary
❑ Personnel Assistant
❑ Secretary
❑ Travel Clerk

SOCIAL AND GOVERNMENT
High school/vocational diploma
❑ Corrections Officer
❑ Police Officer
❑ Security Guard
❑ Store Detective
Up to two years beyond high school
❑ Detective (police)
❑ Hazardous Waste Technician
❑ Recreation Leader
❑ Personal/Customer Services

STORAGE AND DISPATCHING
High school/vocational diploma
❑ Dispatcher
❑ Mail Carrier
❑ Railroad Conductor
❑ Shipping/Receiving Clerk
❑ Stock Clerk
❑ Tool Crib Attendant
❑ Warehouse Worker
Up to two years beyond high school
❑ Warehouse Supervisor

VEHICLE OPERATION AND REPAIR
High school/vocational diploma
❑ Automotive Painter
❑ Bus Driver
❑ Chauffeur
❑ Diesel Mechanic
❑ Farm Equipment Mechanic
❑ Forklift Operator
❑ Heavy Equipment Mechanic
❑ Locomotive Engineer
❑ Railroad Braker
❑ Refuse Collector
❑ Service Station Attendant
❑ Taxicab Driver
❑ Truck Driver
Up to two years beyond high school
❑ Aircraft Mechanic
❑ Airplane Pilot
❑ Auto Body Repairer
❑ Automotive Mechanic
❑ Garage Supervisor
❑ Motorcycle Mechanic

Parts of a Resume

At the very least, your resume should include the following components:

Heading: Centered at the top of the page should be your name, address, phone number, and e-mail address.

Objective: In one sentence, tell the employer what type of work you are looking for.

Education: Beginning with your most recent school or program, include the date (or expected date) of completion, the degree or certificate earned, and the address of the institution. Don't overlook any workshops or seminars, self-study, or on-the-job training in which you have been involved. If any courses particularly lend themselves to the type of work you'd be doing on that job, include them. Mention grade point averages and class rank when they are especially impressive.

Skills and abilities: Until you've actually listed these on paper, you can easily overlook many of them. They may be as varied as the ability to work with computers or being captain of the girl's basketball team.

Work experience: If you don't have any, skip this section. If you do, begin with your most recent employer and include the date you left the job, your job title, the company name, and the company address. If you are still employed there, simply enter your start date and "to present" for the date. Include notable accomplishments for each job. High school and college students with little work experience shouldn't be shy about including summer, part-time, and volunteer jobs, such as lifeguarding, babysitting, delivering pizzas, or volunteering at the local parks and recreation department.

Personal: Here's your opportunity to include your special talents and interests as well as notable accomplishments or experiences.

SAMPLE FUNCTIONAL RESUME

Michele A. Thomas
3467 Main Street
Atlanta, Georgia 30308
404-555-3423
E-mail: mthomas_987654321@yahoo.com

OBJECTIVE

Seeking a sales position in the wireless phone industry

EDUCATION

High School Diploma, June 2003

John F. Kennedy High School, Atlanta, Georgia

SKILLS

Computer literate, IBM: MS Works, MS Word, WordPerfect, Netscape; Macintosh: MS Word, Excel

ACTIVITIES/LEADERSHIP

Student Government secretary, 2002–2003

Key Club vice president, 2001–2002

Future Business Leaders of America

AWARDS

Varsity Swim Club (Captain; MVP Junior, Senior; Sportsmanship Award)
Outstanding Community Service Award, 2002

EXPERIENCE

Sales Clerk, The Limited, Atlanta, Georgia; part-time, September 2001 to present

Cashier, Winn-Dixie Supermarkets, Atlanta, Georgia, Summers 2000 and 2001

INTERESTS

Swimming, reading, computers

REFERENCES

Available upon request

References: Most experts agree that it's best to simply state that references are available upon request. However, if you do decide to list names, addresses, and phone numbers, limit yourself to no more than three. Make sure you inform any people whom you have listed that they may be contacted. Take a look at the sample resume on the previous page, and use it as a model when you create your resume.

SAMPLE COVER LETTER

Take a look at how this student applied the facts outlined in her resume to the job she's applying for in the cover letter below. You can use this letter to help you get started on your own cover letters. Text that appears in all caps below indicates the kind of information you need to include in that section. Before you send your letter, proofread it for mistakes and ask a parent or friend you trust to look it over as well.

(DATE)
June 29, 2003

(YOUR ADDRESS)
3467 Main Street
Atlanta, Georgia 30308
E-mail: mthomas_987654321@yahoo.com
Phone: 404-555-6721

(PERSON—BY NAME—TO WHOM YOU'RE SENDING THE LETTER)
Mr. Charles E. Pence
Manager, Human Resources
NexAir Wireless
20201 East Sixth Street
Atlanta, Georgia 30372

Dear Mr. Pence:

(HOW YOU HEARD OF THE POSITION)
Your job announcement in the Atlanta Gazette for an entry-level sales position asked for someone who has both computer and sales skills. (SOMETHING EXTRA THAT WILL INTEREST THE READER) My training and past job experience fit both of those categories. I also bring an enthusiasm and desire to begin my career in a communications firm such as NexAir.

(WHAT PRACTICAL SKILLS YOU CAN BRING TO THE POSITION)
A few weeks ago, I graduated from John F. Kennedy High School here in Atlanta. While in school, I concentrated on gaining computer skills on both IBM and Macintosh machines and participated in organizations such as the Key Club, in which I was vice president, and the Future Business Leaders of America.

(RELATE PAST EXPERIENCE TO DESIRED JOB)
As you will see from my resume, I worked as a cashier at Winn-Dixie Supermarket for two summers and am currently employed as a sales clerk at The Limited. From these two positions, I have gained valuable customer service skills and an attention to detail, qualities which I'm sure are of utmost importance to you as you make your hiring decision.

I would very much like to interview for the position and am available at your convenience. I look forward to hearing from you soon.

Sincerely,

Michele A. Thomas

Resume-Writing Tips

These tips will help as you begin constructing your resume:

- Keep the resume short and simple. Although senior executives may use as many as two or three pages, recent graduates should limit themselves to one page.
- Capitalize headings.
- Keep sentences short; avoid writing in paragraphs.
- Use language that is simple, not flowery or complex.
- Be specific, and offer examples when appropriate.
- Emphasize achievements.
- Be honest.
- Don't include information about salary or wages.
- Use high-quality, white, beige, or gray, 8½" × 11" paper.
- Make good use of white space by leaving adequate side and top margins on the paper.
- Make what you write presentable, using good business style and typing it on a computer or word processor.
- Because your resume should be a reflection of your personality, write it yourself.
- Avoid gimmicks such as colored paper, photos, or clip art.
- Make good use of bullets or asterisks, underlining, and bold print.
- Proofread your work, and have someone you trust proofread it also.
- Be neat and accurate.
- Never send a resume without a cover letter.

The Cover Letter

Every resume should be accompanied by a cover letter. This is often the most crucial part of your job search because the letter will be the first thing that a potential employer reads. When you include a cover letter, you're showing the employer that you care enough to take the time to address him or her personally and that you are genuinely interested in the job.

Always call the company and verify the name and title of the person to whom you are addressing the letter. Although you will want to keep your letter brief, introduce yourself and begin with a statement that will catch the reader's attention. Indicate the position you are applying for and mention if someone referred you or if you are simply responding to a newspaper ad. Draw attention to yourself by including something that will arouse the employer's curiosity about your experience and accomplishments. A cover letter should request something, most commonly an interview. Sign and date your letter. Then follow up with a phone call a few days after you're sure the letter has been received. Persistence pays. The sample cover letter on the next page can help you as you begin writing your cover letter.

JOB HUNTING 101

High school is a time for taking classes and learning, developing relationships with others, becoming involved in extracurricular activities that teach valuable life skills, and generally preparing for college or a job. Regardless of where you're headed after high school, you need to learn how to create a favorable impression. That can mean setting some clear, attainable goals for yourself, putting them down on paper in the form of a resume and cover letter, and convincing interviewers that you are, indeed, the person for whom they are looking. In short, learn how to sell yourself. A brief course in Job Hunting 101 will help you do just that.

Marketing Yourself

You can use several approaches to market yourself successfully. Networking, the continual process of contacting friends and relatives, is a great way to get information about job openings. Seventy-five percent of the job openings in this country are not advertised but are filled by friends, relatives, and acquaintances of people who already work there. From the employer's perspective, there is less risk associated with hiring someone recommended by an employee than by hiring someone unknown. Networking is powerful. Everyone has a primary network of people they know and talk to frequently. Those acquaintances know and talk to networks of their own, thereby creating a secondary network for you and multiplying the number of individuals who know what you're looking for in a job.

Broadcasting is another marketing method in which you gather a list of companies that interest you and then mail them letters asking for job interviews. Although the rate of return on your mailings is small, two thirds of all job hunters use this approach, and half of those who use it find a job. You will increase your response rate by addressing your letter to a particular person—the one who has the power to hire you—and by following up with a phone call a few days after the letter has been received. To obtain the manager's name, simply call the company and ask the receptionist for the person's name, job title, and correct spelling. Good resources for finding potential employers include referrals, community agencies, job fairs, newspaper ads, trade directories, trade journals, state indexes, the local chamber of commerce, the Yellow Pages, and the Web. See page 121 for a listing of career Web resources. These tips can help as you begin hunting for the perfect job.

- Job-hunting is time intensive. Do your homework, and take it seriously by using every opportunity available to you.

- Prepare yourself for the fact that there will be far more rejections than acceptances.

- Consider taking a temporary job while you continue the job hunt. It will help pay the bills and give you new skills to boost your resume at the same time.

- Research the activities of potential employers, and show that you have studied them when you're being interviewed.

- Keep careful records of all contacts and follow-up activities.

- Don't ignore any job leads—act on every tip you get.

- Stay positive.

With all these thoughts in mind, you should be ready to begin the process of making people believe in you, and that's a major part of being successful in your job hunt.

THE JOB INTERVIEW

You can prevent some of the preinterview jitters by adequately preparing. Remember that you have nothing to lose and that you, too, are doing the choosing. Just as you are waiting and hoping to be offered a job, you have the option of choosing whether or not to accept an offer. It's all right to feel somewhat anxious, but keep everything in perspective. This is an adventure, and you are in control. Most important, remember to be yourself. With all of this in mind, consider some of the following points of the interview process.

- Speak up during the interview, and furnish the interviewer with the information he or she needs in order to make an informed decision. It is especially impressive if you can remember the names of people to whom you've been introduced. People like to be called by name, and it shows that you took the initiative to remember them.

- Always arrive a few minutes early for the interview, and look your best. The way you act and dress tells the interviewer plenty about your attitude and personality. Sloppy dress, chewing gum, and cigarettes have no place at an interview and will probably cut your interview short. Instead, dress professionally and appropriately for the job. Avoid heavy makeup, short skirts, jeans, and untidy or flashy clothing of any kind. Although a business suit may be appropriate for certain jobs, a person who is applying for an outdoor position should probably interview in clean, neatly pressed dress slacks and a golf shirt or a skirt and blouse.

The best way to prepare for the interview is to practice. Have a friend or relative play the role of the interviewer, and go over some of the most commonly asked questions. Learn as much as you can about the company you're interviewing with—it pays to do your homework. When you show a potential employer that you've taken the time and initiative to learn about his or her company, you're showing that you will be a motivated and hardworking employee. Employers fear laziness and minimal effort, looking instead for workers who don't always have to be told what to do and when to do it.

Here is a list of interview questions you can expect to have to answer:

- **Tell me a little bit about yourself.** This is your chance to pitch your qualifications for the job in two minutes. Provide a few details about your education, previous jobs you've held, and extracurricular activities that relate to the position that you're interviewing for.

- **Are you at your best when working alone or in a group?** The safest answer is "Both." Most companies today cluster their employees into work groups, so you will need strong interpersonal skills. However, on occasion, you may be required to work on projects alone.

- **What did you like the most about your last job? What did you dislike the most about it?** Always accentuate the positives in an interview, so focus primarily on what you liked. Also be honest about what you disliked, but then explain how facing the negatives helped you grow as an employee.

- **What are your career goals?** Be sure you've done some research on the company and industry before your interview. When this question comes up, talk realistically about how far you believe your skills and talents will take you and what actions you plan to take to ensure this happens, such as pursuing more education.

- **Do you have any questions for me?** Absolutely! See "Asking Questions" below.

FINDING JOBS ON THE WEB

As we mentioned, you can find jobs through your network of friends, family, and acquaintances; through classified ads in the newspaper; and through career Web pages. Here is a listing of popular Web sites that not only offer job search technology but also information on resume writing, interviewing, and other important career advice.

www.monster.com   **www.careerbuilder.com**

www.hotjobs.com   **www.vault.com**

Take the time to prepare some answers to these commonly asked questions. For instance, if you haven't set at least one career goal for yourself, do it now. Be ready to describe it to the interviewer. Likewise, you should be able to talk about your last job, including what you liked the most and the least. Adapt your answers so they apply to the job for which you are presently interviewing. Other questions that might be asked include:

- What qualifications do you have?

- Why do you want to work for us?

- Do you enjoy school? Why or why not?

- Do you plan to continue your education?

- What do you plan to be doing for work five years from now?

- What motivates you to do a good job?

If you are seeking a job as a manager, you might respond by saying you liked the varied responsibilities of your past job. Recall that you enjoyed the unexpected challenges and flexible schedule. And when describing what you liked least, make sure you respond with some function or area of responsibility that has nothing to do with the responsibilities of the job you hope to get.

More than likely, the first question you'll be asked is to tell the interviewer something about yourself. This is your chance to "toot your horn," but don't ramble. You might ask the interviewer specifically what he or she would like to hear about: your educational background or recent experiences and responsibilities in your present or last job. After he or she chooses, stick to the basics; the next move belongs to the interviewer.

When asked about personal strengths and weaknesses, given that the question is two parts, begin with a weakness so you can end on a strong note with your strengths. Again, try to connect your description of a strength or weakness with the requirements for the job. Naturally, it wouldn't be wise to reveal a serious weakness about yourself, but you can mention how you have changed your shortcomings. You might say, "I like to get my work done fast, but I consciously try to slow down a little to make sure I'm careful and accurate." When it comes to strengths, don't exaggerate, but don't sell yourself short.

Asking Questions

You can ask questions, too. In fact, the interviewer expects you to ask questions to determine if the job is right for you, just as he or she will be trying to find out if you'll be successful working for his or her company. When you ask questions, it shows that you're interested and want to learn more. When the type of question you ask indicates that you've done your homework regarding the job and the company, your interviewer will be impressed. Avoid asking questions about salary or fringe benefits, anything adversarial, or questions that show you have a negative opinion of the company. It's all right to list your questions on a piece of paper; it's the quality of the question that's important, not whether you can remember it. Here are a few sample questions that you should consider asking if the topics don't come up in your interview:

- What kind of responsibilities come with this job?

- How is the department organized?

- What will be the first project for the new hire to tackle?

- What is a typical career advancement path for a person in this position?

- Who will the supervisor be for this position, and can I meet him or her?

- What is the office environment like? Is it casual or corporate?

- When do you expect to reach a hiring decision?

SAMPLE THANK-YOU LETTER

After you've interviewed for a job, it's important to reiterate your interest in the position by sending a thank-you letter to those who interviewed you. Take a look at Michele's letter to the manager she interviewed with at NexAir. You can use this letter as a model when the time comes for you to write some thank-you letters.

July 17, 2003

Michele A. Thomas
3467 Main Street
Atlanta, Georgia 30308
E-mail: mthomas_987654321@yahoo.com
Phone: 404-555-6721

Mr. Charles E. Pence
Manager, Human Resources
NexAir Wireless
20201 East Sixth Street
Atlanta, Georgia 30372

Dear Mr. Pence:

It was a pleasure meeting with you Monday to discuss the sales opportunity at NexAir's downtown location. After learning more about the position, it is clear to me that with my background and enthusiasm, I would be an asset to your organization.

As we discussed, my experiences as a cashier at Winn-Dixie Supermarket and as a sales clerk at The Limited have provided me with the basic skills necessary to perform the responsibilities required of a sales representative at NexAir. I believe that with my ability to learn quickly and communicate effectively, I can help NexAir increase sales of its wireless products.

Thank you for the opportunity to interview with your organization. If there is any additional information I can provide about myself, please do not hesitate to call me. I look forward to hearing your decision soon.

Sincerely,

Michele A. Thomas

Following Up

After the interview, follow up with a thank-you note to the interviewer. Not only is it a thoughtful gesture, it triggers the interviewer's memory about you and shows that you have a genuine interest in the job. Your thank-you note should be written in a business letter format and should highlight the key points in your interview. The sample thank-you note above can help.

During the interview process, remember that you will not appeal to everyone who interviews you. If your first experience doesn't work out, don't get discouraged. Keep trying.

WHAT EMPLOYERS EXPECT FROM EMPLOYEES

As part of the National City Bank personnel team in Columbus, Ohio, Rose Graham works with Cooperative Business Education (CBE) coordinators in the area who are trying to place high school students in the workplace. When asked what skills she looks for in potential employees, she quickly replies that basic communication skills are at the top of her list. She stresses, "The ability to construct a sentence and put together words cannot be overemphasized." She cites knowledge of the personal computer, with good keyboarding skills, as essential.

In an article published in the *Nashville Business Journal*, Donna Cobble of Staffing Solutions outlined these basic skills for everyday life in the workplace:

Communication: Being a good communicator not only means having the ability to express oneself properly in the English language, but it also means being a good listener. If you feel inferior in any of these areas, it's a good idea to sign up for a public speaking class, read books on the subject, and borrow techniques from professional speakers.

Organization: Organization is the key to success in any occupation or facet of life. The ability to plan, prioritize, and complete a task in a timely fashion is a valuable skill. Check out the next section for tips on improving your time-management skills.

Problem solving: Companies are looking for creative problem solvers, people who aren't afraid to act on a situation and follow through with their decision. Experience and practice play a major role in your ability to determine the best solution. You can learn these techniques by talking with others about how they solve problems as well as observing others in the problem-solving process.

Sensitivity: In addition to being kind and courteous to their fellow workers, employees need to be sensitive to a coworker's perspective. That might mean putting yourself in the other person's shoes to gain a better understanding of that person's feelings. Employers look for individuals who are able to work on a team instead of those concerned only with their own personal gain.

Judgment: Although closely related to problem solving, good judgment shows up on many different levels in the workplace. It is the ability of a person to assess a situation, weigh the options, consider the risks, and make the necessary decision. Good judgment is built on experience and self-confidence.

Concentration: Concentration is the ability to focus on one thing at a time. Learning to tune out distractions and relate solely to the task at hand is a valuable asset for anyone.

Cooperation: Remember that you're being paid to do a job, so cooperate.

Honesty: Dishonesty shows up in many different ways, ranging from stealing time or property to divulging company secrets. Stay honest.

Initiative: Don't always wait to be told exactly what to do. Show some initiative and look around to see what needs to be done next.

Willingness to learn: Be willing to learn how things are done at the company instead of doing things the way you want to do them.

Dependability: Arrive at work on time every day, and meet your deadlines.

Enthusiasm: Although not every task you're assigned will be stimulating, continue to show enthusiasm for your work at all times.

Acceptance of criticism: Corrective criticism is necessary for any employee to learn how things should be done. Employees who view criticism as a way to improve themselves will benefit from it.

Loyalty: There is no place for negativity in the workplace. You simply won't be happy working for an employer to whom you're not loyal.

Never fail to show pride in your work, the place where you work, and your appearance. By making these traits a part of your personality and daily performance, you will demonstrate that you are a cut above other employees with equal or better qualifications.

JUMPING ON THE SALARY FAST-TRACK

So the job offer comes, and it's time to talk about money. Unless you are an undiscovered genius, you most likely will start near the bottom of the salary scale if you're heading straight to the workplace after graduating from high school. There's not much room to negotiate a salary since you probably won't be able to say, "Well, I've done this, this, and this. I know what my experience is worth." You will find that most people hiring first-time employees will have a "take-it-or-leave-it" attitude about salary offers. However, according to Amryl Ward, a human resources consultant who has been hiring employees for more than twenty-five years in various human resource positions, there are some things that entry-level employees can do to make themselves more easily hired and, once hired, to get themselves on the fast-track toward more pay.

1. **As you interview for the job, be prepared to tell a potential employer why you're worth hiring.** "Bring your skills to the table," says Ward. For instance, you might not think that the job you had during the summer at that big office supply store did anything more than earn you spending money.

On the contrary, you learned valuable skills, such as how to be part of a team and how to deal with customers. What about that after-school office job you had? You learned how to answer the phones and how to work with certain software. Think carefully about the jobs you had in high school and what you learned from them. Those are called transferable skills.

2. **Once you're hired, be willing to do more than just what the job requires.** Sure, you may be frying fries at the start. But if you come in early and stay late, if you pitch in to help another employee with his or her job, or if you voluntarily clean up the counters and sweep the floor, that says to management, "This employee is a winner. Let's keep him or her in mind the next time a promotion comes up." Soon, you might be managing a crew, then the store.

ON THE JOB

Once you snag that perfect job, there's no time to rest easy. You need to keep your manager happy and instill trust in your coworkers. And at the same time you're doing this, you'll want to watch out for yourself, keep yourself happy, and stay ahead of the learning curve. Here are some ways for you to do just that.

Minding Your Office Etiquette

Okay, so maybe you didn't know which was the salad fork at your cousin Sally's wedding reception. Most likely, though, you can name a few basic rules of etiquette, like not chewing with your mouth open at the dinner table. Now, what about when it comes to the manners you're supposed to have in the workplace? That usually draws a blank if you've never worked in an office setting. How would you know what's the right way to answer the phone or talk to your boss or customers?

Shannon McBride, of the Golden Crescent Tech Prep School to Career Partnership in Victoria, Texas, has seen many students come through his program and land good jobs. He's also seen many of them succeed because they knew how to present themselves in a professional situation. Unfortunately, he can also relate stories of high school graduates who had no clue how to act in the workplace. They didn't realize that when they're working in an office with a group of people, they have to go out of their way to get along and follow the unwritten rules of that workplace. They didn't realize that the office is not the place to make personal statements about their individuality in how they dress or in how they conduct themselves that conflict with the environment.

McBride says that means you'll have to size up how others are dressing and match what the office is geared to. For instance, if you work in a business office, most likely you'd wear slacks and a button-down shirt or a nice skirt and top. If you worked in a golf pro shop, you'd wear a golf shirt and shorts. "As much as you want to be an individual," says McBride, "you have to fit in when you're in a business setting. If you want an adult job, you have to act like an adult."

A lot of young people don't grasp how important office etiquette is and blow it off as just some silly rules imposed by adults. But McBride cautions that not following the norms of office etiquette can make or break a job. You can have all the technical talent and know all the latest software applications, but if you're not up on how people dress, talk, and conduct business, your job probably won't last very long. When it comes to getting a job, McBride warns, "First impressions are so important. Bad office etiquette can hurt that first impression." The best advice that we can give is that if you're not sure what the policy is about answering phones, using e-mail or the Internet on the job, or dress codes, you should ask your boss. He or she won't steer you wrong and will be pleased that you were concerned enough to ask.

Finding a Friendly Face at Work

There you are on the first day of a new job. Everyone looks like they know what they're doing while you stand there feeling really dumb. Even for the most seasoned employee, those first few weeks on the job are tough. Of course, everyone else looks like they know what they're doing because they've been doing it for quite some time. Wouldn't it be nice, though, if you had someone to help you adjust? Someone who would give you those little inside tips everyone else learns with experience. Someone to caution you about things that could go wrong or to give you a heads-up when you're doing something that could lead to a reprimand. If you look around the office, you'll find such a person, says Robert Fait, Career Counselor and Instructional Specialist, who is associated with Career and Technology Education in the Katy Independent School district in Katy, Texas.

You might not realize that such a person is a mentor, but in the strict definition of the word, that's what he or she is. Or, as Fait puts it, "Mentors are role models who are willing to assist others with personal education and career goal setting and planning. This caring person shares a listening ear, a comforting shoulder, and an understanding heart." In other words, a mentor is someone who will make you feel comfortable in a new working environment, show you the procedures, and, in the end, help you become more productive.

Unless the company you're working for has a formal mentoring program, mentors don't come with huge signs around their necks that read, "Look here. I'm a mentor. Ask me anything." You have to look for them. Fait advises new employees to look closely at their coworkers and take notice of who demonstrates positive behavior, has strong work habits, and seems trustworthy. Those are the people to approach. "Such workers are usually willing to share their knowledge and insights with others," says Fait.

Who knows? Given some time, you could become a mentor yourself after you've been on the job for a while. Maybe you'll be able to help some new employee who looks kind of bewildered and in need of a friendly hand because you'll remember what it was like to be the new person.

12 chapter

SURVIVAL SKILLS

Whether you're headed to college or work, you're going to come face to face with some intimidating stuff after graduation.

Your LEVEL OF STRESS will most likely increase due to the demands of your classes or job and to your exposure to alcohol or drugs; various forms of conflict will rise, and you're going to have to keep up with your own health and nutrition. Seem daunting? It's really not if you keep a level head about you and stick to your core values. This section will help you work through the muddier side of life after high school.

SKILLS TO MAKE YOU STRESS-HARDY

Jump out of bed and into the shower. What to wear? Throw that on. Yuck—what's that stain? "Mom, where are my clean socks?" Tick, tock. No time to grab a bite if you want to make the homeroom bell. Skid around the corner and race for the classroom just as the final bell rings. Whoops, forgot your bio book. Sports, clubs, job, homework, friends on the phone, and finally (sigh) sleep.

Sound like your life? If you're like most high school students, that description probably hits pretty close to home. So now we'll take your already hectic schedule and throw in the fact that you'll soon be graduating and have to figure out what to do with your life. Can you say "stress"?

Some people say that stress actually motivates them to perform better, but we won't talk about those perfect people. For most of you, stress means that you

may snap at the dog, slam a few doors, get mad at your mom, and feel down. Maybe you'll even have physical symptoms—stomach disturbances, rapid heartbeat, sweaty palms, dizziness. The list goes on. Not a good place to be when you're dealing with a huge list of things to do, plus graduation is staring you in the face.

How to handle stress has been written about countless times, but out of all the advice that's out there, a few simple pointers can really help you prevent the sweaty palms and nauseated feeling in the pit of your stomach.

- **French fries out, good food in.** Eat at least one hot, balanced meal a day. Healthy, as in veggies, fruits, meats, cheese, grains. Read further along in this section for more information about nutrition and health.

- **Sleep.** Seven, eight, ten hours a day. Easier said than done, but well worth it. Sleep will not only get you through high school but also your college and career lives, and it will help you stop feeling like such a frazzled bunch of nerve endings.

- **Hug your dog, cat, rabbit, friend, or mom.** Loneliness breeds stress because then all you've got is yourself and those stressed-out thoughts zooming around in your head.

- **Get with friends.** That takes time, but being with people you like and doing fun things eases stress—as long as you don't overdo it.

- **Exercise.** This does not include running down the hall to make the bell. We're talking 20 minutes of heart-pounding perspiration at least three times a week. It's amazing what a little sweat can do to relax you. Believe it or not, good posture helps too.

- **Don't smoke, drink, or use excessive amounts of caffeine.** Whoever told you that partying is the way to relieve stress got it all wrong. Nicotine and alcohol actually take away the things your body needs to fight stress.

- **Simplify your expenses.** Money can be a big stress factor. Think of ways to eliminate where you're spending money so that the money you have doesn't have to be stretched so far. Be creative. Share resources. Sell items you no longer use. Maybe put off buying something you've been wanting.

- **Let your feelings out of your head.** It takes time and energy to keep them bottled up inside. Have regular conversations with your parents and siblings so that minor annoyances can be solved when they're still small.

- **Organize your time.** As in prioritizing and dealing with one small part of your life instead of trying to solve everything in one shot. Read on for more information about time management. This is just a teaser.

- **Lighten up.** When you've graduated and are into whatever it is you'll end up doing, you'll look back and realize that this was a teensy little part of your life. So look on the bright side. The decisions you'll be making about your future are heavy, but they won't be cut in stone. You can change them if they don't work out.

Stress Busters

Most people get stressed when things are out of control—too many things to do, too many decisions to make, or too much information to digest. If you add not having enough time, enough money, or enough energy to get it all done, you have the perfect recipe for stress.

In the space below, identify what's causing you stress:

_____

_____

_____

_____

_____

Then, choose from these three stress-busting options:

1. **Alter the situation.** Some things you can't control, some things you can. Change the ones you can. If you have too much on your plate and can't possibly do it all, push a few things aside. There's got to be something on the list you can get rid of. (And no, homework is not an acceptable answer.) Maybe you need to be able to say no to extra demands. Concentrate on what is important. Make a list of your priorities from the most important to the least, and work your way down.

2. **Avoid the situation—for now.** Step back and ask, "Is this really a problem? Do I really need to solve it now?" This doesn't mean you should procrastinate on things that need to get done. Think of this stress buster as buying some time, taking a break, catching your breath, getting advice, and airing out the situation so that you can deal with it when you're more prepared to handle it.

3. **Accept the situation.** How you perceive your circumstances has a lot to do with how you make decisions about them. Put whatever is stressing you in the perspective of the big picture. How will this really affect me next year or even ten years from now? Look at your circumstances through the lens of your personal values. Think about what feels right to you, not someone else.

Quick Fixes for Stressful Moments

So, you've done all the things we talked about earlier in this section, and you're still feeling like you're being pulled in a million directions. If your stress thermometer has hit the top, use these quick fixes to help calm you down.

- Make the world slow down for a bit. Take a walk. Take a shower. Listen to some soothing music.

- Breathe deeply. Get in tune with the rhythm of your own breathing. Lie or sit down for 15 minutes and just concentrate on relaxing.

- Relax those little knots of tension. Start at your head and work down to your toes.

- Close your eyes and clear your mind. Oops, there comes that nagging thought. Out, out, out. Get rid of the clutter. Imagine yourself in your favorite place: the beach, under a tree, whatever works.

- Close the door to your bedroom, and let out a blood-curdling scream. Walt Whitman knew what he was talking about when he said, "I sound my barbaric yawp over the roofs of the world." Just let your family know what you're doing so they don't come running to your room in fear. You'll be amazed at how much better you feel.

- When all else fails, watch a funny movie. Read the comics. Get in a giggly frame of mind. Those big challenges will quickly be brought down to size.

WINNING THE TIME MANAGEMENT GAME

What is the value of time? Six dollars an hour? The price of a scholarship because the application is a day late? Time can be a very expensive resource or something you can use to your advantage. Even if you recognize the value of time, managing it is a challenge.

When you live with enough time, life is relaxed and balanced. In order to find that balance, you have to prioritize and plan. Decide what you want and what is important to you. Organize logically and schedule realistically. Overcome obstacles. Change bad habits. Simplify and streamline. Save time when you can.

Sound impossible? It's not easy, but you can do it. The secret is held in a Chinese proverb: The wisdom of life is the elimination of nonessentials.

It's All about Control

The good thing about time is that much of it is yours to do with as you wish. You may feel out of control and as if you must run to keep up with the conflicting demands and expectations of your life. But we all have the same number of hours in each day. The key is in how we spend them. The following tips are designed to help you spend your time wisely and to keep you in control of your life.

Prepare a list of your goals and the tasks necessary to accomplish them. This could be by day, week, month, semester, or even year. You may also want to break the list into sections, such as friends and family, school, work, sports, health and fitness, home, personal development, and college preparation.

Prioritize based on time-sensitive deadlines. Use a grading system to code how important each task is. A is "Do It Now," B is "Do It Soon," C is "Do It Later." Understand the difference between "important" and "urgent."

Be realistic about how much you can really do. Analyze how you spend your time now. What can you cut? How much time do you truly have for each task?

Think ahead. How many times have you underestimated how long it will take to do something? Plan for roadblocks, and give yourself some breathing space.

Accept responsibility. Once you decide to do something, commit yourself to it. That doesn't mean that a task that was on the "A" list can't be moved to the "C" list. But be consistent and specific about what you want to accomplish.

Divide and conquer. You may need to form a committee, delegate tasks to your parents, or ask for help from a friend. That is why it is called time management.

Take advantage of your personal prime time. Don't schedule yourself to get up and do homework at 6 a.m.

if you are a night owl. It won't work. Instead, plan complex tasks when you are most efficient.

Avoid procrastination. There are a million ways to procrastinate. And not one of them is a good reason if you really want to get something done. Have you ever noticed that you always find time to do the things you enjoy?

Do the most unpleasant task first. Get it over with. Then it will be all downhill from there.

Don't over-prepare. That is just another way to procrastinate.

Learn to say no to the demands on your time that you cannot afford.

Be enthusiastic, and share your goals with others.

If you set too many goals at once, you will overwhelm yourself from the start. Remember, what is important is the quality of the time you spend on a task, not the quantity. It doesn't make any difference if you study for 10 hours if you don't recall a thing you've reviewed. The overall goal is to be productive, efficient, and effective, not just busy. You'll also need to pace yourself. All work and no play makes for an unbalanced person.

Use all the benefits of modern technology to help you manage time. You can save lots of time by using a fax, e-mail, or voice mail. If you don't already use a day planner or calendar, you would be wise to invest in one. Write in all the important deadlines, and refer to it often. Block out commitments you know you have so you won't over-schedule yourself. When you do over-schedule yourself or underestimate the time it takes to accomplish a task, learn from your mistakes. But don't get too down on yourself. Give yourself a pep talk every now and then to keep yourself positive and motivated.

MOVING OUT ON YOUR OWN?

As you consider moving away from home either to a college dorm or your own place, some pretty wonderful expectations of what it will be like no doubt will come floating into your head. No more parental rules. On your own. Making your own decisions. Hamburgers forever. Coming and going when you want to. Oops, what's this? Looks like you're out of clothes to wear. No more cereal bowls—they're all in the sink, and they're dirty. Out of milk and the refrigerator's empty. Yikes! What happened to all those warm, fuzzy thoughts about freedom?

Sure, it's nice to be able to come and go as you please, but before you get too far into that pleasant—and unrealistic—mind mode, here are some thoughts you might want to consider as you make plans to become independent. Ozzie Hashley, a guidance counselor at Clinton Community Schools in Clinton, Michigan, works with juniors and seniors in high school. Here is what he says to inform students about the realities of independent life.

1. If you rent your own place, have you thought about the extra charges in addition to the rent? Says Hashley, "Many students think only of paying the rent. They don't realize that they'll be responsible for utilities in many cases. Or the money it will take to wash and dry your clothes."

2. Subsisting on hamburgers and fries sounds yummy, but as you watch a fast food diet eat its way into your paycheck, you'll most likely think about cooking up something yourself. What will you cook? Who will buy the food? More importantly, who will do the dishes? Dividing up the responsibilities of preparing food is a big aspect of being on your own, especially when sharing a living space.

3. Medical insurance may not be on your mind as you prepare to graduate—you're probably on your parent's insurance plans right now. However, once you are established as an independent person at age 18 and you're living on your own, insurance becomes a big consideration. If you need health care and don't have medical insurance, the bills will be big. So when

you get a job, make sure that you have medical coverage. If you're going off to college after high school, you'll most likely be covered under your parent's insurance until age 23.

4. There's no one to tell you when to come home when you're on your own. There's also no one to tell you that you're really disorganized when it comes to managing your time. Time management might not sound like a big deal now, but when you have to juggle all the facets of being independent— your job, taking care of your living space and car, your social life—then being able to manage time becomes an important part of life.

5. Managing your money moves into a whole other realm when you are on your own. You have to make sure you have enough to pay the rent, your car loan, and insurance, not to mention that movie you wanted to see, the CD you wanted to buy, or those funky jeans you saw at the mall last week. If you want to eat at the end of the month, budgeting will become an important part of your new independent vocabulary. Ask your parents or an adult you trust to help you set up your budget. Also learn how to balance your checkbook. It's a lot easier to manage your money when you keep track of how much you have in your bank account and how much you spend!

DRUGS AND ALCOHOL: ARE YOU AT RISK?

At risk? Wait a minute. How could you be at risk when the legal drinking age in all fifty states is 21? Chances are, if you're reading this, you're not 21 yet. It's also illegal to smoke or buy any tobacco product before age 18, and possession of any drug for recreational use is illegal, period. So if you drink alcohol before age 21; smoke or buy cigarettes, cigars,

or chewing tobacco before age 18; or take any illegal drugs, you could:

- Be arrested for driving under the influence (DUI)
- Be convicted
- Be required to pay steep fines
- Have your driving privileges suspended
- Get kicked out of school (that's any kind of school, college included)
- Get fired
- Go to jail
- Have a criminal record

A criminal record . . . so what?

Consider this true story. A 29-year-old man who recently received his graduate degree in business was offered a job with a major Fortune-100 corporation. We're talking big bucks, stock options, reserved parking space—the whole nine yards. When the company did a background check and found that he was arrested for a DUI during his freshman year of college, they rescinded their offer. The past can and will come back to haunt you. Let's not even think about what would happen down the line if you decide to run for public office.

Think about why you might want to try drinking or doing drugs. For fun? To forget your troubles? To be cool? Are your reasons good enough? Remember the consequences before you make a decision.

How Can I Say No without Looking like a Geek?

"It takes a lot more guts to stay sober, awake, and aware than to just get high, get numb, and learn nothing about life," says one former user. "Laugh at people who suggest you drink or take drugs, and then avoid them like the plague."

Friends worth having will respect your decision to say no. And girls—if a guy pressures you to drink or get high, ditch him pronto. You can vice-versa that for guys, too. According to the National Institute on Drug Abuse (NIDA), alcohol and club drugs like GHB or Rohypnol (roofies) make you an easy target for date rape.

The Nitty Gritty

Along with the temporary pleasure they may give you, all drugs (including club drugs, alcohol, and nicotine) have a downside. Alcohol, for example, is a depressant. Even one drink slows down the part of your brain that controls your reasoning. So your judgment gets dull just when you're wondering, "Should I drive my friends home? Should I talk to this guy? Should I have another drink?"

Your body needs about an hour to burn up the alcohol in one drink. Nothing, including coffee, will sober you up any faster. Here's what "one drink" means: one shot of hard liquor (straight or mixed in a cocktail), one glass of wine, one 12-ounce beer, or one wine cooler.

Alcohol helps smart people make bad decisions. In fact, many drugs make you believe that you're thinking even more clearly than usual. Well, guess what? You aren't. Depending on what drug you take, how much, and what you do while you're on it, you're also risking confusion, nausea, headache, sleep problems, depression, paranoia, rape (especially "date rape"), unwanted pregnancy, sexually transmitted diseases (STDs) ranging from herpes to HIV/AIDS, having a baby with a birth defect, memory impairment, persistent psychosis, lung damage, cancer, injuring or killing someone else, and death.

Take a moment now, when your brain is razor sharp, to decide if those consequences are worth the

DID YOU KNOW...

... that nicotine is as addictive as cocaine and heroin, according to the American Cancer Society?

... that drinking a lot of alcohol fast can kill you on the spot, according to Keystone College?

... that MDMA (Ecstasy, X, Adam, Clarity, Lover's Speed), according to NIDA, may permanently damage your memory?

DO I HAVE A PROBLEM?

Take the quiz below to see if you're in real trouble with drugs or alcohol.

1. **Do you look forward to drinking or using drugs?**

2. **Do most of your friends drink or do drugs?**

3. **Do you keep a secret supply of alcohol or drugs?**

4. **Can you drink a lot without appearing drunk?**

5. **Do you "power-hit" to get high faster, by binge-drinking, funneling, or slamming?**

6. **Do you ever drink or do drugs alone, including in a group where no one else is doing so?**

7. **Do you ever drink or use drugs when you hadn't planned to?**

8. **Do you ever have blackouts where you can't remember things that happened when you were drunk or high?**

If you answered yes to any of these questions, you probably need help. If you have a friend who fits the picture, find a respectful way to bring up your concerns. Don't be surprised if he or she tells you to back off—but don't give up, either. If someone in your family has an alcohol or drug problem, be aware that you may be prone to the same tendency.

Source: Keystone College, La Plume, Pennsylvania

---

escape you get for 20 minutes one night. You may be saying, "Oh, come on. Only addicts have problems like that." Getting drunk or high doesn't necessarily mean that you're an alcoholic or an addict—but it always means a loss of control.

"So much of addiction is about denial," says one member of Alcoholics Anonymous. "I just didn't think I looked or acted or thought or smelled or lied or cheated or failed like an alcoholic or addict. It was when the drugs and alcohol use started to cause problems in multiple areas of my life that I began to think the problem might reside with me. Friends leaving—in disgust—was what opened my eyes."

Where Can I Get Help?

If you think you have a problem, or if you think a friend has a problem, try Alcoholics Anonymous or Narcotics Anonymous. If you're not sure, ask yourself the questions in "Do I Have a Problem?" on the top of this page.

Talk to any adult you trust: maybe your doctor, a clergy member, a counselor, or your parents. Health clinics and hospitals offer information and treatment. The American Cancer Society can help you quit smoking. These are only a few places to turn—check out the Yellow Pages and the Web for more.

Alcoholics Anonymous
212-870-3400
www.aa.org

American Cancer Society
800-ACS-2345
www.cancer.org

Narcotics Anonymous
818-773-9999
www.na.org

So, that's the straight stuff. You're at a tough but wonderful age, when your life is finally your own and your decisions really matter. Think about what you value most—and then make your choices.

CONFLICT: HOW TO AVOID IT AND DEFUSE IT

You're walking along and you see a group of kids up ahead . . . and suddenly you're afraid. Or you're about to talk to someone you have a disagreement with, and already you're tense. Or your boyfriend's jealousy is spooking you. What should you do?

All of these situations involve potential conflicts that could get out of hand. Even if you never get into a violent situation, you'll face conflicts with others, as we all do. Learning to spot the warning signs of violence and to handle conflicts well will bring you lifelong benefits.

What's Your Style?

What do you do when you're faced with a potential conflict? Do you try to get away, no matter what? Do you find yourself bowing to pressure from others? Do you feel like you have to stand and fight, even if you don't want to? Do you wish you had some new ways to handle conflict?

Different situations call for different strategies. First, let's talk about situations where violence is a real possibility. Most of us get a bad feeling before things get violent, but too often, we ignore the feeling. Trust your gut feeling! And whether you're on the street or in school, Fred Barfoot of the Crime Prevention Association of Philadelphia suggests that you keep in mind these tips for avoiding violence:

- Walk like you're in charge and you know where you're going.

- Stick to lighted areas.

- Travel with a trusted friend when possible. On campus, get an escort from security at night. Loners are targets.

- If a person or group up ahead makes you nervous, cross the street immediately—and calmly—as if you'd intended to anyway.

- Call out to an imaginary friend, "Hey, Joe! Wait up!" and then run toward your "friend," away from whoever is scaring you.

- Go right up to the nearest house and ring the bell. Pretend you're expected: "Hey Joe, it's me!" You can explain later.

- If someone threatens you physically, scream.

- If someone assaults you, scream, kick where it hurts, scratch—anything.

- Don't ever get in a car with someone you don't know well or trust, even if you've seen that person around a lot.

- Strike up a conversation with an innocent bystander if you feel threatened by someone else, just to make yourself less vulnerable for a few minutes.

- Wear a whistle around your neck or carry a personal alarm or pepper spray.

- If someone mugs you, hand over your purse, wallet, jewelry—whatever he or she asks for. None of it is worth your life.

- Don't go along with something your gut says is wrong, no matter who says it's okay.

Remember that it's not a sign of weakness to back down if someone's egging you on to fight. Bill Tomasco, principal of Furness High School in Philadelphia, says that pressure from other kids to fight creates much of the violence in schools. If you're being pushed to fight, show true strength: Know that your opponent has a good side too, speak only to that good side, and don't give in to the pressure of the crowd.

Are You Safe at Home?

Locking doors and windows makes sense—but sometimes the danger lies within. A lot of violence occurs in abusive relationships, says Amy Gottlieb, a marriage family therapist intern at the California Family Counseling Center in Encino. To find out if you're at risk, ask yourself whether your partner, roommate, or family member:

- Uses jealousy to justify controlling you

- Puts you down, humiliates you, or pulls guilt trips on you

- Threatens to reveal your secrets or tells lies about you

- Makes all the decisions

- Frightens you, especially if it's on purpose

- Threatens you in any way

- Makes light of abusive behavior or says you provoked it

If any of these things are going on in your relationship, talk about it to an adult you trust, and ask for help.

Talking It Out

If your instincts tell you to get away from a situation, do it. But you can resolve many actual or potential conflicts face to face and gracefully so that everyone walks away feeling good. Read on for some tips on handling conflict from Kare Anderson, a communications expert in Sausalito, California.

Most of us make the mistake of reacting quickly, thinking only of our own needs, and not listening, says Anderson. Try doing the opposite. First and foremost, think about what you really want from the situation, and keep your goal in mind the whole time. But bring up the other person's concerns first. Then, discuss how the situation affects you both. Offer a solution that will benefit you both—and only then talk about how your solution addresses your own needs.

When the other person is talking, really listen—don't just come up with retorts in your head. Always show that you've heard the person before you give your response, especially if you're talking with someone of a different sex, size, or race. Those differences can distract us so much that we actually hear less. If you're female, you may need to s-l-o-w yourself down. Say less than you think you need to. Guys, don't shut down altogether—keep the communication going.

Even if the other person acts like a jerk, be gracious and respectful. Ask questions instead of criticizing. Let someone save face instead of looking like a fool. If you insult or embarrass someone, you may never have that person's full attention again. In short, treat the other person as you'd like to be treated.

What should you do if you're really angry? One teen said, "Thinking about things calms me down." Another said, "Once in a while, we have to cool off for a day and then come back to the discussion." Anger almost always covers up fear. What are you afraid of? Is the reward you want out of this negotiation bigger than your fear? Focus on that reward. Don't forget to breathe—long, slow breaths.

Think about these strategies often, so you'll be more likely to use them when a situation gets hot, instead of just reacting blindly. Use them to plan for negotiations ahead of time, too. Learning to resolve problems with people takes most of us a lifetime—get a jump on it now!

THE LOWDOWN ON SEXUAL HARASSMENT

Has someone ever looked at you, talked to you, or touched you in a way that gave you the creeps, made you self-conscious about your body, or created a sexual mood when it wasn't appropriate? And did you begin to dread seeing this person because he or she just wouldn't quit?

If so, you've encountered sexual harassment. Sexual harassment is inappropriate behavior that

- is happening to you because of your sex
- is unwanted (you don't like it)
- is objectively offensive (to a hypothetical "reasonable" man or woman)
- is either severe, persistent, or pervasive
- interferes with your work or school experience

Paul Edison, a domestic and sexual violence prevention educator in Portland, Oregon, says that mostly—just as with crimes like rape—men harass women. But teenage girls are a bit more likely than older women to sexually harass someone, more girl-on-girl harassment goes on with teens, and guys get harassed, too. In some of the most brutal cases coming to light now, gay men (or men perceived to be gay) are the targets.

People who sexually harass others fall into three camps, says Edison. Some just seem to be misguided and insensitive. Others get turned on by harassing someone. And a third group does it to intimidate—for example, to drive someone away from a job or just to make them feel bad about themselves.

So What Do I Do if Someone's Harassing Me?

Experts in self-defense say the best technique is to name the behavior that's bugging you and request that it stop. You might say, "Your hand is on my knee. Please remove it." If the person doesn't quit, you might try writing a letter spelling out what's bothering you and requesting that the person stop—this way, you've confronted the situation directly and you also have a record of your complaint.

But here's the good news, says Edison: You are not expected to handle harassment on your own, especially if the person harassing you is in a position of authority over you, such as a teacher, sergeant, or boss. The authorities at your school or your job should handle it—but they can't do that unless you tell them what's going on.

If you file a complaint, be prepared to describe what happened, when, and where. And make sure you report your concerns to someone who has clear authority to handle sexual harassment complaints, such as the principal or the personnel director.

Often, the person harassing you will stop as soon as he or she gets the clear message that the behavior isn't okay with you, especially if your complaint goes to someone higher up as well. Edison notes that most harassment cases don't end up involving lawyers and lawsuits. You may choose, in serious cases, to register your complaint with the Office of Civil Rights (if you're being harassed at school) or the Equal Employment Opportunity Commission (if you're being harassed at work). You can also file your complaint on different levels at the same time: for example, with your school and the police.

You have the legal right to a school and workplace free from discrimination based on your race, color, religion, sex, national origin, and—depending on where you live, as state and local laws vary—your sexual orientation. You have the right to protection from retaliation if you file a complaint of harassment. So don't be afraid to report a situation if it truly offends you and interferes with your life.

What if I'm Just Being Hypersensitive?

If someone's words or actions make you uncomfortable, that's all the reason you need to ask that person to stop the behavior, no matter how innocent the behavior may be. Trust your feelings—especially if you find you're trying to convince yourself that nothing is wrong.

What Will Happen to the Person Who Has Been Harassing Me?

If your complaint is successfully handled, says Edison, the main thing that will happen is that the person will stop harassing you. People aren't "charged" with sexual harassment unless their behavior includes criminal conduct. But your harasser may face disciplinary action, loss of privileges, suspension, expulsion, lawsuits, or criminal action, depending on the severity of his or her behavior.

How Can I Avoid Harassing Someone?

Sometimes the line between harmless flirting, joking, or complimenting and harassment is pretty thin. How can you stay on the right side of that line?

First, pay attention to your own motives. Be honest with yourself. Do you enjoy watching someone get uncomfortable when you say or do certain things? Do you feel angry with the person for some reason? Do you enjoy exercising your authority over this person in some way? Do you find yourself obsessing about the person? If any of these are true, whatever you're saying or doing probably isn't harmless.

Even if your motives seem harmless to you, be extraordinarily careful about whom and how you touch. You may be comfortable touching people casually—perhaps you'll touch someone's hand or shoulder in conversation—but remember that other people's boundaries may differ from yours.

Pay attention to the person's reactions to you. Are you getting clear green signals when you do or say things around this person, or does the person seem to shrink away from you? Does the person shut down or seem upset when you do or say certain things? Of course, if someone's told you clearly that she or he doesn't like it when you do or say certain things, apologize and stop at once. And remember, no means no.

So, if you're faced with something that feels like sexual harassment, remember to trust your feelings, convey them clearly, and get help promptly if you need it.

STAYING HEALTHY IN SPITE OF YOURSELF

When someone—like your mom—asks if you're eating right, do you ever want to say, "Hey, have you looked at my life lately? Do you see a lot of time there for eating right?" Well, how about exercise—are you getting enough? "Yeah, right. I bench-press my backpack when I'm not doing wind sprints to my next class," may be how you reply.

If you're feeling like you can't escape your stress and fatigue, you might be surprised by how much better you'll feel if you keep active and don't just eat junk. Your workload will seem easier. You'll sleep better. You'll look fantastic. And you can stay healthy—even if your time and money are in short supply.

But Really, Who Has Time to Exercise?

As one teen says, "Schoolwork gets in the way, and then I want to relax when I have a moment that isn't filled with schoolwork." You can make time for anything, if you choose to. But if you aren't athletic by nature or your school or work keeps you going nonstop, exercise is the first thing to go out the window.

However, you don't have to become a gym rat or run miles to get enough exercise. Longer workouts are great if you do them consistently, but you're better off getting little bits of regular exercise than just doing a huge workout every so often or never doing anything. And by "little bits," we mean 15- to 20-minute chunks. Add that to a fast walk to the bus, a frenzied private dance session in your room, or running up the stairs instead of taking the elevator, and you're exercising!

Regardless of how you choose to pump that muscle in the middle of your chest, the important thing is that you're doing something. You'll not only feel better about yourself, but you'll have increased energy to do other things, like study, go to work, or go out with friends.

What Does "Eating Right" Mean Anyway?

Eating right means eating a balance of good foods in moderate amounts. Your diet needn't be complicated or expensive. Dr. Michele Wilson, a specialist in adolescent medicine at the Children's Hospital of Philadelphia, notes that a teen's diet should be heavy in grains—especially whole grains—and light in sugars and fats. It should include a lot of fruits and vegetables and provide you with plenty of protein, calcium, vitamin A, B vitamins, iron, and zinc. Sound complicated?

Well, what's complicated about a bean burrito with cheese? How about pasta with vegetables, meat, or both in the sauce? A banana or some cantaloupe? Stir-fried vegetables with tofu? Carrot sticks with peanut butter? Yogurt? Cereal with milk and fruit? All of these are cheap, quick to make, and great for you.

One teen swears by microwaveable veggie burgers and adds, "Staying away from deep-fried anything is a good plan." Try to avoid things like chips and sweets, says Dr. Wilson, adding that if you're a vegetarian—and especially if you don't eat dairy products or fish—you should make sure you're getting enough protein and iron. And no matter what your diet, drink water—eight glasses a day.

As Long as I'm in Control of What I Eat, I'm Okay, Right?

That depends. Of course, having no control over what you eat is a problem. But "in control" can be good or bad. How severely do you control what and how you eat? Are you obsessed with getting thinner? Do people who love you tell you that you're too thin, and do you take that as a compliment? Do you ever binge secretly or make yourself throw up after a meal? If any of these are true, you may be suffering from anorexia or bulimia.

According to the National Association of Anorexia Nervosa and Associated Disorders (ANAD), eating disorders affect about 7 million women and 1 million men in this country and can lead to serious health problems—even death. "The thing that convinced me to get help was fear—I had to be hospitalized, as I was literally dying from my anorexia," says one woman. Most Americans who are anorexic or bulimic developed their eating disorders in their teens.

We asked some women being treated for eating disorders what they used to see when they looked in the mirror. "Total ugliness," said one. "The smallest dimple in my flesh looked immense," said another. And a third said, "I got rid of the mirrors because they would set me off to where I wouldn't eat for days." Their advice to teens struggling with an eating disorder? "Treat yourself as you wish your parents had treated you," "Ask people you feel close to not to discuss your weight with you," and "Find ways outside of yourself to feel in control." Above all—get help! That means going to someone you trust, whether it be a parent, relative, sibling, friend, doctor, or teacher. Or call ANAD's national hotline at 847-831-3438 for a listing of support groups and referrals in your area.

So if I Eat Right and Exercise, I'm Healthy?

Well, probably. But Dr. Wilson suggests that you keep a few other things in mind too. If you smoke, drink, or do drugs, you're asking for trouble. Aside from their many scarier side effects, all these habits can steal nutrients that you need. If all this sounds like the recipe for a dull and totally uncool life, remember that feeling and looking great are never boring and that vomiting (or dying) after downing the most tequilas in the fastest time looks really uncool. If you're making short-term decisions that will hurt you in the long run, take some time to figure out why. Good health is priceless—just ask any grandparent.

APPENDICIES

NOW THAT YOU HAVE DECIDED what types of opportunities you wish to pursue after graduation, you need a jumping-off point for getting more information. The appendices that follow will provide you with additional data to help you with your decision-making process.

NOTE: Because of Peterson's comprehensive editorial review and because all material comes directly from institution or organization officials, we believe that the information presented in these appendices is accurate. Nonetheless, errors and omissions are possible in a data collection and processing endeavor of this scope. You should check with the specific institution or organization at the time of application to verify pertinent data that may have changed since the publication of this book.

WESTERN REGION

AK
Fairbanks •
★ Anchorage
• Juneau
• Seward

WA
• Seattle
Spokane •
• Tacoma
Olympia
• Yakima
Walla Walla •
Vancouver
• Pendleton
Portland •
★ Salem

MT
• Havre
• Great Falls
Sidney •
MT
• Missoula
★ Helena
• Butte
Billings •

OR
• Eugene
ID
Ontario •
★ Boise
Idaho Falls •
Pocatello •
• Twin Falls
• Medford

WY
• Sheridan
• Casper
• Rock Springs
★ Cheyenne

NV
• Eureka
CA
• Eureka
Reno •
★ Carson City
Sacramento
★
Santa Rosa •
Berkley •
San Francisco • Oakland
• San Jose
Santa Cruz •
• Fresno

Brigham City •
Ogden •
Salt Lake City ★
• Provo
UT
• Cedar City

CO
Boulder •
★ Denver
• Grand
Junction
Colorado Springs •
• Pueblo
• Durango

Glendale
Las Vegas •
Boulder •
City
• Bakersfield
Santa Barbara •
• Glendale
• Los Angeles

AZ
• Flagstaff
Prescott •
★ Phoenix
San Diego •
Yuma •
• Tucson

Farmington •
• Taos
★ Santa Fe
• Albuquerque
NM
Clovis •
• Silver City
• Alamogordo
• Las Cruces

Kauai
Oahu
Honolulu ★
HI
Molokai
Maui

Hawaii

HIGH SCHOOL DIPLOMA TEST REQUIREMENTS

Alaska

All Alaska high school students must pass an examination in reading, writing, and mathematics before they receive a high school diploma. Students must pass the Alaska High School Graduation Qualifying Examination in addition to completing all course requirements to earn a high school diploma. Beginning with the graduating class of 2004, all students must pass the exam. The examination will be administered to tenth grade students in all subjects. For more information, visit the Alaska Department of Education Web site at www.eed.state.ak.us or call 907-465-8691.

Arizona

Effective for the graduation classes of 2002 and 2003, students must pass the minimum course of study and competency requirements and receive a passing score on the reading and writing portion of the Arizona's Instrument to Measure Standards (AIMS) assessment for the graduation of pupils from high school or to receive of a high school diploma, and receipt of a passing score on the reading, writing, and mathematics portions of AIMS for the graduation class of 2004. For more information, visit the Arizona Department of Education Web site at www.ade.state.az.us or call 602-542-5031.

California

Beginning for grade 10 in the 2001–2002 school year and continuing on through each subsequent administration or until the examination has been passed, California high school students are required to take the California High School Exit Exam (CAHSEE). Beginning in 2002, the option for ninth graders to take the exam was removed. The exam has two parts: English-language arts and mathematics. Students must pass both portions of the CAHSEE to receive their high school diploma, beginning in the 2003–2004 school year. Students must also meet the district's requirements for graduation. For more information, visit the California Department of Education Web site at www.cde.ca.gov/statetests/cahsee/background/info or call the California Department of Education Standards and Assessment Division at 916-657-3011.

Colorado

Colorado currently does not require high school students to pass a proficiency test in order to receive a high school diploma.

Hawaii

Hawaii currently does not require high school students to pass a proficiency test in order to receive a high school diploma.

Idaho

Idaho currently does not require high school students to pass a proficiency test in order to receive a high school diploma.

Montana

Montana currently does not require high school students to pass a proficiency test in order to receive a high school diploma.

Nevada

High school students must pass the Nevada High School Proficiency Exams in mathematics, reading, and writing. Students who enter grade 10 during the 2002–2003 school year must also pass a proficiency examination in science. These exams were developed as exit content standards of what students should know and be able to do upon graduation from Nevada public schools. High school grade level content tests are given in grades 10, 11, and 12. For more information about the exit exam, visit the Nevada Department of Education Web site at www.nde.state.nv.us or call 775-687-9186.

New Mexico

A High School Competency Exam is given in language arts, math, reading, science, writing, and social studies. It is administered in the tenth grade in all subjects. Results are released to the public. They are in the process of developing a new test at the high school level that is based on state standards. For more information, visit the New Mexico Department of Education Web site at http://sde.state.nm.us or call 505-827-6524.

Oregon

Oregon currently does not require high school students to pass a proficiency test in order to receive a high school diploma.

Utah

There is no high school exit exam given at this time; however, starting in the class of 2004, a tenth-grade Competency Exam will be given in the spring in the following subjects: English language arts, reading, and math. For more information, visit the Utah Department of Education Web site at www.state.ut.us/education/k-12.html or call 801-538-7810.

Washington

There is no test required for high school graduation at this time; however, beginning with the tenth grade in 2001, the Washington Assessment of Student Learning—Tenth Grade (WAST-10) was implemented and given in the following subjects: reading, writing, communications, math, and science. For more information, visit the Washington Department of Education Web site at www.k12.wa.us/assessment/.

Wyoming

Wyoming currently does not require high school students to pass a proficiency test in order to receive a high school diploma. Beginning with the 2006 graduating class, students must demonstrate proficiency in five of nine content areas in order to receive a high school diploma.

4-YEAR COLLEGES AND UNIVERSITIES

Alaska

Alaska Bible College
Box 289
Glennallen, AK 99588-0289
907-822-3201
www.akbible.edu

Alaska Pacific University
4101 University Drive
Anchorage, AK 99508-4672
907-561-1266
www.alaskapacific.edu

Sheldon Jackson College
801 Lincoln Street
Sitka, AK 99835-7699
907-747-5222
www.sj-alaska.edu

University of Alaska
Anchorage
3211 Providence Drive
Anchorage, AK 99508-8060
907-786-1800
www.uaa.alaska.edu

University of Alaska
Fairbanks
PO Box 757480
Fairbanks, AK 99775-7480
907-474-7211
www.uaf.edu

University of Alaska
Southeast
11120 Glacier Highway
Juneau, AK 99801
907-465-6457
www.jun.alaska.edu

Arizona

American Indian College of
the Assemblies of God, Inc.
10020 North Fifteenth Ave
Phoenix, AZ 85021-2199
602-944-3335

Arizona State University
Tempe, AZ 85287
480-965-9011
www.asu.edu

Arizona State University East
7001 East Williams Field Rd.
Mesa, AZ 85212
480-727-3278
www.east.asu.edu

Arizona State University West
PO Box 37100, 4701 W
Thunderbird Rd
Phoenix, AZ 85069-7100
602-543-5500
www.west.asu.edu

The Art Institute of Phoenix
2233 West Dunlap Avenue
Phoenix, AZ 85021-2859
602-678-4300
www.aipx.edu

Collins College: A School of
Design and Technology
1140 South Priest Drive
Tempe, AZ 85281-5206
480-966-3000
www.collinscollege.edu

DeVry Institute of Technology
2149 West Dunlap Avenue
Phoenix, AZ 85021-2995
602-870-9222
www.devry-phx.edu

Education America, Tempe
Campus
875 West Elliot Road,
Suite 216
Tempe, AZ 85284
480-834-1000
educationamerica.com

Embry-Riddle Aeronautical
University
3200 Willow Creek Road
Prescott, AZ 86301-3720
928-708-3728
www.embryriddle.edu

Grand Canyon University
3300 W Camelback Road,
PO Box 11097
Phoenix, AZ 85061-1097
602-249-3300
www.grand-canyon.edu

International Baptist College
2150 East Southern Avenue
Tempe, AZ 85282
480-838-7070

Mesa State College
1100 North Avenue
Grand Junction, CO 81501
970-248-1020
www.mesastate.edu

Metropolitan College of
Court Reporting
4640 East Elwood Street,
Suite 12
Phoenix, AZ 85040
602-955-5900
www.metropolitancollege.edu

Northcentral University
600 East Gurley Street #E
Prescott, AZ 86301
520-541-7777
www.ncu.edu

Northern Arizona University
Box 4132
Flagstaff, AZ 86011
520-523-9011
www.nau.edu

Prescott College
220 Grove Avenue
Prescott, AZ 86301-2990
520-778-2090
www.prescott.edu

Southwestern College
2625 East Cactus Road
Phoenix, AZ 85032-7042
602-992-6101
www.southwesterncollege.edu

University of Advancing
Computer Technology
2625 West Baseline Road
Tempe, AZ 85283-1042
602-383-8228
www.uact.edu

The University of Arizona
Tucson, AZ 85721
520-621-2211
www.arizona.edu

University of
Phoenix–Phoenix Campus
4635 East Elwood Street
Phoenix, AZ 85040-1958
480-557-2000
www.phoenix.edu

University of
Phoenix–Southern Arizona
Campus
5099 East Grant Road
Tucson, AZ 85712
520-881-6512
www.phoenix.edu

Western International
University
9215 North Black Canyon
Highway
Phoenix, AZ 85021-2718
602-943-2311
www.wintu.edu

California

Academy of Art College
79 New Montgomery Street
San Francisco, CA 94105-
3410
415-274-2200
www.academyart.edu

Alliant International
University
10455 Pomerado Road
San Diego, CA 92131-1799
858-271-4300
www.usiu.edu

American InterContinental
University
12655 West Jefferson Blvd
Los Angeles, CA 90066
310-302-2000
www.aiuniv.edu

Antioch University Los
Angeles
13274 Fiji Way
Marina del Rey, CA
90292-7090
310-578-1080
www.antiochla.edu

Antioch University Santa
Barbara
801 Garden Street
Santa Barbara, CA 93101-1581
805-962-8179
www.antiochsb.edu

Argosy University-Los Angeles
3745 Chapman Avenue,
Suite 100
Orange, CA 92868
714-940-0025
www.sarasota.edu

Armstrong University
1608 Webster Street
Oakland, CA 94612
510-835-7900
www.armstrong-u.edu

Art Center College of Design
1700 Lida Street
Pasadena, CA 91103-1999
626-396-2200
www.artcenter.edu

The Art Institute of California
10025 Mesa Rim Road
San Diego, CA 92121
858-546-0602
www.aica.artinstitutes.edu

Art Institute of Southern
California
2222 Laguna Canyon Road
Laguna Beach, CA
92651-1136
949-376-6000
www.aisc.edu

Art Institutes International at
San Francisco
1170 Market Street
San Francisco, CA
94102-4908
415-865-0198
www.aisf.artinstitutes.edu

Azusa Pacific University
901 East Alosta Avenue,
PO Box 7000
Azusa, CA 91702-7000
626-815-6000
www.apu.edu

Bethany College of the
Assemblies of God
800 Bethany Drive
Scotts Valley, CA 95066-2820
831-438-3800
www.bethany.edu

Bethesda Christian University
730 North Euclid Street
Anaheim, CA 92801
714-517-1945
www.bcu.edu

Biola University
13800 Biola Avenue
La Mirada, CA 90639-0001
562-903-6000
www.biola.edu

Brooks Institute of
Photography
801 Alston Road
Santa Barbara, CA
93108-2399
805-966-3888
www.brooks.edu

California Baptist University
8432 Magnolia Avenue
Riverside, CA 92504-3206
909-689-5771
www.calbaptist.edu

California Christian College
4881 East University Avenue
Fresno, CA 93703-3533
559-251-4215
www.calchristiancollege.org

California College for Health
Sciences
2423 Hoover Avenue
National City, CA 91950-6605
619-477-4800
www.cchs.edu

California College of Arts and
Crafts
1111 Eighth Street
San Francisco, CA 94107
415-703-9500
www.ccac-art.edu

California Institute of Integral
Studies
1453 Mission Street
San Francisco, CA 94103
415-575-6100
www.ciis.edu

California Institute of
Technology
1200 East California
Boulevard
Pasadena, CA 91125-0001
626-395-6811
www.caltech.edu

California Institute of the Arts
24700 McBean Parkway
Valencia, CA 91355-2340
661-255-1050
www.calarts.edu

California Lutheran
University
60 West Olsen Road
Thousand Oaks, CA
91360-2787
805-492-2411
www.clunet.edu

California Maritime Academy
PO Box 1392, 200 Maritime
Academy Drive
Vallejo, CA 94590-0644
707-654-1000
www.csum.edu

California National University
for Advanced Studies
16909 Parthenia Street
North Hills, CA 91343
818-830-2411
www.cnuas.edu

California Polytechnic State
University, San Luis Obispo
San Luis Obispo, CA 93407
805-756-1111
www.calpoly.edu

California State Polytechnic
University, Pomona
3801 West Temple Avenue
Pomona, CA 91768-2557
909-869-7659
www.csupomona.edu

California State University
San Marcos
San Marcos, CA 92096-0001
760-750-4000
ww2.csusm.edu

California State University,
Bakersfield
9001 Stockdale Highway
Bakersfield, CA 93311-1099
661-664-2011
www.csubak.edu

California State University,
Chico
400 West First Street
Chico, CA 95929-0722
530-898-6116
www.csuchico.edu

California State University,
Dominguez Hills
1000 East Victoria Street
Carson, CA 90747-0001
310-243-3300
www.csudh.edu

California State University,
Fresno
5241 North Maple Avenue
Fresno, CA 93740-8027
559-278-4240
www.csufresno.edu

California State University,
Fullerton
PO Box 34080
Fullerton, CA 92834-9480
714-278-2011
www.fullerton.edu

California State University,
Hayward
25800 Carlos Bee Boulevard
Hayward, CA 94542-3000
510-885-3000
www.csuhayward.edu

California State University,
Long Beach
1250 Bellflower Boulevard
Long Beach, CA 90840
562-985-4111
www.csulb.edu

California State University,
Los Angeles
5151 State University Drive
Los Angeles, CA 90032-8530
323-343-3000
www.calstatela.edu

California State University,
Monterey Bay
100 Campus Center
Seaside, CA 93955-8001
831-582-3000
www.monterey.edu

California State University,
Northridge
18111 Nordhoff Street
Northridge, CA 91330
818-677-1200
www.csun.edu

California State University,
Sacramento
6000 J Street
Sacramento, CA 95819-6048
916-278-6011
www.csus.edu

California State University,
San Bernardino
5500 University Parkway
San Bernardino, CA
92407-2397
909-880-5000
www.csusb.edu

California State University,
Stanislaus
801 West Monte Vista Avenue
Turlock, CA 95382
209-667-3122
www.csustan.edu

Chapman University
One University Drive
Orange, CA 92866
714-997-6815
www.chapman.edu

Charles R. Drew University of
Medicine and Science
1731 East 120th Street
Los Angeles, CA 90059
323-563-4800
www.cdrewu.edu

Christian Heritage College
2100 Greenfield Drive
El Cajon, CA 92019-1157
619-441-2200
www.christianheritage.edu

Claremont McKenna College
500 East 9th Street
Claremont, CA 91711
909-621-8000
www.claremontmckenna.edu

Cleveland Chiropractic
College-Los Angeles Campus
590 North Vermont Avenue
Los Angeles, CA 90004-2196
323-660-6166
www.clevelandchiropractic.edu

Cogswell Polytechnical
College
1175 Bordeaux Drive
Sunnyvale, CA 94089-1299
408-541-0100
www.cogswell.edu

Coleman College
7380 Parkway Drive
La Mesa, CA 91942-1532
619-465-3990
www.coleman.edu

Columbia
College–Hollywood
18618 Oxnard Street
Tarzana, CA 91356
818-345-8414
www.columbiacollege.edu

Concordia University
1530 Concordia West
Irvine, CA 92612-3299
949-854-8002
www.cui.edu

Design Institute of San Diego
8555 Commerce Avenue
San Diego, CA 92121-2685
858-566-1200

DeVry Institute of Technology
22801 West Roscoe Blvd
West Hills, CA 91304
801-713-8111
www.wh.devry.edu

DeVry Institute of Technology
6600 Dumbarton Circle
Fremont, CA 94555
510-574-1100
www.fre.devry.edu

DeVry Institute of Technology
3880 Kilroy Airport Way
Long Beach, CA 90806
562-427-0861
www.lb.devry.edu

DeVry Institute of Technology
901 Corporate Center Drive
Pomona, CA 91768-2642
909-622-8866
www.pom.devry.edu

Dominican School of
Philosophy and Theology
2401 Ridge Road
Berkeley, CA 94709-1295
510-849-2030
www.dspt.edu

Dominican University of
California
50 Acacia Avenue
San Rafael, CA 94901-2298
415-457-4440
www.dominican.edu

Education America
University
123 Camino de la Reina,
North Building, Suite 100
San Diego, CA 92108
619-686-8600

Emmanuel Bible College
1605 East Elizabeth Street
Pasadena, CA 91104
626-791-2575
www.emmanuelbiblecollege.
edu

Fresno Pacific University
1717 South Chestnut Avenue
Fresno, CA 93702-4709
559-453-2000
www.fresno.edu

Golden Gate University
536 Mission Street
San Francisco, CA
94105-2968
415-442-7000
www.ggu.edu

Harvey Mudd College
301 East 12th Street
Claremont, CA 91711-5994
909-621-8000
www.hmc.edu

Holy Names College
3500 Mountain Boulevard
Oakland, CA 94619-1699
510-436-1000
www.hnc.edu

Hope International University
2500 East Nutwood Avenue
Fullerton, CA 92831-3138
714-879-3903
www.hiu.edu

Humboldt State University
1 Harpst Street
Arcata, CA 95521-8299
707-826-3011
www.humboldt.edu

Humphreys College
6650 Inglewood Avenue
Stockton, CA 95207-3896
209-478-0800
www.humphreys.edu

Institute of Computer
Technology
3200 Wilshire Boulevard,
400
Los Angeles, CA 90010-1308
213-381-3333
www.ictcollege.edu

Interior Designers Institute
1061 Camelback Road
Newport Beach, CA 92660
949-675-4451
www.idi.edu/main.html

International Technological
University
1650 Warburton Avenue
Santa Clara, CA 95050
408-556-9010
www.itu.edu

John F. Kennedy University
12 Altarinda Road
Orinda, CA 94563-2603
925-254-0200
www.jfku.edu

La Sierra University
4700 Pierce Street
Riverside, CA 92515-8247
909-785-2000
www.lasierra.edu

LIFE Bible College
1100 Covina Boulevard
San Dimas, CA 91773-3298
909-599-5433
www.lifebible.edu

Lincoln University
401 15th Street
Oakland, CA 94612
510-628-8010
www.lincolnuca.edu

Loma Linda University
Loma Linda, CA 92350
909-558-1000
www.llu.edu

Loyola Marymount
University
One LMU Drive
Los Angeles, CA 90045-2659
310-338-2700

The Master's College and
Seminary
21726 Placerita Canyon Road
Santa Clarita, CA 91321-1200
661-259-3540
www.masters.edu

Menlo College
1000 El Camino Real
Atherton, CA 94027-4301
650-688-3753
www.menlo.edu

Mills College
5000 MacArthur Boulevard
Oakland, CA 94613-1000
510-430-2255
www.mills.edu

Mount St. Mary's College
12001 Chalon Road
Los Angeles, CA 90049-1599
310-954-4000
www.msmc.la.edu

Mt. Sierra College
101 East Huntington Drive
Monrovia, CA 91016
626-873-2144
www.mtsierra.edu

Musicians Institute
1655 North McCadden Place
Hollywood, CA 90028
323-462-1384

The National Hispanic
University
14271 Story Road
San Jose, CA 95127-3823
408-254-6900
www.nhu.edu

National University
11255 North Torrey Pines Rd.
La Jolla, CA 92037-1011
619-563-7100
www.nu.edu

New College of California
50 Fell Street
San Francisco, CA
94102-5206
415-241-1300
www.newcollege.edu

NewSchool of Architecture &
Design
1249 F Street
San Diego, CA 92101-6634
619-235-4100
www.newschoolarch.edu

Northwestern Polytechnic
University
117 Fourier Avenue
Fremont, CA 94539-7482
510-657-5911
www.npu.edu

Notre Dame de Namur
University
1500 Ralston Avenue
Belmont, CA 94002-1997
650-593-1601
www.cnd.edu

Occidental College
1600 Campus Road
Los Angeles, CA 90041-3314
323-259-2500
www.oxy.edu

Otis College of Art and
Design
9045 Lincoln Boulevard
Los Angeles, CA 90045-9785
310-665-6800
www.otisart.edu

Pacific Oaks College
5 Westmoreland Place
Pasadena, CA 91103
626-397-1300
www.pacificoaks.edu

Pacific States University
1516 South Western Avenue
Los Angeles, CA 90006
323-731-2383
www.psuca.edu

Pacific Union College
One Angwin Avenue
Angwin, CA 94508-9707
707-965-6311
www.puc.edu

Patten College
2433 Coolidge Avenue
Oakland, CA 94601-2699
510-261-8500
www.diac.com/~patten

Pepperdine University
24255 Pacific Coast Highway
Malibu, CA 90263-0002
310-506-4000
www.pepperdine.edu

Pitzer College
1050 North Mills Avenue
Claremont, CA 91711-6101
909-621-8000
www.pitzer.edu

Point Loma Nazarene
University
3900 Lomaland Drive
San Diego, CA 92106-2899
619-849-2200
www.ptloma.edu

Pomona College
550 North College Avenue
Claremont, CA 91711
909-621-8000
www.pomona.edu

Saint Mary's College of
California
1928 Saint Mary's Road
Moraga, CA 94556
925-631-4000
www.stmarys-ca.edu

Samuel Merritt College
370 Hawthorne Avenue
Oakland, CA 94609-3108
510-869-6511
www.samuelmerritt.edu

San Diego State University
5500 Campanile Drive
San Diego, CA 92182
619-594-5200
www.sdsu.edu

San Francisco Art Institute
800 Chestnut Street
San Francisco, CA 94133
415-771-7020
www.sfai.edu

San Francisco Conservatory
of Music
1201 Ortega Street
San Francisco, CA
94122-4411
415-564-8086
www.sfcm.edu

San Francisco State
University
1600 Holloway Avenue
San Francisco, CA
94132-1722
415-338-1100
www.sfsu.edu

San Jose Christian College
790 South Twelfth Street
San Jose, CA 95112-2381
408-278-4300
www.sjchristiancol.edu

San Jose State University
One Washington Square
San Jose, CA 95192-0001
408-924-1000
www.sjsu.edu

Santa Clara University
500 El Camino Real
Santa Clara, CA 95053
408-554-4000
www.scu.edu

Scripps College
1030 Columbia Avenue
Claremont, CA 91711-3948
909-621-8000
www.scrippscol.edu

Shasta Bible College
2980 Hartnell Avenue
Redding, CA 96002
530-221-4275
www.shasta.edu

Simpson College and
Graduate School
2211 College View Drive
Redding, CA 96003-8606
530-224-5600
www.simpsonca.edu

Sonoma State University
1801 East Cotati Avenue
Rohnert Park, CA 94928-3609
707-664-2880
www.sonoma.edu

Southern California Bible
College & Seminary
2075 East Madison Avenue
El Cajon, CA 92019
619-442-9841
www.scbcs.edu

Southern California Institute
of Architecture
350 Merrick Street
Los Angeles, CA 90013
213-613-2200
www.sciarc.edu

St. John's Seminary College
5118 Seminary Road
Camarillo, CA 93012-2599
805-482-2755
www.west.net/~sjsc

Stanford University
Stanford, CA 94305-9991
650-723-2300
www.stanford.edu

Thomas Aquinas College
10000 North Ojai Road
Santa Paula, CA 93060-9980
805-525-4417
www.thomasaquinas.edu

Touro University
International
Suite 102, 10542 Calle Lee
Los Alamitos, CA 90720
714-816-0366
www.tourouniversity.edu

University of California,
Berkeley
Berkeley, CA 94720-1500
510-642-6000
www.berkeley.edu

University of California,
Davis
One Shields Avenue
Davis, CA 95616
530-752-1011
www.ucdavis.edu

University of California,
Irvine
Irvine, CA 92697
949-824-5011
www.uci.edu

University of California,
Los Angeles
405 Hilgard Avenue
Los Angeles, CA 90095
310-825-4321
www.ucla.edu

University of California,
Riverside
900 University Avenue
Riverside, CA 92521-0102
909-787-1012
www.ucr.edu

University of California,
San Diego
9500 Gilman Drive
La Jolla, CA 92093
858-534-2230
www.ucsd.edu

University of California,
Santa Barbara
Santa Barbara, CA 93106
805-893-8000
www.ucsb.edu

University of California,
Santa Cruz
1156 High Street
Santa Cruz, CA 95064
831-459-0111
www.ucsc.edu

University of Judaism
15600 Mulholland Drive
Bel Air, CA 90077-1599
310-476-9777
www.uj.edu

University of La Verne
1950 Third Street
La Verne, CA 91750-4443
909-593-3511
www.ulv.edu

University of Phoenix–
Northern California Campus
7901 Stoneridge Drive,
Suite 100
Pleasanton, CA 94588
877-4-STUDENT
www.phoenix.edu

University of Phoenix–
Sacramento Campus
1760 Creekside Oaks Drive,
Suite 100
Sacramento, CA 95833
800-266-2107
www.phoenix.edu

University of Phoenix–
San Diego Campus
3890 Murphy Canyon Road,
Suite 100
San Diego, CA 92123
888-UOP-INFO
www.phoenix.edu

University of Phoenix–
Southern California Campus
10540 Talbert Avenue, West
Building, Suite 100
Fountain Valley, CA 92708
800-GO-TO-UOP
www.phoenix.edu

University of Redlands
1200 E. Colton Avenue,
PO Box 3080
Redlands, CA 92373-0999
909-793-2121
www.redlands.edu

University of San Diego
5998 Alcala Park
San Diego, CA 92110-2492
619-260-4600
www.sandiego.edu

University of San Francisco
2130 Fulton Street
San Francisco, CA 94117-1080
415-422-6886
www.usfca.edu

University of Southern
California
University Park Campus
Los Angeles, CA 90089
213-740-2311
www.usc.edu

University of the Pacific
3601 Pacific Avenue
Stockton, CA 95211-0197
209-946-2011
www.uop.edu

University of West
Los Angeles
1155 West Arbor Vitae Street
Inglewood, CA 90301-2902
310-342-5200
www.uwla.edu

Vanguard University of
Southern California
55 Fair Drive
Costa Mesa, CA 92626-6597
714-556-3610
www.vanguard.edu

Westmont College
955 La Paz Road
Santa Barbara, CA
93108-1099
805-565-6000
www.westmont.edu

Westwood College of
Aviation Technology–
Los Angeles
8911 Aviation Boulevard
Inglewood, CA 90301-2904
310-337-4444
www.westwood.edu

Whittier College
13406 E Philadelphia Street
Whittier, CA 90608-0634
562-907-4200
www.whittier.edu

Woodbury University
7500 Glenoaks Boulevard
Burbank, CA 91504-1099
818-767-0888
www.woodbury.edu

Yeshiva Ohr Elchonon
Chabad/West Coast
Talmudical Seminary
7215 Waring Avenue
Los Angeles, CA 90046-7660
213-937-3763

Colorado

Adams State College
208 Edgemont Boulevard
Alamosa, CO 81102
719-587-7011
www.adams.edu

The Art Institute of Colorado
1200 Lincoln Street
Denver, CO 80203
303-837-0825
www.aic.artinstitutes.edu

Colorado Christian University
180 South Garrison Street
Lakewood, CO 80226-7499
303-202-0100
www.ccu.edu

The Colorado College
14 East Cache La Poudre
Colorado Springs, CO
80903-3294
719-389-6000
www.coloradocollege.edu

Colorado School of Mines
1500 Illinois Street
Golden, CO 80401-1887
303-273-3000
www.mines.edu

Colorado State University
Fort Collins, CO 80523-0015
970-491-1101
www.colostate.edu

Colorado Technical University
4435 North Chestnut Street
Colorado Springs, CO
80907-3896
719-598-0200
www.coloradotech.edu

Colorado Technical University
Denver Campus
5775 Denver Tech Center Blvd
Greenwood Village, CO 80111
303-694-6600
www.coloradotech.edu

Denver Technical College
925 South Niagara Street
Denver, CO 80224-1658
303-329-3000
www.den.devry.edu

Denver Technical College at
Colorado Springs
225 South Union Boulevard
Colorado Springs, CO
80910-3138
719-632-3000
www.dtc.edu

DeVry Institute of Technology
225 South Union Boulevard
Colorado Springs, CO 80910
719-632-3000
www.cs.devry.edu

Education America, Colorado
Springs Campus
6050 Erin Park Drive, #250
Colorado Springs, CO 80918
719-532-1234

Education America,
Denver Campus
11011 West 6th Avenue
Lakewood, CO 80215-0090
303-445-0500

Fort Lewis College
1000 Rim Drive
Durango, CO 81301-3999
970-247-7010
www.fortlewis.edu

Johnson & Wales University
7150 Montview Boulevard
Denver, CO 80220
303-256-9300
www.jwu.edu

Jones International
University
9697 East Mineral Avenue
Englewood, CO 80112
303-784-8045
www.jonesinternational.edu

Metropolitan State College of
Denver
PO Box 173362
Denver, CO 80217-3362
303-556-3018
www.mscd.edu

Naropa University
2130 Arapahoe Avenue
Boulder, CO 80302-6697
303-444-0202
www.naropa.edu

National American University
5125 North Academy Blvd
Colorado Springs, CO 80918
719-277-0588

National American University
1325 South Colorado Blvd,
Suite 100
Denver, CO 80222
303-758-6700

Nazarene Bible College
1111 Academy Park Loop
Colorado Springs, CO
80910-3704
719-884-5000
www.nbc.edu

Regis University
3333 Regis Boulevard
Denver, CO 80221-1099
303-458-4100
www.regis.edu

Rocky Mountain College of
Art & Design
6875 East Evans Avenue
Denver, CO 80224-2329
303-753-6046
www.rmcad.edu

Teikyo Loretto Heights
University
3001 South Federal Blvd
Denver, CO 80236-2711
303-937-4200

United States Air Force
Academy
HQ USAFA/XPR,
2304 Cadet Drive, Suite 200
USAF Academy, CO
80840-5025
719-333-1818
www.usafa.edu/rr

University of Colorado at
Boulder
Boulder, CO 80309
303-492-1411
www.colorado.edu

University of Colorado at
Colorado Springs
PO Box 7150
Colorado Springs, CO
80933-7150
719-262-3000
www.uccs.edu

University of Colorado at
Denver
PO Box 173364
Denver, CO 80217-3364
303-556-2400
www.cudenver.edu

University of Colorado
Health Sciences Center
4200 East Ninth Avenue
Denver, CO 80262
303-399-1211
www.uchsc.edu

University of Denver
University Park,
2199 South University Park
Denver, CO 80208
303-871-2000
www.du.edu

University of Northern
Colorado
Greeley, CO 80639
970-351-1890
www.unco.edu

University of Phoenix–
Colorado Campus
10004 Park Meadows Drive
Lone Tree, CO 80124
303-755-9090
www.phoenix.edu

University of Phoenix–
Southern Colorado Campus
5475 Tech Center, Suite 130
Colorado Springs, CO 80919
719-599-5282
www.phoenix.edu

University of Southern
Colorado
2200 Bonforte Boulevard
Pueblo, CO 81001-4901
719-549-2100
www.uscolo.edu

Western State College of
Colorado
600 North Adams Street
Gunnison, CO 81231
970-943-0120
www.western.edu

Westwood College of
Technology–Denver North
7350 North Broadway
Denver, CO 80221-3653
303-426-7000
www.westwood.edu

Yeshiva Toras Chaim
Talmudical Seminary
1400 Quitman Street
Denver, CO 80204-1415
303-629-8200

Hawaii

Brigham Young
University–Hawaii
55-220 Kulanui Street
Laie, HI 96762-1294
808-293-3211
www.byuh.edu

Chaminade University of
Honolulu
3140 Waialae Avenue
Honolulu, HI 96816-1578
808-735-4711
www.chaminade.edu

Education America, Honolulu
Campus
1111 Bishop Street, Suite 400
Honolulu, HI 96813
808-942-1000

Hawai`i Pacific University
1166 Fort Street
Honolulu, HI 96813-2785
808-544-0200
www.hpu.edu

International College and
Graduate School
20 Dowsett Avenue
Honolulu, HI 96817
808-595-4247
home.hawaii.rr.com/
international/icgs.html

University of Hawaii at Hilo
200 West Kawili Street
Hilo, HI 96720-4091
808-974-7311
www.uhh.hawaii.edu

University of Hawaii at
Manoa
2444 Dole Street
Honolulu, HI 96822
808-956-8111
www.uhm.hawaii.edu

University of Hawaii–
West Oahu
96-129 Ala Ike
Pearl City, HI 96782-3366
808-454-4700

University of Phoenix–
Hawaii Campus
827 Fort Street
Honolulu, HI 96813
866-2-ENROLL
www.phoenix.edu

Idaho

Albertson College of Idaho
2112 Cleveland Boulevard
Caldwell, ID 83605-4494
208-459-5011
www.albertson.edu

Boise Bible College
8695 West Marigold Street
Boise, ID 83714-1220
208-376-7731
www.boisebible.edu

Boise State University
1910 University Drive
Boise, ID 83725-0399
208-426-1011
www.boisestate.edu

Idaho State University
741 South 7th Avenue
Pocatello, ID 83209
208-282-0211
www.isu.edu

Lewis-Clark State College
500 Eighth Avenue
Lewiston, ID 83501-2698
208-792-5272
www.lcsc.edu

Northwest Nazarene University
623 Holly Street
Nampa, ID 83686-5897
208-467-8011
www.nnu.edu

University of Idaho
875 Perimeter Drive
Moscow, ID 83844-2282
208-885-6111
www.its.uidaho.edu/uihome

Montana

Carroll College
1601 North Benton Avenue
Helena, MT 59625-0002
406-447-4300
www.carroll.edu

Montana State University–
Billings
1500 North 30th Street
Billings, MT 59101-0298
406-657-2011
www.msubillings.edu

Montana State
University–Bozeman
Bozeman, MT 59717
406-994-0211
www.montana.edu

Montana State University–
Northern
PO Box 7751
Havre, MT 59501-7751
406-265-3700
www.msun.edu

Montana Tech of The
University of Montana
1300 West Park Street
Butte, MT 59701-8997
406-496-4101
www.mtech.edu

Rocky Mountain College
1511 Poly Drive
Billings, MT 59102-1796
406-657-1000
www.rocky.edu

University of Great Falls
1301 Twentieth Street South
Great Falls, MT 59405
406-761-8210
www.ugf.edu

The University of Montana–
Missoula
Missoula, MT 59812-0002
406-243-0211
www.umt.edu

The University of Montana–
Western
710 South Atlantic
Dillon, MT 59725-3598
406-683-7011
www.umwesten.edu

Nevada

Morrison University
140 Washington Street
Reno, NV 89503-5600
775-323-4145
www.morrison.edu

Sierra Nevada College
999 Tahoe Boulevard
Incline Village, NV 89451
775-831-1314
www.sierranevada.edu

University of Nevada,
Las Vegas
4505 Maryland Parkway
Las Vegas, NV 89154-9900
702-895-3011
www.unlv.edu

University of Nevada, Reno
Reno, NV 89557
775-784-1110
www.unr.edu

University of Phoenix–
Nevada Campus
333 North Rancho Drive,
Suite 300
Las Vegas, NV 89106
702-638-7868
www.phoenix.edu

New Mexico

College of Santa Fe
1600 Saint Michael's Drive
Santa Fe, NM 87505-7634
505-473-6011
www.csf.edu

College of the Southwest
6610 Lovington Highway
Hobbs, NM 88240-9129
505-392-6561
www.csw.edu

Eastern New Mexico
University
Portales, NM 88130
505-562-1011
www.enmu.edu

Metropolitan College of
Court Reporting
1717 Louisiana Blvd NE,
Suite 207
Albuquerque, NM 87110-7027
505-888-3400
www.metropolitancollege.edu

National American University
1202 Pennsylvania Ave, NE
Albuquerque, NM 87110
505-265-7517

Nazarene Indian Bible
College
2315 Markham Road, SW
Albuquerque, NM 87105
505-877-0240

New Mexico Highlands
University
PO Box 9000
Las Vegas, NM 87701
505-454-3000
www.nmhu.edu

New Mexico Institute of
Mining and Technology
801 Leroy Place
Socorro, NM 87801
505-835-5011
www.nmt.edu

New Mexico State University
PO Box 30001
Las Cruces, NM 88003-8001
505-646-0111
www.nmsu.edu

St. John's College
1160 Camino Cruz Blanca
Santa Fe, NM 87501-4599
505-984-6000
www.sjcsf.edu

University of New Mexico
Albuquerque, NM
87131-2039
505-277-0111
www.unm.edu

University of Phoenix–New
Mexico Campus
7471 Pan American Freeway NE
Albuquerque, NM 87109
505-821-4800
www.phoenix.edu

Western New Mexico
University
PO Box 680
Silver City, NM 88062-0680
505-538-6011
www.wnmu.edu

Oregon

The Art Institute of Portland
2000 Southwest Fifth Avenue
Portland, OR 97201-4907
503-228-6528
www.aipd.artinstitutes.edu

Cascade College
9101 East Burnside Street
Portland, OR 97216-1515
503-255-7060
www.cascade.edu

Concordia University
2811 Northeast Holman
Portland, OR 97211-6099
503-288-9371
www.cu-portland.edu

Eastern Oregon University
1 University Boulevard
La Grande, OR 97850-2899
541-962-3672
www.eou.edu

Eugene Bible College
2155 Bailey Hill Road
Eugene, OR 97405-1194
541-485-1780
www.ebc.edu

George Fox University
414 North Meridian
Newberg, OR 97132-2697
503-538-8383
www.georgefox.edu

Lewis & Clark College
0615 SW Palatine Hill Road
Portland, OR 97219-7899
503-768-7000
www.lclark.edu

Linfield College
900 SE Baker Street
McMinnville, OR 97128-6894
503-434-2200
www.linfield.edu

Marylhurst University
PO Box 261
Marylhurst, OR 97036-0261
503-636-8141
www.marylhurst.edu

Mount Angel Seminary
Saint Benedict, OR 97373
503-845-3951

Multnomah Bible College
and Biblical Seminary
8435 Northeast Glisan Street
Portland, OR 97220-5898
503-255-0332
www.multnomah.edu

Northwest Christian College
828 East 11th Avenue
Eugene, OR 97401-3745
541-343-1641
www.nwcc.edu

Oregon College of Art & Craft
8245 Southwest Barnes Road
Portland, OR 97225
503-297-5544
www.ocac.edu

Oregon Health & Science
University
3181 SW Sam Jackson Park Rd
Portland, OR 97201-3098
503-494-8311
www.ohsu.edu

Oregon Institute of
Technology
3201 Campus Drive
Klamath Falls, OR 97601-8801
541-885-1000
www.oit.edu

Oregon State University
Corvallis, OR 97331
541-737-1000
osu.orst.edu

Pacific Northwest College of
Art
1241 NW Johnson Street
Portland, OR 97209
503-226-4391
www.pnca.edu

Pacific University
2043 College Way
Forest Grove, OR 97116-1797
503-357-6151
www.pacificu.edu

Portland State University
PO Box 751
Portland, OR 97207-0751
503-725-3000
www.pdx.edu

Reed College
3203 Southeast Woodstock
Boulevard
Portland, OR 97202-8199
503-771-1112
www.reed.edu

Southern Oregon University
1250 Siskiyou Boulevard
Ashland, OR 97520
541-552-7672
www.sou.edu

University of Oregon
Eugene, OR 97403
541-346-3111
www.uoregon.edu

University of
Phoenix–Oregon Campus
13221 SW 68th Parkway,
Suite 500
Portland, OR 97223
503-670-0590
www.phoenix.edu

University of Portland
5000 North Willamette
Boulevard
Portland, OR 97203-5798
503-943-7911
www.up.edu

Warner Pacific College
2219 Southeast 68th Avenue
Portland, OR 97215-4099
503-517-1000
www.warnerpacific.edu

Western Baptist College
5000 Deer Park Drive, SE
Salem, OR 97301-9392
503-581-8600
www.wbc.edu

Western Oregon University
345 North Monmouth Ave
Monmouth, OR 97361-1394
503-838-8000
www.wou.edu

Western States Chiropractic
College
2900 Northeast 132nd Ave
Portland, OR 97230-3099
503-256-3180
www.wschiro.edu

Willamette University
900 State Street
Salem, OR 97301-3931
503-370-6300
www.willamette.edu

Utah

Brigham Young University
Provo, UT 84602-1001
801-378-1211
www.byu.edu

Southern Utah University
351 West Center
Cedar City, UT 84720-2498
435-586-7700
www.suu.edu

University of Phoenix–Utah
Campus
5251 Green Street
Salt Lake City, UT 84123
801-263-1444
www.phoenix.edu

University of Utah
201 South University Street
Salt Lake City, UT 84112-1107
801-581-7200
www.utah.edu

Utah State University
Old Main Hill
Logan, UT 84322
435-797-1000
www.usu.edu

Weber State University
1001 University Circle
Ogden, UT 84408-1001
801-626-6000
weber.edu

Western Governors
University
2040 East Murray Holladay,
Suite 106
Salt Lake City, UT 84117
801-274-3280
www.wgu.edu

Westminster College
1840 South 1300 East
Salt Lake City, UT 84105-3697
801-484-7651
www.wcslc.edu

Washington

Antioch University Seattle
2326 Sixth Avenue
Seattle, WA 98121-1814
206-441-5352
www.antiochsea.edu

Bastyr University
14500 Juanita Drive, NE
Kenmore, WA 98028-4966
425-823-1300
www.bastyr.edu

Central Washington
University
400 East 8th Avenue
Ellensburg, WA 98926-7463
509-963-1111
www.cwu.edu

City University
11900 NE First Street
Bellevue, WA 98005
425-637-1010
www.cityu.edu

Cornish College of the Arts
710 East Roy Street
Seattle, WA 98102-4696
206-323-1400
www.cornish.edu

DeVry Institute of Technology
3600 South 34th Way
Federal Way, WA 98001
253-943-2800
www.sea.devry.edu

Eastern Washington
University
526 5th Street
Cheney, WA 99004-2431
509-359-6200
www.ewu.edu

The Evergreen State College
2700 Evergreen Parkway, NW
Olympia, WA 98505
360-866-6000
www.evergreen.edu

Gonzaga University
502 East Boone Avenue
Spokane, WA 99258
509-328-4220
www.gonzaga.edu

Henry Cogswell College
3002 Colby Avenue
Everett, WA 98201
425-258-3351
www.henrycogswell.edu

Heritage College
3240 Fort Road
Toppenish, WA 98948-9599
509-865-8500
www.heritage.edu

The Leadership Institute of
Seattle
14506 Juanita Drive, NE
Kenmore, WA 98028-4966
425-939-8100
www.lios.org

Northwest College
PO Box 579
Kirkland, WA 98083-0579
425-822-8266
www.nwcollege.edu

Northwest College of Art
16464 State Highway 305
Poulsbo, WA 98370
360-779-9993
www.nca.edu

Pacific Lutheran University
Tacoma, WA 98447
253-531-6900
www.plu.edu

Puget Sound Christian
College
410 4th Avenue North
Edmonds, WA 98020-3171
425-775-8686

Saint Martin's College
5300 Pacific Avenue, SE
Lacey, WA 98503-7500
360-491-4700
www.stmartin.edu

Seattle Pacific University
3307 Third Avenue West
Seattle, WA 98119-1997
206-281-2000
www.spu.edu

Seattle University
900 Broadway
Seattle, WA 98122
206-296-6000
www.seattleu.edu

Trinity Lutheran College
4221 228th Avenue, SE
Issaquah, WA 98029-9299
425-392-0400
www.tlc.edu

University of
Phoenix–Washington
Campus
7100 Fort Dent Way,
Suite 100
Seattle, WA 98188
877-877-4867
www.phoenix.edu

University of Puget Sound
1500 North Warner Street
Tacoma, WA 98416
253-879-3100
www.ups.edu

University of Washington
Seattle, WA 98195
206-543-2100
www.washington.edu

Walla Walla College
204 South College Avenue
College Place, WA 99324-1198
509-527-2615
www.wwc.edu

Washington State University
Pullman, WA 99164
509-335-3564
www.wsu.edu

Western Washington
University
516 High Street
Bellingham, WA 98225-5996
360-650-3000
www.wwu.edu

Whitman College
345 Boyer Avenue
Walla Walla, WA 99362-2083
509-527-5111
www.whitman.edu

Whitworth College
300 West Hawthorne Road
Spokane, WA 99251-0001
509-777-1000
www.whitworth.edu

Wyoming

University of Wyoming
Laramie, WY 82071
307-766-1121
www.uwyo.edu

2-YEAR COLLEGES AND UNIVERSITIES

Alaska

Charter College
2221 East Northern Lights
Boulevard, Suite 120
Anchorage, AK 99508-4157
Phone: 907-277-1000
www.chartercollege.org

University of Alaska
Anchorage, Kenai Peninsula
College
34820 College Drive
Soldotna, AK 99669-9798
Phone: 907-262-0300
www.uaa.alaska.edu/kenai

University of Alaska
Anchorage, Kodiak College
117 Benny Benson Drive
Kodiak, AK 99615-6643
Phone: 907-486-4161
www.koc.alaska.edu

University of Alaska
Anchorage, Matanuska-
Susitna College
PO Box 2889
Palmer, AK 99645-2889
Phone: 907-745-9774
www.uaa.alaska.edu/matsu/
msc.htm

University of Alaska
Southeast, Ketchikan Campus
2600 7th Avenue
Ketchikan, AK 99901-5798
Phone: 907-225-6177
www.ketch.alaska.edu

University of Alaska
Southeast, Sitka Campus
1332 Seward Avenue
Sitka, AK 99835-9418
Phone: 907-747-6653
www.uas-sitka.net

University of Alaska, Prince
William Sound Community
College
PO Box 97
Valdez, AK 99686-0097
Phone: 907-834-1600
www.uaa.alaska.edu/pwscc/
home.html

Arizona

Apollo College–Phoenix, Inc.
8503 North 27th Avenue
Phoenix, AZ 85051
Phone: 602-864-1571
www.apollocollege.com

Apollo College–Tri-City, Inc.
630 West Southern Avenue
Mesa, AZ 85210-5004
Phone: 480-831-6585
www.apollocollege.com

Apollo College–Tucson, Inc.
3870 North Oracle Road
Tucson, AZ 85705-3227
Phone: 520-888-5885
www.apollocollege.com

Apollo College–Westside, Inc.
2701 West Bethany Home Rd
Phoenix, AZ 85017
Phone: 602-433-1333
www.apollocollege.com

Arizona Automotive Institute
6829 North 46th Avenue
Glendale, AZ 85301-3597
Phone: 602-934-7273
www.azautoinst.com

Arizona Institute of Business
& Technology
6049 North 43rd Avenue
Phoenix, AZ 85019
Phone: 602-242-6265
www.aibt.edu

Arizona Western College
PO Box 929
Yuma, AZ 85366-0929
Phone: 928-317-6000
www.awc.cc.az.us

Central Arizona College
8470 North Overfield Road
Coolidge, AZ 85228-9779
Phone: 520-426-4444
www.cac.cc.az.us

Chandler-Gilbert Community
College
2626 East Pecos Road
Chandler, AZ 85225-2479
Phone: 480-732-7000
www.cgc.maricopa.edu

Chaparral College
4585 East Speedway, No 204
Tucson, AZ 85712
Phone: 520-327-6866
www.chap-col.edu

Cochise College
4190 West Highway 80
Douglas, AZ 85607-9724
Phone: 520-364-7943
www.cochise.cc.az.us

Cochise College
901 North Columbo
Sierra Vista, AZ 85635-2317
Phone: 520-515-0500
www.cochise.cc.az.us

Coconino Community College
3000 North 4th Street,
Suite 17, PO Box 80000
Flagstaff, AZ 86003
Phone: 520-527-1222

Diné College
PO Box 98
Tsaile, AZ 86556
Phone: 520-724-6600
www.crystal.ncc.cc.nm.us

Eastern Arizona College
PO Box 769
Thatcher, AZ 85552-0769
Phone: 520-428-8322
www.easternarizona.com

Estrella Mountain Community
College
3000 North Dysart Road
Avondale, AZ 85323-1000
Phone: 602-935-8000
www.emc.maricopa.edu

GateWay Community College
108 North 40th Street
Phoenix, AZ 85034-1795
Phone: 602-392-5000
www.gwc.maricopa.edu

Glendale Community College
6000 West Olive Avenue
Glendale, AZ 85302-3090
Phone: 623-845-3000
www.gc.maricopa.edu

High-Tech Institute
1515 East Indian School Road
Phoenix, AZ 85014-4901
Phone: 602-279-9700
www.high-techinstitute.com

ITT Technical Institute
4837 East McDowell Road
Phoenix, AZ 85008-4292
Phone: 602-252-2331

ITT Technical Institute
1455 West River Road
Tucson, AZ 85704
Phone: 520-408-7488
www.itt-tech.edu

Lamson College
1126 North Scottsdale Road,
Suite 17
Tempe, AZ 85281
Phone: 480-898-7000
www.lamsoncollege.com

Mesa Community College
1833 West Southern Avenue
Mesa, AZ 85202-4866
Phone: 602-461-7000

Mohave Community College
1971 Jagerson Avenue
Kingman, AZ 86401
Phone: 520-757-4331
www.mohave.cc.az.us

Northland Pioneer College
PO Box 610
Holbrook, AZ 86025-0610
Phone: 520-524-7600
www.northland.cc.az.us

Paradise Valley Community
College
18401 North 32nd Street
Phoenix, AZ 85032-1200
Phone: 602-787-6500
www.pvc.maricopa.edu

Phoenix College
1202 West Thomas Road
Phoenix, AZ 85013-4234
Phone: 602-264-2492
www.pc.maricopa.edu

Pima Community College
4905 East Broadway
Tucson, AZ 85709-1010
Phone: 520-206-4666
www.pima.edu

Pima Medical Institute
3350 East Grant Road
Tucson, AZ 85716
Phone: 520-326-1600
www.pimamedical.com

Pima Medical Institute
957 South Dobson Road
Mesa, AZ 85202
Phone: 602-644-0267
www.pimamedical.com

Rhodes College
2525 West Beryl Avenue
Phoenix, AZ 85021
Phone: 602-942-4141
rhodes-college.com

Rio Salado College
2323 West 14th Street
Tempe, AZ 85281-6950
Phone: 480-517-8000
www.rio.maricopa.edu

Scottsdale Community
College
9000 East Chaparral Road
Scottsdale, AZ 85256-2626
Phone: 602-423-6000
www.sc.maricopa.edu

Scottsdale Culinary Institute
8100 East Camelback Road,
Suite 1001
Scottsdale, AZ 85251-3940
Phone: 480-990-3773
www.scichefs.com

South Mountain Community
College
7050 South Twenty-fourth St
Phoenix, AZ 85040
Phone: 602-243-8000
www.smc.maricopa.edu

The Art Center
2525 North Country Club Rd
Tucson, AZ 85716-2505
Phone: 520-325-0123
www.theartcenter.edu

The Bryman School
4343 North 16th Street
Phoenix, AZ 85016-5338
Phone: 602-274-4300
www.hightechschools.com

The Paralegal Institute, Inc.
2933 West Indian School Rd
Phoenix, AZ 85017
Phone: 602-212-0501
www.theparalegalinstitute.
com

The Refrigeration School
4210 East Washington Street
Phoenix, AZ 85034-1816
Phone: 602-275-7133
www.refrigerationschool.
com

Universal Technical Institute
3121 West Weldon Avenue
Phoenix, AZ 85017-4599
Phone: 602-264-4164
www.uticorp.com

Yavapai College
1100 East Sheldon Street
Prescott, AZ 86301-3297
Phone: 520-445-7300
www.yavapai.cc.az.us

California

Allan Hancock College
800 South College Drive
Santa Maria, CA 93454-6399
Phone: 805-922-6966
www.hancock.cc.ca.us

American Academy of
Dramatic Arts/Hollywood
1336 North La Brea Avenue
Hollywood, CA 90028
Phone: 323-464-2777
www.aada.org

American River College
4700 College Oak Drive
Sacramento, CA 95841-4286
Phone: 916-484-8011
www.arc.losrios.cc.ca.us

Antelope Valley College
3041 West Avenue K
Lancaster, CA 93536-5426
Phone: 661-722-6300
www.avc.edu

Bakersfield College
1801 Panorama Drive
Bakersfield, CA 93305-1299
Phone: 661-395-4011
www.kccd.cc.ca.us

Barstow College
2700 Barstow Road
Barstow, CA 92311-6699
Phone: 760-252-2411
www.barstow.cc.ca.us

Brooks College
4825 East Pacific Coast
Highway
Long Beach, CA 90804-3291
Phone: 562-498-2441
Fax: 562-597-7412
www.brookscollege.edu/

Butte College
3536 Butte Campus Drive
Oroville, CA 95965-8399
Phone: 530-895-2511
Fax: 530-895-2345

Cañada College
4200 Farm Hill Boulevard
Redwood City, CA
94061-1099
Phone: 650-306-3100
www.canadacollege.net

Cabrillo College
6500 Soquel Drive
Aptos, CA 95003-3194
Phone: 831-479-6100
www.cabrillo.cc.ca.us

California College of
Technology
4330 Watt Avenue, Suite 400
Sacramento, CA 95660
Phone: 916-649-8168
www.californiacollegetech.
com

California Culinary Academy
625 Polk Street
San Francisco, CA
94102-3368
Phone: 415-771-3500
www.baychef.com

California Design College
3440 Wilshire Boulevard,
Seventh Floor
Los Angeles, CA 90010
Phone: 213-251-3636
www.cdc.edu

Cerritos College
11110 Alondra Boulevard
Norwalk, CA 90650-6298
Phone: 562-860-2451
www.cerritos.edu

Cerro Coso Community
College
3000 College Heights Blvd
Ridgecrest, CA 93555-9571
Phone: 760-384-6100
www.cc.cc.ca.us

Chabot College
25555 Hesperian Boulevard
Hayward, CA 94545-5001
Phone: 510-723-6600
www.chabot.cc.ca.us

Chaffey College
5885 Haven Avenue
Rancho Cucamonga, CA
91737-3002
Phone: 909-987-1737
www.chaffey.cc.ca.us

Citrus College
1000 West Foothill Boulevard
Glendora, CA 91741-1899
Phone: 626-963-0323
www.citrus.cc.ca.us

City College of San Francisco
50 Phelan Avenue
San Francisco, CA
94112-1821
Phone: 415-239-3000
www.ccsf.org

Coastline Community
College
11460 Warner Avenue
Fountain Valley, CA
92708-2597
Phone: 714-546-7600
www.coastline.cccd.edu

College of Alameda
555 Atlantic Avenue
Alameda, CA 94501-2109
Phone: 510-522-7221
www.peralta.cc.ca.us

College of Marin
835 College Avenue
Kentfield, CA 94904
Phone: 415-457-8811
www.marin.cc.ca.us

College of Oceaneering
272 South Fries Avenue
Wilmington, CA 90744-6399
Phone: 310-834-2501
www.diveco.com

College of San Mateo
1700 West Hillsdale Blvd
San Mateo, CA 94402-3784
Phone: 650-574-6161
www.gocsm.net

College of the Canyons
26455 Rockwell Canyon Road
Santa Clarita, CA
91355-1899
Phone: 661-259-7800
www.coc.cc.ca.us

College of the Desert
43-500 Monterey Avenue
Palm Desert, CA 92260-9305
Phone: 760-346-8041
www.desert.cc.ca.us

College of the Redwoods
7351 Tompkins Hill Road
Eureka, CA 95501-9300
Phone: 707-476-4100

College of the Sequoias
915 South Mooney Blvd
Visalia, CA 93277-2234
Phone: 559-730-3700
www.sequoias.cc.ca.us

College of the Siskiyous
800 College Avenue
Weed, CA 96094-2899
Phone: 530-938-4461
www.siskiyous.edu

Columbia College
11600 Columbia College Dr
Sonora, CA 95370
Phone: 209-588-5100

Compton Community
College
1111 East Artesia Boulevard
Compton, CA 90221-5393
Phone: 310-900-1600

Contra Costa College
2600 Mission Bell Drive
San Pablo, CA 94806-3195
Phone: 510-235-7800
www.contracosta.cc.ca.us

Copper Mountain College
6162 Rotary Way
Joshua Tree, CA 92252
Phone: 760-366-3791
www.cmccd.cc.ca.us

Cosumnes River College
8401 Center Parkway
Sacramento, CA 95823-5799
Phone: 916-691-7451
www.wserver.crc.losrios.cc.
ca.us

Crafton Hills College
11711 Sand Canyon Road
Yucaipa, CA 92399-1799
Phone: 909-794-2161

Cuesta College
PO Box 8106
San Luis Obispo, CA
93403-8106
Phone: 805-546-3100
www.cuesta.org

Cuyamaca College
900 Rancho San Diego Pkwy
El Cajon, CA 92019-4304
Phone: 619-660-4000
www.cuyamaca.net

Cypress College
9200 Valley View
Cypress, CA 90630-5897
Phone: 714-484-7000
www.cypress.cc.ca.us

D-Q University
PO Box 409
Davis, CA 95617-0409
Phone: 530-758-0470

De Anza College
21250 Stevens Creek Blvd
Cupertino, CA 95014-5793
Phone: 408-864-5678
www.deanza.fhda.edu

Deep Springs College
HC 72, Box 45001
Deep Springs, CA
89010-9803
Phone: 760-872-2000
www.deepsprings.edu

Diablo Valley College
321 Golf Club Road
Pleasant Hill, CA
94523-1544
Phone: 925-685-1230
www.dvc.edu

Don Bosco College of
Science and Technology
1151 San Gabriel Boulevard
Rosemead, CA 91770-4299
Phone: 626-940-2000
www.boscotech.org

East Los Angeles College
1301 Avenida Cesar Chavez
Monterey Park, CA
91754-6001
Phone: 323-265-8650
www.elac.cc.ca.us

El Camino College
16007 Crenshaw Boulevard
Torrance, CA 90506-0001
Phone: 310-532-3670

Empire College
3035 Cleveland Avenue
Santa Rosa, CA 95403
Phone: 707-546-4000
www.empcol.com

Evergreen Valley College
3095 Yerba Buena Road
San Jose, CA 95135-1598
Phone: 408-274-7900

Fashion Careers of California
College
1923 Morena Boulevard
San Diego, CA 92110
Phone: 619-275-4700
www.fashioncollege.com

Fashion Institute of Design
and Merchandising,
Los Angeles
919 South Grand Avenue
Los Angeles, CA 90015-1421
Phone: 213-624-1200
www.fidm.com

Fashion Institute of Design
and Merchandising,
San Diego Campus
1010 Second Avenue,
Suite 200
San Diego, CA 92101-4903
Phone: 619-235-2049
www.fidm.com

Fashion Institute of Design
and Merchandising,
San Francisco Campus
55 Stockton Street
San Francisco, CA
94108-5829
Phone: 415-675-5200
www.fidm.com

Feather River Community
College District
570 Golden Eagle Avenue
Quincy, CA 95971-9124
Phone: 530-283-0202
www.frcc.cc.ca.us

Foothill College
12345 El Monte Road
Los Altos Hills, CA
94022-4599
Phone: 650-949-7777
www.foothillcollege.org

Foundation College
5353 Mission Center Road,
Suite 100
San Diego, CA 92108-1306
Phone: 619-683-3273
www.foundationcollege.org

Fresno City College
1101 East University Avenue
Fresno, CA 93741-0002
Phone: 559-442-4600
www.scccd.cc.ca.us

Fullerton College
321 East Chapman Avenue
Fullerton, CA 92832-2095
Phone: 714-992-7000
www.fullcoll.edu

Gavilan College
5055 Santa Teresa Boulevard
Gilroy, CA 95020-9599
Phone: 408-847-1400
www.gavilan.cc.ca.us

Glendale Community College
1500 North Verdugo Road
Glendale, CA 91208-2894
Phone: 818-240-1000
www.glendale.cc.ca.us

Golden West College
PO Box 2748,
15744 Golden West Street
Huntington Beach, CA
92647-2748
Phone: 714-892-7711
www.gwc.cccd.edu

Grossmont College
8800 Grossmont College Dr
El Cajon, CA 92020-1799
Phone: 619-644-7000

Hartnell College
156 Homestead Avenue
Salinas, CA 93901-1697
Phone: 831-755-6700

Heald College Concord
5130 Commercial Circle
Concord, CA 94520
Phone: 925-228-5800
www.heald.edu

Heald College, School of
Business
2150 John Glenn Drive
Concord, CA 94520-5618
Phone: 510-827-1300

Heald College, School of
Business
1450 North Main Street
Salinas, CA 93906
Phone: 408-443-1700
www.heald.edu

Heald College, School of
Business
1605 East March Lane
Stockton, CA 95210
Phone: 209-477-1114

Heald College, School of
Business
2425 Mendocino Avenue
Santa Rosa, CA 95403-3116
Phone: 707-525-1300

Heald College, Schools of
Business and Technology
341 Great Mall Parkway
Milpitas, CA 95035
Phone: 408-934-4900
www.heald.edu

Heald College, Schools of
Business and Technology
255 West Bullard Avenue
Fresno, CA 93704-1706
Phone: 559-438-4222
www.heald.edu

Heald College, Schools of
Business and Technology
2910 Prospect Park Drive
Rancho Cordova, CA
95670-6005
Phone: 916-638-1616
www.heald.edu

Heald College, Schools of
Business and Technology
Seven Sierra Gate Plaza
Roseville, CA 95678
Phone: 916-789-8600
www.heald.edu

Heald College, Schools of
Business and Technology
24301 Southland Drive,
Suite 500
Hayward, CA 94545-1557
Phone: 510-783-2100
www.heald.edu

Heald College, Schools of
Business and Technology
350 Mission Street
San Francisco, CA
94105-2206
Phone: 415-808-3000
www.heald.edu

Imperial Valley College
PO Box 158, 380 East Aten Rd
Imperial, CA 92251-0158
Phone: 760-352-8320
www.imperial.cc.ca.us

Irvine Valley College
5500 Irvine Center Drive
Irvine, CA 92620-4399
Phone: 949-451-5100
www.ivc.cc.ca.us

ITT Technical Institute
16916 South Harlan Road
Lathrop, CA 95330
Phone: 209-858-0077
www.itt-tech.edu

ITT Technical Institute
10863 Gold Center Drive
Rancho Cordova, CA
95670-6034
Phone: 916-851-3900
www.itt-tech.edu

ITT Technical Institute
630 East Brier Drive,
Suite 150
San Bernardino, CA
92408-2800
Phone: 909-889-3800
www.itt-tech.edu

ITT Technical Institute
5104 Old Ironsides Drive
Santa Clara, CA 95050
Phone: 408-496-0655
www.itt-tech.edu

ITT Technical Institute
3979 Trust Way
Hayward, CA 94545
Phone: 510-785-8522

ITT Technical Institute
2051 Solar Drive, Suite 150
Oxnard, CA 93030
Phone: 805-988-0143

ITT Technical Institute
1530 West Cameron Avenue
West Covina, CA 91790-2711
Phone: 626-960-8681
www.itt-tech.edu

ITT Technical Institute
20050 South Vermont Avenue
Torrance, CA 90502
Phone: 310-380-1555
www.itt-tech.edu

ITT Technical Institute
525 North Muller Street
Anaheim, CA 92801-9938
Phone: 714-535-3700
www.itt-tech.edu

ITT Technical Institute
12669 Encinitas Avenue
Sylmar, CA 91342-3664
Phone: 818-364-5151
www.itt-tech.edu

ITT Technical Institute
9680 Granite Ridge Drive,
Suite 100
San Diego, CA 92123
Phone: 858-571-8500
www.itt-tech.edu

Kelsey Jenney College
201 A Street
San Diego, CA 92101
Phone: 619-233-7418
www.kelsey-jenney.com

Lake Tahoe Community
College
One College Drive
South Lake Tahoe, CA
96150-4524
Phone: 530-541-4660
www.ltcc.cc.ca.us

Laney College
900 Fallon Street
Oakland, CA 94607-4893
Phone: 510-834-5740
laney.peralta.cc.ca.us

Las Positas College
3033 Collier Canyon Road
Livermore, CA 94550-7650
Phone: 925-373-5800
www.clpccd.cc.ca.us/lpc

Lassen Community College
District
Highway 139, PO Box 3000
Susanville, CA 96130
Phone: 530-257-6181
www.lassen.cc.ca.us

Long Beach City College
4901 East Carson Street
Long Beach, CA 90808-1780
Phone: 562-938-4111
de.lbcc.cc.ca.us

Los Angeles City College
855 North Vermont Avenue
Los Angeles, CA 90029-3590
Phone: 323-953-4000
www.lacc.cc.ca.us

Los Angeles County College
of Nursing and Allied Health
1200 N State St, Muir Hall,
Rm 114
Los Angeles, CA 90033-1084
Phone: 213-226-4911

Los Angeles Harbor College
1111 Figueroa Place
Wilmington, CA 90744-2397
Phone: 310-522-8200
www.lahc.cc.ca.us

Los Angeles Mission College
13356 Eldridge Avenue
Sylmar, CA 91342-3245
Phone: 818-364-7600
www.lamission.cc.ca.us

Los Angeles Pierce College
6201 Winnetka Avenue
Woodland Hills, CA
91371-0001
Phone: 818-347-0551
www.lapc.cc.ca.us

Los Angeles Southwest
College
1600 West Imperial Highway
Los Angeles, CA 90047-4810
Phone: 323-241-5225

Los Angeles Trade-Technical
College
400 West Washington Blvd
Los Angeles, CA 90015-4108
Phone: 213-744-9500

Los Angeles Valley College
5800 Fulton Avenue
Valley Glen, CA 91401-4096
Phone: 818-947-2600
www.lavc.cc.ca.us

Los Medanos College
2700 East Leland Road
Pittsburg, CA 94565-5197
Phone: 925-439-2181

Maric College
3666 Kearny Villa Road
San Diego, CA 92123-1995
Phone: 858-279-4500
www.mariccollege.edu

Marymount College, Palos Verdes, California
30800 Palos Verdes Dr East
Rancho Palos Verdes, CA 90275-6299
Phone: 310-377-5501
www.marymountpv.edu

Mendocino College
PO Box 3000
Ukiah, CA 95482-0300
Phone: 707-468-3000
www.mendocino.cc.ca.us

Merced College
3600 M Street
Merced, CA 95348-2898
Phone: 209-384-6000

Merritt College
12500 Campus Drive
Oakland, CA 94619-3196
Phone: 510-531-4911

MiraCosta College
One Barnard Drive
Oceanside, CA 92056-3899
Phone: 760-757-2121
www.miracosta.cc.ca.us

Mission College
3000 Mission College Boulevard
Santa Clara, CA 95054-1897
Phone: 408-988-2200
www.wvmccd.cc.ca.us/mc

Modesto Junior College
435 College Avenue
Modesto, CA 95350-5800
Phone: 209-575-6498
mjc.yosemite.cc.ca.us

Monterey Peninsula College
980 Fremont Street
Monterey, CA 93940-4799
Phone: 831-646-4000
www.mpc.edu

Moorpark College
7075 Campus Road
Moorpark, CA 93021-1695
Phone: 805-378-1400
www.moorpark.cc.ca.us

Mt. San Antonio College
1100 North Grand Avenue
Walnut, CA 91789-1399
Phone: 909-594-5611
www.mtsac.edu

Mt. San Jacinto College
1499 North State Street
San Jacinto, CA 92583-2399
Phone: 909-487-6752
www.msjc.cc.ca.us

MTI College
2011 West Chapman Avenue, Suite 100
Orange, CA 92868-2632
Phone: 714-385-1132

MTI College of Business and Technology
5221 Madison Avenue
Sacramento, CA 95841
Phone: 916-339-1500
www.mticollege.com

Napa Valley College
2277 Napa-Vallejo Highway
Napa, CA 94558-6236
Phone: 707-253-3000
www.nvc.cc.ca.us

Ohlone College
43600 Mission Boulevard
Fremont, CA 94539-5884
Phone: 510-659-6000
www.ohlone.cc.ca.us

Orange Coast College
2701 Fairview Road,
PO Box 5005
Costa Mesa, CA 92628-5005
Phone: 714-432-0202
www.orangecoastcollege.com

Oxnard College
4000 South Rose Avenue
Oxnard, CA 93033-6699
Phone: 805-986-5800
www.oxnard.cc.ca.us

Palo Verde College
811 West Chanslorway
Blythe, CA 92225-1118
Phone: 760-922-6168
www.paloverde.cc.ca.us

Palomar College
1140 West Mission Road
San Marcos, CA 92069-1487
Phone: 760-744-1150
www.palomar.edu

Pasadena City College
1570 East Colorado Blvd
Pasadena, CA 91106-2041
Phone: 626-585-7123
www.paccd.cc.ca.us

Pima Medical Institute
780 Bay Boulevard
Chula Vista, CA 91910
Phone: 619-425-3200

Platt College
3700 Inland Empire Boulevard, Suite 400
Ontario, CA 91764
Phone: 909-941-9410
www.plattcollege.edu

Platt College
3901 MacArthur Boulevard
Newport Beach, CA 92660
Phone: 949-833-2300
www.plattcollege.edu

Platt College
10900 East 183rd St, Suite 290
Cerritos, CA 90703-5342
Phone: 562-809-5100
www.platt.edu

Platt College San Diego
6250 El Cajon Boulevard
San Diego, CA 92115-3919
Phone: 619-265-0107
www.platt.edu

Platt College–Los Angeles, Inc
7470 North Figueroa Street
Los Angeles, CA 90041-1717
Phone: 323-258-8050
www.plattcollege.edu

Porterville College
100 East College Avenue
Porterville, CA 93257-6058
Phone: 559-791-2200
www.pc.cc.ca.us

Professional Golfers Career College
PO Box 892319
Temecula, CA 92589
Phone: 909-693-2963

Queen of the Holy Rosary College
PO Box 3908
Mission San Jose, CA 94539-0391
Phone: 510-657-2468
www.msjdominicans.org/college.html

Reedley College
995 North Reed Avenue
Reedley, CA 93654-2099
Phone: 559-638-3641
www.rc.cc.ca.us

Rhodes College
9616 Archibald Ave, Suite 100
Rancho Cucamonga, CA 91730
Phone: 909-484-4311
rhodes-college.com

Rio Hondo College
3600 Workman Mill Road
Whittier, CA 90601-1699
Phone: 562-692-0921
www.rh.cc.ca.us

Riverside Community College
4800 Magnolia Avenue
Riverside, CA 92506-1299
Phone: 909-222-8000
www.rccd.cc.ca.us

Sacramento City College
3835 Freeport Boulevard
Sacramento, CA 95822-1386
Phone: 916-558-2111
www.scc.losrios.cc.ca.us

Saddleback College
28000 Marguerite Parkway
Mission Viejo, CA 92692-3697
Phone: 949-582-4500
www.saddleback.cc.ca.us

Salvation Army College for Officer Training
30840 Hawthorne Boulevard
Rancho Palos Verdes, CA 90275
Phone: 310-377-0481

San Bernardino Valley College
701 South Mt Vernon Avenue
San Bernardino, CA 92410-2748
Phone: 909-888-6511

San Diego City College
1313 Twelfth Avenue
San Diego, CA 92101-4787
Phone: 619-388-3400
www.city.sdccd.cc.ca.us

San Diego Golf Academy
1910 Shadowridge Drive, Suite 111
Vista, CA 92083
Phone: 760-734-1208
www.sdgagolf.com

San Diego Mesa College
7250 Mesa College Drive
San Diego, CA 92111-4998
Phone: 619-388-2600
www.sdmesa.sdccd.cc.ca.us

San Diego Miramar College
10440 Black Mountain Road
San Diego, CA 92126-2999
Phone: 619-536-7800
www.miramar.sdccd.cc.ca.us

San Francisco College of
Mortuary Science
1598 Dolores Street
San Francisco, CA
94110-4927
Phone: 415-824-1313
www.sfcms.org

San Joaquin Delta College
5151 Pacific Avenue
Stockton, CA 95207-6370
Phone: 209-954-5151
www.deltacollege.org

San Joaquin Valley College
8400 West Mineral King
Avenue
Visalia, CA 93291
Phone: 559-651-2500
www.sjvc.com

San Jose City College
2100 Moorpark Avenue
San Jose, CA 95128-2799
Phone: 408-298-2181
www.sjcc.edu

Santa Ana College
1530 West 17th Street
Santa Ana, CA 92706-3398
Phone: 714-564-6000
www.rsccd.org

Santa Barbara City College
721 Cliff Drive
Santa Barbara, CA
93109-2394
Phone: 805-965-0581
www.sbcc.net

Santa Monica College
1900 Pico Boulevard
Santa Monica, CA
90405-1628
Phone: 310-434-4000
www.smc.edu

Santa Rosa Junior College
1501 Mendocino Avenue
Santa Rosa, CA 95401-4395
Phone: 707-527-4011
www.santarosa.edu

Santiago Canyon College
8045 East Chapman Avenue
Orange, CA 92869
Phone: 714-564-4000
www.sccollege.org

Sequoia Institute
200 Whitney Place
Fremont, CA 94539-7663
Phone: 510-490-6900
www.sequoiainstitute.com

Shasta College
PO Box 496006
Redding, CA 96049-6006
Phone: 530-225-4600
www.shastacollege.edu

Sierra College
5000 Rocklin Road
Rocklin, CA 95677-3397
Phone: 916-624-3333
www.sierra.cc.ca.us

Silicon Valley College
41350 Christy Street
Fremont, CA 94538
Phone: 510-623-9966
www.siliconvalley.edu

Silicon Valley College
6201 San Ignacio Boulevard
San Jose, CA 95119
Phone: 408-360-0840
www.siliconvalley.edu

Silicon Valley College
2800 Mitchell Drive
Walnut Creek, CA 94598
Phone: 925-280-0235
www.siliconvalley.edu

Skyline College
3300 College Drive
San Bruno, CA 94066-1698
Phone: 650-738-4100
skylinecollege.net

Solano Community College
4000 Suisun Valley Road
Suisun, CA 94585-3197
Phone: 707-864-7000
www.solano.cc.ca.us

Southern California College
of Business and Law
595 West Lambert Road
Brea, CA 92821-3909
Phone: 714-256-8830

Southern California Institute
of Technology
1900 West Crescent Avenue,
Building B
Anaheim, CA 92801
Phone: 714-520-5552

Southwestern College
900 Otay Lakes Road
Chula Vista, CA 91910-7299
Phone: 619-421-6700
www.swc.cc.ca.us

Taft College
29 Emmons Park Drive
Taft, CA 93268-2317
Phone: 661-763-7700
www.taft.cc.ca.us

The Art Institute of Los
Angeles
2900 31st Street
Santa Monica, CA
90405-3035
Phone: 310-752-4700
www.aila.aii.edu

Ventura College
4667 Telegraph Road
Ventura, CA 93003-3899
Phone: 805-654-6400
www.ventura.cc.ca.us

Victor Valley College
18422 Bear Valley Road
Victorville, CA 92392-5849
Phone: 760-245-4271
www.vvcconline.com

Vista Community College
2020 Milvia Street, 3rd Floor
Berkeley, CA 94704-5102
Phone: 510-981-2800
www.peralta.cc.ca.us

West Hills Community
College
300 Cherry Lane
Coalinga, CA 93210-1399
Phone: 559-935-0801
www.westhills.cc.ca.us

West Los Angeles College
4800 Freshman Drive
Culver City, CA 90230-3519
Phone: 310-287-4200
www.wlac.cc.ca.us

West Valley College
14000 Fruitvale Avenue
Saratoga, CA 95070-5698
Phone: 408-867-2200
www.westvalley.edu

Western Institute of Science
and Health
130 Avram Avenue
Rohnert Park, CA 94928
Phone: 707-664-9267
www.westerni.org

Yuba College
2088 North Beale Road
Marysville, CA 95901-7699
Phone: 530-741-6700
www.yuba.cc.ca.us

Colorado

Aims Community College
Box 69
Greeley, CO 80632-0069
Phone: 970-330-8008
www.aims.edu

Arapahoe Community
College
5900 South Santa Fe Drive,
PO Box 9002
Littleton, CO 80160-9002
Phone: 303-797-4222
www.arapahoe.edu

Bel-Rea Institute of Animal
Technology
1681 South Dayton Street
Denver, CO 80231-3048
Phone: 303-751-8700
www.bel-rea.com

Blair College
828 Wooten Road
Colorado Springs, CO 80915
Phone: 719-574-1082
www.cci.edu

Cambridge College
12500 East Iliff Avenue, # 100
Aurora, CO 80014
Phone: 303-338-9700
www.hightechschools.com

CollegeAmerica-Denver
1385 South Colorado Blvd
Denver, CO 80222-1912
Phone: 303-691-9756
www.collegeamerica.com

CollegeAmerica-Fort Collins
4601 South Mason Street
Fort Collins, CO 80525-3740
Phone: 970-223-6060
www.collegeamerica.com

Colorado Mountain College,
Alpine Campus
1330 Bob Adams Drive
Steamboat Springs, CO
80487
Phone: 970-870-4444
www.coloradomtn.edu

Colorado Mountain College,
Spring Valley Campus
3000 County Road 114
Glenwood Springs, CO
81601
Phone: 970-945-7481
www.coloradomtn.edu

Colorado Mountain College,
Timberline Campus
901 South Highway 24
Leadville, CO 80461
Phone: 719-486-2015
www.coloradomtn.edu

Colorado Northwestern
Community College
500 Kennedy Drive
Rangely, CO   81648-3598
Phone: 970-675-2261
www.cncc.cc.co.us

Colorado School of Trades
1575 Hoyt Street
Lakewood, CO   80215-2996
Phone: 303-233-4697
www.schooloftrades.com

Community College of
Aurora
16000 East Centre Tech Pkwy
Aurora, CO   80011-9036
Phone: 303-360-4700
www.cca.cccoes.edu

Community College of
Denver
PO Box 173363
Denver, CO   80217-3363
Phone: 303-556-2600
www.ccd.rightchoice.org

Denver Academy of Court
Reporting
7290 Samuel Drive, Suite 200
Denver, CO   80221-2792
Phone: 303-427-5292
www.dacr.com

Denver Automotive and
Diesel College
460 South Lipan Street
Denver, CO   80223-2025
Phone: 303-722-5724
www.denverautodiesel.com

Front Range Community
College
3645 West 112th Avenue
Westminster, CO
80031-2105
Phone: 303-466-8811
www.frcc.cc.co.us

Institute of Business &
Medical Careers
1609 Oakridge Drive,
Suite 102
Fort Collins, CO   80525
Phone: 970-223-2669

IntelliTec College
772 Horizon Drive
Grand Junction, CO   81506
Phone: 970-245-8101

IntelliTec College
2315 East Pikes Peak Avenue
Colorado Springs, CO
80909-6030
Phone: 719-632-7626

IntelliTec Medical Institute
2345 North Academy
Boulevard
Colorado Springs, CO   80909
Phone: 719-596-7400

ITT Technical Institute
500 East 84th Avenue,
Suite B12
Thornton, CO   80229
Phone: 303-288-4488
www.itt-tech.edu

Lamar Community College
2401 South Main Street
Lamar, CO   81052-3999
Phone: 719-336-2248

Morgan Community College
17800 County Road 20
Fort Morgan, CO
80701-4399
Phone: 970-542-3100
www.mcc.cccoes.edu

Northeastern Junior College
100 College Drive
Sterling, CO   80751-2399
Phone: 970-521-6600
www.nejc.cc.co.us

Otero Junior College
1802 Colorado Avenue
La Junta, CO   81050-3415
Phone: 719-384-6831

Parks College
9065 Grant Street
Denver, CO   80229-4339
Phone: 303-457-2757
www.cci.edu

Pikes Peak Community
College
5675 South Academy Blvd
Colorado Springs, CO
80906-5498
Phone: 719-576-7711
www.ppcc.cccoes.edu

Pima Medical Institute
1701 West 72nd Avenue, #130
Denver, CO   80221
Phone: 303-426-1800
www.pimamedical.com

Platt College
3100 South Parker Road,
Suite 200
Aurora, CO   80014-3141
Phone: 303-369-5151
www.plattcolorado.edu

Pueblo Community College
900 West Orman Avenue
Pueblo, CO   81004-1499
Phone: 719-549-3200
www.pcc.cccoes.edu

Red Rocks Community
College
13300 West 6th Avenue
Lakewood, CO   80228-1255
Phone: 303-988-6160

Trinidad State Junior College
600 Prospect
Trinidad, CO   81082-2396
Phone: 719-846-5011
www.tsjc.cccoes.edu

Westwood College of
Aviation Technology–Denver
10851 West 120th Avenue
Broomfield, CO   80021-3465
Phone: 303-466-1714
www.westwood.edu

Hawaii

Hawaii Business College
33 South King Street,
Fourth Floor
Honolulu, HI   96813-4316
Phone: 808-524-4014
www.hbc.edu

Hawaii Community College
200 West Kawili Street
Hilo, HI   96720-4091
Phone: 808-974-7611
www.hawcc.hawaii.edu

Hawaii Tokai International
College
2241 Kapiolani Boulevard
Honolulu, HI   96826-4310
Phone: 808-983-4100
www.tokai.edu

Heald College, Schools of
Business and Technology
1500 Kapiolani Boulevard
Honolulu, HI   96814-3797
Phone: 808-955-1500
www.heald.edu

Honolulu Community
College
874 Dillingham Boulevard
Honolulu, HI   96817-4598
Phone: 808-845-9211
www.hcc.hawaii.edu

Kapiolani Community
College
4303 Diamond Head Road
Honolulu, HI   96816-4421
Phone: 808-734-9111

Kauai Community College
3-1901 Kaumualii Highway
Lihue, HI   96766-9591
Phone: 808-245-8311
www.kauaicc.hawaii.edu

Leeward Community College
96-045 Ala Ike
Pearl City, HI   96782-3393
Phone: 808-455-0011
www.lcc.hawaii.edu

Maui Community College
310 Kaahumanu Avenue
Kahului, HI   96732
Phone: 808-984-3500
mauicc.hawaii.edu

TransPacific Hawaii College
5257 Kalanianaole Highway
Honolulu, HI   96821-1884
Phone: 808-377-5402
www.transpacific.org

Windward Community
College
45-720 Keaahala Road
Kaneohe, HI   96744-3528
Phone: 808-235-7400
www.wcc.hawaii.edu

Idaho

American Institute of Health
Technology, Inc.
1200 North Liberty Road
Boise, ID   83704
Phone: 208-377-8080
www.aiht.com

Brigham Young University–
Idaho
Rexburg, ID   83460-1650
Phone: 208-496-2011
www.byui.edu

College of Southern Idaho
PO Box 1238
Twin Falls, ID   83303-1238
Phone: 208-733-9554
www.csi.edu

Eastern Idaho Technical
College
1600 South 25th East
Idaho Falls, ID   83404-5788
Phone: 208-524-3000
www.eitc.edu

ITT Technical Institute
12302 West Explorer Drive
Boise, ID 83713
Phone: 208-322-8844
www.itt-tech.edu

North Idaho College
1000 West Garden Avenue
Coeur d'Alene, ID
83814-2199
Phone: 208-769-3300
www.nic.edu

Montana

Blackfeet Community College
PO Box 819
Browning, MT 59417-0819
Phone: 406-338-5441
www.montana.edu/wwwbcc

Dawson Community College
Box 421
Glendive, MT 59330-0421
Phone: 406-377-3396
www.dawson.cc.mt.us

Dull Knife Memorial College
PO Box 98
Lame Deer, MT 59043-0098
Phone: 406-477-6215
www.dkmc.cc.mt.us

Flathead Valley Community
College
777 Grandview Drive
Kalispell, MT 59901-2622
Phone: 406-756-3822
www.fvcc.cc.mt.us

Fort Belknap College
PO Box 159
Harlem, MT 59526-0159
Phone: 406-353-2607
www.montana.edu/wwwse/
fbc/fbc.html

Fort Peck Community College
PO Box 398
Poplar, MT 59255-0398
Phone: 406-768-5551
www.fpcc.cc.mt.us

Helena College of Technology
of The University of Montana
1115 North Roberts Street
Helena, MT 59601
Phone: 406-444-6800
www.hct.umontana.edu

Little Big Horn College
Box 370
Crow Agency, MT
59022-0370
Phone: 406-638-2228

Miles Community College
2715 Dickinson
Miles City, MT 59301-4799
Phone: 406-234-3031
www.mcc.cc.mt.us

Montana State University–
Great Falls College of
Technology
2100 16th Avenue, South
Great Falls, MT 59405
Phone: 406-771-4300
www.msugf.edu

Salish Kootenai College
PO Box 117
Pablo, MT 59855-0117
Phone: 406-675-4800
www.skc.edu

Stone Child College
RR1, Box 1082
Box Elder, MT 59521
Phone: 406-395-4313

Nevada

Career College of Northern
Nevada
1195-A Corporate Boulevard
Reno, NV 89502
Phone: 775-856-2266
www.ccnn4u.com

Community College of
Southern Nevada
3200 East Cheyenne Avenue
North Las Vegas, NV
89030-4296
Phone: 702-651-4000
www.ccsn.nevada.edu

Great Basin College
1500 College Parkway
Elko, NV 89801-3348
Phone: 775-738-8493

Heritage College
3305 Spring Mountain Road,
Suite 7
Las Vegas, NV 89102
Phone: 702-368-2338
www.heritage-college.com

ITT Technical Institute
168 Gibson Road
Henderson, NV 89014
Phone: 702-558-5404
www.itt-tech.edu

Las Vegas College
4100 West Flamingo Road,
Suite 2100
Las Vegas, NV 89103-3926
Phone: 702-368-6200
www.cci.edu

Truckee Meadows
Community College
7000 Dandini Boulevard
Reno, NV 89512-3901
Phone: 775-673-7000
www.tmcc.edu

Western Nevada Community
College
2201 West College Parkway
Carson City, NV 89703-7316
Phone: 775-445-3000
www.wncc.nevada.edu

New Hampshire
Hesser College
3 Sundial Avenue
Manchester, NH 03103-7245
603-668-6660
www.hesser.edu

McIntosh College
23 Cataract Avenue
Dover, NH 03820-3990
603-742-1234
www.mcintoshcollege.com

New Hampshire Community
Technical College,
Berlin/Laconia
2020 Riverside Drive
Berlin, NH 03570-3717
603-752-1113
www.berl.tec.nh.us

New Hampshire Community
Technical College,
Manchester
1066 Front Street
Manchester, NH 03102-8518
603-668-6706
www.manc.tec.nh.us

New Hampshire Community
Technical College, Nashua/
Claremont
505 Amherst Street
Nashua, NH 03063-1026
603-882-6923
www.nashua.tec.nh.us

New Hampshire Technical
Institute
11 Institute Drive
Concord, NH 03301-7412
603-271-6484
www.nhti.net

New Mexico

Albuquerque Technical
Vocational Institute
525 Buena Vista, SE
Albuquerque, NM
87106-4096
Phone: 505-224-3000
www.tvi.cc.nm.us

Clovis Community College
417 Schepps Boulevard
Clovis, NM 88101-8381
Phone: 505-769-2811
www.clovis.cc.nm.us

Doña Ana Branch
Community College
MSC-3DA, Box 30001,
3400 South Espina Street
Las Cruces, NM 88003-8001
Phone: 505-527-7500
dabcc-www.nmsu.edu

Eastern New Mexico
University–Roswell
PO Box 6000
Roswell, NM 88202-6000
Phone: 505-624-7000
www.enmu.edu/roswell/
buchanaj/ENMU-R

Institute of American Indian
Arts
83 Avan Nu Po Road
Santa Fe, NM 87508
Phone: 505-424-2300
www.iaiancad.org

ITT Technical Institute
5100 Masthead, NE
Albuquerque, NM
87109-4366
Phone: 505-828-1114
www.itt-tech.edu

Luna Community College
PO Box 1510
Las Vegas, NM 87701
Phone: 505-454-2500
www.lvti.cc.nm.us

Mesa Technical College
911 South Tenth Street
Tucumcari, NM 88401
Phone: 505-461-4413
www.mesatc.cc.nm.us

New Mexico Junior College
5317 Lovington Highway
Hobbs, NM 88240-9123
Phone: 505-392-4510
www.nmjc.cc.nm.us

New Mexico Military Institute
101 West College Boulevard
Roswell, NM 88201-5173
Phone: 505-622-6250
www.nmmi.cc.nm.us

New Mexico State
University–Alamogordo
2400 North Scenic Drive
Alamogordo, NM
88311-0477
Phone: 505-439-3600
alamo.nmsu.edu

New Mexico State
University–Carlsbad
1500 University Drive
Carlsbad, NM 88220-3509
Phone: 505-234-9200
cavern.nmsu.edu

New Mexico State
University–Grants
1500 3rd Street
Grants, NM 87020-2025
Phone: 505-287-7981

Northern New Mexico
Community College
921 Paseo de Oñate
Española, NM 87532
Phone: 505-747-2100
www.nnm.cc.nm.us

Pima Medical Institute
2201 San Pedro NE,
Building 3, Suite 100
Albuquerque, NM 87110
Phone: 505-881-1234
www.pimamedical.com

San Juan College
4601 College Boulevard
Farmington, NM 87402-4699
Phone: 505-326-3311
www.sjc.cc.nm.us

Santa Fe Community College
6401 Richards Avenue
Santa Fe, NM 87505-4887
Phone: 505-428-1000
www.santa-fe.cc.nm.us

Southwestern Indian
Polytechnic Institute
9169 Coors, NW, Box 10146
Albuquerque, NM
87184-0146
Phone: 505-346-2347
www.sipi.bia.edu

The Art Center
5041 Indian School Road, NE,
Suite 100
Albuquerque, NM 87110
Phone: 505-254-7575
www.theartcenter.edu

University of New Mexico–
Gallup
200 College Road
Gallup, NM 87301-5603
Phone: 505-863-7500
www.gallup.unm.edu

University of New Mexico–
Los Alamos Branch
4000 University Drive
Los Alamos, NM
87544-2233
Phone: 505-662-5919

University of New Mexico–
Valencia Campus
280 La Entrada
Los Lunas, NM 87031-7633
Phone: 505-925-8500

Oregon

Blue Mountain Community
College
2411 Northwest Carden
Avenue, PO Box 1000
Pendleton, OR 97801-1000
Phone: 541-276-1260
www.bmcc.cc.or.us

Central Oregon Community
College
2600 Northwest College Way
Bend, OR 97701-5998
Phone: 541-383-7700
www.cocc.edu

Chemeketa Community
College
PO Box 14007
Salem, OR 97309-7070
Phone: 503-399-5000
www.chemeketa.edu

Clackamas Community
College
19600 South Molalla Avenue
Oregon City, OR 97045-7998
Phone: 503-657-6958
www.clackamas.cc.or.us

Clatsop Community College
1653 Jerome
Astoria, OR 97103-3698
Phone: 503-325-0910
www.clatsopcollege.com

Heald College, Schools of
Business and Technology
625 SW Broadway, 2nd Floor
Portland, OR 97205
Phone: 503-229-0492
www.heald.edu

ITT Technical Institute
6035 Northeast 78th Court
Portland, OR 97218-2854
Phone: 503-255-6500
Fax: 503-255-6135
www.itt-tech.edu

Lane Community College
4000 East 30th Avenue
Eugene, OR 97405-0640
Phone: 541-747-4501
www.lanecc.edu

Linn-Benton Community
College
6500 Southwest Pacific Blvd
Albany, OR 97321
Phone: 541-917-4999
www.lbcc.cc.or.us

Mt. Hood Community
College
26000 Southeast Stark Street
Gresham, OR 97030-3300
Phone: 503-491-6422
www.mhcc.cc.or.us

Pioneer Pacific College
27501 Southwest Parkway Ave
Wilsonville, OR 97070
Phone: 503-682-3903
www.pioneerpacificcollege.
com

Portland Community College
PO Box 19000
Portland, OR 97280-0990
Phone: 503-244-6111
www.pcc.edu

Rogue Community College
3345 Redwood Highway
Grants Pass, OR 97527-9298
Phone: 541-956-7500
www.rogue.cc.or.us

Southwestern Oregon
Community College
1988 Newmark Avenue
Coos Bay, OR 97420-2912
Phone: 541-888-2525
www.southwestern.cc.or.us

Treasure Valley Community
College
650 College Boulevard
Ontario, OR 97914-3423
Phone: 541-889-6493
www.tvcc.cc.or.us

Umpqua Community College
PO Box 967
Roseburg, OR 97470-0226
Phone: 541-440-4600
www.umpqua.cc.or.us

Western Business College
425 Southwest Washington
Portland, OR 97204
Phone: 503-222-3225

Utah

Certified Careers Institute
1455 West 2200 South,
Suite 200
Salt Lake City, UT 84119
Phone: 801-973-7008
www.cciutah.edu

College of Eastern Utah
451 East 400 North
Price, UT 84501-2699
Phone: 435-637-2120
www.ceu.edu

Dixie State College of Utah
225 South 700 East
St. George, UT 84770-3876
Phone: 435-652-7500
www.dixie.edu

ITT Technical Institute
920 West Levoy Drive
Murray, UT 84123-2500
Phone: 801-263-3313
www.itt-tech.edu

LDS Business College
411 East South Temple Street
Salt Lake City, UT
84111-1392
Phone: 801-524-8100
www.ldsbc.edu

Mountain West College
3280 West 3500 South
West Valley City, UT 84119
Phone: 801-840-4800
www.mwcollege.com

Salt Lake Community
College
PO Box 30808
Salt Lake City, UT
84130-0808
Phone: 801-957-4111
www.slcc.edu

Snow College
150 East College Avenue
Ephraim, UT 84627-1203
Phone: 435-283-7000
www.snow.edu

Stevens-Henager College
2168 Washington Boulevard
Ogden, UT 84401-1420
Phone: 801-394-7791
www.stevenshenager.com

Utah Career College
1902 West 7800 South
West Jordan, UT 84088
Phone: 801-304-4224
www.utahcollege.com

Utah Valley State College
800 West 1200 South Street
Orem, UT   84058-5999
Phone: 801-222-8000
www.uvsc.edu

Washington

Bates Technical College
1101 South Yakima Avenue
Tacoma, WA   98405-4895
Phone: 253-596-1500
www.bates.ctc.edu

Bellevue Community College
3000 Landerholm Circle, SE
Bellevue, WA   98007-6484
Phone: 425-564-1000
www.bcc.ctc.edu

Bellingham Technical College
3028 Lindbergh Avenue
Bellingham, WA   98225
Phone: 360-738-0221
www.beltc.ctc.edu

Big Bend Community
College
7662 Chanute Street
Moses Lake, WA   98837-3299
Phone: 509-762-5351
www.bbcc.ctc.edu

Cascadia Community College
Suite 102, 19017 120th Ave,
NE
Bothell, WA   98011
Phone: 425-398-5400
www.cascadia.ctc.edu

Centralia College
600 West Locust
Centralia, WA   98531-4099
Phone: 360-736-9391
www.centralia.ctc.edu

Clark College
1800 East McLoughlin Blvd
Vancouver, WA   98663-3598
Phone: 360-992-2000
www.clark.edu

Clover Park Technical College
4500 Steilacoom Blvd, SW
Lakewood, WA   98499
Phone: 253-589-5678
www.cptc.ctc.edu

Columbia Basin College
2600 North 20th Avenue
Pasco, WA   99301-3397
Phone: 509-547-0511
www.cbc2.org

Court Reporting Institute
929 North 130th Street,
Suite 2
Seattle, WA   98133
Phone: 206-363-8300

Crown College
8739 South Hosmer
Tacoma, WA   98444-1836
Phone: 253-531-3123
www.crowncollege.edu

Edmonds Community
College
20000 68th Avenue West
Lynnwood, WA   98036-5999
Phone: 425-640-1500
www.edcc.edu

Everett Community College
2000 Tower Street
Everett, WA   98201-1327
Phone: 425-388-9100
www.evcc.ctc.edu

Grays Harbor College
1620 Edward P Smith Drive
Aberdeen, WA   98520-7599
Phone: 360-532-9020
ghc.ctc.edu

Green River Community
College
12401 Southeast 320th Street
Auburn, WA   98092-3699
Phone: 253-833-9111
www.greenriver.ctc.edu

Highline Community College
PO Box 98000
Des Moines, WA   98198-9800
Phone: 206-878-3710
www.hcc.ctc.edu

ITT Technical Institute
2525 223rd Street, SE,
Canyon Park East
Bothell, WA   98021
Phone: 425-485-0303
www.itt-tech.edu

ITT Technical Institute
12720 Gateway Drive,
Suite 100
Seattle, WA   98168-3333
Phone: 206-244-3300
www.itt-tech.edu

ITT Technical Institute
1050 North Argonne Road
Spokane, WA   99212-2682
Phone: 509-926-2900
www.itt-tech.edu

Lake Washington Technical
College
11605 132nd Avenue NE
Kirkland, WA   98034-8506
Phone: 425-739-8100

Lower Columbia College
PO Box 3010
Longview, WA   98632-0310
Phone: 360-577-2300
lcc.ctc.edu

North Seattle Community
College
9600 College Way North
Seattle, WA   98103-3599
Phone: 206-527-3600
www.northseattle.edu

Northwest Aviation College
506 23rd, NE
Auburn, WA   98002
Phone: 253-854-4960
www.afsnac.com

Northwest Indian College
2522 Kwina Road
Bellingham, WA   98226
Phone: 360-676-2772
www.nwic.edu

Olympic College
1600 Chester Avenue
Bremerton, WA   98337-1699
Phone: 360-792-6050
www.oc.ctc.edu/~oc

Peninsula College
1502 East Lauridsen Blvd
Port Angeles, WA
98362-2779
Phone: 360-452-9277
www.pc.ctc.edu

Pierce College
9401 Farwest Drive, SW
Lakewood, WA   98498-1999
Phone: 253-964-6500
www.pierce.ctc.edu

Pima Medical Institute
1627 Eastlake Avenue East
Seattle, WA   98102
Phone: 206-322-6100
www.pimamedical.com

Renton Technical College
3000 NE Fourth Street
Renton, WA   98056-4195
Phone: 425-235-2352
www.renton-tc.ctc.edu

Seattle Central Community
College
1701 Broadway
Seattle, WA   98122-2400
Phone: 206-587-3800
seattlecentral.org

Shoreline Community
College
16101 Greenwood Avenue N
Seattle, WA   98133-5696
Phone: 206-546-4101
www.shoreline.ctc.edu

Skagit Valley College
2405 College Way
Mount Vernon, WA
98273-5899
Phone: 360-416-7600
www.svc.ctc.edu

South Puget Sound
Community College
2011 Mottman Road, SW
Olympia, WA   98512-6292
Phone: 360-754-7711
www.spscc.ctc.edu

South Seattle Community
College
6000 16th Avenue, SW
Seattle, WA   98106-1499
Phone: 206-764-5300
www.sccd.ctc.edu

Spokane Community College
1810 North Greene Street
Spokane, WA   99217-5399
Phone: 509-533-7000
www.scc.spokane.cc.wa.us

Spokane Falls Community
College
3410 West Fort George
Wright Drive
Spokane, WA   99224-5288
Phone: 509-533-3500
www.sfcc.spokane.cc.wa.us

Tacoma Community College
6501 South 19th Street
Tacoma, WA   98466
Phone: 253-566-5000
Fax: 253-566-5376
www.tacoma.ctc.edu

The Art Institute of Seattle
2323 Elliott Avenue
Seattle, WA   98121-1642
Phone: 206-448-0900
www.ais.edu

Walla Walla Community
College
500 Tausick Way
Walla Walla, WA   99362-9267
Phone: 509-522-2500
www.wallawalla.cc

Wenatchee Valley College
1300 Fifth Street
Wenatchee, WA   98801-1799
Phone: 509-662-1651
www.wvc.ctc.edu

Whatcom Community
College
237 West Kellogg Road
Bellingham, WA   98226-8003
Phone: 360-676-2170
Fax: 360-676-2171
www.whatcom.ctc.edu

Yakima Valley Community
College
PO Box 22520
Yakima, WA   98907-2520
Phone: 509-574-4600
www.yvcc.cc.wa.us

Wyoming

Casper College
125 College Drive
Casper, WY   82601-4699
Phone: 307-268-2110
www.cc.whecn.edu

Central Wyoming College
2660 Peck Avenue
Riverton, WY   82501-2273
Phone: 307-855-2000
www.cwc.cc.wy.us

Eastern Wyoming College
3200 West C Street
Torrington, WY   82240-1699
Phone: 307-532-8200
ewcweb.ewc.cc.wy.us

Laramie County Community
College
1400 East College Drive
Cheyenne, WY   82007-3299
Phone: 307-778-5222
www.lccc.cc.wy.us

Northwest College
231 West 6th Street
Powell, WY   82435-1898
Phone: 307-754-6000
www.nwc.cc.wy.us

Sheridan College
PO Box 1500
Sheridan, WY   82801-1500
Phone: 307-674-6446
www.sc.cc.wy.us

Western Wyoming
Community College
PO Box 428
Rock Springs, WY
82902-0428
Phone: 307-382-1600
www.wwcc.cc.wy.us

Wyoming Technical Institute
4373 North Third Street
Laramie, WY   82072-9519
Phone: 307-742-3776
www.wyotech.com

VOCATIONAL AND TECHNICAL COLLEGES

Alaska

Alaska Vocational Institute
210 Ferry Way, Suite 200
Juneau, AK 99801

Alaska Vocational Technical
Center
PO Box 889
Seward, AK 99664
907-224-4153

Career Academy
1415 East Tudor Road
Anchorage, AK 99507-1033
907-563-7575

Charter College
2221 East Northern Lights
Boulevard, Suite 120
Anchorage, AK 99508-4140
907-777-1341

Shear Allusions 2000, A
Training Salon
44539 Sterling Highway
The Blazy Mall
Soldotna, AK 99669
907-262-6525

Arizona

Academy of Radio
Broadcasting
4914 East McDowell Rd, #107
Phoenix, AZ 85008
602-267-8001

Alta Center For
Communication Arts
9014 North 23rd Avenue,
Suite 1
Phoenix, AZ 85021
888-729-4954

Apollo College-Phoenix, Inc.
8503 North 27th Avenue
Phoenix, AZ 85051
602-864-1571

Apollo College-Tri-City, Inc.
630 West Southern Avenue
Mesa, AZ 85210-5004
480-831-6585

Apollo College-Tucson, Inc.
3870 North Oracle Road
Tucson, AZ 85705
520-888-5885

Apollo College-Westside, Inc.
2701 West Bethany Home Rd
Phoenix, AZ 85017
602-433-1333 Ext. 251

Arizona Automotive Institute
6829 North 46th Avenue
Glendale, AZ 85301
623-934-7273

Arizona College of Allied
Health
1940 West Indian School Rd
Phoenix, AZ 85015
602-222-9300

Arizona Paralegal Training
Program
111 West Monroe St, Suite 800
Phoenix, AZ 85003
602-252-2171

The Art Institute of Phoenix
2233 West Dunlap Avenue
Phoenix, AZ 85021
800-474-2479

The Bryman School
2250 West Peoria Avenue
Phoenix, AZ 85029
602-274-4300

Chaparral College
4585 East Speedway Blvd,
Suite 204
Tucson, AZ 85712
520-327-6866

Charles of Italy Beauty College
1987 McCulloch Boulevard
Lake Havasu City, AZ 86403

Collins College: A School of
Design and Technology
1140 South Priest Drive
Tempe, AZ 85281-5206
480-966-3000

Conservatory of Recording
Arts and Sciences
2300 East Broadway Road
Tempe, AZ 85282
800-562-6383

DeVoe College of Beauty
750 Bartow Drive
Sierra Vista, AZ 85635
520-458-8660

Education America, Tempe
Campus
875 West Elliot Road
Tempe, AZ 85284
480-834-1000

GateWay Community College
108 North 40th Street
Phoenix, AZ 85034-1795
602-392-5194

High-Tech Institute
1515 East Indian School Road
Phoenix, AZ 85014-4901
602-279-9700

High-Tech Institute
2250 West Peoria Avenue
Phoenix, AZ 85029
602-279-9700

International Academy of Hair
Design
4415 South Rural Road,
Suite 2
Tempe, AZ 85282

International Import/Export
Institute
2432 West Peoria, Suite 1026
Phoenix, AZ 85029
602-648-5750

ITT Technical Institute
1455 West River Road
Tucson, AZ 85704
520-408-7488

ITT Technical Institute
4837 East McDowell Road
Phoenix, AZ 85008-4292
602-231-0871

Metropolitan College of
Court Reporting
4640 East Elwood St, Suite 12
Phoenix, AZ 85040
602-955-5900

Mohave Community College
1971 Jagerson Avenue
Kingman, AZ 86401
520-757-0898

Motorcycle Mechanics
Institute
2844 West Deer Valley Road
Phoenix, AZ 85027-2399
623-869-9644

Northern Arizona College of
Health Careers
5200 East Cortland
Boulevard, Suite A19
Flagstaff, AZ 86004
928-526-0763

Northland Pioneer College
PO Box 610
Holbrook, AZ 86025-0610
928-536-6257

Pima Medical Institute
957 South Dobson
Mesa, AZ 85202
480-345-7777

The Refrigeration School
4210 East Washington Street
Phoenix, AZ 85034
602-275-7133

Rhodes College
2525 West Beryl Avenue
Phoenix, AZ 85021-1641
602-942-4141

Scottsdale Culinary Institute
8100 East Camelback Road,
Suite 1001
Scottsdale, AZ 85251-3940
602-990-3773

Universal Technical Institute
3121 West Weldon Avenue
Phoenix, AZ 85017
602-264-4164

University of Phoenix-
Phoenix Campus
4605 East Elwood Street
Phoenix, AZ 85040
480-557-2000

University of Phoenix-
Southern Arizona Campus
5099 East Grant Road, #120
Tucson, AZ 85712
520-881-6512

California

Academy of Art College
79 New Montgomery Street
San Francisco, CA 94105
415-263-7757

Academy of Radio
Broadcasting
16052 Beach Boulevard,
Suite 263
Huntington Beach, CA 92647
714-842-0100

The Advanced Career
College
41765 N. 12th St. Ste. B.
West Palmdale, CA 93551
661-948-4141

American Career College,
Inc.
4021 Rosewood Avenue
Los Angeles, CA 90004
323-666-7555

American InterContinental
University
12655 West Jefferson Blvd
Los Angeles, CA 90066
888-248-7390

Andon College
1201 North El Dorado Street
Stockton, CA 95202
209-462-8777

Andon College
1700 McHenry Village Way
Modesto, CA 95350
209-571-8777

Antelope Valley College
3041 West Avenue K
Lancaster, CA 93536-5426
661-722-6338

The Art Institute of California
10025 Mesa Rim Road
San Diego, CA 92121-2913
866-275-2422 Ext. 3117

The Art Institute of
Los Angeles
2900 31st Street
Santa Monica, CA
90405-3035
310-752-4700

Art Institute of Los Angeles-
Orange County
3601 West Sunflower Avenue
Santa Ana, CA 92704
888-549-3055

Art Institutes International at
San Francisco
1170 Market Street
San Francisco, CA 94102
888-493-3261

Asian-American International
Beauty College
7871 Westminster Boulevard
Westminster, CA 92683
714-891-0508

Bethany College of the
Assemblies of God
800 Bethany Drive
Scotts Valley, CA 95066-2820
831-438-3800 Ext. 1400

Brooks College
4825 East Pacific Coast Hwy
Long Beach, CA 90804
800-421-3775 Ext. 271

Brooks Institute of
Photography
801 Alston Road
Santa Barbara, CA
93108-2399
805-966-3888

Bryman College
1045 West Redondo Beach
Boulevard, Suite 275
Gardena, CA 90247
310-527-7105 Ext. 102

Bryman College
12446 Putnam Street
Whittier, CA 90602
562-945-9191

Bryman College
1245 South Winchester
Boulevard, Suite 102
San Jose, CA 95128
408-246-4171

Bryman College
22336 Main Street
Hayward, CA 94541
510-582-9500

Bryman College
3000 South Robertson
Boulevard, 3rd Floor
Los Angeles, CA 90034
310-840-5777

Bryman College
3208 Rosemead Boulevard,
Suite 100
El Monte, CA 91731
626-573-5470

Bryman College
3460 Wilshire Boulevard,
Suite 500
Los Angeles, CA 90010
213-388-9950

Bryman College
511 North Brookhurst Street,
Suite 300
Anaheim, CA 92801
714-953-6500

Bryman College
520 North Euclid Avenue
Ontario, CA 91762-3591
909-984-5027

Bryman College
814 Mission Street, Suite 500
San Francisco, CA 94103
415-777-2500

Bryan College of Court
Reporting
2333 Beverly Boulevard
Los Angeles, CA 90057
213-484-8850

California College for Health
Sciences
2423 Hoover Avenue
National City, CA 91950-6605
619-477-4800 Ext. 301

California College of
Technology
4330 Watt Avenue, Suite 400
Sacramento, CA 95660
916-649-8168

California Motel Training
801 Riverside Avenue,
Suite 104
Roseville, CA 95678

California Paramedical and
Technical College
4550 La Sierra Avenue
Riverside, CA 92505-2907
909-687-9006

California Paramedical and
Technical College
3745 Long Beach Boulevard
Long Beach, CA 90807-3377
562-427-4217

California School of Culinary
Arts
521 East Green Street
Pasadena, CA 91101
888-900-2433 Ext. 1352

California Vocational College
3951 Balboa Street
San Francisco, CA 94121
415-668-0103

Career Networks Institute
986 Town & Country Road
Orange, CA 92868-4714
714-568-1566

Central Coast College
480 South Main Street
Salinas, CA 93901
831-753-6660

City College of San Francisco
50 Phelan Avenue
San Francisco, CA
94112-1821
415-239-3285

Coleman College
1284 West San Marcos Blvd
San Marcos, CA 92069
760-747-3990

Coleman College
7380 Parkway Drive
La Mesa, CA 91942
619-465-3990 Ext. 131

Computer Training Academy
235 Charcot Avenue
San Jose, CA 95131
408-441-6990 Ext. 112

Concorde Career Institute
570 W. 4th St. Ste. 107
San Bernardino, CA 92401
714-884-8891

Concord University School of
Law
1133 Westwood Boulevard,
Suite 2010
Los Angeles, CA 90024
800-439-4794

De Anza College
21250 Stevens Creek Blvd
Cupertino, CA 95014-5793

Dell'Arte School of Physical
Theatre
PO Box 816
Blue Lake, CA 95525
541-488-9180

Detective Training Institute
PO Box 909
San Juan Capistrano, CA
92693

Education America
University
123 Camino De La Reina,
Suite 100
San Diego, CA 92108
619-686-8600 Ext. 202

Empire College
3035 Cleveland Avenue
Santa Rosa, CA 95403
707-546-4000

Galen College of California,
Inc.
1604 Ford Avenue, Suite 10
Modesto, CA 95350
209-527-5084

Galen College of California,
Inc.
3908 West Caldwell Avenue,
Suite A
Visalia, CA 93277
559-732-5200

Galen College of California,
Inc.
1325 North Wishon Avenue
Fresno, CA 93728
559-264-9700

Gemological Institute of
America, Inc.
550 South Hill Street,
Suite 901
Los Angeles, CA 90013
213-833-0115

Gemological Institute of
America, Inc.
5345 Armada Drive
Carlsbad, CA 92008
760-603-4001

Glendale Career College
1015 Grandview Avenue
Glendale, CA 91201
818-243-1131

Glendale Career College-
Oceanside
Tri-City Medical Center,
4002 Vista Way
Oceanside, CA 92056
760-945-9896

Harbor Medical College
1231 Cabrillo Avenue,
Suite 201
Torrance, CA 90501
310-320-3200

Heald College, Schools of
Business and Technology
255 West Bullard Avenue
Fresno, CA 93704-1706
559-438-4222 Ext. 4134

High-Tech Institute
1111 Howe Avenue, #250
Sacramento, CA 95825
916-929-9700

Institute for Business and
Technology
2550 Scott Boulevard
Santa Clara, CA 95050
408-727-1060

International Air Academy,
Inc.
2980 Inland Empire
Boulevard
Ontario, CA 91764-4804
909-989-5222 Ext. 224

ITT Technical Institute
630 East Brier Drive,
Suite 150
San Bernardino, CA 92408-
2800
909-889-3800

ITT Technical Institute
9680 Granite Ridge Drive
San Diego, CA 92123-2662
858-571-8500

ITT Technical Institute
10863 Gold Center Drive
Rancho Cordova, CA
95670-6034
916-851-3900

ITT Technical Institute
Lake Marriott Business
Center, 5104 Old Ironside
Santa Clara, CA 95054
408-496-0655

ITT Technical Institute
20050 South Vermont Avenue
Torrance, CA 90502
310-380-1555 Ext. 105

ITT Technical Institute
12669 Encinitas Avenue
Sylmar, CA 91342-3664
818-364-5151

ITT Technical Institute
2051 North Solar Drive,
Suite 150
Oxnard, CA 93030
805-988-0143

ITT Technical Institute
525 North Muller Avenue
Anaheim, CA 92801
714-535-3700

ITT Technical Institute
3979 Trust Way, Britannia
Point Eden
Hayward, CA 94545
510-785-8522 Ext. 23

ITT Technical Institute
16916 South Harlan Road
Lathrop, CA 95330
209-858-0077

ITT Technical Institute
1530 West Cameron Avenue
West Covina, CA 91790-2767
626-960-8681

Kensington College
2428 North Grand Avenue,
Suite D
Santa Ana, CA 92705

Las Positas College
3033 Collier Canyon Road
Livermore, CA 94550-7650
501-373-5800

Loving Hands Institute of
Healing Arts
639 11th Street
Fortuna, CA 95540-2346
707-725-9627

Maric College
3666 Kearny Villa Road,
Suite 100
San Diego, CA 92123
858-279-4500

Maric College
2030 University Drive
Vista, CA 92083
760-630-1555

Marinello School of Beauty
1226 University Avenue
San Diego, CA 92103
800-648-3413

Martinez Adult School
600 F Street
Martinez, CA 94553-3298
925-228-3276 Ext. 230

Mendocino College
PO Box 3000
Ukiah, CA 95482-0300
707-468-3101

Modern Technology College
6180 Laurel Canyon
Boulevard, #101
North Hollywood, CA 91606
818-763-2563 Ext. 223

MTI Business College of
Stockton Inc.
6006 North El Dorado Street
Stockton, CA 95207-4349
209-957-3030 Ext. 314

National Career Education
6060 Sunrise Vista Drive
Citrus Heights, CA 95610
916-969-4900

National Institute of
Technology
236 East Third Street
Long Beach, CA 90802
562-437-0501

New School of Architecture &
Design
1249 F Street
San Diego, CA 92101-6634
619-235-4100 Ext. 103

North-West College
134 W. Holt Avenue
Pomona, CA 91768
626-960-5046

North-West College
2121 W. Garvey Avenue
West Covina, CA 91790
626-960-5046

North-West College
530 E. Union Street
Pasadena, CA 91101

North-West College
124 S. Glendale Avenue
Glendale, CA 91205
818-242-0205

Orange Coast College
2701 Fairview Road,
PO Box 5005
Costa Mesa, CA 92628-5005
714-432-5773

Pacific College of Oriental
Medicine
7445 Mission Valley Road,
Suite 105
San Diego, CA 92108
619-574-6909

Pacific School of Massage
and Healing Arts
44800 Fish Rock Road
Gualala, CA 95445
707-884-3138

Platt College
3700 Inland Empire Blvd
Ontario, CA 91764
909-941-9410

Platt College
3901 MacArthur Boulevard
Newport Beach, CA 92660
949-833-2300

Platt College-Los Angeles, Inc
7470 North Figueroa Street
Los Angeles, CA 90041-1717
323-258-8050

Platt College San Diego
6250 El Cajon Boulevard
San Diego, CA 92115-3919
619-265-0107

Rhodes College
9616 Archilbald Ave, Suite 100
Rancho Cucamonga, CA
91730
909-484-4311

Sacramento City College
3835 Freeport Boulevard
Sacramento, CA 95822-1386
916-558-2438

San Joaquin Valley College
10641 Church Street
Rancho Cucamonga, CA
91730
909-948-7582

San Joaquin Valley College
295 East Sierra Avenue
Fresno, CA 93710-3616
559-229-7800

San Joaquin Valley College
8400 West Mineral King Ave
Visalia, CA 93291-9283
559-651-2500

San Joaquin Valley College
4985 East Anderson Avenue
Fresno, CA 93727
559-453-0123

Santa Barbara Business
College
5266 Hollister Avenue
Santa Barbara, CA 93111
805-967-9677

Santa Barbara Business
College
305 East Plaza Drive
Santa Maria, CA 93454
805-922-8256

Santa Barbara Business
College
211 South Real Road
Bakersfield, CA 93309
805-835-1100

Silicon Valley College
2800 Mitchell Road
Walnut Creek, CA 94598
925-280-0235

Silicon Valley College
41350 Christy Street
Fremont, CA 94538
510-623-9966

Silicon Valley College
6201 San Ignacio Avenue
San Jose, CA 95119
408-360-0840

Simi Valley Adult School
3192 Los Angeles Avenue
Simi Valley, CA 93065
805-579-6200

Skadron College
295 East Caroline, Suite D
San Bernardino, CA 92408
909-783-8810

Spectrum Community
Services, Inc.
1435 Grove Way
Hayward, CA 94546
510-881-0300 Ext. 227

Travel-World College and
Agency
2990 South Sepulveda
Boulevard, Suite 205
West Los Angeles, CA 90064
310-479-6093

United Education Corp
3380 Shelby Street, Suite 150
Ontario, CA 91764
909-476-2424

United Education
Corporation
7335 Van Nuys Boulevard
Van Nuys, CA 91405
818-756-1200

United Education Corp
1323 6th Avenue
San Diego, CA 92101
619-544-9800

United Education
Corporation
6812 Pacific Boulevard
Huntington Park, CA 90255
323-277-8000

United Education
Corporation
310 3rd Avenue, Suite C6/C7
Chula Vista, CA 91910
619-409-4111

United Education
Corporation
295 East Caroline Street,
Suite E
San Bernardino, CA 92408
909-554-1999

United Education
Corporation
3727 West 6th Street
Los Angeles, CA 90020
213-427-3700

Universal Technical Institute
15530 6th Street, Suite #110
Rancho Cucamonga, CA
91730
909-484-1929

University of Phoenix-
Northern California Campus
7901 Stoneridge Drive,
Suite 100
Pleasanton, CA 94588
877-478-8336

University of Phoenix-
Sacramento Campus
1760 Creekside Oaks Drive,
#100
Sacramento, CA 95833
800-266-2107

University of Phoenix-
San Diego Campus
11682 El Camino Real,
2nd Floor
San Diego, CA 92130
888-867-4636

University of Phoenix-
Southern California Campus
10540 Talbert Avenue, #120
Fountain Valley, CA 92708
800-468-6867

Valley Travel College
1368 W. Herndon Ste. 101
Fresno, CA 93711
559-436-1027

Western Career College
380 Civic Drive, Suite 300
Pleasant Hill, CA 94523
925-609-6650

Western Career College
8909 Folsom Boulevard
Sacramento, CA 95826
916-361-1660 Ext. 615

Westwood College of
Aviation Technology-
Los Angeles
8911 Aviation Boulevard
Inglewood, CA 90301
310-642-5440 Ext. 203

Westwood College of
Technology-Anaheim
2461 West La Palma Avenue
Anaheim, CA 92801
714-226-9990 Ext. 100

Westwood College of
Technology-Inland Empire
20 West 7th Street
Upland, CA 91786
909-931-7550 Ext. 100

Westwood College of
Technology-Los Angeles
3460 Wilshire, Suite 700
Los Angeles, CA 90010
213-739-9999 Ext. 100

Colorado

Americana Beauty College II
3650 Austin Bluffs Parkway,
Suite 174
Colorado Springs, CO 80918
719-598-4188

The Art Institute of Colorado
1200 Lincoln Street
Denver, CO 80203
800-275-2420

Bel-Rea Institute of Animal
Technology
1681 South Dayton Street
Denver, CO 80231-3048
303-751-8700

Cambridge College
12500 East Iliff Avenue
Aurora, CO 80014
303-338-9700

CollegeAmerica
1385 South Colorado
Boulevard, 5th Floor
Denver, CO 80222
303-691-9756

Colorado School of Trades
1575 Hoyt Street
Lakewood, CO 80215-2996
303-233-4697 Ext. 16

Denver Automotive and
Diesel College
460 South Lipan Street,
PO Box 9366
Denver, CO 80223-9960
303-722-5724

Denver Career College
1401 19th Street
Denver, CO 80202-1213
303-295-0550

Education America, Colorado
Springs Campus
6050 Erin Park Drive,
Suite 250
Colorado Springs, CO
80918-3401
719-532-1234

Education America, Denver
Campus
11011 West 6th Avenue
Lakewood, CO 80215-5501
303-445-0500

Institute of Business and
Medical Careers
1609 Oakridge Drive,
Suite 102
Fort Collins, CO 80525

International Guide Academy
Inc.
PMB 318, 2888 Bluff Street
Boulder, CO 80301
303-530-3420

ITT Technical Institute
500 East 84 Avenue
Thornton, CO 80229-5338
303-288-4488

Johnson & Wales University
7150 Montview Boulevard
Denver, CO 80220
303-256-9300

Otero Junior College
1802 Colorado Avenue
La Junta, CO 81050-3415
719-384-6831

Parks College
9065 Grant Street
Denver, CO 80229
303-457-2757

Parks College
6 Abilene Street
Aurora, CO 80011
303-367-2757

Platt College
3100 South Parker Road,
Suite 200
Aurora, CO 80014-3141
303-369-5151

Real Estate College of
Colorado
33 Inverness Place
Durango, CO 81301

Rocky Mountain College of
Art & Design
6875 East Evans Avenue
Denver, CO 80224-2359
303-753-6046

Sage Technical Services
365 South Main Street
Brighton, CO 80601
800-867-9856

Sage Technical Services
764 Horizon Drive, Suite 201
Grand Junction, CO 81506

Technical Trades Institute
2315 East Pikes Peak Avenue
Colorado Springs, CO
80909-6030
719-632-7626

T. H. Pickens Technical Center
500 Airport Boulevard
Aurora, CO 80011
303-344-4910 Ext. 27935

Trinidad State Junior
College-Valley Campus
1011 Main Street
Alamosa, CO 81101
719-589-1513

University of Phoenix-
Colorado Campus
10004 Park Meadows Drive
Lone Tree, CO 80124
303-755-9090

University of Phoenix-
Southern Colorado Campus
5475 Tech Center Drive,
Suite 130
Colorado Springs, CO 80919
719-599-5282 Ext. 114

Westwood College of
Aviation Technology-Denver
10851 West 120th Avenue
Broomfield, CO 80021-3465
303-466-1714

Westwood College of
Technology-Denver North
7350 North Broadway
Denver, CO 80221-3653
303-426-7000 Ext. 100

Westwood College of
Technology-Denver South
3150 South Sheridan Blvd
Denver, CO 80227
303-934-1122 Ext. 100

Hawaii

Education America, Honolulu
Campus
1111 Bishop Street, Suite 400
Honolulu, HI 96813
808-942-1000

Hawaii Business College
33 South King Street,
4th Floor
Honolulu, HI 96813
808-524-4014

Hawaii Institute of Hair
Design
71 South Hotel Street
Honolulu, HI 96813-3112
808-533-6596

Heald College, Schools of
Business and Technology
1500 Kapiolani Boulevard
Honolulu, HI 96814-3797
808-955-1500 Ext. 512

Hollywood Beauty College
99-084 Kauhale Street,
Building A
Aiea, HI 96701

Honolulu Community
College
874 Dillingham Boulevard
Honolulu, HI 96817-4598
808-845-9129

Institute of Body
Therapeutics
PO Box 11777
Lahaina, HI 96761

Kauai Community College
3-1901 Kaumualii Highway
Lihue, HI 96766-9591
808-245-8225

New York Technical Institute
of Hawaii
1375 Dillingham Boulevard
Honolulu, HI 96817-4415
808-841-5827

Travel Institute of the Pacific
1314 Sourth King Street,
Suite 1164
Honolulu, HI 96814-4401
808-591-2708

University of Phoenix-Hawaii
Campus
827 Fort Street
Honolulu, HI 96813
866-236-7655

Idaho

Aero Technicians, Inc.
Rexburg Airport, PO Box 7
Rexburg, ID 83440
208-245-4446

American Institute of Health
Technology
1200 North Liberty Street
Boise, ID 83704
208-377-8080 Ext. 22

Eastern Idaho Technical
College
1600 South 25th East
Idaho Falls, ID 83404-5788
208-524-3000 Ext. 3371

Headmasters School of Hair
Design II
602 Main Street
Lewiston, ID 83501
208-743-1512

ITT Technical Institute
12302 West Explorer Drive
Boise, ID 83713-1529
208-322-8844

Mr. Juan's College of Hair
Design
577 Lynwood Mall
Twin Falls, ID 83301
208-733-7777

Sage Technical Services
207 South 34th Avenue
Caldwell, ID 83605
800-858-6304

Sage Technical Services
1420 East 3rd Avenue
Post Falls, ID 83854
800-400-0079

The School of Hairstyling
257 North Main Street
Pocatello, ID 83204

Shadow Mountain Business
Careers
11911 Ustick Road
Boise, ID 83706

Montana

Jerry Malson's Montana
Guide Training Center
22 Swamp Creek Road
Trout Creek, MT 59874
406-847-5582

Miles Community College
2715 Dickinson
Miles City, MT 59301-4799
406-234-3518

Rocky Mountain College
1511 Poly Drive
Billings, MT 59102-1796
406-657-1148

Sage Technical Services
3044 Hesper Road
Billings, MT 59102
406-652-3030

Nevada

Computer-Ed Institute
2290 Corporate Circle Drive,
Suite 100
Henderson, NV 89074
702-269-7600 Ext. 201

ITT Technical Institute
168 North Gibson Road
Henderson, NV 89014
702-558-5404

Las Vegas College
4100 West Flamingo Road,
#2100
Las Vegas, NV 89103
702-368-6200

Nevada Career Institute
3025 East Desert Inn Road,
Suite 11
Las Vegas, NV 89121
702-893-3300

Prestige Travel School
6175 West Spring Mountain Rd
Las Vegas, NV 89146
702-251-5552

Southern Nevada School of
Real Estate
3441 West Sahara Avenue,
Suite C1
Las Vegas, NV 89102-6059

Truckee Meadows
Community College
7000 Dandini Boulevard
Reno, NV 89512-3901
775-673-7041

University of Phoenix-
Nevada Campus
333 North Rancho Drive, #300
Las Vegas, NV 89106
702-638-7868

New Mexico

Clovis Community College
417 Schepps Boulevard
Clovis, NM 88101-8381
505-769-4021

ITT Technical Institute
5100 Masthead Street, NE
Albuquerque, NM
87109-4366
505-828-1114

Mesa Technical College
911 South Tenth Street
Tucumcari, NM 88401
505-461-4413 Ext. 103

Metropolitan College of
Court Reporting
1717 Louisiana, NE, Suite 207
Albuquerque, NM
87110-4129
505-888-3400

New Mexico State
University-Alamogordo
2400 North Scenic Drive
Alamogordo, NM
88311-0477

New Mexico State
University-Carlsbad
1500 University Drive
Carlsbad, NM 88220-3509
505-234-9220

Phoenix-New Mexico
Campus
7471 Pan American Fwy, NE
Albuquerque, NM 87109
505-821-4800

Oregon

Apollo College
2600 Southeast 98th Avenue
Portland, OR 97266
503-761-6100

The Art Institute of Portland
2000 Southwest Fifth Avenue
Portland, OR 97201
888-228-6528

College of Hair Design
Careers
3322 Lancaster Drive, NE
Salem, OR 97305-1354

ITT Technical Institute
6035 Northeast 78th Court
Portland, OR 97218-2854
800-234-5488

Linn-Benton Community
College
6500 Southwest Pacific Blvd
Albany, OR 97321
541-917-4817

Northwest Nannies Institute,
Inc.
11830 SW Kerr Parkway,
Suite 100
Lake Oswego, OR 97035
503-245-5288

Oregon Institute of
Technology
3201 Campus Drive
Klamath Falls, OR
97601-8801
541-885-1000

Portland Community College
PO Box 19000
Portland, OR 97280-0990
503-977-4519

University of Phoenix-
Oregon Campus
13221 Southwest 68th
Parkway, Suite 500
Portland, OR 97223
503-670-0590

Western Business College
425 Southwest Washington St
Portland, OR 97204
503-222-3225

Western Culinary Institute
1201 Southwest 12th Avenue,
Suite 100
Portland, OR 97205
503-223-2245 Ext. 335

Utah

Bon Losee Academy of Hair
Artistry
2230 North University Pkwy,
Building 5
Provo, UT 84604
801-375-8000

Bridgerland Applied
Technology Center
1301 North 600 West
Logan, UT 84321
435-750-3250

Cameo College of Beauty
Skin and Electrolysis
1600 South State Street
Salt Lake City, UT 84115

Center for Travel Education
9489 South 700 East
Sandy, UT 84088

Certified Careers Institute
1455 West 2200 South,
Suite 103
Salt Lake City, UT
84119-7218
801-973-7008

Certified Careers Institute
775 South 2000 East
Clearfield, UT 84015
801-774-9900

ITT Technical Institute
920 West Levoy Drive
Murray, UT 84123-2500
801-263-3313

LDS Business College
411 East South Temple Street
Salt Lake City, UT 84111-1392
801-524-8144

Mountain West College
3280 West 3500 South
West Valley City, UT 84119
801-840-4800

Provo College
1450 West 820 North
Provo, UT 84601
801-375-1861

Stevens-Henager College
2168 Washington Boulevard
Ogden, UT 84401
800-977-5455

Stevens-Henager College of
Business-Provo
25 E. 1700 S.
Provo, UT 84606-6157
801-375-5455

Stevens-Henager College-
Provo
25 East 1700 South
Provo, UT 84606
800-977-5455

Stevens-Henager College-
Salt Lake City
635 West 5300 South
Salt Lake City, UT 84123
800-977-5455

Uintah Basin Applied
Technology Center
1100 East Lagoon 124-5
Roosevelt, UT 84066
435-722-4523

University of Phoenix-Utah
Campus
5251 Green Street
Salt Lake City, UT 84123
800-224-2844

Weber State University
1001 University Circle
Ogden, UT 84408-1001
801-626-6067

Western Governors
University
2040 East Murray Holladay,
Suite 106
Salt Lake City, UT 84117
801-274-3280 Ext. 15

Washington

Apollo College
1101 North Fancher Avenue
Spokane, WA 99212
509-532-8888

The Art Institute of Seattle
2323 Elliott Avenue
Seattle, WA 98121
206-239-2242

Bellingham Beauty School
211 West Holly Street
Bellingham, WA 98225
360-739-1494

Big Bend Community
College
7662 Chanute Street
Moses Lake, WA 98837-3299
509-762-5351 Ext. 226

Bryman College
17900 Pacific Highway South,
Suite 400
Seatac, WA 98188
206-241-5825

Clover Park Technical College
4500 Steilacoom Blvd, SW
Lakewood, WA 98499
253-589-5541

Columbia Basin College
2600 North 20th Avenue
Pasco, WA 99301-3397
509-547-0511 Ext. 2761

Eton Technical Institute
209 East Casino Road
Everett, WA 98208
425-353-4888

Gene Juarez Academy of
Beauty
2222 South 314th Street
Federal Way, WA 98003
206-368-0210

Glen Dow Academy of Hair
Design
309 West Riverside Avenue
Spokane, WA 99201
509-624-3244

International Air Academy
2901 East Mill Plain Blvd
Vancouver, WA 98661-4899
360-695-2500 Ext. 319

ITT Technical Institute
Argonne Office Park, North
1050 Argonne Road
Spokane, WA 99212-2610
509-926-2900

ITT Technical Institute
Canyon Park East,
2525 223rd Street, SE
Bothell, WA 98021
425-485-0303

ITT Technical Institute
12720 Gateway Drive,
Suite 100
Seattle, WA 98168-3333
206-244-3300

North Seattle Community
College
9600 College Way North
Seattle, WA 98103-3599

Pierce College
9401 Farwest Drive, SW
Lakewood, WA 98498-1999
253-964-6501

Pierce College-Puyallup
1601 39th Avenue SE
Puyallup, WA 98374
253-840-8470

Pima Medical Institute
1627 Eastlake Avenue East
Seattle, WA 98102
206-324-6100 Ext. 28

Renton Technical College
3000 Fourth Street, NE
Renton, WA 98056
425-235-2463

Seattle Midwifery School
2524 16th Avenue S. Rm 300
Seattle, WA 98144
206-322-8834

Skagit Valley College
2405 College Way
Mount Vernon, WA
98273-5899
360-416-7620

Tacoma Community College
6501 South 19th Street
Tacoma, WA 98466
253-566-5120

University of Phoenix-
Washington Campus
7100 Fort Dent Way,
Suite 100
Seattle, WA 98188
877-877-4867

Western Business College
Stonemill Center,
120 Northeast 136th Avenue
Vancouver, WA 98684
360-254-3282

Wyoming

Casper College
125 College Drive
Casper, WY 82601-4699
307-268-2213

Central Wyoming College
2660 Peck Avenue
Riverton, WY 82501-2273
307-855-2231

Laramie County Community
College
1400 East College Drive
Cheyenne, WY 82007-3299
307-778-1212

Northwest College
231 West 6th Street
Powell, WY 82435-1898

Sage Technical Services
2368 Oil Drive
Casper, WY 82604
307-234-0242

Wyoming Technical Institute
4373 North 3rd Street
Laramie, WY 82072-9519
307-742-3776

SCHOLARSHIPS AND FINANCIAL AID

Alaska

Alaska Commission on Post-Secondary Education Teacher Education Scholarship Loan
Renewable loans for Alaska residents who are graduates of an Alaskan high school and pursuing teaching careers in rural elementary and secondary schools in Alaska. Must be nominated by rural school district. Eligible for 100 percent forgiveness if loan recipient teaches in Alaska upon graduation. Several awards of up to $7500 each. Must maintain good standing at institution. Contact for deadline. **Award:** Forgivable loan for use in freshman, sophomore, junior, or senior years; renewable. **Number:** 100. **Amount:** up to $7500. **Eligibility Requirements:** Applicant must be enrolled full-time at a four-year institution or university; resident of Alaska and studying in Alaska. **Application Requirements:** Application, transcript. **Contact:** Lori Stedman, Administrative Assistant, Special Programs, Alaska Commission on Post-Secondary Education, 3030 Vintage Boulevard, Juneau, AK 99801-7100. **Phone:** 907-465-6741

Michael Murphy Memorial Scholarship Loan Fund
Assists full-time undergraduate or graduate students enrolled in a program relating to law enforcement. Recipient receives forgiveness of 20 percent of the full loan amount for each year employed in law enforcement. Must be Alaska resident. **Award:** Forgivable loan for use in any year; renewable. **Number:** 3–6. **Amount:** up to $1000. **Eligibility Requirements:** Applicant must be enrolled full-time at a two-year or four-year institution or university and resident of Alaska. Available to U.S. citizens. **Application Requirements:** Application. **Application deadline:** April 1. **Contact:** Rodney Dial, Lieutenant, Alaska State Troopers, 5700 East Tudor Road, Anchorage, AK 99507. **Phone:** 907-269-5759. **E-mail:** rodney_dial@dps.state.ak.us

Western Undergraduate Exchange (WUE) Program
Program allowing Alaska residents to enroll at two-or four-year institutions in participating states at a reduced tuition level, which is the in-state tuition plus 50 percent of that amount. To be used for full-time undergraduate studies. Contact for application procedures, requirements, deadlines, and further information. **Award:** Grant for use in freshman, sophomore, junior, or senior years; renewable. **Eligibility Requirements:** Applicant must be enrolled full-time at a two-year or four-year institution and resident of Alaska. **Contact:** Lori Stedman, Administrative Assistant, Special Programs, Alaska Commission on Post-Secondary Education, 3030 Vintage Boulevard, Juneau, AK 99801-7100. **Phone:** 907-465-6741

California

California State University Real Estate Scholarship and Internship Grant Program
Targeted at low income and educationally disadvantaged undergraduate and graduate students at one of twenty-three California State University campuses. Must be enrolled at least half-time in a program related to land use or real estate. Minimum GPA is 2.5 for undergraduate students and 3.0 for graduate students. **Award:** Scholarship for use in any year; not renewable. **Number:** 22–31. **Amount:** $500–$2350. **Eligibility Requirements:** Applicant must be enrolled full or part-time at a four-year institution or university and studying in California. Applicant must have 2.5 GPA or higher. Available to U.S. citizens. **Application Requirements:** Application, essay, financial need analysis, transcript. **Application deadline:** Continuous. **Contact:** Pam Amundsen, Project Manager, Real Estate and Land Use Institute, 7700 College Town Drive, Suite 200, Sacramento, CA 95826-2304. **Phone:** 916-278-6633. **E-mail:** amundsenpl@csus.edu

Cooperative Agencies Resources for Education Program
Renewable award available to California resident attending a two-year California community college. Must have no more than 70 degree-applicable units, currently receive CALWORKS/TANF, and have at least one child under 14 years of age. Must be in EOPS, single head of household, and 18 or older. Contact local college EOPS-CARE office. **Award:** Grant for use in freshman or sophomore years; renewable. **Number:** 11,000. **Eligibility Requirements:** Applicant must be age 18; enrolled full-time at a two-year institution; single; resident of California; studying in California and member of Extended Opportunity Program Service. Available to U.S. citizens. **Application Requirements:** Application, financial need analysis, test scores, transcript. **Application deadline:** Continuous. **Contact:** Local Community College EOPS/CARE Program, California Community Colleges, 1102 Q Street, Sacramento, CA 95814-6511

Japanese Studies Scholarship
One-time award open to university-enrolled students ages 18 through 29 (university must be outside Japan). One-year course designed to develop Japanese language aptitude and knowledge of the country's culture, areas that the applicant must currently be studying. Scholarship comprises transportation, accommodations, medical expenses, and monthly and arrival allowances. Contact for more information. **Award:** Scholarship for use in freshman, sophomore, junior, or senior years; not renewable. **Eligibility Requirements:** Applicant must be age 18–29; enrolled full-time at an institution or university and must have an interest in Japanese language. Available to U.S. and non-U.S. citizens. **Application Requirements:** Application, autobiography, essay, interview, photo, references, test scores, transcript. **Contact:** Japanese Government/The Monbusho Scholarship Program, 350 South Grand Avenue, Suite 1700, Los Angeles, CA 90071

Colorado

Colorado Leveraging Educational Assistance Partnership (CLEAP) and SLEAP
Renewable awards for Colorado residents who are attending Colorado state-supported post-secondary institutions at the undergraduate level. Must document financial need. Contact colleges for complete information and deadlines. **Award:** Grant for use in freshman, sophomore, junior, or senior years; not renewable. **Number:** 2000–2500. **Amount:** $50–$900. **Eligibility Requirements:** Applicant must be enrolled full- or part-time at a two-year, four-year, or technical institution or university; resident of Colorado and studying in Colorado. Available to U.S. citizens. **Application Requirements:** Application, financial need analysis.

Contact: Financial Aid Office at college/institution, Colorado Commission on Higher Education, 1380 Lawrence Street, Suite 1200, Denver, CO 80204-2059

Colorado Nursing Scholarships

Renewable awards for Colorado residents pursuing nursing education programs at Colorado state-supported institutions. Applicant must agree to practice nursing in Colorado upon graduation. Contact colleges for complete information and deadlines. **Award:** Scholarship for use in freshman, sophomore, junior, or senior years; not renewable. **Number:** 100. **Eligibility Requirements:** Applicant must be enrolled full- or part-time at a two-year, four-year, or technical institution or university; resident of Colorado and studying in Colorado. **Application Requirements:** Application, financial need analysis. **Application deadline:** April 1. **Contact:** Financial Aid Office at college/institution, Colorado Commission on Higher Education, 1380 Lawrence Street, Suite 1200, Denver, CO 80204-2059

Colorado Student Grant

Assists Colorado residents attending eligible public, private, or vocational institutions within the state. Application deadlines vary by institution. Renewable award for undergraduates. Contact the financial aid office at the college/institution for more information and an application. **Award:** Grant for use in freshman, sophomore, junior, or senior years; renewable. **Eligibility Requirements:** Applicant must be enrolled at a two-year, four-year, or technical institution or university; resident of Colorado and studying in Colorado. **Application Requirements:** Application, financial need analysis. **Contact:** Financial Aid Office at college/institution, Colorado Commission on Higher Education, 1380 Lawrence Street, Suite 1200, Denver, CO 80204-2059

Colorado Undergraduate Merit Scholarships

Renewable awards for students attending Colorado state-supported institutions at the undergraduate level. Must demonstrate superior scholarship or talent. Contact college financial aid office for complete information and deadlines. **Award:** Scholarship for use in freshman, sophomore, junior, or senior years; renewable. **Eligibility Requirements:** Applicant must be enrolled at a two-year, four-year, or technical institution or

university and studying in Colorado. Applicant must have 3.0 GPA or higher. **Application Requirements:** Application. **Contact:** Financial Aid Office at college/institution, Colorado Commission on Higher Education, 1380 Lawrence Street, Suite 1200, Denver, CO 80204-2059

Law Enforcement/POW/MIA Dependents Scholarship—Colorado

Aid available for dependents of Colorado law enforcement officers, fire, or national guard personnel killed or disabled in the line of duty and for dependents of prisoner-of-war or service personnel listed as missing in action. Award covers tuition and room and board. **Award:** Scholarship for use in freshman, sophomore, junior, or senior years; renewable. **Eligibility Requirements:** Applicant must be enrolled full- or part-time at a two-year, four-year, or technical institution or university. Applicant must have 2.5 GPA or higher. **Application Requirements:** Application. **Application deadline:** Continuous. **Contact:** Rita Beachem, Colorado Commission on Higher Education, 1380 Lawrence Street, Suite 1200, Denver, CO 80204. **Phone:** 303-866-2723

Western Undergraduate Exchange Program

Residents of Arkansas, Colorado, Hawaii, Idaho, Montana, Nevada, New Mexico, North Dakota, Oregon, South Dakota, Utah, Washington, and Wyoming can enroll in designated two- and four-year undergraduate programs at institutions in participating states at reduced tuition level (resident tuition plus half). Contact Western Interstate Commission for Higher Education for list and deadlines. **Award:** Scholarship for use in freshman, sophomore, junior, or senior years; renewable. **Eligibility Requirements:** Applicant must be enrolled full-time at a two-year or four-year institution; resident of Alaska, Colorado, Hawaii, Idaho, Montana, Nevada, New Mexico, North Dakota, Oregon, South Dakota, Utah, Washington, or Wyoming and studying in Alaska, Colorado, Hawaii, Idaho, Montana, Nevada, New Mexico, North Dakota, Oregon, South Dakota, Utah, or Wyoming. Available to U.S. citizens. **Application Requirements:** Application. **Contact:** Ms. Sandy Jackson, Program Coordinator, Western Interstate Commission for Higher Education, PO Box 9752, Boulder, CO 80301-9752.

Phone: 303-541-0210.
E-mail: info-sep@wiche.edu

Hawaii

Hawaii State Student Incentive Grant

Grants are given to residents of Hawaii who are enrolled in a Hawaiian state school. Funds are for undergraduate tuition only. Applicants must submit a financial need analysis. **Award:** Grant for use in freshman, sophomore, junior, or senior years; renewable. **Eligibility Requirements:** Applicant must be enrolled full- or part-time at a two-year or four-year institution or university; resident of Hawaii and studying in Hawaii. Available to U.S. citizens. **Application Requirements:** Financial need analysis. **Contact:** Jo Ann Yoshida, Financial Aid Specialist, Hawaii State Post-Secondary Education Commission, University of Hawaii at Manoa, Honolulu, HI 96822. **Phone:** 808-956-6066

Idaho

Education Incentive Loan Forgiveness Contract—Idaho

Renewable award assists Idaho residents enrolling in teacher education or nursing programs within state. Must rank in top 15 percent of high school graduating class, have a 3.0 GPA or above, and agree to work in Idaho for two years. Deadlines vary. Contact financial aid office at institution of choice. **Award:** Forgivable loan for use in freshman, sophomore, junior, or senior years; renewable. **Number:** 29. **Eligibility Requirements:** Applicant must be enrolled full-time at a four-year institution or university; resident of Idaho and studying in Idaho. Applicant must have 3.0 GPA or higher. Available to U.S. citizens. **Application Requirements:** Application, test scores, transcript. **Contact:** Financial Aid Office

Idaho Minority and "At Risk" Student Scholarship

Renewable award for Idaho residents who are disabled or members of a minority group and have financial need. Must attend one of eight post-secondary institutions in the state for undergraduate study. Deadlines vary by institution. Must be a U.S. citizen and be a graduate of an Idaho high school. Contact college financial aid office. **Award:** Scholarship for use in freshman, sophomore, junior, or senior years; renewable. **Number:** 38–40. **Amount:** $3000.**Eligibility Requirements:** Applicant must be Native American or Eskimo, African American, or Hispanic; enrolled full-time at a two-year or four-year institution or university; resident of Idaho and studying in Idaho. Available to U.S. citizens. **Application Requirements:** Application, financial need analysis. **Contact:** Financial Aid Office

Idaho Promise Category A Scholarship Program
Renewable award available to Idaho residents who are graduating high school seniors. Must attend an approved Idaho college full-time. Based on class rank (must be verified by school official), GPA, and ACT scores. Professional-technical student applicants must take COMPASS. **Award:** Scholarship for use in freshman, sophomore, junior, or senior years; renewable. **Number:** 25–30. **Amount:** $3000.**Eligibility Requirements:** Applicant must be high school student; planning to enroll full-time at a two-year, four-year, or technical institution or university; resident of Idaho and studying in Idaho. Applicant must have 3.5 GPA or higher. Available to U.S. citizens. **Application Requirements:** Application, test scores. **Application deadline:** December 15. **Contact:** Caryl Smith, Scholarship Assistant, Idaho State Board of Education, PO Box 83720, Boise, ID 83720-0037. **Phone:** 208-332-1576. **E-mail:** csmith@osbe.state.id.us

Idaho Promise Category B Scholarship Program
Available to Idaho residents entering college for the first time prior to the age of 22. Must have completed high school or its equivalent in Idaho and have a minimum GPA of 3.0 or an ACT score of 20 or higher. Renewable one time only. **Award:** Scholarship for use in freshman or sophomore years; renewable. **Amount:** $500.**Eligibility Requirements:** Applicant must be age 22 or under; enrolled full-time at a two-year, four-year, or technical institution or university; resident of Idaho and studying in Idaho. Applicant must have 3.0 GPA or higher. Available to U.S. citizens. **Application Requirements:** Application. **Application deadline:** Continuous. **Contact:** Lynn Humphrey, Academic Program Coordinator, Idaho State Board of Education, PO Box 83720, Boise, ID 83720-0037.**Phone:** 208-332-1574

Leveraging Educational Assistance State Partnership Program (LEAP)
One-time award assists students attending participating Idaho colleges and universities majoring in any field except theology or divinity. Idaho residence is not required but must be U.S. citizen or permanent resident. Must show financial need. Application deadlines vary by institution. **Award:** Grant for use in any year; not renewable. **Amount:** up to $5000.**Eligibility Requirements:** Applicant must be enrolled full-or part-time at a two-year or four-year institution or university and studying in Idaho. Available to U.S. citizens. **Application Requirements:** Application, financial need analysis, self-addressed stamped envelope. **Contact:** Lynn Humphrey, Academic Program Coordinator, Idaho State Board of Education, PO Box 83720, Boise, ID 83720-0037. **Phone:** 208-332-1574

Montana

Indian Student Fee Waiver
This award is a fee waiver awarded by the Montana University System to undergraduate and graduate students meeting the criteria. It waives the registration and tuition fee. The award amount varies, depending on the tuition and registration fee at each participating college. Students must provide documentation of one-fourth Indian blood or more; must be a resident of Montana for at least one year prior to enrolling in school and must demonstrate financial need. Full- or part-time study qualifies. Complete and submit the FAFSA by March 1 and a Montana Indian Fee Waiver application form. Contact the financial aid office at the college of attendance to determine eligibility. **Award:** Scholarship for use in freshman, sophomore, junior, senior, or graduate years; renewable. **Number:** 600. **Amount:** $2000. **Eligibility Requirements:** Applicant must be Native American or Eskimo; enrolled full- or part-time at a two-year or four-year institution or university; resident of Montana and studying in Montana. Available to U.S. citizens. **Application Requirements:** Application, financial need analysis, FAFSA. **Contact:** Financial Aid Office. **E-mail:** scholars@mgslp.state.mt.us

Life Member Montana Federation of Garden Clubs Scholarship
Applicant must be at least a sophomore, majoring in conservation, horticulture, park or forestry, floriculture, greenhouse management, land management, or related subjects. Must be in need of assistance. Must have a potential for a successful future. Must be ranked in upper half of class or have a minimum 2.8 GPA. Must be a Montana resident and all study must be done in Montana. Deadline: May 1. **Award:** Scholarship for use in sophomore, junior, or senior years; not renewable. **Number:** 1. **Amount:** $1000. **Eligibility Requirements:** Applicant must be enrolled full-time at a four-year institution or university; resident of Montana and studying in Montana. Available to U.S. citizens. **Application Requirements:** Autobiography, financial need analysis, photo, references, transcript. **Application deadline:** May 1. **Contact:** Elizabeth Kehmeier, Life Members Scholarship Chairman, Montana Federation of Garden Clubs, 214 Wyant Lane, Hamilton, MT 59840. **Phone:** 406-363-5693

Montana Board of Regents High School Honor Scholarship
Scholarship provides a one-year non-renewable fee waiver of tuition and registration and is awarded to graduating high school seniors from accredited high schools in Montana. Five hundred scholarships are awarded each year averaging $2000 per recipient. The value of the award varies, depending on the tuition and registration fee at each participating college. Must have a minimum 3.0 GPA, meet all college-preparatory requirements, and be enrolled in an accredited high school for at least three years prior to graduation. Awarded to highest-ranking student in class attending a participating school. Contact high school counselor to apply. Deadline: April 15. **Award:** Scholarship for use in freshman year; not renewable. **Number:** 500. **Amount:** $2000. **Eligibility Requirements:** Applicant must be high school student; planning to enroll full- or part-time at a two-year or four-year institution or university; resident of Montana and studying in Montana. Applicant must have 3.0 GPA or higher. Available to U.S. citizens. **Application Requirements:** Application, transcript. **Application deadline:** April 15. **Contact:** High School Counselor. **E-mail:** scholars@mgslp.state.mt.us

Montana Higher Education Grant
This grant is awarded based on need to undergraduate students attending either part-time or full-time who are residents

of Montana and attending participating Montana schools. Awards are limited to the most needy students. A specific major or program of study is not required. This grant does not need to be repaid, and students may apply each year. Apply by filing a Free Application for Federal Student Aid by March 1 and contacting the financial aid office at the admitting college. **Award:** Grant for use in freshman, sophomore, junior, or senior years; not renewable. **Number:** 500. **Amount:** $400–$600. **Eligibility Requirements:** Applicant must be enrolled full- or part-time at a two-year or four-year institution or university; resident of Montana and studying in Montana. Available to U.S. citizens. **Application Requirements:** Financial need analysis, FAFSA. **Contact:** Financial Aid Office.
E-mail: scholars@mgslp.state.mt.us

Montana Tuition Assistance Program—Baker Grant
This grant is based on need to Montana residents attending participating Montana schools and who have earned at least $2575 during the previous calendar year. Must be enrolled full-time. Grant does not need to be repaid. Award covers the first undergraduate degree or certificate. Apply by filing a Free Application for Federal Student Aid by March 1 and contacting the financial aid office at the admitting college. **Award:** Grant for use in freshman, sophomore, junior, or senior years; not renewable. **Amount:** $100–$1000. **Eligibility Requirements:** Applicant must be enrolled full-time at a two-year or four-year institution or university; resident of Montana and studying in Montana. Available to U.S. citizens. **Application Requirements:** Financial need analysis, Free Application for Federal Student Aid (FAFSA). **Contact:** Financial Aid Office.
E-mail: scholars@mgslp.state.mt.us

Nevada

Nevada Student Incentive Grant
Award available to Nevada residents for use at an accredited Nevada college or university. Must show financial need. Any field of study eligible. High school students may not apply. One-time award of up to $5000. Contact financial aid office at local college. **Award:** Grant for use in any year; not renewable. **Number:** 400–800. **Amount:** $100–$5000. **Eligibility Requirements:** Applicant must be

enrolled full- or part-time at a two-year, four-year, or technical institution or university; resident of Nevada and studying in Nevada. Available to U.S. citizens. **Application Requirements:** Application, financial need analysis. **Application deadline:** Continuous. **Contact:** Financial aid office at local college, Nevada Department of Education, 700 East 5th Street, Carson City, NV 89701

New Mexico

3% Scholarship Program
Award equal to tuition and required fees for New Mexico residents who are undergraduate students attending public post-secondary institutions in New Mexico. Contact financial aid office of any public post-secondary institution in New Mexico for deadline. **Award:** Scholarship for use in freshman, sophomore, junior, or senior years; not renewable. **Eligibility Requirements:** Applicant must be enrolled full- or part-time at a two-year or four-year institution; resident of New Mexico and studying in New Mexico. Available to U.S. citizens. **Application Requirements:** Application. **Contact:** Barbara Serna, Clerk Specialist, New Mexico Commission on Higher Education, PO Box 15910, Santa Fe, NM 87506-5910. **Phone:** 505-827-4026

Allied Health Student Loan Program—New Mexico
Renewable loans for New Mexico residents enrolled in an undergraduate allied health program. Loans can be forgiven through service in a medically underserved area or can be repaid. Penalties apply for failure to provide service. May borrow up to $12,000 per year for four years. Apply by calling the Commission at the CHE Student Helpline: 800-279-9777. **Award:** Forgivable loan for use in freshman, sophomore, junior, or senior years; renewable. **Number:** 1–40. **Amount:** up to $12,000. **Eligibility Requirements:** Applicant must be enrolled full- or part-time at a two-year or four-year institution or university; resident of New Mexico and studying in New Mexico. Available to U.S. citizens. **Application Requirements:** Application, financial need analysis, transcript. **Application deadline:** July 1. **Contact:** Barbara Serna, Clerk Specialist, New Mexico Commission on Higher Education, PO Box 15910, Santa Fe, NM 87506-5910. **Phone:** 505-827-4026

Children of Deceased Veterans Scholarship—New Mexico
Award for New Mexico residents who are children of veterans killed or disabled as a result of service, prisoner-of-war, or veterans missing-in-action. Must be between ages 16 to 26. For use at New Mexico schools for undergraduate study. Submit parent's death certificate and DD form 214. **Award:** Scholarship for use in freshman, sophomore, junior, or senior years; renewable. **Amount:** $250–$750. **Eligibility Requirements:** Applicant must be age 16–26; enrolled full- or part-time at an institution or university; resident of New Mexico and studying in New Mexico. Applicant or parent must meet one or more of the following requirements: general military experience; retired from active duty; disabled or killed as a result of military service; prisoner-of-war; or missing in action. **Application Requirements:** Application, transcript. **Application deadline:** Continuous. **Contact:** Alan Martinez, Manager of State Benefits, New Mexico Veterans' Service Commission, PO Box 2324, Sante Fe, NM 87504. **Phone:** 505-827-6300

Legislative Endowment Scholarships
Awards for undergraduate students with substantial financial need who are attending public post-secondary institutions in New Mexico. Preference given to returning adult students at two-year and four-year institutions and students transferring from two-year to four-year institutions. Deadline set by each institution. Must be resident of New Mexico. Contact financial aid office of any New Mexico public post-secondary institution to apply. **Award:** Scholarship for use in freshman, sophomore, junior, or senior years; not renewable. **Amount:** $1000–$2500. **Eligibility Requirements:** Applicant must be enrolled full- or part-time at a two-year or four-year institution; resident of New Mexico and studying in New Mexico. Available to U.S. citizens. **Application Requirements:** Application, financial need analysis. **Contact:** Barbara Serna, Clerk Specialist, New Mexico Commission on Higher Education, PO Box 15910, Santa Fe, NM 87506-5910. **Phone:** 505-827-7383

Lottery Success Scholarships
Awards equal to 100 percent of tuition at New Mexico public post-secondary institution. Must have New Mexico high school degree and be enrolled at New Mexico public college or university in

first regular semester following high school graduation. Must obtain 2.5 GPA during this semester. May be eligible for up to eight consecutive semesters of support. Deadlines vary by institution. Apply through financial aid office of any New Mexico public post-secondary institution. **Award:** Scholarship for use in freshman, sophomore, junior, or senior years; renewable. **Eligibility Requirements:** Applicant must be enrolled full-time at a two-year or four-year institution; resident of New Mexico and studying in New Mexico. Applicant must have 2.5 GPA or higher. Available to U.S. citizens. **Application Requirements:** Application. **Contact:** Barbara Serna, Clerk Specialist, New Mexico Commission on Higher Education, PO Box 15910, Santa Fe, NM 87506-5910. **Phone:** 505-827-4026

New Mexico Competitive Scholarship

Scholarship available to encourage out-of-state students who have demonstrated high academic achievement to enroll in public institutions of higher education in New Mexico. One-time award for undergraduate students. Deadlines set by each institution. Contact financial aid office of any New Mexico public post-secondary institution to apply. **Award:** Scholarship for use in freshman, sophomore, junior, or senior years; not renewable. **Amount:** $100. **Eligibility Requirements:** Applicant must be enrolled full- or part-time at a two-year or four-year institution or university and studying in New Mexico. Applicant must have 3.0 GPA or higher. Available to U.S. citizens. **Application Requirements:** Application, essay, references, test scores. **Contact:** Barbara Serna, Clerk Specialist, New Mexico Commission on Higher Education, PO Box 15910, Santa Fe, NM 87506-5910. **Phone:** 505-827-4026

New Mexico Scholars Program

Several scholarships to encourage New Mexico high school graduates to enroll in college at a public or selected private nonprofit post-secondary institution in New Mexico before their 22nd birthday. Selected private colleges are College of Santa Fe, St. John's College in Santa Fe, and College of the Southwest. Must have graduated in top 5 percent of their class or obtained an ACT score of 25 or SAT score of 1140. One-time scholarship for tuition, books, and fees. Contact financial aid office at college to apply. **Award:** Scholarship for use in freshman, sophomore, junior, or senior years; not renewable. **Eligibility Requirements:**

Applicant must be age 22 or under; enrolled full- or part-time at a two-year or four-year institution; resident of New Mexico and studying in New Mexico. Available to U.S. citizens. **Application Requirements:** Application, financial need analysis, test scores. **Contact:** Barbara Serna, Clerk Specialist, New Mexico Commission on Higher Education, PO Box 15910, Santa Fe, NM 87506-5910. **Phone:** 505-827-4026

New Mexico Student Incentive Grant

Several grants available for resident undergraduate students attending public and selected private nonprofit institutions in New Mexico. Must demonstrate financial need. Several one-time awards of varying amounts. To apply, contact financial aid office at any public or private nonprofit post-secondary institution in New Mexico. **Award:** Grant for use in freshman, sophomore, junior, or senior years; not renewable. **Amount:** $200–$2500. **Eligibility Requirements:** Applicant must be enrolled at a two-year or four-year institution or university; resident of New Mexico and studying in New Mexico. Available to U.S. citizens. **Application Requirements:** Application, financial need analysis. **Contact:** Barbara Serna, Clerk Specialist, New Mexico Commission on Higher Education, PO Box 15910, Santa Fe, NM 87506-5910. **Phone:** 505-827-4026

Nursing Student Loan-For-Service Program

Award for New Mexico residents accepted or enrolled in nursing program at New Mexico public post-secondary institution. Must practice as nurse in designated health professional shortage area in New Mexico. Award dependent upon financial need but may not exceed $12,000. Deadline: July 1. To apply, call the Commission at the CHE Student Helpline: 800-279-9777. **Award:** Forgivable loan for use in freshman, sophomore, junior, or senior years; not renewable. **Amount:** up to $12,000. **Eligibility Requirements:** Applicant must be enrolled full- or part-time at a two-year or four-year institution; resident of New Mexico and studying in New Mexico. Available to U.S. citizens. **Application Requirements:** Application, financial need analysis. **Application deadline:** July 1. **Contact:** Barbara Serna, Clerk Specialist, New Mexico Commission on Higher Education, PO Box 15910, Santa Fe, NM 87506-5910. **Phone:** 505-827-4026

Oregon

Albina Fuel Company Scholarship

One scholarship available to a dependent child of a current Albina Fuel Company employee. The employee must have been employed for at least one full year as of October 1 prior to the scholarship deadline. One-time award. **Award:** Scholarship for use in freshman, sophomore, junior, or senior years; not renewable. **Eligibility Requirements:** Applicant must be resident of Oregon; affiliated with Albina Fuel Company and have employment experience in designated career field. Available to U.S. citizens. **Application Requirements:** Application, essay, financial need analysis, transcript, activity chart. **Application deadline:** March 1. **Contact:** Director of Grant Programs, Oregon Student Assistance Commission, 1500 Valley River Drive, Suite 100, Eugene, OR 97401-7020. **Phone:** 800-452-8807 Ext. 7395. **E-mail:** awardinfo@mercury.osac.state.or.us

Alpha Delta Kappa/Harriet Simmons Scholarship

One-time award for elementary and secondary education majors entering their senior year or graduate students enrolled in a fifth-year program leading to a teaching certificate. Visit Web site (http://www.osac.state.or.us) for more information. **Award:** Scholarship for use in senior or graduate years; not renewable. **Eligibility Requirements:** Applicant must be enrolled at a four-year institution or university and resident of Oregon. Available to U.S. citizens. **Application Requirements:** Application, essay, financial need analysis, transcript, activity chart. **Application deadline:** March 1. **Contact:** Director of Grant Programs, Oregon Student Assistance Commission, 1500 Valley River Drive, Suite 100, Eugene, OR 97401-7020. **Phone:** 800-452-8807 Ext. 7395. **E-mail:** awardinfo@mercury.osac.state.or.us

American Ex-Prisoner of War Scholarships: Peter Connacher Memorial Scholarship

Renewable award for American prisoners-of-war and their descendants. Written proof of prisoner-of-war status and discharge papers from the U.S. Armed Forces must accompany application. Statement of relationship between applicant and former prisoner-of-war is required. See Web site for details. **Award:** Scholarship for use in any year; renewable. **Eligibility Requirements:**

Applicant must be enrolled at a two-year or four-year institution and resident of Oregon. Available to U.S. citizens. Applicant or parent must meet one or more of the following requirements: general military experience; retired from active duty; disabled or killed as a result of military service; prisoner-of-war; or missing in action. **Application Requirements:** Application, essay, financial need analysis, transcript. **Application deadline:** March 1. **Contact:** Director of Grant Programs, Oregon Student Assistance Commission, 1500 Valley River Drive, Suite 100, Eugene, OR 97401-7020. **Phone:** 800-452-8807 **Ext.** 7395. **E-mail:** awardinfo@mercury. osac.state.or.us

Ben Selling Scholarship

Award for Oregon residents enrolling as sophomores or higher in college. College GPA 3.50 or higher required. Apply/compete annually. Must be U.S. citizen or permanent resident. Wells Fargo employees, their children, or near relatives must provide complete disclosure of employment status to receive this award. **Award:** Scholarship for use in sophomore, junior, or senior years; not renewable. **Eligibility Requirements:** Applicant must be resident of Oregon. Applicant must have 3.5 GPA or higher. Available to U.S. citizens. **Application Requirements:** Application, essay, financial need analysis, references, transcript, activity chart. **Application deadline:** March 1. **Contact:** Director of Grant Programs, Oregon Student Assistance Commission, 1500 Valley River Drive, Suite 100, Eugene, OR 97401-7020. **Phone:** 800-452-8807 **Ext.** 7395. **E-mail:** awardinfo@mercury.osac.state.or.us

David Family Scholarship

Award for residents of Clackamas, Lane, Linn, Marion, Multnomah, Washington, and Yamill counties. First preference to applicants enrolling at least half-time in upper-division or graduate programs at four-year colleges. Second preference to graduating high school seniors from West Linn-Wilsonville, Lake Oswego, Portland, Tigard-Tualatin, or Beaverton school districts. **Award:** Scholarship for use in any year; not renewable. **Eligibility Requirements:** Applicant must be enrolled full- or part-time at a four-year institution and resident of Oregon. Applicant must have 2.5 GPA or higher. Available to U.S. citizens. **Application Requirements:** Application, essay, financial need analysis, test scores, transcript, activity chart. **Application dead-line:** March 1. **Contact:** Director of Grant Programs, Oregon Student Assistance Commission, 1500 Valley River Drive, Suite 100, Eugene, OR 97401-7020. **Phone:** 800-452-8807 **Ext.** 7395. **E-mail:** awardinfo@mercury.osac.state.or.us

Dorothy Campbell Memorial Scholarship

Renewable award for female Oregon high school senior with a minimum 2.75 GPA. Must submit essay describing strong, continuing interest in golf and the contribution that sport has made to applicant's development. See Web site for more information. **Award:** Scholarship for use in freshman, sophomore, junior, or senior years; renewable. **Eligibility Requirements:** Applicant must be high school student; planning to enroll at a four-year institution; female; resident of Oregon; studying in Oregon and must have an interest in golf. Available to U.S. citizens. **Application Requirements:** Application, essay, financial need analysis, test scores, transcript, activity chart. **Application dead-line:** March 1. **Contact:** Director of Grant Programs, Oregon Student Assistance Commission, 1500 Valley River Drive, Suite 100, Eugene, OR 97401-7020. **Phone:** 800-452-8807 **Ext.** 7395. **E-mail:** awardinfo@mercury.osac.state.or.us

Ford Opportunity Program

Award for Oregon residents who are single heads of household with custody of a dependent child or children. Only for use at Oregon colleges. Minimum 3.0 GPA or 260 GED score required. If minimum requirements not met, Special Recommendation Form (see high school counselor or contact OSAC) must be submitted. May apply for this program or Ford Scholars. **Award:** Scholarship for use in freshman, sophomore, junior, or senior years; renewable. **Eligibility Requirements:** Applicant must be enrolled at a two-year or four-year institution; single; resident of Oregon and studying in Oregon. Applicant must have 3.0 GPA or higher. **Application Requirements:** Application, essay, financial need analysis, test scores, transcript, activity chart. **Application dead-line:** March 1. **Contact:** Director of Grant Programs, Oregon Student Assistance Commission, 1500 Valley River Drive, Suite 100, Eugene, OR 97401-7020. **Phone:** 800-452-8807 **Ext.** 7395. **E-mail:** awardinfo@mercury.osac.state.or.us

Ford Scholars

Award for Oregon graduating seniors, Oregon high school graduates not yet full-time undergraduates, or those who have completed two years of under-graduate study at an Oregon community college and will enter junior year at a four-year Oregon college. Minimum cumulative 3.0 GPA or 260 GED score. If minimum requirements not met, Special Recommendation Form (see high school counselor or contact OSAC) must be submitted. May apply for this program or Ford Opportunityt. **Award:** Scholarship for use in freshman, sophomore, or junior years; renewable. **Eligibility Requirements:** Applicant must be enrolled at a four-year institution; resident of Oregon and studying in Oregon. Applicant must have 3.0 GPA or higher. Available to U.S. citizens. **Application Requirements:** Application, essay, financial need analysis, test scores, transcript, activity chart. **Application dead-line:** March 1. **Contact:** Director of Grant Programs, Oregon Student Assistance Commission, 1500 Valley River Drive, Suite 100, Eugene, OR 97401-7020. **Phone:** 800-452-8807 **Ext.** 7395. **E-mail:** awardinfo@mercury.osac.state.or.us

Glenn Jackson Scholars Scholarships (OCF)

Award for graduating high school seniors who are dependents of employees or retirees of Oregon Department of Transportation or Parks and Recreation Department. Employees must have worked in their department at least three years. Award for maximum twelve undergraduate quarters or six quarters at a two-year institution. Must be U.S. citizen or permanent resident. Visit Web site (http://www.osac.state.or.us) for more details. **Award:** Scholarship for use in freshman, sophomore, junior, or senior years; renewable. **Eligibility Requirements:** Applicant must be high school student; planning to enroll at a four-year institution; resident of Oregon; affiliated with Oregon Department of Transportation Parks and Recreation and have employment experience in designated career field. Available to U.S. citizens. **Application Requirements:** Application, essay, financial need analysis, references, transcript, activity chart. **Application deadline:** March 1. **Contact:** Director of Grant Programs, Oregon Student Assistance Commission, 1500 Valley River Drive, Suite 100, Eugene, OR 97401-7020. **Phone:** 800-452-8807 **Ext.** 7395. **E-mail:** awardinfo@mercury.osac. state.or.us

Ida M. Crawford Scholarship

One-time scholarship awarded to Oregon high school seniors with a cumulative GPA of 3.5. Not available to applicants majoring in law, medicine, theology, teaching, or music. U.S. Bancorp employees and their children or near relatives are not eligible. Must supply proof of birth in the continental U.S. **Award:** Scholarship for use in freshman year; not renewable. **Eligibility Requirements:** Applicant must be high school student and resident of Oregon. Applicant must have 3.5 GPA or higher. Available to U.S. citizens. **Application Requirements:** Application, essay, financial need analysis, test scores, transcript. **Application deadline:** March 1. **Contact:** Director of Grant Programs, Oregon Student Assistance Commission, 1500 Valley River Drive, Suite 100, Eugene, OR 97401-7020. **Phone:** 800-452-8807 **Ext. 7395. E-mail:** awardinfo@mercury.osac.state.or.us

Lawrence R. Foster Memorial Scholarship

One-time award to students enrolled or planning to enroll in a public health degree program. First preference given to those working in the public health field and those pursuing a graduate degree in public health. Undergraduates entering junior or senior year health programs may apply if seeking a public health career—and not private practice. Must provide 3 references. Additional essay required. Must be resident of Oregon. **Award:** Scholarship for use in junior, senior, graduate, or postgraduate years; not renewable. **Eligibility Requirements:** Applicant must be enrolled at a four-year institution and resident of Oregon. Available to U.S. citizens. **Application Requirements:** Application, essay, financial need analysis, references, transcript, activity chart. **Application deadline:** March 1. **Contact:** Director of Grant Programs, Oregon Student Assistance Commission, 1500 Valley River Drive, Suite 100, Eugene, OR 97401-7020. **Phone:** 800-452-8807 **Ext. 7395. E-mail:** awardinfo@mercury.osac.state.or.us

Mentor Graphics Scholarship

One-time award for computer science, computer engineering, or electrical engineering majors entering junior or senior year at a four-year institution. Preference for one award to female, African-American, Native American, or Hispanic applicant. **Award:** Scholarship for use in junior or senior years; not renewable.

Eligibility Requirements: Applicant must be Native American or Eskimo, African American, or Hispanic; enrolled at a four-year institution; female and resident of Oregon. Available to U.S. citizens. **Application Requirements:** Application, essay, financial need analysis, references, transcript, activity chart. **Application deadline:** March 1. **Contact:** Director of Grant Programs, Oregon Student Assistance Commission, 1500 Valley River Drive, Suite 100, Eugene, OR 97401-7020. **Phone:** 800-452-8807 **Ext. 7395. E-mail:** awardinfo@mercury.osac.state.or.us

Oregon Collectors Association Bob Hasson Memorial Scholarship

One-time award for graduating Oregon high school seniors and recent Oregon high school graduates enrolling in college within one year of graduation. Children and grandchildren of owners and officers of collection agencies registered in Oregon are not eligible. Award is based on a 3–4 page essay titled "The Proper Use of Credit." See Web site (http://www.osac.state.or.us) for important application information. **Award:** Scholarship for use in freshman year; not renewable. **Amount:** $1500–$3000. **Eligibility Requirements:** Applicant must be enrolled at a two-year, four-year, or technical institution; resident of Oregon and studying in Oregon. Available to U.S. citizens. **Application Requirements:** Application, applicant must enter a contest, essay, financial need analysis, test scores, transcript, activity chart. **Application deadline:** March 1. **Contact:** Director of Grant Programs, Oregon Student Assistance Commission, 1500 Valley River Drive, Suite 100, Eugene, OR 97401-7020. **Phone:** 800-452-8807 **Ext. 7395. E-mail:** awardinfo@mercury.osac.state.or.us

Oregon Dungeness Crab Commission Scholarship

One scholarship available to graduating high school senior who is a dependent of licensed Oregon Dungeness Crab fisherman or crew member. One-time award. Identify name of vessel in place of work site. **Award:** Scholarship for use in freshman year; not renewable. **Number:** 1. **Eligibility Requirements:** Applicant must be high school student; resident of Oregon; affiliated with Oregon Dungeness Crab Commission and have employment experience in designated career field. Available to U.S. citizens. **Application Requirements:** Application, essay, financial need analy-

sis, transcript, activity chart. **Application deadline:** March 1. **Contact:** Director of Grant Programs, Oregon Student Assistance Commission, 1500 Valley River Drive, Suite 100, Eugene, OR 97401-7020. **Phone:** 800-452-8807 **Ext. 7395. E-mail:** awardinfo@mercury.osac.state.or.us

Oregon Metro Federal Credit Union Scholarship

One scholarship available to an Oregon high school graduate who is a Oregon Metro Federal Credit Union member. Preference given to graduating high school senior and applicant who plans to attend an Oregon college. One-time award. **Award:** Scholarship for use in freshman, sophomore, junior, or senior years; not renewable. **Number:** 1. **Eligibility Requirements:** Applicant must be enrolled at a four-year institution; resident of Oregon; studying in Oregon and affiliated with Oregon Metro Federal Credit Union. Available to U.S. citizens. **Application Requirements:** Application, essay, financial need analysis, references, transcript, activity chart. **Application deadline:** March 1. **Contact:** Director of Grant Programs, Oregon Student Assistance Commission, 1500 Valley River Drive, Suite 100, Eugene, OR 97401-7020. **Phone:** 800-452-8807 **Ext. 7395. E-mail:** awardinfo@mercury.osac.state.or.us

Oregon Trucking Association Scholarship

One scholarship available to a child of an Oregon Trucking Association member or child of employee of member. Applicants must be Oregon residents who are graduating high school seniors from an Oregon high school. One-time award. **Award:** Scholarship for use in freshman year; not renewable. **Number:** 1. **Eligibility Requirements:** Applicant must be high school student; planning to enroll at a four-year institution; resident of Oregon; affiliated with Oregon Trucking Association and have employment experience in designated career field. Available to U.S. citizens. **Application Requirements:** Application, essay, financial need analysis, references, transcript, activity chart. **Application deadline:** March 1. **Contact:** Director of Grant Programs, Oregon Student Assistance Commission, 1500 Valley River Drive, Suite 100, Eugene, OR 97401-7020. **Phone:** 800-452-8807 **Ext. 7395. E-mail:** awardinfo@mercury.osac.state.or.us

Pacific NW Federal Credit Union Scholarship

One scholarship available to graduating high school senior who is a member of Pacific North West Federal Credit Union. A special essay is required employing the theme, "Why is My Credit Union an Important Consumer Choice?" Employers and officials of the Credit Union and their dependents are not eligible. One-time award. **Award:** Scholarship for use in freshman year; not renewable. **Number:** 1.**Eligibility Requirements:** Applicant must be high school student; planning to enroll at a four-year institution; resident of Oregon and affiliated with Pacific Northwest Federal Credit Union. Available to U.S. citizens. **Application Requirements:** Application, essay, financial need analysis, references, transcript, activity chart. **Application deadline:** March 1. **Contact:** Director of Grant Programs, Oregon Student Assistance Commission, 1500 Valley River Drive, Suite 100, Eugene, OR 97401-7020. **Phone:** 800-452-8807 **Ext.** 7395. **E-mail:** awardinfo@mercury. osac.state.or.us

Robert D. Forster Scholarship

One scholarship available to a dependent child of a Walsh Construction Co. employee who has completed 1,000 hours or more in each of three consecutive fiscal years. Award may be received for a maximum of twelve quarters of undergraduate study and may only be used at four-year colleges. **Award:** Scholarship for use in freshman, sophomore, junior, or senior years; renewable. **Number:** 1. **Eligibility Requirements:** Applicant must be enrolled at a four-year institution; resident of Oregon; affiliated with Walsh Construction Company and have employment experience in designated career field. Available to U.S. citizens. **Application Requirements:** Application, essay, financial need analysis, references, transcript, activity chart. **Application deadline:** March 1. **Contact:** Director of Grant Programs, Oregon Student Assistance Commission, 1500 Valley River Drive, Suite 100, Eugene, OR 97401-7020. **Phone:** 800-452-8807 **Ext.** 7395. **E-mail:** awardinfo@mercury. osac.state.or.us

Roger W. Emmons Memorial Scholarship

One scholarship available to a graduating Oregon high school senior who is a child or grandchild of an employee (for at least three years) of member of the Oregon Refuse and Recycling

Association. One-time award for use at an Oregon college. **Award:** Scholarship for use in freshman year; renewable. **Number:** 1.**Eligibility Requirements:** Applicant must be high school student; planning to enroll at a four-year institution; resident of Oregon; studying in Oregon; affiliated with Oregon Refuse and Recycling Association and have employment experience in designated career field. Available to U.S. citizens. **Application Requirements:** Application, essay, financial need analysis, references, transcript, activity chart. **Application deadline:** March 1. **Contact:** Director of Grant Programs, Oregon Student Assistance Commission, 1500 Valley River Drive, Suite 100, Eugene, OR 97401-7020. **Phone:** 800-452-8807 **Ext.** 7395. **E-mail:** awardinfo@mercury. osac.state.or.us

Teamsters Clyde C. Crosby/Joseph M. Edgar Memorial Scholarship

One scholarship available for a graduating high school senior with a minimum 3.0 cumulative GPA who is a child or dependent stepchild of an active, retired, disabled, or deceased member of local union affiliated with Teamsters #37. Member must have been active for at least one year. Award may be received for a maximum of twelve quarters. **Award:** Scholarship for use in freshman, sophomore, junior, or senior years; renewable. **Number:** 1. **Eligibility Requirements:** Applicant must be high school student; planning to enroll full- or part-time at an institution or university; resident of Oregon; member of Teamsters and have employment experience in designated career field. Applicant must have 3.0 GPA or higher. Available to U.S. citizens. **Application Requirements:** Application, essay, financial need analysis, transcript, activity chart. **Application deadline:** March 1. **Contact:** Director of Grant Programs, Oregon Student Assistance Commission, 1500 Valley River Drive, Suite 100, Eugene, OR 97401-7020. **Phone:** 800-452-8807 **Ext.** 7395. **E-mail:** awardinfo@mercury.osac.state.or.us

Troutman's Emporium Scholarship

One scholarship available to Troutman's Emporium full-time or part-time employees and dependents. Employee must have been employed for at least one year. Applicants must be planning to enroll at least half-time in an undergraduate course of study. Preference given to those planning to attend college in California, Idaho, Oregon, or

Washington. One-time award. **Award:** Scholarship for use in freshman, sophomore, junior, or senior years; not renewable. **Eligibility Requirements:** Applicant must be enrolled full- or part-time at a two-year or four-year institution; resident of Oregon; studying in California, Idaho, Oregon, or Washington; affiliated with Troutman's Emporium and have employment experience in designated career field. Available to U.S. citizens. **Application Requirements:** Application, essay, financial need analysis, references, transcript, activity chart. **Application deadline:** March 1. **Contact:** Director of Grant Programs, Oregon Student Assistance Commission, 1500 Valley River Drive, Suite 100, Eugene, OR 97401-7020. **Phone:** 800-452-8807 **Ext.** 7395. **E-mail:** awardinfo@mercury. osac.state.or.us

Walter and Marie Schmidt Scholarship

One scholarship available to a student who is enrolled or planning to enroll in a program of training to become a registered nurse. Applicants must submit an additional essay describing their desire to pursue a nursing career in geriatrics. U.S. Bancorp employees and their relatives are not eligible. One-time award. **Award:** Scholarship for use in freshman or sophomore years; not renewable. **Number:** 1.**Eligibility Requirements:** Applicant must be enrolled full- or part-time at a two-year or four-year institution and resident of Oregon. Available to U.S. citizens. **Application Requirements:** Application, essay, financial need analysis, references, transcript, activity chart. **Application deadline:** March 1. **Contact:** Director of Grant Programs, Oregon Student Assistance Commission, 1500 Valley River Drive, Suite 100, Eugene, OR 97401-7020. **Phone:** 800-452-8807 **Ext.** 7395. **E-mail:** awardinfo@mercury. osac.state.or.us

Woodard Family Scholarship

Scholarships are available to employees and children of employees of Kimwood Corporation or Middlefield Estates. Applicants must have graduated from a U.S. high school. Awards may be used at Oregon colleges only and may be received for a maximum of twelve quarters of undergraduate study. **Award:** Scholarship for use in freshman, sophomore, junior, or senior years; renewable. **Eligibility Requirements:** Applicant must be enrolled at a two-year or four-year institution; resident of Oregon; studying in Oregon; affiliated with Kimwood

Corporation or Middlefield Village and have employment experience in designated career field. Available to U.S. citizens. **Application Requirements:** Application, essay, financial need analysis, references, transcript. **Application deadline:** March 1. **Contact:** Director of Grant Programs, Oregon Student Assistance Commission, 1500 Valley River Drive, Suite 100, Eugene, OR 97401-7020. **Phone:** 800-452-8807 **Ext.** 7395. **E-mail:** awardinfo@mercury. osac.state.or.us

Utah

New Century Scholarship
Scholarship for qualified high school graduates of Utah. Must attend Utah state-operated college. Award depends on number of hours student enrolled. Please contact for further eligibility requirements. Students must complete an associate degree at a Utah state-operated institution by September 1 of the year they graduate from a UT-accredited high school. Eligible recipients receive an award equal to 75 percent of tuition for 60 credit hours toward the completion of a bachelor's degree. **Award:** Scholarship for use in junior or senior years; renewable. **Amount:** $500–$1000. **Eligibility Requirements:** Applicant must be high school student; planning to enroll full- or part-time at a four-year institution or university; resident of Utah and studying in Utah. Available to U.S. citizens. **Application Requirements:** Application, test scores, transcript, GPA/Copy of Enrollment verification from an eligible UT four-year institute. **Application deadline:** Continuous. **Contact:** Angie Loving, Manager for Programs/Administration, State of Utah, 3 Triad Center, Suite 500, Salt Lake City, UT 84180-1205. **Phone:** 801-321-7124. **E-mail:** aloving@utahsbr.edu

T.H. Bell Teaching Incentive Loan—Utah
Renewable awards for Utah residents who are high school seniors and wish to pursue teaching careers. Award pays for tuition and fees at a Utah institution. Must agree to teach in a Utah public school or pay back loan through monthly installments. Must be a U.S. citizen. **Award:** Forgivable loan for use in freshman, sophomore, junior, or senior years; renewable. **Number:** 50. **Eligibility Requirements:** Applicant must be high school student; planning to enroll full-

time at a two-year or four-year institution or university; resident of Utah and studying in Utah. Available to U.S. citizens. **Application Requirements:** Application, essay, test scores, transcript. **Application deadline:** March 29. **Contact:** Diane DeMan, Executive Secretary, Utah State Office of Education, 250 East 500 South, Salt Lake City, UT 84111. **Phone:** 801-538-7741

Terrel H. Bell Teaching Incentive Loan
Designed to provide financial assistance to outstanding Utah students pursuing a degree in education. The incentive loan funds full-time tuition and general fees for eight semesters. After graduation/certification, the loan may be forgiven if the recipient teaches in a Utah public school or accredited private school (K–12). Loan forgiveness is done on a year for year basis. Application deadline depends on institution. **Award:** Forgivable loan for use in freshman, sophomore, junior, or senior years; renewable. **Number:** 365. **Amount:** $600–$1500. **Eligibility Requirements:** Applicant must be enrolled full-time at a two-year or four-year institution or university; resident of Utah and studying in Utah. Available to U.S. citizens. **Application Requirements:** Application, essay, test scores, transcript. **Contact:** Angie Loving, Manager for Programs and Administration, State of Utah, 3 Triad Center, Suite 500, Salt Lake City, UT 84180-1205. **Phone:** 801-321-7124 **E-mail:** aloving@utahsbr.edu

Utah Society of Professional Engineers Scholarship
One-time award for entering freshman pursuing studies in the field of engineering (civil, chemical, electrical, or engineering related technologies.) Minimum 3.0 GPA required. Must be a U.S. citizen and Utah resident attending school in Utah. Application deadline is April 29. **Award:** Scholarship for use in freshman year; not renewable. **Number:** 2. **Amount:** $1000. **Eligibility Requirements:** Applicant must be high school student; planning to enroll full- or part-time at a four-year institution or university; resident of Utah and studying in Utah. Applicant must have 3.0 GPA or higher. Available to U.S. citizens. **Application Requirements:** Application, essay, references, test scores, transcript, certification. **Application deadline:** March 29. **Contact:** Owen Mills, Scholarship Coordinator, Utah Society of Professional Engineers, 488 East

Winchester Street, Suite 400, Murray, UT 84107. **Phone:** 801-262-3735. **E-mail:** omills@uta.cog.ut.us

Washington

Washington National Guard Scholarship Program
A state-funded retention incentive/loan program for both Washington Army and Air Guard members meeting all eligibility requirements. The loans are forgiven if soldiers/airmen complete their service requirements. Failure to meet/complete service obligations incurs the requirement to repay the loan plus 8 percent interest. Minimum 2.5 GPA required. Deadline is April 30. **Award:** Forgivable loan for use in any year; not renewable. **Number:** 25–30. **Eligibility Requirements:** Applicant must be enrolled full- or part-time at a two-year, four-year, or technical institution or university and resident of Washington. Applicant must have 2.5 GPA or higher. Available to U.S. and non-U.S. citizens. Applicant must have served in the Air Force National Guard or Army National Guard. **Application Requirements:** Application, transcript, enlistment/extension documents. **Application deadline:** April 30. **Contact:** Mark Rhoden, Educational Officer, Washington National Guard, Building 1, Camp Murray, Tacoma, WA 98430-5073. **Phone:** 253-512-8899. **E-mail:** mark.rhoden@wa.ngb.army.mil

Wyoming

Superior Student in Education Scholarship—Wyoming
Available to Wyoming high school graduates who have demonstrated high academic achievement and plan to teach in Wyoming public schools. Award is for tuition at Wyoming institutions. Must maintain 3.0 GPA. **Award:** Scholarship for use in freshman, sophomore, junior, or senior years; renewable. **Number:** 16–80. **Eligibility Requirements:** Applicant must be enrolled full-time at a two-year or four-year institution or university; resident of Wyoming; studying in Wyoming and must have an interest in leadership. Applicant must have 3.0 GPA or higher. Available to U.S. citizens. **Application Requirements:** Application, references, test scores, transcript. **Application deadline:** October 31. **Contact:** JoelAnne Berrigan, Assistant Director, Scholarships, State of Wyoming, PO Box 3335, Laramie, WY 82071-3335. **Phone:** 307-766-2117

INTERNSHIPS

Alaska

KJNP AM-FM Radio-TV
General Information: Christian radio and television station for Alaska and the Northern Hemisphere
Contact: Julie Beaver, Secretary to President, 2501 Mission Road, PO Box 56359, North Pole, AK 99705-1359
Phone: 907-488-2216
Fax: 907-488-5246
E-mail: kjnp@mosquitonet.com
Web site: www.mosquitonet.com/~kjnp

Pike's Waterfront Lodge
General Information: Hotel, restaurant, lounge, and riverboat musical entertainment
Contact: Lloyd Huskey, General Manager, 1850 Hoselton Road, Fairbanks, AK 99709
Fax: 907-456-4515
E-mail: northwave1@gci.net
Web site: www.Pikeslodge.com

Arizona

Sunset Crater Volcano, Walnut Canyon, and Wupatki National Monuments
General Information: Three national monuments managed by the National Park Service including a volcano, cliff dwellings, and pueblo archaeological sites; provides for visitor enjoyment, education, and resource protection
Contact: Kris Cole, Volunteer Coordinator, Route 3, Box 149, Flagstaff, AZ 86004
Phone: 520-526-0502
Fax: 520-714-0565
E-mail: flag-sunset_crater@nps.gov
Web site: www.nps.gov/sucr

World Hunger Ecumenical Arizona Task Force (WHEAT)
General Information: Nonprofit organization that educates, advocates, and empowers individuals to action in the fight against hunger
Contact: Tamera Zivic, Executive Director, 4423 North 24th Street, Suite 540, Phoenix, AZ 85016
Phone: 602-955-5076
Fax: 602-955-5290
E-mail: wheat@hungerhurts.org
Web site: www.HungerHurts.org

California

Arthritis Foundation, Northern California Chapter
General Information: Foundation that seeks to improve lives through leadership in the prevention, control, and cure of arthritis and related diseases
Contact: Molly Klarman, Summer Science Coordinator, 657 Mission Street, Suite 603, San Francisco, CA 94105
Fax: 415-356-1240
E-mail: mklarman@arthritis.org
Web site: www.arthritis.org

California National Organization for Women
General Information: Women's rights organization working primarily on legislation in the state of California
Contact: Elena Perez, Program Director, 926 J Street, Suite 820, Sacramento, CA 95814
Phone: 916-442-3414
Fax: 916-442-6942
E-mail: canow@canow.org
Web site: www.canow.org

CARAL-California Abortion & Reproductive Rights Action League
General Information: Political lobbying, educational organization dedicated to creating and sustaining a constituency that uses the political process to guarantee the full range of reproductive rights to all women
Contact: Krisitn Hilton, Administrative Coordinator, 32 Monterey Boulevard, San Francisco, CA 94131
Phone: 415-334-1502
Fax: 415-334-6510
E-mail: caral@aol.com
Web site: www.caral.org or www.choice.org

Educational Communications, Inc.;ECONEWS Television;Environmental Directions Radio;Ecology Center of Southern California;Project Ecotourism,Compendium
General Information: Environmental broadcasting and conservation organization specializing in ecological activism and audio/video production and distribution
Contact: Leslie Lewis, Administrative Assistant, PO Box 351419, Los Angeles, CA 90035-9119
Phone: 310-559-9160
Fax: 310-559-9160
E-mail: ecnp@aol.com
Web site: www.ecoprojects.org

Farm Sanctuary–West
General Information: National nonprofit organization dedicated to ending animal agricultural abuses through public education programs, legislation, farm animal cruelty investigations and campaigns, in addition to providing shelters for rescuing and rehabilitating
Contact: Michelle Waffner, Education Coordinator, 19080 Newville Road, Orland, CA 95963
Phone: 607-583-2225
Fax: 607-583-4349
E-mail: educate@farmsanctuary.org
Web site: www.farmsanctuary.org

First Chance/ Y-CHOW, Inc.
General Information: Nonprofit prevention/outreach education organization
Contact: Faith Bolton, Program Administrator, 1800 Western Avenue, Suite 104, San Bernardino, CA 92411
Fax: 909-473-0881
E-mail: ychows@gte.net

Global Children's Organization
General Information: Nonprofit organization whose mission is to "restore children to childhood" through providing summer camp program that serve children traumatized by intolerance and violence in Croatia and Los Angeles
Contact: Judith Jenya, Founder and Executive Director, 10524 West Pico Boulevard, Suite 216, Los Angeles, CA 90064
Phone: 310-842-9235
Fax: 310-842-9236
E-mail: gw@globalchild.org
Web site: www.globalchild.org

International Documentary Association
General Information: Nonprofit organization founded to promote and support the work of nonfiction and documentary film and video makers and to promote international understanding through the documentary arts and sciences
Contact: Amitai Adler, Membership Administrator, 1201 West 5th Street, Suite M320, Los Angeles, CA 90017
Phone: 213-534-3600
Fax: 213-534-3610
E-mail: membership@documentary.org
Web site: www.documentary.org

Judah L. Magnes Museum

General Information: Jewish art museum that preserves and collects historical Jewish objects and contemporary fine art on Jewish themes or by Jewish artists, and that houses the Blumenthal Rare Book Manuscript Library and the Western Jewish History Center
Contact: Julie Ulmer, Educator, 2911 Russell Street, Berkeley, CA 94705
Phone: 510-549-6943
Fax: 510-849-3673
E-mail: education@magnesmuseum.org
Web site: www.magnesmuseum.org

JustAct: Youth ACTion for Global JUSTice

General Information: Nonprofit organization that links students to organizations and grassroots movements working for sustainable and just communities around the world
Contact: Elaine Peterson, Education Coordinator, 333 Valencia Street, Suite 101, San Francisco, CA 94103
Phone: 415-431-4204
Fax: 415-431-5953
E-mail: elaine@justact.org
Web site: www.justact.org

KVIE-TV

General Information: Public television station serving the nation's 21st-largest media market; covers Sacramento, CA and 28 surrounding counties; strives to educate, enlighten, and entertain its viewers and members
Contact: Lillian Nelson, Volunteer Intern Coordinator, PO Box 6, 2595 Capitol Oaks Drive, Sacramento, CA 95833
Phone: 916-923-7474, Ext. 6482
Fax: 916-929-7215
E-mail: lnelson@kvie.org

Levine Communications Office

General Information: Entertainment public relations firm
Contact: Internship Coordinator, 10333 Ashton Avenue, Los Angeles, CA 90024
Phone: 310-248-6222, Ext. 14
Fax: 310-248-6227
E-mail: iowa@levinepr.com
Web site: www.levinepr.com

Media Watch

General Information: Organization that challenges the biases found in commercial media
Contact: Ann Simonton, Director, PO Box 618, Santa Cruz, CA 95061-0618
Phone: 831-423-6355
Fax: 831-423-6355
E-mail: mwatch@cruzio.com
Web site: www.mediawatch.com

National Student Campaign Against Hunger and Homelessness

General Information: Coalition of student and community members who are working to end hunger and homelessness through education, service, and organizing; trains students to create or improve service programs and promotes campus and community collaborations
Contact: Jen Hecker, Director, 3435 Wilshire Boulevard, Suite 380, Los Angeles, CA 90010
Phone: 800-664-8647
Fax: 413-256-6435
E-mail: nscah@aol.com
Web site: www.nscahh.org

The New Conservatory Theatre Center

General Information: Nonprofit theater school and performing arts company for children ages 4-19 emphasizing new and socially aware plays for family audiences; school consists of three educational theater touring companies for youths in grades K-12
Contact: Ed Decker, Executive Director, 25 Van Ness Avenue, Lower Lobby, San Francisco, CA 94102
Web site: www.nctcsf.org

Resource Publications, Inc.

General Information: Communications firm dealing in resources for ministry, education, and personal growth
Contact: William Burns, President, 160 East Virginia Street, Suite 290, San Jose, CA 95112-5876
Fax: 408-287-8748
E-mail: wjb@rpinet.com
Web site: www.rpinet.com/

San Francisco Bay Guardian

General Information: San Francisco-based liberal alternative news and arts/entertainment weekly paper
Contact: Camille Taiara, Editorial Coordinator, 520 Hampshire Street, San Francisco, CA 94110
Phone: 415-255-3100
Fax: 415-255-8762
E-mail: camille@sfbg.com
Web site: www.sfbg.com

San Francisco Cinematheque

General Information: Nonprofit film exhibition organization
Contact: Steve Polta, Office Manager, 480 Potrero Avenue, San Francisco, CA 94110
Phone: 415-822-2885
Fax: 415-822-1952
E-mail: sfc@sfcinematheque.org
Web site: www.sfcinematheque.org

San Jose Repertory Theatre

General Information: Professional theater company that produces all types of theater, from new works to classics to musicals, in a six-show season running from September to June
Contact: Karen Piemme, Educational and Outreach Programs Manager, 101 Paseo de San Antonio, San Jose, CA 95113
Fax: 408-367-7237
E-mail: karenp@sjrep.com
Web site: www.sjrep.com

Schneider Publishing

General Information: Magazine publisher
Contact: Ann Shepphird, Managing Editor, 11835 West Olympic Boulevard, Suite 1265, Los Angeles, CA 90064
Fax: 310-577-3715
E-mail: ann@schneiderpublishing.com

Sonoma County Legal Services Foundation

General Information: Foundation that provides legal education, referrals, and services to youth and families, especially on the lower end of the economic scale
Contact: Toni Novak, Executive Director, 1212 4th Street, #I, Santa Rosa, CA 95404
Phone: 707-546-2924
Fax: 707-546-0263
E-mail: sclsf@sonic.net

Speak Out

General Information: Nonprofit national speakers and artists agency providing 200 speakers and artists who address issues of social, economic, and political justice, working primarily through campuses and community groups
Contact: Lolan Sevilla, Program Coordinator, PO Box 99096, Emeryville, CA 94662
Phone: 510-601-0182
Fax: 510-601-0183
E-mail: speakout@igc.org
Web site: www.speakersandartists.org

Steen Art Study

General Information: Independent art historian and educator who performs research; involved in publishing, curating, and lecturing; and conducts classes and study trips
Contact: Ronald Steen, 961 East California Boulevard 329, Pasadena, CA 91106-4057
Phone: 323-681-6343
Fax: 323-577-7384
E-mail: ronaldsteen@worldnet.att.net
Web site: www.steenartstudy.com

Summerbridge National

General Information: Education program that provides free academic enrichment to 5th-9th graders and teaching, mentorship, and tutoring opportunities to high school and college students
Contact: Jessica D'Arcy, Admissions Manager, 361 Oak Street, San Francisco, CA 94102
Phone: 415-865-2970, Ext. 100
Fax: 415-865-2979
E-mail: admissions@summerbridge.org
Web site: www.summerbridge.org

Surfrider Foundation

General Information: Nonprofit environmental organization dedicated to the protection, preservation, and restoration of the world's oceans, waves, and beaches through conservation, activism, research, and education
Contact: Michelle Kremer, Deputy Executive Director, 122 South El Camino Real, #67, San Clemente, CA 92672
E-mail: mkremer@surfrider.org
Web site: www.surfrider.org

Teen Line

General Information: Organization that provides teen-to-teen hot line and associated community outreach services
Contact: Elaine Leader, Executive Director, PO Box 48750, Los Angeles, CA 90048
Phone: 310-423-3401, Ext. 1
Fax: 310-423-0456
E-mail: teenlineca@aol.com
Web site: www.teenlineonline.org

U.S. Forest Service, Stanislaus National Forest

General Information: Land management agency
Contact: Joy Barney, Interpretive Specialist/Environmental Education Coordinator, #1 Pinecrest Lake Road, Pinecrest, CA 95364
Phone: 209-965-3434
Fax: 209-965-3372
E-mail: jbarney@fs.fed.us

Y.E.S. to Jobs

General Information: Program designed to introduce minority high school students to career opportunities behind the scenes in the entertainment industry
Contact: Marsha Cole, Program Coordinator, PO Box 3390, Los Angeles, CA 90078
E-mail: yestojobs@aol.com
Web site: www.yestojobs.org

Colorado

Boulder County AIDS Project

General Information: AIDS service organization
Contact: Jenny Schwartz, Intern Coordinator, 2118 14th Street, Boulder, CO 80302
E-mail: jaschwartz@worldnet.att.net
Web site: www.bcap.org

Circle of Neighbors

General Information: Nonprofit community service organization focusing on planning and funding for college-bound students
Contact: Tom Okuto, Director of Consultants, One College Center, Box 76000, Colorado Springs, CO 80970
Phone: 800-743-4731
Fax: 888-743-4731
E-mail: info@circleofneighbors.com
Web site: www.circleofneighbors.org

City of Fort Collins Utility Wellness Program

General Information: Provider of electric power, water, wastewater, stormwater, and street services to the community
Contact: Maureen Balzer, Utility Services Wellness Coordinator, 700 Wood Street, Fort Collins, CO 80522
Phone: 970-221-6349
E-mail: mbalzer@ci.fort-collins.co.us

Ecumenical Social Ministries

General Information: Nonprofit human services agency that provides basic emergency services, food, rental assistance, medicine, and clothing
Contact: Marcia Hanscom, Volunteer Director, 201 North Weber Street, Colorado Springs, CO 80903
Phone: 719-633-1537
Fax: 719-636-3452
E-mail: esmmarcia@juno.com

Rio Grande National Forest

General Information: Natural resource agency that stresses multiple use of its resources and manages Bureau of Land Management lands
Contact: Volunteer Coordinator, 1803 West Highway 160, Monte Vista, CO 81144
Phone: 719-852-5941
Fax: 719-852-6250

Volunteers for Outdoor Colorado

General Information: Organization that seeks to instill a personal sense of responsibility for the stewardship of Colorado's public lands, working in partnership with federal, state, and local land management agencies and other nonprofits to organize volunteers on projects
Contact: Leilani Fintus, Clearinghouse Coordinator, 600 South Marion Parkway, Denver, CO 80209
Phone: 303-715-1010
Fax: 303-715-1212
E-mail: voc@voc.org
Web site: www.voc.org

Montana

Alliance for the Wild Rockies

General Information: Organization whose aim is to preserve and protect the remaining wilderness and biodiversity of the Northern Rockies bio-region by empowering regional conservationists and informing the public about the loss of wildlands
Contact: Cori Chandler-Pepelnjak, Outreach Director, PO Box 8731, Missoula, MT 59807
Fax: 406-721-9917
E-mail: cori@wildrockiesalliance.org
Web site: www.wildrockies.org/awr

Project Vote Smart

General Information: National library of political information on over 13,000 candidates and elected officials per election cycle
Contact: Peter David, Internship Coordinator, One Common Ground, Philipsburg, MT 59858
Phone: 406-859-VOTE
Fax: 406-859-8680
E-mail: intern@vote-smart.org
Web site: www.vote-smart.org

New Mexico

SITE Santa Fe

General Information: Not-for-profit contemporary art space
Contact: Chris Nail, Education Coordinator, 1606 Paseo de Peralta, Santa Fe, NM 87501
Phone: 505-989-1199, Ext. 19
Fax: 505-989-1188
E-mail: chrisnail@sitesantafe.org
Web site: www.sitesantafe.org

Oregon

Monika's House/Domestic Violence Resource Center

General Information: Private nonprofit organization serving men, women, and children victims of domestic violence through support groups, education, shelter, restraining order advocacy, and individual therapy

Contact: Tiffani Smith, Volunteer Coordinator, PO Box 494, Hillsboro, OR 97123
Phone: 503-640-5352, Ext. 305
E-mail: smith_tiffani@hotmail.com
Web site: shelterdvrc.webjump.com

Northwest Coalition for Alternatives to Pesticides

General Information: Nonprofit 5-state grassroots membership organization that works to protect people and the environment by advancing healthy solutions to pest problems
Contact: Pollyanna Lind, Information Services Coordinator, PO Box 1393, Eugene, OR 97440
Phone: 541-344-5044
Fax: 541-344-6923
E-mail: info@pesticide.org
Web site: www.pesticide.org

Washington

Eating Disorders Awareness and Prevention–EDAP

General Information: Nonprofit organization working to eliminate eating disorders and body dissatisfaction though prevention efforts, education, advocacy, and research
Contact: Holly Hoff, Director of Programs, 603 Stewart Street, Seattle, WA 98101
Phone: 206-382-3587
Fax: 206-829-8501
E-mail: hhoff@edap.org
Web site: www.edap.org

Seattle Opera

General Information: Opera company producing 5 full-scale operas per season, plus one educational outreach show
Contact: Paula Podemski, Production Supervisor, PO Box 9248, Seattle, WA 98109
Phone: 206-676-5812
Fax: 206-389-7651
E-mail: paula.podemski@seattleopera.org
Web site: www.seattleopera.org

Seattle Youth Involvement Network

General Information: Organization that advocates for youth in order to create positive changes in the community through civic involvement, leadership development, and volunteer service
Contact: Liz Vivian, Executive Director, 172 20th Avenue, Seattle, WA 98122
Fax: 206-323-8731
E-mail: liz@seattleyouth.org
Web site: www.seattleyouth.org

Wyoming

Albany County SAFE Project

General Information: Project that advocates for victims of domestic violence and sexual assault
Contact: Linda Torres, Executive Director, 312 Steele, Laramie, WY 82070
Phone: 307-742-7273
Fax: 307-745-4510
E-mail: safeproject@vcn.com

SUMMER OPPORTUNITIES

Alaska

Adventures Cross-Country, Alaska Adventure
General Information: Coed residential outdoor/wilderness program established in 1983.
Contact: Scott von Eschen, Director, 242 Redwood Highway, Mill Valley, CA 94941
Phone: 415-332-5075 or 415-332-2130
E-mail: arcc@adventurescrosscountry.com
Web site: www.adventurescrosscountry.com

Alaska Pacific University Wilderness Expedition Course
Anchorage, AK
General Information: Coed residential adventure and outdoor/wilderness program established in 1996.
Contact: Gavin Vaughn, Outdoor Programs, 4101 University Drive, Anchorage, AK 99508
Phone: 907-564-8388 or 907-564-8806
E-mail: gavinvau@alaskapacific.edu
Web site: www.alaskapacific.edu

Cordova 4 H Bluegrass and Old Time Music and Dance Camp
Cordova, AK
General Information: Coed residential and day arts program established in 1995.
Contact: Mrs. Linda Brown, 4H Camp Coordinator, Box 1053, Cordova, AK 99574
Phone: 907-424-5143 or 907-424-3277
E-mail: linda@cordovanet.com

EARTHWATCH INSTITUTE–Biodiversity–Sea Otters of Alaska
General Information: Coed residential outdoor/wilderness program.
Contact: General Information Desk, PO Box 75, Maynard, MA 01754
Phone: 800-776-0188 or 978-461-2332
E-mail: info@earthwatch.org
Web site: www.earthwatch.org

NBC Camps–Basketball Speed–Alaska
General Information: Coed residential sports program.
Contact: Ms. Bonnie Tucker, Office Manager, 10003 North Milan Road, #100, Spokane, WA 99218
Phone: 509-466-4690 or 509-467-6289
E-mail: btucker@nbccamps.com
Web site: www.nbccamps.com

NBC Camps–Basketball–Team (Boys)–Alaska
General Information: Boys residential sports program.
Contact: Danny Beard, 10003 North Milan Road, #100, Spokane, WA 99218
Phone: 509-466-4690 or 509-467-6289
E-mail: danny@nbccamps.com
Web site: www.nbccamps.com

NBC Camps–Basketball–Team (Girls)–Alaska
General Information: Girls residential sports program.
Contact: Danny Beard, 10003 North Milan Road, #100, Spokane, WA 99218
Phone: 509-466-4690 or 509-467-6289
E-mail: danny@nbccamps.com
Web site: www.nbccamps.com

NBC Camps–Volleyball–Alaska
General Information: Girls residential sports program.
Contact: Ms. Bonnie Tucker, Office Manager, 10003 North Milan Road, #100, Spokane, WA 99218
Phone: 509-466-4690 or 509-467-6289
E-mail: btucker@nbccamps.com
Web site: www.nbccamps.com

Putney Student Travel–Community Service–Alaska
General Information: Coed residential community service program established in 1951.
Contact: Jeff Shumlin, Director, 345 Hickory Ridge Road, Putney, VT 05346
Phone: 802-387-5885, 802-387-4276
E-mail: info@goputney.com
Web site: www.goputney.com

Visions–Alaska
General Information: Coed residential cultural program established in 1989.
Contact: Joanne Pinaire, Director, PO Box 220, Newport, PA 17074
Phone: 717-567-7313 or 717-567-7853
E-mail: visions@pa.net
Web site: www.visionsadventure.com

Arizona

Breakthroughs Abroad–Navajo
Chinle, AZ
General Information: Coed residential community service and cultural program established in 2001.
Contact: Garth Lewis, Director, 1160-B Woodstock, Estes Park, CO 80517
Phone: 970-577-1908 or 970-577-9855
E-mail: info@breakthroughsabroad.com
Web site: www.breakthroughsabroad.org

Deer Hill Expeditions, Arizona
General Information: Coed residential community service and outdoor/wilderness program established in 1984.
Contact: Beverly Capelin, Founder and Owner, PO Box 180, Mancos, CO 81328
Phone: 800-533-7221 or 970-533-7221
E-mail: info@deerhillexpeditions.com
Web site: www.deerhillexpeditions.com

Oak Creek Ranch Summer School
West Sedona, AZ
General Information: Coed residential academic program established in 1972.
Contact: Mr. Jay Wick, Headmaster, PO Box 4329, West Sedona, AZ 86340
Phone: 928-634-5571 or 928-634-4915
E-mail: admissions@ocrs.com
Web site: www.ocrs.com

Orme Summer Camp
Mayer, AZ
General Information: Coed residential academic program established in 1929.
Contact: Mr. Doug Bartlett, Camp Director, HC 63 Box 3040, Mayer, AZ 86333
Phone: 520-632-7601 or 520-632-7605
E-mail: dbartlett@ormeschool.org
Web site: www.ormecamp.org

St. Paul's Preparatory Academy Summer Program
Phoenix, AZ
General Information: Boys residential and day academic program established in 1994.
Contact: David C. Johnson, Director of Admission, PO Box 32650, Phoenix, AZ 85064-2650
Phone: 602-956-9090 or 602-956-3018
E-mail: admissions@stpaulsacademy.com
Web site: www.stpaulsacademy.com

Southwestern Adventures
Rimrock, AZ
General Information: Coed residential academic program established in 1924.
Contact: Mr. Troy Boyle, Director of Admissions, 2800 Monterey Road, San Marino, CA 91108
Phone: 626-799-5010 ext. 204 or 626-799-0407
E-mail: admissions@southwesternacademy.edu
Web site: www.southwesternacademy.edu

California

Academic Study Associates–ASA at the University of California, Berkeley
Berkeley, CA
General Information: Coed residential and day academic program established in 2001.
Contact: Marcia Evans, President, 10 New King Street, White Plains, NY 10604
Phone: 914-686-7730 or 914-686-7740
E-mail: summer@asaprogams.com
Web site: www.asaprograms.com

Academy By The Sea
Carlsbad, CA
General Information: Coed residential and day academic program established in 1943.
Contact: Ms. Lori Adlfinger, Associate Director, PO Box 3000, Carlsbad, CA 92018-3000
Phone: 760-434-7564 or 760-729-1574
E-mail: info@abts.com
Web site: www.abts.com

Acting Workshop by Education Unlimited
Berkeley, CA
General Information: Coed residential and day arts program established in 1997.
Contact: Mr. Andy Spear, Program Director, 1678 Shattuck Avenue, #305, Berkeley, CA 94709
Phone: 800-548-6612 or 510-548-0212
E-mail: camps@educationunlimited.com
Web site: www.educationunlimited.com

Adventures Cross-Country, California Adventure
General Information: Coed residential outdoor/wilderness program established in 1983.
Contact: Scott von Eschen, Director, 242 Redwood Highway, Mill Valley, CA 94941
Phone: 415-332-5075 or 415-332-2130
E-mail: arcc@adventurescrosscountry.com
Web site: www.adventurescrosscountry.com

Adventures Cross-Country, Mountaineering Adventure
General Information: Coed residential outdoor/wilderness program established in 1983.
Contact: Scott von Eschen, Director, 242 Redwood Highway, Mill Valley, CA 94941
Phone: 415-332-5075 or 415-332-2130

E-mail: arcc@adventurescrosscountry.com
Web site: www.adventurescrosscountry.com

American Legal Experience
Berkeley, CA
General Information: Coed residential academic program.
Contact: Director, 1678 Shattuck Avenue, #305, Berkeley, CA 94709
Phone: 800-548-6612
Web site: www.educationunlimited.com

American Legal Experience
Los Angeles, CA
General Information: Coed residential academic program.
Contact: Director, 1678 Shattuck Avenue, #305, Berkeley, CA 94709
Phone: 800-548-6612
Web site: www.educationunlimited.com

American Legal Experience
Stanford, CA
General Information: Coed residential academic program.
Contact: Director, 1678 Shattuck Avenue, #305, Berkeley, CA 94709
Phone: 800-548-6612
Web site: www.educationunlimited.com

Art Center College of Design–Saturday High
Pasadena, CA
General Information: Coed day arts program established in 0.
Contact: Christina Stafford, Administrative Assistant, 1700 Lida Street, Pasadena, CA 91103
Phone: 626-396-2319 or 626-796-9564
E-mail: acan@artcenter.edu
Web site: www.artcenter.edu

Astrocamp
Idyllwild, CA
General Information: Coed residential academic program established in 1990.
Contact: Jeri Karp, Summer Camp Secretary, PO Box 1360, Claremont, CA 91711
Phone: 800-645-1423
E-mail: jkarp@guideddiscoveries.org
Web site: www.astrocamp.org

Aviation Challenge–California
Atwater, CA
General Information: Coed residential academic program established in 1997.
Contact: Reservations Department, PO Box 070015, Huntsville, AL 35807
Phone: 800-63-SPACE or 256-837-6137
Web site: www.spacecamp.com

Bay Area Shakespeare Camp
General Information: Coed day arts program established in 1994.
Contact: Mr. John Western, Marketing Director, PO Box 590479, San Francisco, CA 94159
Phone: 415-422-2313 or 415-221-0643
E-mail: sfshakes@usfca.edu
Web site: www.sfshakes.org

Brotherhood-Sisterhood Camp
Los Angeles, CA
General Information: Coed residential cultural program established in 1950.
Contact: Ben Wright, Administrative Specialist, 1055 Wilshire Boulevard, Suite 1615, Los Angeles, CA 90017-2499
Phone: 213-250-8787 ext. 212 or 213-250-8799
E-mail: bwright@nccj.org
Web site: www.nccjla.org

California College of Arts and Crafts Pre-College Program
Oakland, CA
General Information: Coed residential and day arts program established in 1986.
Contact: Molly Ryan, Director of Undergraduate Admissions, 1111 Eighth St, San Francisco, CA 94107
Phone: 415-703-9523 or 415-703-9539
E-mail: enroll@ccac-art.edu
Web site: www.ccac-art.edu

California National Debate Institute
Berkeley, CA
General Information: Coed residential and day academic program established in 1992.
Contact: Mr. Robert Thomas, Associate Director, 1678 Shattuck Avenue, #305, Berkeley, CA 94709
Phone: 510-548-4800 or 510-548-0212
E-mail: debate@educationunlimited.com
Web site: www.educationunlimited.com

Cal Poly State University PSAT & SAT I Prep Camp
San Luis Obispo, CA
General Information: Coed residential and day academic program established in 1986.
Contact: Carroll Busselen, Director, 807 Skyline Drive, San Luis Obispo, CA 93405
Phone: 805-544-6777
Web site: www.calpoly.edu

Cal Poly State University Summer Young Scholars Program
San Luis Obispo, CA
General Information: Coed day academic

program established in 1982.
Contact: Carroll Busselen, Director, 807 Skyline Drive, San Luis Obispo, CA 93405
Phone: 805-544-6777
Web site: www.calpoly.edu

Camp Pacific's Surf and Bodyboard Camp
Carlsbad, CA
General Information: Coed residential and day sports program established in 1943.
Contact: Ms. Lori Adlfinger, Associate Director, PO Box 3000, Carlsbad, CA 92008
Phone: 760-434-7564 or 760-729-1574
E-mail: info@abts.com
Web site: www.surfcamp.org

Camp $tart-Up–California
Danville, CA
General Information: Girls residential academic program established in 1994.
Contact: Valjeanne Estes, Camp Director, 126 Powers Avenue, Santa Barbara, CA 93103
Phone: 800-350-1816 or 805-965-3148
E-mail: vestes@independentmeans.com
Web site: www.independentmeans.com

College Admission Prep Camp–Stanford University
Stanford, CA
General Information: Coed residential and day academic program established in 1993.
Contact: Matthew Fraser, Executive Director, 1678 Shattuck Avenue, #305, Berkeley, CA 94709
Phone: 800-548-6612 or 510-548-0212
E-mail: camps@educationunlimited.com
Web site: www.educationunlimited.com

College Admission Prep Camp–UC Berkeley
Berkeley, CA
General Information: Coed residential and day academic program established in 1993.
Contact: Matthew Fraser, Executive Director, 1678 Shattuck Avenue, #305, Berkeley, CA 94709
Phone: 800-548-6612 or 510-548-0212
E-mail: camps@educationunlimited.com
Web site: www.educationunlimited.com

College Admission Prep Camp–UC Davis
Davis, CA
General Information: Coed residential and day academic program established in 1993.
Contact: Mr. Matthew Fraser, Executive

Director, 1678 Shattuck Avenue, #305, Berkeley, CA 94709
Phone: 800-548-6612 or 510-548-0212
E-mail: camps@educationunlimited.com
Web site: www.educationunlimited.com

College Admission Prep Camp–UCLA
Los Angeles, CA
General Information: Coed residential and day academic program established in 1993.
Contact: Matthew Fraser, Executive Director, 1678 Shattuck Avenue, #305, Berkeley, CA 94709
Phone: 800-548-6612 or 510-548-0212
E-mail: camps@educationunlimited.com
Web site: www.educationunlimited.com

Computer Camp by Education Unlimited–Los Angeles
Los Angeles, CA
General Information: Coed residential and day academic program established in 1995.
Contact: Matthew Fraser, Executive Director, 1678 Shattuck Avenue, #305, Berkeley, CA 94709
Phone: 800-548-6612 or 510-548-0212
E-mail: camps@educationunlimited.com
Web site: www.educationunlimited.com

Computer Camp by Education Unlimited–Stanford
Palo Alto, CA
General Information: Coed residential and day academic program established in 1995.
Contact: Matthew Fraser, Executive Director, 1678 Shattuck Avenue, #305, Berkeley, CA 94709
Phone: 800-548-6612 or 510-548-0212
E-mail: camps@educationunlimited.com
Web site: www.educationunlimited.com

Computer Camp by Education Unlimited–UC Berkeley
Berkeley, CA
General Information: Coed residential and day academic program established in 1995.
Contact: Matthew Fraser, Executive Director, 1678 Shattuck Avenue, #305, Berkeley, CA 94709
Phone: 800-548-6612 or 510-548-0212
E-mail: camps@educationunlimited.com
Web site: www.educationunlimited.com

Computer Camp by Education Unlimited–UC Davis
Davis, CA
General Information: Coed residential and day academic program established in 1995.

Contact: Mr. Matthew Fraser, Executive
Director, 1678 Shattuck Avenue, #305, Berkeley, CA 94709
Phone: 800-548-6612 or 510-548-0212
E-mail: camps@educationunlimited.com
Web site: www.educationunlimited.com

Crossroads School–Aquatics
Santa Monica, CA
General Information: Coed day sports program.
Contact: Angela Smith, Director of Summer Programs, 1714 21st Street, Santa Monica, CA 90404
Phone: 310-829-7391 ext. 506 or 310-828-8147
E-mail: asmith@xrds.org
Web site: www.xrds.org

Crossroads School–Roadrunners Basketball Camp
Santa Monica, CA
General Information: Coed day sports program.
Contact: Angela Smith, Director of Summer Programs, 1714 21st Street, Santa Monica, CA 90404
Phone: 310-829-7391 ext. 506 or 310-828-8147
E-mail: summer@xrds.org
Web site: www.xrds.org

Crossroads School–Soccer Camps
Santa Monica, CA
General Information: Coed day sports program.
Contact: Angela Smith, Director of Summer Programs, 1714 21st Street, Santa Monica, CA 90404
Phone: 310-829-7391 ext. 506 or 310-828-8147
E-mail: summer@xrds.org
Web site: www.xrds.org

Crossroads School Summer Educational Journey
Santa Monica, CA
General Information: Coed day academic and arts program established in 1980.
Contact: Angela Smith, Director of Summer Programs, Crossroads School, 1714 21st Street, Santa Monica, CA 90404
Phone: 310-829-7391 ext. 506 or 310-828-8147
E-mail: asmith@xrds.org
Web site: www.xrds.org

Cybercamps–Cal State Polytechnic University
Pomona, CA
General Information: Coed residential and day academic program established in 1997.

Contact: Celia Paz, Customer Care Representative, 12131 113th Avenue NE, Suite 102, Kirkland, WA 98034
Phone: 888-904-CAMP or 425-825-4601
E-mail: info@cybercamps.com
Web site: www.cybercamps.com

Cybercamps–Cal State University Hayward
Hayward, CA
General Information: Coed residential and day academic program established in 1997.
Contact: Celia Paz, Customer Care Representative, 12131 113th Avenue NE, Suite 102, Kirkland, WA 98034
Phone: 888-904-CAMP or 425-825-4601
E-mail: info@cybercamps.com
Web site: www.cybercamps.com

Cybercamps–Cal State University Northridge
Northridge, CA
General Information: Coed residential and day academic program established in 1997.
Contact: Celia Paz, Customer Care Representative, 12131 113th Avenue NE, Suite 102, Kirkland, WA 98034
Phone: 888-904-CAMP or 425-825-4601
E-mail: info@cybercamps.com
Web site: www.cybercamps.com

Cybercamps–Chapman University
Orange, CA
General Information: Coed residential and day academic program established in 1997.
Contact: Celia Paz, Customer Care Representative, 12131 113th Avenue NE, Suite 102, Kirkland, WA 98034
Phone: 888-904-CAMP or 425-825-4601
E-mail: info@cybercamps.com
Web site: www.cybercamps.com

Cybercamps–Concordia University
Irvine, CA
General Information: Coed residential and day academic program established in 1997.
Contact: Celia Paz, Customer Care Representative, 12131 113th Avenue NE, Suite 102, Kirkland, WA 98034
Phone: 888-904-CAMP or 425-825-4601
E-mail: info@cybercamps.com
Web site: www.cybercamps.com

Cybercamps–Las Positas College
Livermore, CA
General Information: Coed residential and day academic program established in 1997.
Contact: Celia Paz, Customer Care Representative, 12131 113th Avenue NE,

Suite 102, Kirkland, WA 98034
Phone: 888-904-CAMP or 425-825-4601
E-mail: info@cybercamps.com
Web site: www.cybercamps.com

Cybercamps–Menlo College
Atherton, CA
General Information: Coed residential and day academic program established in 1997.
Contact: Celia Paz, Customer Care Representative, 12131 113th Avenue NE, Suite 102, Kirkland, WA 98034
Phone: 888-904-CAMP or 425-825-4601
E-mail: info@cybercamps.com
Web site: www.cybercamps.com

Cybercamps–Mills College
Oakland, CA
General Information: Coed residential and day academic program established in 1997.
Contact: Celia Paz, Customer Care Representative, 12131 113th Avenue NE, Suite 102, Kirkland, WA 98034
Phone: 888-904-CAMP or 425-825-4601
E-mail: info@cybercamps.com
Web site: www.cybercamps.com

Cybercamps–San Jose State University
San Jose, CA
General Information: Coed residential and day academic program established in 1997.
Contact: Celia Paz, Customer Care Representative, 12131 113th Avenue NE, Suite 102, Kirkland, WA 98034
Phone: 888-904-CAMP or 425-825-4601
E-mail: info@cybercamps.com
Web site: www.cybercamps.com

Cybercamps–Santa Clara University
Santa Clara, CA
General Information: Coed residential and day academic program established in 1997.
Contact: Celia Paz, Customer Care Representative, 12131 113th Avenue NE, Suite 102, Kirkland, WA 98034
Phone: 888-904-CAMP or 425-825-4601
E-mail: info@cybercamps.com
Web site: www.cybercamps.com

Cybercamps–UCLA
Los Angeles, CA
General Information: Coed residential and day academic program established in 1997.
Contact: Celia Paz, Customer Care Representative, 12131 113th Avenue NE, Suite 102, Kirkland, WA 98034
Phone: 888-904-CAMP or 425-825-4601
E-mail: info@cybercamps.com
Web site: www.cybercamps.com

Cybercamps–UC San Diego (UCSD)
La Jolla, CA
General Information: Coed residential and day academic program established in 1997.
Contact: Celia Paz, Customer Care Representative, 12131 113th Avenue NE, Suite 102, Kirkland, WA 98034
Phone: 888-904-CAMP or 425-825-4601
E-mail: info@cybercamps.com
Web site: www.cybercamps.com

Cybercamps–University of California at Berkeley
Berkeley, CA
General Information: Coed residential and day academic program established in 1997.
Contact: Celia Paz, Customer Care Representative, 12131 113th Avenue NE, Suite 102, Kirkland, WA 98034
Phone: 888-904-CAMP or 425-825-4601
E-mail: info@cybercamps.com
Web site: www.cybercamps.com

Cybercamps–University of San Diego
San Diego, CA
General Information: Coed residential and day academic program established in 1997.
Contact: Celia Paz, Customer Care Representative, 12131 113th Avenue NE, Suite 102, Kirkland, WA 98034
Phone: 888-904-CAMP or 425-825-4601
E-mail: info@cybercamps.com
Web site: www.cybercamps.com

Cybercamps–West Valley College
Saratoga, CA
General Information: Coed residential and day academic program established in 1997.
Contact: Celia Paz, Customer Care Representative, 12131 113th Avenue NE, Suite 102, Kirkland, WA 98034
Phone: 888-904-CAMP or 425-825-4601
E-mail: info@cybercamps.com
Web site: www.cybercamps.com

Elite Baseball Camp
Los Angeles, CA
General Information: Boys residential sports program established in 2001.
Contact: Mr. Steve Foral, Associate Director, Summer and Special Programs, Bovard Administration #115, Los Angeles, CA 90084-4019
Phone: 213-740-5679 or 213-740-6417
E-mail: sforal@usc.edu
Web site: www.usc.edu/summer-programs

Elite Educational Center Elementary Enrichment

General Information: Coed day academic program established in 1987.

Contact: Christian Park, Program Director, 19735 Colima Road, #2, Rowland Heights, CA 91748

Phone: 909-444-0876 or 909-444-0877

Elite Educational Center SAT Bootcamp

General Information: Coed day academic program established in 1987.

Contact: Christian Park, Program Director, 19735 Colima Road #2, Rowland Heights, CA 91748

Phone: 909-444-0876 or 909-444-0877

Elite Educational Center SAT Preparation

General Information: Coed day academic program established in 1987.

Contact: Christian Park, Program Director, 19735 Colima Road, #2, Rowland Heights, CA 91748

Phone: 909-444-0876 or 909-444-0877

Elite Junior Ambassador Program

Los Angeles, CA

General Information: Coed residential and day academic program established in 2000.

Contact: David Siegel, Program Director, 4009 Wilshire Boulevard, #200, Los Angeles, CA 90010

Phone: 213-365-8008 or 213-365-1253

ELS Language Centers–Malibu Teen Vacations

Malibu, CA

General Information: Coed residential academic and cultural program established in 1977.

Contact: Beverly Familar, Vacation Programs Supervisor, 400 Alexander Park, Princeton, NJ 08540-6306

Phone: 609-750-3516 or 609-750-3594

E-mail: bfamilar@els.com

Web site: www.els.com

ELS Language Centers–Redlands Youth Camp

Redlands, CA

General Information: Coed residential cultural program established in 1977.

Contact: Beverly Familiar, Vacation Programs Supervisor, 400 Alexander Park, Princeton, NJ 08540-6306

Phone: 609-750-3516 or 609-750-3594

E-mail: bfamilar@els.com

Web site: www.els.com

ELS Language Centers–Santa Barbara High School Prep

Goleta, CA

General Information: Coed residential academic and cultural program established in 1977.

Contact: Beverly Familar, Vacation Programs Supervisor, 400 Alexander Park, Princeton, NJ 08540-6306

Phone: 609-750-3516 or 609-750-3594

E-mail: bfamilar@els.com

Web site: www.els.com

EXCEL–Sonoma State University

Rohnert Park, CA

General Information: Coed day academic and arts program established in 1982.

Contact: Greer Upton, Coordinator, Office of Extended Education, 1801 East Cotati Avenue, Rohnert Park, CA 94928

Phone: 707-664-2394 or 707-664-2613

Web site: www.sonoma.edu/exed/excel

Exploration of Architecture

Los Angeles, CA

General Information: Coed residential academic program established in 1983.

Contact: Ms. Jody Cherry, Director of Admission, Watt Hall, Room 204, Los Angeles, CA 90089-0291

Phone: 213-740-2420 or 213-740-8884

E-mail: cherry@bmf.usc.edu

Web site: www.usc.edu/dept/architecture/explor/

Gallagher's High Adventure Camp

General Information: Boys residential outdoor/wilderness program established in 1996.

Contact: John Champion Gallagher, Director/Owner, PO Drawer 240, Meadow Valley, CA 95956

Phone: 530-283-5502

E-mail: highcamp@psln.com

Web site: www.psln.com/highcamp

Hamlin Summer Camp

General Information: Coed day adventure program established in 1998.

Contact: Mr. Tyler Fonarow, Camp Director, 2120 Broadway, San Francisco, CA

Phone: 415-674-5457 or 415-674-5445

E-mail: fonarow@hamlin.org

Web site: www.hamlin.org

Harker Summer Programs

San Jose, CA

General Information: Coed day academic program established in 1957.

Contact: Kelly Espinosa, Summer Programs Director, 4300 Bucknall Road, San Jose, CA 95130

Phone: 408-871-4622 or 408-871-4320

E-mail: kellye@harker.org

Web site: www.harker.org

The Harker Summer Institute

San Jose, CA

General Information: Coed day academic program established in 1999.

Contact: Jada Burrell, Summer Programs Assistant, 500 Saratoga Avenue, San Jose, CA 95129

Phone: 408-349-2510 or 408-984-2325

E-mail: campinfo@harker.org

Web site: www.harker.org

iD Tech Camps–College of Notre Dame, Belmont, CA

Belmont, CA

General Information: Coed residential and day academic program established in 1999.

Contact: Mr. Pete Ingram-Cauchi, President, 2103 South Bascom Avenue, Campbell, CA 95008

Phone: 888-709-TECH or 408-626-9505

E-mail: info@internaldrive.com

Web site: www.internaldrive.com

iD Tech Camps–CSUMB, Monterey Bay, CA

Monterey, CA

General Information: Coed residential and day academic program established in 1999.

Contact: Mr. Pete Ingram-Cauchi, President, 2103 South Bascom Avenue, Campbell, CA 95008

Phone: 888-709-TECH or 408-626-9505

E-mail: info@internaldrive.com

Web site: www.idtechcamps.com

iD Tech Camps–Dominican University, San Rafael, CA

San Rafael, CA

General Information: Coed residential and day academic program established in 1999.

Contact: Mr. Pete Ingram-Cauchi, President, 2103 South Bascom Avenue, Campbell, CA 95008

Phone: 888-709-TECH or 408-626-9505

E-mail: info@internaldrive.com

Web site: www.internaldrive.com

iD Tech Camps–Loyola Marymount, Los Angeles, CA

Los Angeles, CA

General Information: Coed residential and day academic program established in 1999.

Contact: Mr. Pete Ingram-Cauchi, President, 2103 South Bascom Avenue, Campbell, CA 95008

Phone: 888-709-TECH or 408-626-9505

E-mail: info@internaldrive.com

Web site: www.internaldrive.com

iD Tech Camps–Menlo College, Atherton, CA

Atherton, CA

General Information: Coed residential and day academic program established in 1999.

Contact: Mr. Pete Ingram-Cauchi, President, 2103 South Bascom Avenue, Campbell, CA 95008

Phone: 888-709-TECH or 408-626-9505

E-mail: info@internaldrive.com

Web site: www.internaldrive.com

iD Tech Camps–Santa Clara University, San Jose, CA

Santa Clara, CA

General Information: Coed residential and day academic program established in 1999.

Contact: Mr. Pete Ingram-Cauchi, President, 2103 South Bascom Avenue, Campbell, CA 95008

Phone: 888-709-TECH or 408-626-9505

E-mail: info@internaldrive.com

Web site: www.idtechcamps.com

iD Tech Camps–St. Mary's College, Moraga, CA

Moraga, CA

General Information: Coed residential and day academic program established in 1999.

Contact: Mr. Pete Ingram-Cauchi, President, 2103 South Bascom Avenue, Campbell, CA 95008

Phone: 888-709-TECH or 408-626-9505

E-mail: info@internaldrive.com

Web site: www.idtechcamps.com

iD Tech Camps–Stanford, Palo Alto, CA

Palo Alto, CA

General Information: Coed residential and day academic program established in 1999.

Contact: Mr. Pete Ingram-Cauchi, President, 2103 South Bascom Avenue, Campbell, CA 95008

Phone: 888-709-TECH or 408-626-9505

E-mail: info@internaldrive.com

Web site: www.internaldrive.com

iD Tech Camps–UC Berkeley, Berkeley, CA

Berkeley, CA

General Information: Coed residential and day academic program established in 1999.

Contact: Mr. Pete Ingram-Cauchi, President, 2103 South Bascom Avenue, Campbell, CA 95008

Phone: 888-709-TECH or 408-626-9505

E-mail: info@internaldrive.com

Web site: www.internaldrive.com

iD Tech Camps–UC Irvine, Irvine, CA

Irvine, CA

General Information: Coed residential and day academic program established in 1999.

Contact: Mr. Pete Ingram-Cauchi, President, 2103 South Bascom Avenue, Campbell, CA 95008

Phone: 888-709-TECH or 408-626-9505

E-mail: info@internaldrive.com

Web site: www.idtechcamps.com

iD Tech Camps–UCLA, Brentwood, CA

Brentwood, CA

General Information: Coed residential and day academic program established in 1999.

Contact: Mr. Pete Ingram-Cauchi, President, 2103 South Bascom Avenue, Campbell, CA 95008

Phone: 888-709-TECH or 408-626-9505

E-mail: info@internaldrive.com

Web site: www.internaldrive.com

iD Tech Camps–UCSD, LaJolla, CA

La Jolla, CA

General Information: Coed residential and day academic program established in 1999.

Contact: Mr. Pete Ingram-Cauchi, President, 2103 South Bascom Avenue, Campbell, CA 95008

Phone: 888-709-TECH or 408-626-9505

E-mail: info@internaldrive.com

Web site: www.internaldrive.com

iD Tech Camps–USD, San Diego, CA

San Diego, CA

General Information: Coed residential and day academic program established in 1999.

Contact: Mr. Pete Ingram-Cauchi, President, 2103 South Bascom Avenue, Campbell, CA 95008

Phone: 888-709-TECH or 408-626-9505

E-mail: info@internaldrive.com

Web site: www.internaldrive.com

Idyllwild Arts Summer Program–American Experience for International Students

Idyllwild, CA

General Information: Coed residential arts program established in 1998.

Contact: Ms. Diane Dennis, Summer Program Registrar, PO Box 38, Idyllwild, CA 92549

Phone: 909-659-2171 ext. 365 or 909-659-5463

E-mail: summerprogram@idyllwildarts. org

Web site: www.idyllwildarts.org

Idyllwild Arts Summer Program–Children's Center

Idyllwild, CA

General Information: Coed residential and day arts program established in 1950.

Contact: Ms. Diane Dennis, Summer Program Registrar, PO Box 38, Idyllwild, CA 92549

Phone: 909-659-2171 ext. 365 or 909-659-5463

E-mail: summerprogram@idyllwildarts. org

Web site: www.idyllwildarts.org

Idyllwild Arts Summer Program–Junior Artists' Center

Idyllwild, CA

General Information: Coed residential and day arts program established in 1950.

Contact: Ms. Diane Dennis, Summer Program Registrar, PO Box 38, Idyllwild, CA 92549

Phone: 909-659-2171 ext. 365 or 909-659-5463

E-mail: summerprogram@idyllwildarts. org

Web site: www.idyllwildarts.org

Idyllwild Arts Summer Program–Youth Arts Center

Idyllwild, CA

General Information: Coed residential and day arts program established in 1950.

Contact: Diane Dennis, Registrar, Summer Program, PO Box 38, Idyllwild, CA 92549

Phone: 909-659-2171 ext. 365 or 909-659-5463

E-mail: summerprogram@idyllwildarts. org

Web site: www.idyllwildarts.org

Inside/Outside Basketball Camp

Los Angeles, CA

General Information: Boys residential sports program established in 2000.

Contact: Mr. Steve Foral, Associate Director, Summer and Special Programs, Bovard Administration #115, Los Angeles, CA 90084-4019

Phone: 213-740-5679 or 213-740-6417

E-mail: sforal@usc.edu

Web site: www.usc.edu/summer-programs

Junior Statesmen Summer School–Stanford University

Stanford, CA

General Information: Coed residential academic program established in 1941.

Contact: Preeta Nayak, Program Director,

60 East 3rd Avenue, Suite 320, San Mateo, CA 94401
Phone: 650-347-1600 or 650-347-7200
E-mail: jsa@jsa.org
Web site: www.jsa.org

Junior Statesmen Symposium on California State Politics and Government
Davis, CA
General Information: Coed residential academic program established in 1990.
Contact: Preeta Nayak, Program Director, 60 East 3rd Avenue, Suite 320, San Mateo, CA 94401
Phone: 650-347-1600 or 650-347-7200
E-mail: jsa@jsa.org
Web site: www.jsa.org

Landmark Volunteers: California
General Information: Coed residential community service program established in 1992.
Contact: Ann Barrett, Executive Director, PO Box 455, Sheffield, MA 01257
Phone: 413-229-0255 or 413-229-2050
E-mail: landmark@volunteers.com
Web site: www.volunteers.com

Le Camp Français en Californie
Mendocino, CA
General Information: Coed residential academic and cultural program established in 1998.
Contact: Mr. Etienne Vallee, Camp Director, 210 Post Street, Suite 502, San Francisco, CA 94108
Phone: 888-841-0024 or 415-477-3669
E-mail: le-camp@frenchfoundation.com
Web site: www.ivpsf.com/frenchcamp

LSA Los Angeles, United States
Los Angeles, CA
General Information: Coed residential academic and cultural program established in 1978.
Contact: Director, 103 Londonderry Court, Reno, NV 89511-2718
Phone: 800-424-5522 or 775-849-9217
E-mail: info@languagestudiesabroad.com
Web site: www.languagestudiesabroad.com

LSA Palo Alto, United States
Palo Alto, CA
General Information: Coed residential academic and cultural program established in 1979.
Contact: Director, 103 Londonderry Court, Reno, NV 89511-2718
Phone: 800-424-5522 or 775-849-9217
E-mail: info@languagestudiesabroad.com
Web site: www.languagestudiesabroad.com

LSA Santa Barbara, United States–Junior Summer Course
Santa Barbara, CA
General Information: Coed residential cultural program established in 1978.
Contact: Director, 103 Londonderry Court, Reno, NV 89511-2718
Phone: 800-424-5522 or 775-849-9217
E-mail: info@languagestudiesabroad.com
Web site: www.languagestudiesabroad.com

Media Workshops
Los Angeles, CA
General Information: Coed residential academic and arts program established in 1984.
Contact: Ms. Carol Gemovese, Administrative Director, 291 South La Cienega Boulevard, Suite 735, Beverly Hills, CA 90211
Phone: 800-223-4561
E-mail: mworkshop1@aol.com
Web site: www.mediaworkshops.org

National Computer Camps at Pitzer College
Claremont, CA
General Information: Coed residential and day academic program established in 1977.
Contact: Dr. Michael Zabinski, President, PO Box 585, Orange, CT 06477
Phone: 203-795-9667
E-mail: info@nccamp.com
Web site: www.nccamp.com

National Computer Camps at Santa Clara University
Santa Clara, CA
General Information: Coed residential and day academic program established in 1977.
Contact: Dr. Michael Zabinski, President, PO Box 585, Orange, CT 06477
Phone: 203-795-9667
E-mail: info@nccamp.com
Web site: www.nccamp.com

National Guitar Workshop–Los Angeles, CA
Los Angeles, CA
General Information: Coed residential and day arts program established in 1984.
Contact: Ms. Paula Abate, Executive Director, PO Box 222, Lakeside, CT 06758
Phone: 860-567-3736 ext. 103 or 860-567-0374
E-mail: paula@guitarworkshop.com
Web site: www.guitarworkshop.com

National Guitar Workshop–San Francisco, CA
Oakland Hills, CA
General Information: Coed residential and day arts program established in 1984.
Contact: Ms. Paula Abate, Executive Director, PO Box 222, Lakeside, CT 06758
Phone: 860-567-3736 ext. 103 or 860-567-0374
E-mail: paula@guitarworkshop.com
Web site: www.guitarworkshop.com

National Student Leadership Conference: Law and Advocacy–California
Palo Alto, CA
General Information: Coed residential academic program established in 1989.
Contact: Dr. Paul M. Lisnek, Executive Director, PO Box 811086, Boca Raton, FL 33481-1086
Phone: 561-362-8585 or 561-362-8383
E-mail: information@nslcleaders.org
Web site: www.nslcleaders.org

NBC Camps–Basketball Individual Training–CA
Redding, CA
General Information: Coed residential sports program.
Contact: Ms. Bonnie Tucker, Office Manager, 10003 North Milan Road, #100, Spokane, WA 99218
Phone: 509-466-4690 or 509-467-6289
E-mail: btucker@nbccamps.com
Web site: www.nbccamps.com

NBC Camps–Basketball Speed Explosion–California
Redding, CA
General Information: Coed residential sports program.
Contact: Ms. Bonnie Tucker, Office Manager, 10003 North Milan Road, #100, Spokane, WA 99218
Phone: 509-466-4690 or 509-467-6289
E-mail: btucker@nbccamps.com
Web site: www.nbccamps.com

NBC Camps–Volleyball Speed Explosion–California
Redding, CA
General Information: Coed residential sports program.
Contact: Ms. Bonnie Tucker, Office Manager, 10003 North Milan Road, #100, Spokane, WA 99218
Phone: 509-466-4690 or 509-467-6289
E-mail: btucker@nbccamps.com
Web site: www.nbccamps.com

NBC Camps–Volleyball–California
Redding, CA
General Information: Girls residential sports program.
Contact: Ms. Bonnie Tucker, Office Manager, 10003 North Milan Road, #100, Spokane, WA 99218
Phone: 509-466-4690 or 509-467-6289
E-mail: btucker@nbccamps.com
Web site: www.nbccamps.com

Ojai Valley Summer School and Camp
Ojai, CA
General Information: Coed residential and day academic program established in 1943.
Contact: Mr. John Williamson, Director of Admission, 723 El Paseo Road, Ojai, CA 93023
Phone: 805-646-1423 or 805-646-0362
Web site: www.ovs.org

Otis Summer of Art Program
Los Angeles, CA
General Information: Coed residential and day arts program established in 1979.
Contact: Ms. Janet Schipper, Summer of Art Coordinator, 9045 Lincoln Boulevard, Los Angeles, CA 90045
Phone: 310-665-6824 or 310-665-6821
E-mail: otisart@otisart.edu
Web site: www.otisart.edu

Oxford School Summer Camp
Rowland Heights, CA
General Information: Coed residential and day academic and cultural program established in 1980.
Contact: Ms. Michelle Cheng, Coordinator, 18760 East Colima Road, Rowland Heights, CA 91748
Phone: 626-964-9588 or 626-913-3919
E-mail: michelle_c@oxfordschool.org
Web site: www.oxfordschool.org

Pre-Freshman Enrichment Program, California State University, Stanislaus
Turlock, CA
General Information: Coed day academic program established in 1989.
Contact: Dr. Viji K. Sundar, Professor of Mathematics, 801 West Monte Vista Avenue, Turlock, CA 95382
Phone: 209-667-3595 or 209-667-3848
E-mail: vsundar@athena.csustan.edu
Web site: www.csustan.edu

Prep Camp Excel–Stanford University
Stanford, CA
General Information: Coed residential

and day academic program established in 2000.
Contact: Ms. Colleen Cadwallader, Director, 1678 Shattuck Avenue, #305, Berkeley, CA 94709
Phone: 800-548-6612 or 510-548-0212
E-mail: camps@educationunlimited.com
Web site: www.educationunlimited.com

Prep Camp Excel–UC Berkeley
Berkeley, CA
General Information: Coed residential and day academic program established in 2000.
Contact: Ms. Colleen Cadwallader, Director, 1678 Shattuck Avenue, #305, Berkeley, CA 94709
Phone: 800-548-6612 or 510-548-0212
E-mail: camps@educationunlimited.com
Web site: www.educationunlimited.com

Public Speaking Institute by Education Unlimited–San Diego
San Diego, CA
General Information: Coed residential and day academic program established in 1995.
Contact: Matthew Fraser, Executive Director, 1678 Shattuck Avenue, #305, Berkeley, CA 94709
Phone: 800-548-6612 or 510-548-0212
E-mail: camps@educationunlimited.com
Web site: www.educationunlimited.com

Public Speaking Institute by Education Unlimited–Stanford
Palo Alto, CA
General Information: Coed residential and day academic program established in 1995.
Contact: Matthew Fraser, Executive Director, 1678 Shattuck Avenue, #305, Berkeley, CA 94709
Phone: 800-548-6612 or 510-548-0212
E-mail: camps@educationunlimited.com
Web site: www.educationunlimited.com

Public Speaking Institute by Education Unlimited–UC Davis
Davis, CA
General Information: Coed residential and day academic program established in 1995.
Contact: Mr. Matthew Fraser, Executive Director, 1678 Shattuck Avenue, #305, Berkeley, CA 94709
Phone: 800-548-6612 or 510-548-0212
E-mail: camps@educationunlimited.com
Web site: www.educationunlimited.com

Science Program for Middle School Girls on Catalina
Los Angeles, CA
General Information: Girls residential

academic program established in 1999.
Contact: Steve Foral, Associate Director, Summer and Special Programs, , Los Angeles, CA 90089-4019**Phone:** 213-740-5679 or 213-740-6417
E-mail: sforal@usc.edu
Web site: www.usc.edu/summer-programs

SEACAMP San Diego
San Diego, CA
General Information: Coed residential academic program established in 1987.
Contact: Mr. Phil Zerofski, Director, 1380 Garnet Avenue, PMB E6, San Diego, CA 92109
Phone: 800-SEACAMP or 619-268-0229
E-mail: seacamp@seacamp.com
Web site: www.seacamp.com

SoccerPlus FieldPlayer Academy (Day)–Mission Viejo, California
Mission Viejo, CA
General Information: Coed day sports program.
Contact: Mr. Shawn Kelly, General Manager, 20 Beaver Road, Suite 102, Wethersfield, CT 06109
Phone: 800-533-7371 or 860-721-8619
E-mail: shawn@goalkeeper.com
Web site: www.soccerpluscamps.com

SoccerPlus Goalkeeper School–Challenge Program–San Diego, CA
San Diego, CA
General Information: Coed residential and day sports program.
Contact: Mr. Shawn Kelly, General Manager, 20 Beaver Road, Suite 102, Wethersfield, CT 06109
Phone: 800-533-7371 or 860-721-8619
E-mail: shawn@goalkeeper.com
Web site: www.soccerpluscamps.com

SoccerPlus Goalkeeper School–Challenge Program–Stockton, CA
Stockton, CA
General Information: Coed residential and day sports program.
Contact: Mr. Shawn Kelly, General Manager, 20 Beaver Road, Suite 102, Wethersfield, CT 06109
Phone: 800-533-7371 or 860-721-8619
E-mail: shawn@goalkeeper.com
Web site: www.soccerpluscamps.com

SoccerPlus Goalkeeper School–Competitive Program (Day)–CA
Mission Viejo, CA
General Information: Coed day sports program.
Contact: Mr. Shawn Kelly, General

Manager, 20 Beaver Road, Suite 102, Wethersfield, CT 06109
Phone: 800-533-7371 or 860-721-8619
E-mail: shawn@goalkeeper.com
Web site: www.soccerpluscamps.com

SoccerPlus Goalkeeper School–National Training Center–Stockton, CA
Stockton, CA
General Information: Coed residential sports program.
Contact: Mr. Shawn Kelly, General Manager, 20 Beaver Road, Suite 102, Wethersfield, CT 06109
Phone: 800-533-7371 or 860-721-8619
E-mail: shawn@goalkeeper.com
Web site: www.soccerpluscamps.com

Southwestern Academy International Summer Semester
San Marino, CA
General Information: Coed residential and day academic program established in 1963.
Contact: Mr. Troy Boyle, Co-Director of Admissions, 2800 Monterey Road, San Marino, CA 91108
Phone: 626-799-5010 ext. 204 or 626-799-0407
E-mail: admissions@ southwesternacademy.edu
Web site: www.southwesternacademy. edu

Stanford National Forensic Institute
Palo Alto, CA
General Information: Coed residential and day academic program established in 1991.
Contact: Mr. Matthew Fraser, Excutive Director, 555 Bryant Street #599, Palo Alto, CA 94301
Phone: 650-723-9086 or 510-548-0212
E-mail: snfi@mail.com
Web site: www.snfi.org

Stanford University Summer College for High School Students
Stanford, CA
General Information: Coed residential and day academic program established in 1960.
Contact: Carolyn Faszholz, Assistant Dean for Summer Session, Building 590, Ground Floor, Stanford, CA 94305-3005
Phone: 650-723-3109 or 650-725-6080
E-mail: summersession@stanford.edu
Web site: summersession.stanford.edu/

Stanford University Summer Discovery Institutes
Stanford, CA
General Information: Coed residential academic program established in 2000.
Contact: Carolyn Faszholz, Assistant Dean for Summer Session, Building 590, Ground Floor, Stanford, CA 94305-3005
Phone: 650-723-3109 or 650-725-6080
E-mail: summersession@stanford.edu
Web site: summerinstitutes.stanford.edu

Stevenson School Summer Camp
Pebble Beach, CA
General Information: Coed residential and day academic program established in 1972.
Contact: Rosemary Tintle, Administrative Secretary, 3152 Forest Lake Road, Pebble Beach, CA 93953
Phone: 831-626-5315 or 831-625-5208
Web site: www.rlstevenson.org

Study Tours in the USA–Citrus
Glendora, CA
General Information: Coed residential academic program established in 1987.
Contact: Ms. Veronica Perez, Director of Admissions, 101 East Green Street, #14, Pasadena, CA 91105
Phone: 626-795-2912 or 626-795-5564
E-mail: veronica@fls.net
Web site: www.fls.net

Study Tours in the USA–Mira Costa College
Oceanside, CA
General Information: Coed residential academic program established in 1999.
Contact: Ms. Veronica Perez, Director of Admissions, 101 East Green Street, #14, Pasadena, CA 91105
Phone: 626-795-2912 or 626-795-5564
E-mail: veronica@fls.net
Web site: www.fls.net

Study Tours in the USA–Oxnard
Oxnard, CA
General Information: Coed residential academic program established in 1987.
Contact: Ms. Veronica Perez, Director of Admissions, 101 East Green Street, #14, Pasadena, CA 91105
Phone: 626-795-2912 or 626-795-5564
E-mail: veronica@fls.net
Web site: www.fls.net

The Summer Science Program
Ojai, CA
General Information: Coed residential academic program established in 1959.
Contact: Mr. Richard Bowdon, Vice President-Recruiting, 108 Whiteberry Drive, Apex, NC 27502

E-mail: rbowden@summerscience.org
Web site: www.summerscience.org

Summer Discovery at UC San Diego
San Diego, CA
General Information: Coed residential academic program established in 1998.
Contact: The Musiker Family, Director, 1326 Old Northern Boulevard, Roslyn Village, NY 11576
Phone: 888-878-6637 or 516-625-3438
E-mail: discovery@summerfun.com
Web site: www.summerfun.com

Summer Discovery at UCLA
Los Angeles, CA
General Information: Coed residential academic program established in 1986.
Contact: The Musiker Family, Director, 1326 Old Northern Boulevard, Roslyn Village, NY 11576
Phone: 888-878-6637 or 516-625-3438
E-mail: discovery@summerfun.com
Web site: www.summerfun.com

Summer Focus at Berkeley
Berkeley, CA
General Information: Coed residential and day academic program established in 1997.
Contact: Ms. Lexy Green, Director of Summer Focus, 1678 Shattuck Avenue, #305, Berkeley, CA 94709
Phone: 800-548-6612 or 510-548-0212
E-mail: camps@educationunlimited.com
Web site: www.educationunlimited.com

SuperCamp–Claremont Colleges
Claremont, CA
General Information: Coed residential academic program established in 1981.
Contact: Enrollments Department, 1725 South Coast Highway, Oceanside, CA 92054
Phone: 800-285-3276 or 760-722-3507
E-mail: info@supercamp.com
Web site: www.supercamp.com

SuperCamp–Stanford University
Palo Alto, CA
General Information: Coed residential academic program established in 1981.
Contact: Enrollments Department, 1725 South Coast Highway, Oceanside, CA 92054
Phone: 800-285-3276 or 760-722-3507
E-mail: info@supercamp.com
Web site: www.supercamp.com

SuperCamp–US International University
San Diego, CA
General Information: Coed residential

academic program established in 1981.
Contact: Enrollments Department, 1725 South Coast Highway, Oceanside, CA 92054
Phone: 800-285-3276 or 760-722-3507
E-mail: info@supercamp.com
Web site: www.supercamp.com

UC San Diego Academic Connections
La Jolla, CA
General Information: Coed residential academic program established in 1990.
Contact: Becky Arce, Assistant Director, 9500 Gilman Drive, La Jolla, CA 92093-0179
Phone: 858-534-0804 or 858-534-8271
E-mail: barce@ucsd.edu
Web site: www.academicconnections.ucsd.edu

University of Southern California Summer Seminars
Los Angeles, CA
General Information: Coed residential academic program established in 1997.
Contact: Steve Foral, Director, Summer and Special Programs, ADM 115, Los Angeles, CA 90089-4019
Phone: 213-740-5679 or 213-740-6417
E-mail: summer@usc.edu
Web site: www.usc.edu/dept/provost/ug-studies

U.S. Space Camp–California
Mountain View, CA
General Information: Coed residential academic program established in 1996.
Contact: Reservations Department, PO Box 070015, Huntsville, AL 35807
Phone: 800-63-SPACE or 256-837-6137
Web site: www.spacecamp.com

Women's Volleyball Camp
Los Angeles, CA
General Information: Girls residential sports program established in 2000.
Contact: Steve Foral, Associate Director, Summer and Special Programs, Bovard Administration #115, Los Angeles, CA 90089-4019
Phone: 213-740-5679 or 213-740-6417
E-mail: sforal@usc.edu
Web site: www.usc.edu/summer-programs

Yo! Basecamp Rock Climbing Camps
General Information: Coed residential adventure and outdoor/wilderness program established in 1998.
Contact: Ms. Lisa Coleman, Co-Director, 130 McCornick Street #7, Santa Cruz, CA 95062

Phone: 408-673-5918
E-mail: climb@yobasecamp.com
Web site: www.yobasecamp.com

Young Actors Workshop
Los Angeles, CA
General Information: Coed day arts program established in 2000.
Contact: Steve Foral, Associate Director, Summer and Special Programs, , Los Angeles, CA 90089-4019
Phone: 213-740-5679 or 213-740-6417
E-mail: sforal@usc.edu
Web site: www.usc.edu/summer-programs

Colorado

Adventures Cross-Country, Colorado Adventure
General Information: Coed residential outdoor/wilderness program established in 1983.
Contact: Scott von Eschen, Owner, 242 Redwood Highway, Mill Valley, CA 94941
Phone: 415-332-5075 or 415-332-2130
E-mail: arcc@adventurescrosscountry.com
Web site: www.adventurescrosscountry.com

Anderson Camps' Colorado River Ranch for Boys/Hilltop Ranch for Girls
Gypsum, CO
General Information: Coed residential outdoor/wilderness program established in 1962.
Contact: Christopher Porter, Director or 7177 Colorado River Road, Gypsum, CO 81637
Phone: 970-524-7766 or 970-524-7107
E-mail: andecamp@rof.net
Web site: www.andersoncamps.com

Colorado Mountain Camps–Expedition Bound
Steamboat Springs, CO
General Information: Coed residential adventure and outdoor/wilderness program established in 1966.
Contact: Matt Merlino, Director, PO Box 658, Oak Creek, CO 80467-0658
Phone: 800-651-8336 or 970-736-8311
E-mail: info@coloradomountaincamps.com
Web site: www.coloradomountaincamps.com

Crow Canyon Archaeological Center High School Excavation Program
Cortez, CO
General Information: Coed residential academic and cultural program established in 1998.
Contact: Theresa Titone, School Programs Marketing Manager, 23390 Road K, Cortez, CO 81321
Phone: 800-422-8975 ext. 130 or 970-565-4859
E-mail: ttitone@crowcanyon.org
Web site: www.crowcanyon.org

Crow Canyon Archaeological Center High School Field School
Cortez, CO
General Information: Coed residential cultural program established in 1982.
Contact: Theresa Titone, School Programs Marketing Manager, 23390 Road K, Cortez, CO 81321
Phone: 800-422-8975 ext. 130 or 970-565-4859
E-mail: ttitone@crowcanyon.org
Web site: www.crowcanyon.org

Deer Hill Expeditions, Colorado
Mancos, CO
General Information: Coed residential community service, cultural, and outdoor/wilderness program established in 1984.
Contact: Beverly Capelin, Program Co-Director, PO Box 180, Mancos, CO 81328
Phone: 800-533-7221 or 970-533-7221
E-mail: info@deerhillexpeditions.com
Web site: www.deerhillexpeditions.com

Eagle Lake Basketball Camp
Colorado Springs, CO
General Information: Coed residential sports program established in 2001.
Contact: Registrar, PO Box 6000, Colorado Springs, CO 80934
Phone: 719-472-1260 or 719-623-0148
E-mail: useagle@navyouth.org
Web site: www.eaglelake.org

Eagle Lake Bike Camp
Colorado Springs, CO
General Information: Coed residential outdoor/wilderness program established in 1997.
Contact: Registrar, PO Box 6000, Colorado Springs, CO 80934
Phone: 719-472-1260 or 719-623-0148
E-mail: useagle@navyouth.org
Web site: www.eaglelake.org

Eagle Lake Camp Crews Program
Colorado Springs, CO
General Information: Coed residential community service program established in 1995.
Contact: Registrar, PO Box 6000, Colorado Springs, CO 80934
Phone: 719-472-1260 or 719-623-0148
E-mail: useagle@navyouth.org
Web site: www.eaglelake.org

iD Tech Camps–UC Colorado Springs, Colorado Springs, CO
Colorado Springs, CO
General Information: Coed residential and day academic program established in 1999.
Contact: Mr. Pete Ingram-Cauchi, President, 2103 South Bascom Avenue, Campbell, CA 95008
Phone: 888-709-TECH or 408-626-9505
E-mail: info@internaldrive.com
Web site: www.idtechcamps.com

Landmark Volunteers: Colorado
General Information: Coed residential community service program established in 1992.
Contact: Ann Barrett, Executive Director, PO Box 455, Sheffield, MA 01257
Phone: 413-229-0255 or 413-229-2050
E-mail: landmark@volunteers.com
Web site: www.volunteers.com

Outpost Wilderness Adventure–Advanced Rock Camp
Lake George, CO
General Information: Coed residential adventure and outdoor/wilderness program established in 1979.
Contact: David Appleton, Director, 20859 County Road 77, Lake George, CO 80827
Phone: 719-748-3080 or 719-748-3046
E-mail: david@owa.com
Web site: www.owa.com

Outpost Wilderness Adventure–Base Camp
Lake George, CO
General Information: Boys residential adventure and outdoor/wilderness program established in 1979.
Contact: David Appleton, Director, 20859 County Road 77, Lake George, CO 80827
Phone: 719-748-3080 or 719-748-3046
E-mail: david@owa.com
Web site: www.owa.com

Outpost Wilderness Adventure–Best of Colorado
Lake George, CO
General Information: Coed residential adventure program established in 1979.
Contact: David Appleton, Director, 20859 County Road 77, Lake George, CO 80827
Phone: 719-748-3080 or 719-748-3046
E-mail: david@owa.com
Web site: www.owa.com

Outpost Wilderness Adventure–Early Rock/Early Bike
Lake George, CO
General Information: Coed residential adventure and outdoor/wilderness program established in 1979.
Contact: David Appleton, Director, 20859 County Road 77, Lake George, CO 80827
Phone: 719-748-3080 or 719-748-3046
E-mail: david@owa.com
Web site: www.owa.com

Outpost Wilderness Adventure–Fly Fishing Camp
Lake George, CO
General Information: Coed residential adventure and outdoor/wilderness program established in 1979.
Contact: David Appleton, Director, 20859 County Road 77, Lake George, CO 80827
Phone: 719-748-3080 or 719-748-3046
E-mail: david@owa.com
Web site: www.owa.com

Outpost Wilderness Adventure–Guide Training Program
Lake George, CO
General Information: Coed residential adventure program established in 1979.
Contact: David Appleton, Director, 20859 County Road 77, Lake George, CO 80827
Phone: 719-748-3080 or 719-748-3046
E-mail: david@owa.com
Web site: www.owa.com

Outpost Wilderness Adventure–Mountain Bike/Rock Camp
Lake George, CO
General Information: Coed residential adventure and outdoor/wilderness program established in 1979.
Contact: David Appleton, Director, 20859 County Road 77, Lake George, CO 80827
Phone: 719-748-3080 or 719-748-3046
E-mail: david@owa.com
Web site: www.owa.com

Pemigewassett West
Crested Butte, CO
General Information: Coed residential outdoor/wilderness program established in 1996.
Contact: Robert L. Grabill, Director, 25 Rayton Road, Hanover, NH 03755
Phone: 603-643-8055 or 603-643-9601
E-mail: robert.grabill@valley.net
Web site: www.camppemi.com

Perry-Mansfield Performing Arts School and Camp
Steamboat Springs, CO
General Information: Coed residential and day arts program established in 1913.
Contact: June Lindenmayer, Executive Director, 40755 Routt County Road 36, Steamboat Springs, CO 80487
Phone: 800-430-2787 or 970-879-5823
E-mail: p-m@cmn.net
Web site: www.perry-mansfield.org

Poulter Colorado Camps
Steamboat Springs, CO
General Information: Coed residential adventure and outdoor/wilderness program established in 1966.
Contact: Mr. Jay B. Poulter, Director, PO Box 772947, Steamboat Springs, CO 80477
Phone: 888-879-4816
E-mail: poulter@poultercamps.com
Web site: www.poultercamps.com

The Road Less Traveled–Trails in Time–Colorado
General Information: Coed residential adventure and outdoor/wilderness program established in 1991.
Contact: Jim Stein, Owner / Director, 2331 North Elston, Chicago, IL 60614
Phone: 773-342-5200 or 773-342-5703
E-mail: rlt1road@aol.com
Web site: www.theroadlesstraveled.com

The Road Less Traveled–Wild, Wild West–Colorado
General Information: Coed residential adventure and outdoor/wilderness program established in 1991.
Contact: Jim Stein, Owner/Director, 2331 North Elston, Chicago, IL 60614
Phone: 773-342-5200 or 773-342-5703
E-mail: rlt1road@aol.com
Web site: www.theroadlesstraveled.com

Summer Study at The University of Colorado at Boulder
Boulder, CO
General Information: Coed residential academic program established in 2001.
Contact: Bill Cooperman, Executive Director, 900 Walt Whitman Road, Melville, NY 11747
Phone: 800-666-2556 or 631-424-0567
E-mail: precollegeprograms@summer-study.com
Web site: www.summerstudy.com

SuperCamp–Colorado College
Colorado Springs, CO
General Information: Coed residential academic program established in 1981.
Contact: Enrollments Department, 1725 South Coast Highway, Oceanside, CA 92054
Phone: 800-285-3276 or 760-722-3507
E-mail: info@supercamp.com
Web site: www.supercamp.com

Hawaii

AAC–Aloha Adventure Photo Camp
Makawao, HI
General Information: Coed residential and day adventure, arts, and cultural program established in 1995.
Contact: Ms. Laura Reed, Camp Coordinator, USPO PO Box 1109, Makawao, Maui, HI 96768
Phone: 877-755-2267 or 310-391-7738
E-mail: aapc@mediaone.net
Web site: www.hawaiicamps.com

Adventures Cross-Country, Hawaii Adventure
General Information: Coed residential outdoor/wilderness program established in 1983.
Contact: Scott von Eschen, Director, 242 Redwood Highway, Mill Valley, CA 94941
Phone: 415-332-5075 or 415-332-2130
E-mail: arcc@adventurescrosscountry.com
Web site: www.adventurescrosscountry.com

EARTHWATCH INSTITUTE–Endangered Ecosystems–Hawai'i's Mountain Streams
General Information: Coed residential adventure program.
Contact: General Information Desk, PO Box 75, Maynard, MA 01754
Phone: 800-776-0188 or 978-461-2332
E-mail: info@earthwatch.org
Web site: www.earthwatch.org

EARTHWATCH INSTITUTE–Oceans–Exploring Dolphin Intelligence
General Information: Coed residential adventure and cultural program.
Contact: General Information Desk, PO Box 75, Maynard, MA 01754
Phone: 800-776-0188 or 978-461-2332
E-mail: info@earthwatch.org
Web site: www.earthwatch.org

Hawaii Preparatory Academy Summer Session
Kamuela, HI
General Information: Coed residential and day academic program established in 1971.
Contact: Special Programs Office, 65-1692 Kohala Mountain Road, Kamuela, HI 96743
Phone: 808-881-4088 or 808-881-4011
E-mail: summer@hpa.edu
Web site: www.hpa.edu/SummerSchool/SummerSchool.html

Maui Surfer Girls
General Information: Girls residential and day adventure and cultural program established in 2001.
Contact: Dustin Tester, Director/Founder, PO Box 1158, Puunene, HI 96784
Phone: 808-250-2019 or 808-879-2019
E-mail: dtester@hotmail.com
Web site: www.mauisurfergirls.com

World Horizons International–Molokai, Hawaii
Molokai, HI
General Information: Coed residential cultural program established in 1999.
Contact: Ms. Judy Manning, Executive Director, PO Box 662, Bethlehem, CT 06751
Phone: 800-262-5874 or 203-266-5874
E-mail: worhorin@snet.net
Web site: www.world-horizons.com

World Horizons International–Oahu, Hawaii
Oahu, HI
General Information: Coed residential community service and cultural program.
Contact: Judy Manning, Executive Director, PO Box 662, Bethlehem, CT 06751
Phone: 800-262-5874 or 230-266-5874
E-mail: worhorin@snet.net
Web site: www.world-horizons.com

Idaho

Landmark Volunteers: Idaho
General Information: Coed residential community service and outdoor/wilderness program established in 1992.
Contact: Ann Barrett, Executive Director, PO Box 455, Sheffield, MA 01257
Phone: 413-229-0255 or 413-229-2050
E-mail: landmark@volunteers.com
Web site: www.volunteers.com

Montana

Landmark Volunteers: Montana
Polson, MT
General Information: Coed residential community service program established in 1992.
Contact: Ann Barrett, Executive Director, PO Box 455, Sheffield, MA 01257
Phone: 413-229-0255 or 413-229-2050
E-mail: landmark@volunteers.com
Web site: www.volunteers.com

NBC Camps–Basketball Individual Training–Montana
Billings, MT
General Information: Coed residential sports program.
Contact: Ms. Bonnie Tucker, Office Manager, 10003 North Milan Road, #100, Spokane, WA 99218
Phone: 509-466-4690 or 509-467-6289
E-mail: btucker@nbccamps.com
Web site: www.nbccamps.com

NBC Camps–Basketball–Team–Billings, MT
Billings, MT
General Information: Coed residential sports program.
Contact: Danny Beard, 10003 North Milan Road, #100, Spokane, WA 99218
Phone: 509-466-4690 or 509-467-6289
E-mail: danny@nbccamps.com
Web site: www.nbccamps.com

NBC Camps–Volleyball–Montana
Billings, MT
General Information: Girls residential sports program.
Contact: Ms. Bonnie Tucker, Office Manager, 10003 North Milan Road, #100, Spokane, WA 99218
Phone: 509-466-4690 or 509-467-6289
E-mail: btucker@nbccamps.com
Web site: www.nbccamps.com

Putney Student Travel–Community Service–Montana
General Information: Coed residential community service program established in 1951.
Contact: Jeff Shumlin, Director, 345 Hickory Ridge Road, Putney, VT 05346
Phone: 802-387-5885 or 802-387-4276
E-mail: info@goputney.com
Web site: www.goputney.com

Visions–Montana
General Information: Coed residential community service and cultural program established in 1989.
Contact: Joanne Pinaire, Director, PO Box 220, Newport, PA 17074

Phone: 717-567-7313 or 717-567-7853
E-mail: visions@pa.net
Web site: www.visionsadventure.com

Nevada

Study Tours in the USA–Southern Nevada
Las Vegas, NV
General Information: Coed residential academic program established in 1987.
Contact: Ms. Veronica Perez, Director of Admissions, 101 East Green Street, #14, Pasadena, CA 91105
Phone: 626-795-2912 or 626-795-5564
E-mail: veronica@fls.net
Web site: www.fls.net

New Mexico

Brush Ranch Camps–Adventure Camp
Tererro, NM
General Information: Coed residential adventure and outdoor/wilderness program established in 1992.
Contact: Kay Rice, Co-Director, PO Box 5759, Santa Fe, NM 87502
Phone: 505-757-8821 or 505-757-8822
E-mail: brc@nm.fiber.com
Web site: www.brushranchcamps.com

Cottonwood Gulch Family Trek Camp
Thoreau, NM
General Information: Coed residential adventure program established in 1975.
Contact: Martin Heinrich, Executive Director, PO Box 969, Thoreau, NM 87323
Phone: 505-862-7503 or 505-862-7503
E-mail: director@go-trek.org
Web site: www.go-trek.org

Deer Hill Expeditions, New Mexico
General Information: Coed residential community service, cultural, and outdoor/wilderness program established in 1984.
Contact: Beverly Capelin, Program Co-Director, PO Box 180, Mancos, CO 81328
Phone: 800-533-7221 or 970-533-7221
E-mail: info@deerhillexpeditions.com
Web site: www.deerhillexpeditions.com

EARTHWATCH INSTITUTE–Origins of Our Future– Prehistoric Pueblos
General Information: Coed residential cultural program.

Contact: General Information Desk, PO Box 75, Maynard, MA 01754
Phone: 800-776-0188 or 978-461-2332
E-mail: info@earthwatch.org
Web site: www.earthwatch.org

The Experiment in International Living–Navajo Nation
Farmington, NM
General Information: Coed residential adventure and cultural program established in 1932.
Contact: Annie Thompson, Enrollment Director, Summer Abroad, Kipling Road, PO Box 676, Brattleboro, VT 05302-0676
Phone: 800-345-2929 or 802-258-3428
E-mail: eil@worldlearning.org
Web site: www.usexperiment.org

Oregon

Adventures in Learning
Corvallis, OR
General Information: Coed day academic program established in 1984.
Contact: Judy Michael, Program Director, 210 Education Hall, Corvallis, OR 97331-3502
Phone: 541-737-1289 or 541-737-2040
E-mail: michaelj@orst.edu
Web site: oregonstate.edu/precollege/ail

Cybercamps–Lewis and Clark College
Portland, OR
General Information: Coed residential and day academic program established in 1997.
Contact: Celia Paz, Customer Care Representative, 12131 113th Avenue NE, Suite 102, Kirkland, WA 98034
Phone: 888-904-CAMP or 425-825-4601
E-mail: info@cybercamps.com
Web site: www.cybercamps.com

Delphi's Summer Session
Sheridan, OR
General Information: Coed residential and day academic program established in 1973.
Contact: Donetta Phelps, Admissions Director, Department 3 or 20950 Southwest Rock Creek Road, Sheridan, OR 97378
Phone: 503-843-3521 or 503-843-4158
E-mail: info@delphian.org
Web site: www.delphian.org

EARTHWATCH INSTITUTE– Biodiversity–Mountain Wildflowers of Oregon
General Information: Coed residential adventure program.

Contact: General Information Desk, PO Box 75, Maynard, MA 01754
Phone: 800-776-0188 or 978-461-2332
E-mail: info@earthwatch.org
Web site: www.earthwatch.org

EARTHWATCH INSTITUTE–Endangered Ecosystems–Saving Crater Lake's Forests
General Information: Coed residential outdoor/wilderness program.
Contact: General Information Desk, PO Box 75, Maynard, MA 01754
Phone: 800-776-0188 or 978-461-2332
E-mail: info@earthwatch.org
Web site: www.earthwatch.org

Expeditions
Corvallis, OR
General Information: Coed day academic program established in 1996.
Contact: Carol Brown, Program Coordinator, 210 Education Hall, Corvallis, OR
Phone: 541-737-2670 or 541-737-2040
E-mail: carol.brown@orst.edu
Web site: osu.orst.edu/precollege/expeditions

Fir Acres Workshop in Writing and Thinking
Portland, OR
General Information: Coed residential academic and arts program established in 1989.
Contact: Diane McDevitt, Administrative Assistant, Lewis and Clark College, 0615 SW Palatine Hill Road, Portland, OR 97219
Phone: 503-768-7745 or 503-768-7747
E-mail: mcdevitt@lclark.edu
Web site: www.lclark.edu/~nwi/high

High Cascade Snowboard Camp
Mt. Hood, OR
General Information: Coed residential sports program established in 1989.
Contact: Amy Butcher, Camp Administrator, PO Box 368, Government Camp, OR 97028
Phone: 800-334-4272 or 503-272-3637
E-mail: highcascade@highcascade.com
Web site: www.highcascade.com

iD Tech Camps–Reed College, Portland, OR
Portland, OR
General Information: Coed residential and day academic program established in 1999.
Contact: Mr. Pete Ingram-Cauchi, President, 2103 South Bascom Avenue, Campbell, CA 95008

Phone: 888-709-TECH or 408-626-9505
E-mail: info@internaldrive.com
Web site: www.idtechcamps.com

IN2BIZ Entrepreneur Camp
Salem, OR
General Information: Coed residential academic program established in 1998.
Contact: Mr. Bret Rios, President, 800 Welcome Way, SE, Salem, OR 97302
Phone: 503-315-8262 or 503-315-8262
E-mail: brios@teleport.com
Web site: www.in2biz.com

NBC Camps–Basketball Individual Training–Newberg, OR
Newberg, OR
General Information: Coed residential sports program.
Contact: Ms. Bonnie Tucker, Office Manager, 10003 North Milan Road, #100, Spokane, WA 99218
Phone: 509-466-4690 or 509-467-6289
E-mail: btucker@nbccamps.com
Web site: www.nbccamps.com

NBC Camps–Basketball–Team–La Grande, OR
La Grande, OR
General Information: Residential sports program.
Contact: Danny Beard, 10003 North Milan Road, #100, Spokane, WA 99218
Phone: 509-466-4690 or 509-467-6289
E-mail: danny@nbccamps.com
Web site: www.nbccamps.com

NBC Camps–Volleyball–Oregon
La Grande, OR
General Information: Girls residential sports program.
Contact: Ms. Bonnie Tucker, Office Manager, 10003 North Milan Road, #100, Spokane, WA 99218
Phone: 509-466-4690 or 509-467-6287
E-mail: btucker@nbccamps.com
Web site: www.nbccamps.com

Oregon Coast Gymnastics Camp
Coos Bay, OR
General Information: Coed residential and day sports program established in 2001.
Contact: Kay Heikkila, Director of Conference and Camp Services, 1988 Newmark, Coos Bay, OR 97420
Phone: 800-962-2838 ext. 7238 or 541-888-7247
E-mail: camps@southwestern.cc.or.us
Web site: www.southwestern.cc.or.us

Oregon Coast–Computer Camp
Coos Bay, OR
General Information: Coed residential and day academic program established in 1999.
Contact: Kay Heikkila, Director of Camp and Conference Services, 1988 Newmark Avenue, Coos Bay, OR 97420
Phone: 800-962-2838 ext. 7238 or 541-888-7247
E-mail: camps@southwestern.cc.or.us
Web site: www.southwestern.cc.or.us

Oregon Coast–Mountain Biking
Coos Bay, OR
General Information: Coed residential and day adventure program established in 1999.
Contact: Kay Heikkila, Director of Camp and Conference Services, 1988 Newmark Avenue, Coos Bay, OR 97420
Phone: 800-962-2838 ext. 7238 or 541-888-7247
E-mail: camps@southwestern.cc.or.us
Web site: www.southwestern.cc.or.us

Oregon Summer Music Camps
Eugene, OR
General Information: Coed residential and day arts program established in 1946.
Contact: Dana Huddleston, Administrative Coordinator, 1225 University of Oregon, School of Music, Eugene, OR 97403-1225
Phone: 541-346-2138 or 541-346-0723
E-mail: dgmartin@oregon.uoregon.edu
Web site: music1.uoregon.edu/EventsNews/Camps/campsgen.html

SoccerPlus Goalkeeper School–Advanced National Training Center–Oregon
Beaverton, OR
General Information: Coed residential sports program established in 1982.
Contact: Mr. Shawn Kelly, General Manager, 20 Beaver Road, Suite 102, Wethersfield, CT 06109
Phone: 800-533-7371 or 860-721-8619
E-mail: shawn@goalkeeper.com
Web site: www.soccerpluscamps.com

Vans Skate Camp
Mt. Hood, OR
General Information: Coed residential sports program established in 2001.
Contact: Ms. Amy Butcher, Camp Administrator, PO Box 368, Government Camp, OR 97028
Phone: 800-334-4272 or 503-272-3637
E-mail: highcascade@highcascade.com
Web site: www.vansskatecamp.com

Young Musicians & Artists
Salem, OR
General Information: Coed residential arts program established in 1965.

Contact: Brian M. Biggs, Executive Director, PO Box 13277, Portland, OR 97213
Phone: 503-281-9528
E-mail: brian@ymainc.org
Web site: www.ymainc.org

Utah

Adventures Cross-Country, Four Corners Adventure
General Information: Coed residential outdoor/wilderness program established in 1983.
Contact: Scott von Eschen, Director, 242 Redwood Highway, Mill Valley, CA 94941
Phone: 415-332-5075 or 415-332-2130
E-mail: arcc@adventurescrosscountry.com
Web site: www.adventurescrosscountry.com

Camp Shakespeare
Cedar City, UT
General Information: Coed residential and day academic and arts program established in 1989.
Contact: Dr. Michael Flachmann, Program Director, Department of English, CSUB, 9001 Stockdale Highway, Bakersfield, CA 93311-1099
Phone: 661-664-2121
E-mail: mflachmann@csub.edu
Web site: www.csub.edu/campshakespeare

Deer Hill Expeditions, Utah
General Information: Coed residential community service and outdoor/wilderness program established in 1984.
Contact: Beverly Capelin, Program Co-Director, PO Box 180, Mancos, CO 81328
Phone: 800-533-7221 or 970-533-7221
E-mail: info@deerhillexpeditions.com
Web site: www.deerhillexpeditions.com

EARTHWATCH INSTITUTE–Endangered Ecosystems–Canyonland Creek Ecology
General Information: Coed residential adventure and cultural program.
Contact: General Information Desk, PO Box 75, Maynard, MA 01754
Phone: 800-776-0188 or 978-461-2332
E-mail: info@earthwatch.org
Web site: www.earthwatch.org

EARTHWATCH INSTITUTE–Origins of Our Future–Utah Canyon Rock Art
General Information: Coed residential adventure and cultural program.
Contact: General Information Desk, PO Box 75, Maynard, MA 01754
Phone: 800-776-0188 or 978-461-2332
E-mail: info@earthwatch.org
Web site: www.earthwatch.org

Mud City Adventures–Park City
Park City, UT
General Information: Coed residential and day adventure program established in 1996.
Contact: Ms. Christine Colangeli, Director, PO Box 4304, Park City, UT 84040
Web site: www.mudcityadventures.com

World Horizons International– Kanab, Utah
General Information: Coed residential community service and cultural program established in 2000.
Contact: Ms. Judy Manning, Executive Director, PO Box 662, Bethlehem, CT 06751
Phone: 800-262-5874, 203-266-5874
E-mail: worhorin@snet.net
Web site: www.world-horizons.com

Washington

A.C.E. Basketball Camp
Seattle, WA
General Information: Boys residential sports program.
Contact: Program Coordinator, 200 West Mercer Street, Suite 504, Seattle, WA 98119
Phone: 206-217-9644 or 206-812-2257
E-mail: summer@cultural.org
Web site: www.cultural.org

A.C.E. Intercultural Institute
General Information: Coed residential academic and cultural program established in 1996.
Contact: Program Coordinator, 200 West Mercer Street, Suite 504, Seattle, WA 98119
Phone: 206-985-1011 or 206-812-2257
E-mail: summer@cultural.org
Web site: www.cultural.org

Adventures in Science and Arts
Bellingham, WA
General Information: Coed residential and day academic program established in 1982.
Contact: Debbie Young Gibbons,

Program Manager, Extended Programs, Mail Stop 5293, Bellingham, WA 98225-5293
Phone: 360-650-6820 or 360-650-6858
E-mail: adventur@cc.wwu.edu
Web site: www.wwu.edu/~adventur

The Art Institute of Seattle–Studio 101
Seattle, WA
General Information: Coed residential and day arts program established in 1985.
Contact: High School and Community Services Office, 2323 Elliot Avenue, Seattle, WA 98121
Phone: 800-275-2471 or 206-269-0275
Web site: www.ais.edu

Camp Kirby Mua Mi Villagers
Bow, WA
General Information: Coed residential adventure program established in 1923.
Contact: Ms. Jenn Brown, Camp Director, 4734 Samish Point Road, Bow, WA 98232
Phone: 360-766-6060 or 360-733-5711
E-mail: tamarjb@aol.com
Web site: www.campkirby.org

Camp Kirby Voyagers
General Information: Coed residential adventure program established in 1923.
Contact: Ms. Jenn Brown, Camp Director, 4734 Samish Point Road, Bow, WA 98232
Phone: 360-766-6060 or 360-733-5711
E-mail: tamarjb@aol.com
Web site: www.campkirby.org

Canoe Island French Camp
Orcas, WA
General Information: Coed residential cultural program established in 1969.
Contact: Richard Carter, Camp Director, PO Box 370, Orcas, WA 98280
Phone: 360-468-2329 or 360-468-3027
E-mail: canoe@rockisland.com
Web site: www.rockisland.com/~canoe

Cybercamps–Bellevue Community College
Bellevue, WA
General Information: Coed residential and day academic program established in 1997.
Contact: Celia Paz, Customer Care Representative, 12131 113th Avenue NE, Suite 102, Kirkland, WA 98034
Phone: 888-904-CAMP or 425-825-4601
E-mail: info@cybercamps.com
Web site: www.cybercamps.com

Cybercamps–University of Puget Sound
Tacoma, WA
General Information: Coed residential and day academic program established in 1997.
Contact: Celia Paz, Customer Care Representative, 12131 113th Avenue NE, Suite 102, Kirkland, WA 98034
Phone: 888-904-CAMP or 425-825-4601
E-mail: info@cybercamps.com
Web site: www.cybercamps.com

Cybercamps–University of Washington
Seattle, WA
General Information: Coed residential and day academic program established in 1997.
Contact: Celia Paz, Customer Care Representative, 12131 113th Avenue NE, Suite 102, Kirkland, WA 98034
Phone: 888-904-CAMP or 425-825-4601
E-mail: info@cybercamps.com
Web site: www.cybercamps.com

Cybercamps–University of Washington, Bothell
Bothell, WA
General Information: Coed residential and day academic program established in 1997.
Contact: Celia Paz, Customer Care Representative, 12131 113th Avenue NE, Suite 102, Kirkland, WA 98034
Phone: 888-904-CAMP or 425-825-4601
E-mail: info@cybercamps.com
Web site: www.cybercamps.com

DigiPen Institute of Technology 3D Computer Animation Workshop
Redmond, WA
General Information: Coed day academic and arts program established in 1998.
Contact: Ms. Gina Corpening, Admissions and Outreach Co-ordinator, 5001-150th Avenue, NE, Redmond, WA 98052
Phone: 425-558-0299 or 425-558-0378
E-mail: gcorpeni@digipen.edu
Web site: www.digipen.edu

EARTHWATCH INSTITUTE– Biodiversity–Caring for Chimpanzees
Ellensburg, WA
General Information: Coed residential adventure program.
Contact: General Information Desk, PO Box 75, Maynard, MA 01754
Phone: 800-776-0188 or 978-461-2332
E-mail: info@earthwatch.org
Web site: www.earthwatch.org

EARTHWATCH INSTITUTE–Oceans–Orca
General Information: Coed residential adventure program.
Contact: General Information Desk, PO Box 75, Maynard, MA 01754
Phone: 800-776-0188 or 978-461-2332
E-mail: info@earthwatch.org
Web site: www.earthwatch.org

e-Camp
Seattle, WA
General Information: Coed residential and day academic program established in 2001.
Contact: Mr. Christopher McCall, Assistant Director Short Term Programs, 200 West Mercer Street #504, Seattle, WA 98119
Phone: 206-217-9644 ext. 211 or 206-217-9643
E-mail: chrism@cultural.org
Web site: www.cultural.org

iD Tech Camps–University of Washington, Seattle, WA
Seattle, WA
General Information: Coed residential and day academic program established in 1999.
Contact: Mr. Pete Ingram-Cauchi, President, 2103 South Bascom Avenue, Campbell, CA 95008
Phone: 888-709-TECH or 408-626-9505
E-mail: info@internaldrive.com
Web site: www.idtechcamps.com

Junior Institute
Seattle, WA
General Information: Coed residential academic program established in 1994.
Contact: Junior Institute Coordinator, 200 West Mercer Street #504, Seattle, WA 98119
Phone: 206-217-9644 or 206-812-2257
E-mail: junior@cultural.org
Web site: www.cultural.org

Junior Statesmen Symposium on Politics and Government–University of Washington
Seattle, WA
General Information: Coed residential academic program established in 1979.
Contact: Preeta Nayak, Program Director, 60 East 3rd Avenue, Suite 320, San Mateo, CA 94401
Phone: 650-347-1600 or 650-347-7200
E-mail: jsa@jsa.org
Web site: www.jsa.org

Landmark Volunteers: Washington
General Information: Coed residential community service program established in 1992.
Contact: Ann Barrett, Executive Director, PO Box 455, Sheffield, MA 01257
Phone: 413-229-0255 or 413-229-2050
E-mail: landmark@volunteers.com
Web site: www.volunteers.com

Marrowstone Music Festival
Bellingham, WA
General Information: Coed residential academic and arts program established in 1943.
Contact: Janice Gatti, Director of Admissions, 11065 5th Avenue, NE, Suite A, Seattle, WA 98125
Phone: 206-362-2300 or 206-361-9254
E-mail: janice@syso.org
Web site: www.marrowstone.org

NBC Camps–Basketball Individual Training (Boys)–Auburn, WA
Auburn, WA
General Information: Boys residential sports program.
Contact: Ms. Bonnie Tucker, Office Manager, 10003 North Milan Road, #100, Spokane, WA 99218
Phone: 509-466-4690 or 509-467-6289
E-mail: btucker@nbccamps.com
Web site: www.nbccamps.com

NBC Camps–Basketball Individual Training (Girls)–Auburn, WA
Auburn, WA
General Information: Girls residential sports program.
Contact: Ms. Bonnie Tucker, Office Manager, 10003 North Milan Road, #100, Spokane, WA 99218
Phone: 509-466-4690 or 509-467-6289
E-mail: btucker@nbccamps.com
Web site: www.nbccamps.com

NBC Camps–Basketball Individual Training–Spangle, WA
Spangle, WA
General Information: Coed residential sports program.
Contact: Ms. Bonnie Tucker, Office Manager, 10003 North Milan Road, #100, Spokane, WA 99218
Phone: 509-466-4690 or 509-467-6289
E-mail: btucker@nbccamps.com
Web site: www.nbccamps.com

NBC Camps–Basketball Individual Training–Spokane, WA
Spokane, WA
General Information: Coed residential sports program.
Contact: Ms. Bonnie Tucker, Office

Manager, 10003 North Milan Road, #100, Spokane, WA 99218
Phone: 509-466-4690 or 509-467-6289
E-mail: btucker@nbccamps.com
Web site: www.nbccamps.com

NBC Camps–Basketball Point Guard Play–Spangle, WA
Spangle, WA
General Information: Coed residential sports program.
Contact: Ms. Bonnie Tucker, Office Manager, 10003 North Milan Road, #100, Spokane, WA 99218
Phone: 509-466-4690 or 509-467-6289
E-mail: btucker@nbccamps.com
Web site: www.nbccamps.com

NBC Camps–Basketball Speed Explosion–Spokane, WA
Spokane, WA
General Information: Coed residential sports program.
Contact: Ms. Bonnie Tucker, Office Manager, 10003 North Milan Road, #100, Spokane, WA 99218
Phone: 509-466-4690 or 509-467-6289
E-mail: btucker@nbccamps.com
Web site: www.nbccamps.com

NBC Camps–Basketball–Adult & Child Hoops–Spokane, WA
Spokane, WA
General Information: Coed residential sports program.
Contact: Ms. Bonnie Tucker, Office Manager, 10003 North Milan Road, #100, Spokane, WA 99218
Phone: 509-466-4690 or 509-467-6289
E-mail: btucker@nbccamps.com
Web site: www.nbccamps.com

NBC Camps–Basketball–Crowell's Intensity–Spokane, WA
Spokane, WA
General Information: Boys residential sports program.
Contact: Ms. Bonnie Tucker, Office Manager, 10003 North Milan Road, #100, Spokane, WA 99218
Phone: 509-466-4690 or 509-467-6289
E-mail: vashon@nbccamps.com
Web site: www.nbccamps.com

NBC Camps–Basketball–Team (Girls)–Spangle, WA
Spangle, WA
General Information: Girls residential sports program.
Contact: Danny Beard, 10003 North Milan Road, #100, Spokane, WA 99218
Phone: 509-466-4690 or 509-467-6289
E-mail: danny@nbccamps.com
Web site: www.nbccamps.com

NBC Camps–Soccer Speed Explosion–Spokane, WA
Spokane, WA
General Information: Coed residential sports program.
Contact: Ms. Bonnie Tucker, Office Manager, 10003 North Milan Road, #100, Spokane, WA 99218
Phone: 509-466-4690 or 509-467-6289
E-mail: btucker@nbccamps.com
Web site: www.nbccamps.com

NBC Camps–Volleyball Speed Explosion–Spokane, WA
Spokane, WA
General Information: Coed residential sports program.
Contact: Ms. Bonnie Tucker, Office Manager, 10003 North Milan Road, #100, Spokane, WA 99218
Phone: 509-466-4690 or 509-467-6289
E-mail: btucker@nbccamps.com
Web site: www.nbccamps.com

The Northwest School Summer Program
Seattle, WA
General Information: Coed residential and day academic and arts program established in 1990.
Contact: Ms. Susan Mueller, Summer Program Director, 1415 Summit Avenue, Seattle, WA 98122
Phone: 206-682-7309 or 206-467-7353
Web site: northwestschool.org

Outdoor Challenge Institute
Bellingham, WA
General Information: Coed residential academic program established in 2000.
Contact: Debbie Young Gibbons, Program Manager, Extended Programs, Mail Stop 5293, Bellingham, WA 98225-5293
Phone: 360-650-6820 or 360-650-6858
E-mail: adventur@cc.wwu.edu
Web site: www.wwu.edu/~adventur

Summer Quest
Bellingham, WA
General Information: Coed residential academic program established in 2000.
Contact: Debbie Young Gibbons, Program Manager, Extended Programs, Mail Stop 5293, Bellingham, WA 98225
Phone: 360-650-6820 or 360-650-6858
E-mail: adventur@cc.wwu.edu
Web site: www.wwu.edu/~adventur/

Wave Trek Adventure Camps
Index, WA
General Information: Coed residential adventure program established in 1984.
Contact: Chris Jonason, President, PO Box 236, Index, WA 98256
Phone: 360-793-1705 or 360-793-2771
E-mail: info@wavetrek.com
Web site: www.wavetrek.com/camps

Wyoming

EARTHWATCH INSTITUTE– Origins of Our Future–Jackson Hole Bison Dig
Jackson Hole, WY
General Information: Coed residential adventure program.
Contact: General Information Desk, PO Box 75, Maynard, MA 01754
Phone: 800-776-0188 or 978-461-2332
E-mail: info@earthwatch.org
Web site: www.earthwatch.org

High School Field Ecology
Kelly, WY
General Information: Coed residential academic program established in 1967.
Contact: Ms. Judy Herman, Registrar, PO Box 68, Kelly, WY 83011
Phone: 307-733-4765 ext. 312 or 307-739-9388
E-mail: judy@tetonscience.org
Web site: www.tetonscience.org

High School Field Natural History
Kelly, WY
General Information: Coed residential academic program established in 1967.
Contact: Ms. Judy Herman, Registrar, PO Box 68, Kelly, WY 83011
Phone: 307-733-4765 ext. 312 or 307-739-9388
E-mail: judy@tetonscience.org
Web site: www.tetonscience.org

Landmark Volunteers: Wyoming
General Information: Coed residential community service program established in 1992.
Contact: Ann Barrett, Executive Director, PO Box 455, Sheffield, MA 01257
Phone: 413-229-0255 or 413-229-2050
E-mail: landmark@volunteers.com
Web site: www.volunteers.com

Middle School Field Ecology
Kelly, WY
General Information: Coed residential academic program established in 1967.
Contact: Ms. Judy Herman, Registrar, PO Box 68, Kelly, WY 83011
Phone: 307-733-4765 or 307-739-9388
E-mail: judy@tetonscience.org
Web site: www.tetonscience.org

The Road Less Traveled–The Great Divide
General Information: Coed residential adventure, cultural, and outdoor/wilderness program established in 1991.
Contact: Jim Stein, Owner / Director, 2331 North Elston, Chicago, IL 60614
Phone: 773-342-5200 or 773-342-5703
E-mail: rlt1road@aol.com
Web site: www.theroadlesstraveled.com

Skinner Brothers Wilderness Camps–Graduate Leadership Session
Pinedale, WY
General Information: Coed residential outdoor/wilderness program established in 1956.
Contact: Monte B. Skinner, Director, PO Box 859, Pinedale, WY 82941-0859
Phone: 800-237-9138, 307-367-4757
E-mail: s6camps@wyoming.com
Web site: www.wyomingoutdoors.com

Skinner Brothers Wilderness Camps–Wilderness School–Boys
Pinedale, WY
General Information: Boys residential outdoor/wilderness program established in 1956.
Contact: Monte B. Skinner, Director, PO Box 859, Pinedale, WY 82941-0859
Phone: 800-237-9138 or 307-367-4757
E-mail: s6camps@wyoming.com
Web site: www.wyomingoutdoors.com

Skinner Brothers Wilderness Camps–Wilderness School–Girls
Pinedale, WY
General Information: Girls residential outdoor/wilderness program established in 1956.
Contact: Monte B. Skinner, Director, PO Box 859, Pinedale, WY 82941-0859
Phone: 800-237-9138 or 307-367-4757
E-mail: s6camps@wyoming.com
Web site: www.wyomingoutdoors.com

Trails Wilderness School–Family Camp
Jackson Hole-Kelly, WY
General Information: Coed residential adventure and outdoor/wilderness program established in 1994.
Contact: Mr. Whigger Mullins, Director/Owner, Teton Valley Ranch, PO Box 123, Jackson Hole-Kelly, WY 83011
Phone: 800-869-8228 or 603-452-4939
E-mail: info@trailsws.ocm
Web site: www.trailsws.com

Trails Wilderness School–Rock Climbing
Jackson Hole-Kelly, WY
General Information: Coed residential adventure program established in 1994.
Contact: Mr. Whigger Mullins, Director/Owner, Teton Valley Ranch, PO Box 123, Jackson Hole-Kelly, WY 83011
Phone: 800-869-8228 or 603-452-4939
E-mail: info@trailsws.com
Web site: www.trailsws.com

Trails Wilderness School–Skiing
Jackson Hole-Kelly, WY
General Information: Coed residential adventure and outdoor/wilderness program established in 1994.
Contact: Mr. Whigger Mullins,

Director/Owner, Teton Valley Ranch, PO Box 123, Jackson Hole-Kelly, WY 83011
Phone: 800-869-8228 or 603-452-4939
E-mail: info@trailsws.com
Web site: www.trailsws.com

Trails Wilderness School–Snowboarding
Jackson Hole-Kelly, WY
General Information: Coed residential outdoor/wilderness program established in 1994.
Contact: Mr. Whigger Mullins, Director/Owner, Teton Valley Ranch, PO Box 123, Jackson Hole-Kelly, WY 83011
Phone: 800-869-8228 or 603-452-4939
E-mail: info@trailsws.com
Web site: www.trailsws.com

Trails Wilderness School–Wyoming
Jackson Hole-Kelly, WY
General Information: Coed residential adventure and outdoor/wilderness program established in 1994.
Contact: Mr. Whigger Mullins, Director/Owner, Teton Valley Ranch, PO Box 123, Jackson Hole-Kelly, WY 83011
Phone: 800-869-8228 or 603-452-4939
E-mail: info@trailsws.com
Web site: www.trailsws.com

Bibliography

ADDITIONAL RESOURCES

BOOKS PUBLISHED BY PETERSON'S AND ARCO

100 Best Careers for the 21st Century, 2nd Edition, by Shelly Field. Arco

Careers without College (Building, Cars, Computers, Emergencies, Entertainment, Fashion, Fitness, Health Care, Kids, Money, Music, Office, Sports, and Travel) . Peterson's

Campus Life Exposed: Advice from the Inside, by Harlan Cohen. Peterson's

Christian Colleges & Universities, 8th Edition. Peterson's

College Applications & Essays, 4th Edition, by Susan D. Van Raalte. Arco

College Money Handbook 2003. Peterson's

Colleges for Students with Learning Disabilities and Attention Deficit Disorders, 6th Edition, Peterson's

College Survival, 6th Edition, by Greg Gottesman and Daniel Baer. Arco

Culinary Schools 2003. Peterson's

Game Plan for Getting into College, by K. Patricia Aviezer. Peterson's

Guide to Career Colleges 2003. Peterson's

Guide to College Visits 2002. Peterson's

Honors Programs & Colleges, 3rd Edition. Peterson's

The Insider's Guide to Writing the Perfect Resume, by Karl Weber and Rick Kaplan. Peterson's

The Insider's Guide to Paying for College, by Don Betterton. Peterson's

Nursing Programs 2003. Peterson's

Peterson's College and University Almanac 2001. Peterson's

Peterson's Competitive Colleges 2002–2003. Peterson's

Peterson's Complete Guide to Financial Aid 2003

Peterson's 2 Year Colleges–2003. Peterson's

Peterson's 4 Year Colleges–2003. Peterson's

Peterson's Sports Scholarships and Athletic Programs. Peterson's

Peterson's Vocational and Technical Schools 2003. Peterson's

Professional Degree Programs in the Visual & Performing Arts 2003. Peterson's

Reading Lists for College-Bound Students, 3rd Edition, by Doug Estell, Michele L. Satchwell, and Patricia S. Wright. Arco

Scholarships, Grants and Prizes 2003. Peterson's

Smart Parents Guide to College, 5th Edition, by Ernest L. Boyer and Paul Boyer. Peterson's

Study Abroad 2003. Peterson's

Summer Jobs in the USA 2003. Peterson's

Summer Opportunities for Kids and Teenagers 2003. Peterson's

The Ultimate College Survival Guide, 2nd Edition, by Janet Farrar Worthington and Ronald Farrar. Peterson's

The Ultimate High School Survival Guide, by Julianne Dueber. Peterson's

Winning Money for College, 4th Edition, by Alan Deutschman. Peterson's

You're Hired! Secrets to a Successful Job Search, by Sharon McDonnell. Arco

ORGANIZATIONS

ACT Assessment, P.O. Box 414, Iowa City, Iowa 52243-0414 (telephone: 319-337-1270)

Air Force Recruiting Services, Air Force Opportunity Center, P.O. Box 3505, Capitol Heights, Maryland 20791-9988 (telephone: 800-423-USAF)

Alcoholics Anonymous, 475 Riverside Drive, 11th Floor, New York, New York 10115 (telephone: 212-870-3400)

American Association of Community Colleges, One Dupont Circle, NW, #410, Washington, D.C. 22206-1176 (telephone: 202-728-0200)

American Cancer Society, 1599 Clifton Rd. NE, Atlanta, Georgia 30329 (telephone: 800-ACS-2345)

Amer-I-Can Program, Inc., 1851 Sunset Plaza Drive, Los Angeles, California 90069 (telephone: 310-652-7884).

Association on Higher Education and Disability, P.O. Box 21192, Columbus, Ohio 43221-0192 (telephone: 614-488-4972)

Brighten Your Future, P.O. Box 991, Logan, Ohio 43138 (telephone: 740-385-5058)

Career College Association, 10 G Street, NE, Ste. 750, Washington, DC 20002 (telephone: 202-336-6800)

Cleveland Scholarship Programs, Inc., 850 Euclid Avenue, Suite 1000, Cleveland, Ohio, 44114 (telephone: 216-241-5587)

Crime Prevention Association of Philadelphia, Suite 4E, 230 South Broad Street, Philadelphia, PA, 19102 (telephone: 215-545-5230)

Department of Veterans Affairs, 1120 Vermont Ave, NW, Washington, DC 20421 (telephone: 202-691-3030)

Disabilities Organizational Development Services, 5984 Pinerock Place, Columbus, Ohio 43231-2334 (telephone: 614-895-0238)

Educational Testing Service, Rosedale Road, Princeton, New Jersey 08541 (telephone: 609-921-9000)

Enlisted Association of the National Guard of the United States, P.O. Box 261, Groveport, Ohio 43125 (telephone: 800-642-6642)

Federal Trade Commission, 600 Pennsylvania Avenue NW, Washington, D.C. 20580 (telephone: 877-FTC-HELP)

Gender Issues Education, 5625 SE 38th Avenue, Portland, Oregon 97202 (telephone: 503-775-6533)

Higher Education Council of Columbus, c/o Ohio State University, Mount Hall, Room 204, 1050 Carmack Road, Columbus, Ohio 43210 (telephone: 614-688-4610)

Hispanic Scholarship Fund, 1 Sansome Street, Suite 1000, San Francisco, California 94104 (telephone: 877-HSF-INFO)

NAACP, National Offices, 4802 Mount Hope Drive, Baltimore, Maryland 21215 (telephone: 877-622-2798)

Narcotics Anonymous, P.O. Box 9999, Van Nuys, California 91409 (telephone: 818-773-9999)

National Association of Anorexia Nervosa and Associated Disorders, P.O. Box 7, Highland Park Illinois 60035 (telephone: 847-831-3438)

National Association of College Admission Counselors, 1631 Prince Street, Alexandria, Virginia 22314-2818 (telephone: 703-836-2222)

National Association of Intercollegiate Athletics, 6120 South Yale Avenue, Suite 1450, Tulsa, Oklahoma 74136 (telephone: 918-494-8828)

National College Access Network, 204 East Lombard Street, Fourth Floor, Baltimore, Maryland 21202 (telephone: 410-244-7218)

National Collegiate Athletic Association Clearinghouse, P.O. Box 4043 , Iowa City, Iowa 52243-4043 (telephone: 319-339-3003)

National Institute on Drug Abuse, Community Drug Alert Bulletin-Club Drugs. 6001 Executive Blvd., Bethesda, Maryland 20892 (telephone: 301-443-1124)

North-American Interfraternity Conference, 3901 West 86th Street, Suite 390, Indianapolis, Indiana 48268 (telephone: 317-872-1112)

Peterson's Education Services, 2000 Lenox Drive, P.O. Box 67005, Lawrenceville, New Jersey 08648 (telephone: 800-338-3282)

The College Fund/UNCF, 8260 Willow Oaks Corporate Drive, P.O. Box 10444, Fairfax, Virginia 22031 (telephone: 703-205-3400)

The Compelling Communications Group, 15 Sausalito Blvd., Sausalito, California (telephone: 415-331-6336)

The Education Resource Institute, 330 Stuart St., Ste. 500, Boston, Massachusetts 02116 (telephone: 800-255- 8374)

U.S. Department of Education, Federal Student Aid Information Center, P.O. Box 84, Washington, D.C. 20044 (telephone: 800-4-FEDAID)

Vocational Instructional Materials Laboratory, The Ohio State University, Columbus, Ohio

NOTES

NOTES